D1001710

Venice, Frail Barrier

Venice,

By Richard de Combray

VENICE, FRAIL BARRIER

ATTITUDES ESPAGNOLES
in collaboration with Michel del Castillo

Frail Barrier

Richard de Combray

Doubleday & Company, Inc. Garden City, New York 1975

Grateful acknowledgment is made to the following for permission to quote from:

INVITATION TO A BEHEADING by Vladimir Nabokov. Copyright © 1959 by Vladimir Nabokov; translated with Dmitri Nabokov. Reprinted by permission of G. P. Putnam's Sons, Inc.

THE LEOPARD by Giuseppe di Lampedusa, translated by Archibald Colquhoun. Copyright © 1960 by Giuseppe de Lampedusa. Reprinted by permission of Pantheon Books, a Division of Random House, Inc.

GIMPEL THE FOOL AND OTHER STORIES by Isaac Bashevis Singer. Copyright © 1953, 1954, 1955, 1957 by Isaac Bashevis Singer. Reprinted by permission of Farrar, Straus & Giroux, Inc.

"A Love" in THE COMPLETE POEMS OF CAVAFY, translated by Rae Dalven. Reprinted by permission of Harcourt Brace Jovanovich, Inc.

FOUR SCREEN PLAYS OF INGMAR BERGMAN by Ingmar Bergman. Copyright © 1960 by Ingmar Bergman. Reprinted by permission of Simon & Schuster, Inc.

Printed in the United States of America
First Edition

Designed by Tracey Penton

for my mother, the memory of my father, and for Sandra

Acknowledgments

The author's grateful thanks are due Professor Giuseppi Mazzariol of the Querini-Stampalia Collection, who so generously gave his permission to photograph the Bella paintings; to Dottore Giovanni Marangoni, also of the Collection, whose help and wit were so valuable and whose book *Giorno per Giorno Tanti Anni Fa* (Libreria Filippi Editrice, Venezia) provided such a storehouse of historical anecdotes; to Mirko Spavento who made so much of living Venice accessible; to Mischa Kiwe and Richard Kamm, who knew so much about discovering its past.

In New York, Messrs. Henry T. Weinstein, Miles Morgan, Michael Grumley, and Robert Ferro were of immeasurable help in assembling this book. The valuable diligence of both Michele Tempesta and Ilaria Rattazzi equalled only their lovely presences. And finally the author wishes to remember Marilyn Allen, in whose walled Mexican garden this project first took life.

Introduction to the Artist
Gabriel Bella

Children say *rich* to define people with a lot of money. Later on they learn the word wealthy, using it to sound at home in the grown-up world of many syllables. When that is over, if they are lucky, they put the word rich back into their vocabulary. We try to approximate what we have lost, sometimes finding that it is still there intact.

My discovery of Bella came about in such a way. On my earliest visits to Venice I happened upon his paintings with a particular pleasure, feeling a youthful kinship with his naïveté in a city filled to the brim and overflowing with Great Art. So full of life, of *feste*, games, promenades, and sailing boats, each with its caption in a language I barely understood, his canvases illuminated the dark gallery in which they hung. It seemed unfair, even then, that Bella's work be given such a lightless home. I delighted in them. And then I forgot them. Canaletto and Guardi and other masters of Venice proved superior in every way. I could not ignore their pre-eminence. Colossal sums were paid for them at auctions. Without shirking, their reproductions greeted the eye on posters, in printshops, bookshops; every cardseller had stacks of them on streetcorners. Poor Bella hung in the dark.

It was while I was on an assignment in Venice that I came upon his canvases once again. One room of the Querini-Stampalia Collection is devoted to them; they crowd the walls with such desperation that certain of them—neither the best nor the worst—are hung four-tiered on rollers, like wallpaper samples. I have only the highest praise for the Querini-Stampalia, a generous organization near San Marco, privately funded, with a particularly fine collection of the works of Longhi. It maintains a remarkable library open to the public late into the day, a rarity in a city where most archives are relatively inaccessible. But the Bella paintings still hang there in the gloom.

Perhaps they do not shine because they have never been particularly noticed. Isn't it the same with certain of the extremely beautiful or wonderfully talented among us who are quite prepared to live their lives neglecting themselves because, it seems, no one has ever mentioned that they were extraordinary? I resolved, then, to investigate Mr. Bella.

The results were disappointing. Before 1960, there is scant mention of him in reference works either about Venice or about art. The Dictionnaire des Peintres et Sculpteurs (1960) and the Thiembecker Kunstler Lexicon (1964) each provide him with a short paragraph. Lorenzetti, whose guide book on Venice is the most scrupulous and probably the best, states:

On the walls (of the Querini-Stampalia) in four rows and screens, 69 pictures: Scenes of Venetian life, by Gabriel Bella (mid-XVIII) amusing works, which are interesting because of their narrative quality and the faithfulness with which details are reproduced of the most characteristic moments in Venetian life, in spite of the fact that they have little artistic value.[1]

Before returning to America at that time, I managed to order a series of 8×10 glossy black-and-white photographs of almost all of Bella's work from the Cini Foundation. Some photographs were missing. The flood of 1966 had destroyed the negatives. When I arrived in New York, I put the box in a drawer and that was that.

It would seem that Gabriel Bella was destined to languish in darkness both in the States and abroad. But my oldest friend was considering writing a book on Lord Byron and I said: "Why not Byron in Venice?" the Bella paintings coming immediately, if inaccurately, to mind (Byron and Bella were fifty years apart) and I rescued the box from the obscurity of a bureau to look at the pictures once again. In the finest tradition of life's inscrutable ways, my friend began a book about slavery in the American South, and Venice became mine.

Bella's story is not easily reconstructed. From the Venetian archives we learn the date of his birth (1730) and we discover that between 1762 and 1776, he and his wife produced six children. There is also a notation that an uncle died in 1788, leaving him five ducats. And there is nothing more. It was in 1797 that Napoleon entered Venice and abolished the thousand-year republic. The four bronze horses above San Marco—stolen by the Venetians from Constantinople during a thirteenth-century crusade—were dismounted and carted off to Paris. The Venetian motto Pax Tibi Marce was removed from all public monuments. The small matter of Bella's death went unrecorded. The Venetian cemetery on the island of San Michele has few

[1] Giulio Lorenzetti, *Venice and its Lagoons* (Istituto Poligrafico dello Stato, 1961).

tombs with old dates. There is no room to retain past Venetians.

During my investigation of Gabriel Bella, I located an extremely fine work published in Florence, *Feste Veneziane.*[2] Its author has thoroughly and enthusiastically examined most of the eighteenth-century Venetian festivals, using Bella's paintings, big as life in black and white, to illustrate them. Her research into Bella's life was inhibited by the scarcity of information about him. But she did discover that he had worked for the patrician family of Andrea Querini in Treviso, near Venice. As an artisan attached to that family, he was given a certain allowance each day to be spent for gesso and paint. We do not know when or why he was commissioned to paint the sixty-nine paintings that form his collection, but we do know that they were created for a family named Guistinian. Somehow the series found its way intact from the walls and ceilings of their palace back to the Querini. There are transportation receipts, there are inventories, there is a back-and-forth, upside-down story somewhere. There always is, in Venetian history.

Bella has used a Venetian formula that served the republic so well throughout its long history: take what you can from wherever you can, and make it yours. His paintings are frequently interpretations of other paintings —did the Guistinian family yearn for the originals, hiring Bella to reproduce them? An example is his *Festival of Giovedi Grasso* (*Maundy Thursday*) *on the Piazzetta*, a direct copy of the Guardi painting in the Louvre executed in Bella's style. Look at the high wire strung from the campanile to the Doges' Palace: in the Guardi work, the wire is empty; in Bella's painting, we see a boy rushing down the wire, attached to it by rollers around his waist, to present a bouquet of flowers to the Doge. It was called *The Flight of the Turk.* Bella has taken Guardi's blue awnings and given them red and white stripes; he has gone on to further stripe the columns of the baroque decoration dominating the Piazzetta, adding a few bas-reliefs of his own here and there. Unlike the serene blue of Guardi, his sky has clouds passing overhead.

Bella borrowed from Guardi, from Canaletto, from Giacomo Franco, an etcher 150 years before Bella's time. He was not averse to taking things from anonymous painters and etchers, though it is possible that they borrowed their subjects from him. He managed to combine local color with the monumental view to create a style of his own.

Each of Bella's paintings pertains to a specific Venetian rite, although in two of them he has reached back into the history of the republic for his subject. One of these is a conspiracy against the government in 1310. The other is the spectacular entrance of Henri III, King of France and Poland, a visit that had taken place two hundred years before the painter's time. It was

[2] Bianca Tamassia Mazzarotto, *Feste Veneziane* (Sansoni, 1961).

Venice at its most lavish; rarely had a visitor been so entertained, and Venice has long been in the business of entertainment. Tintoretto and Veronese elbowed each other in the crowd to get a look at the king. Palladio designed the arch through which he entered Venice. Giovanni Gabrielli wrote two choral compositions in his honor, and Titian received him at his country home. Veronica Franco, the most celebrated poetess-courtesan of the republic, fell in love with him. He was twenty-three. He was French. His mother was Catherine de Médicis and his sister-in-law was Mary Queen of Scots. When Henri III left Venice, Veronica Franco retired to a home for fallen women near the church of San Sebastiano, now closed. It was the golden age in Venice, apparently overwhelming to Henri III. Soon after his Venetian visit he appeared at a ball in Paris *en travesti*, now known as full drag. But that is another story, and Venice and her extravagances should not be implicated.

Venice overwhelms everybody, although many of its summer visitors flee immediately from the crowds and the vapors and the bric-a-brac. It is the one city in the world where truth and illusion fuse, and this is possibly why everyone is so drawn to it. Were those awnings in the Bella painting really red and white, or were they Guardi's blue? While doing the research for this work, I would come upon a fact in one volume, locate it in a slightly different version in another; it would disappear in a third, only to resurface from the depths of a fourth as a combination of the two others. It is the Venetian way. When the Venetian hero Bartolomeo Colleoni, died at a relatively young age, he left two stipulations in his will: all his fortune would go to the republic on the condition that it be used for a campaign against the Turks and to acknowledge his patriotism, the town would erect a statue of him in the main square—the Piazza San Marco. Venice accepted the bequest but immediately began using the money to finance another war, a battle against the Duke of Ferrara. And his monument was erected on the Campo SS Giovanni e Paolo.

Had Bella lived in today's Venice, probably he would have been a photographer. In his paintings he is always absorbed in capturing the human: here, a pair of Albanians sit smoking long pipes; there, a nobleman raises his hand to instruct a gondolier, or a lady turns to gossip with her neighbor in a church pew. Perhaps I feel a particular sympathy with him in his attention to these details, having dragged my camera equipment down narrow alleys throughout long months in an attempt to capture the gestures and life of the city.

Venice is, of course, meant for painters. Often it seems as though there are only two dimensions operating out of the three available elsewhere. Is it the light reflected from the canals? Is it because the buildings are often lighter underneath—an atavism carried from the time long ago of early huts built on high stilts in the lagoons—the Doges' Palace, all arch and air on its lowest floor, a definitive example? This luminescent quality tends to disappear in photographs of the most ornamental Venetian views, just as butterflies, pinned and framed, reflect no light. The woman gossiping in church, that man selling chestnuts, are material for the camera. It is this capability: the scenery of Venice *with* its Venetians (often painted in various sizes according to his whim, outside the laws of perspective) that I most admire in Bella. Also, I rather enjoy his frequent misspellings, another characteristic we share.

Surely Bella looked over my shoulder once or twice while I worked on this book, keeping me reasonably earthbound; free, I trust, from a Tiepolo loftiness so tempting in any description of Venice. His Venice still remains much as it was in the eighteenth century, even though its festivities languish, its spirit is less resourceful, and now it is no longer a very happy place. But perhaps I am getting ahead of my story.

Contents

Part One
SPECTACLE

Everything was coming apart. Everything was falling. A spinning wind was picking up and whirling: dust, rags, chips of painted wood, bits of gilded plaster, pasteboard bricks, posters; an arid gloom fleeted . . .

Vladimir Nabokov: *Invitation to a Beheading*

Everyone has known moments of happiness only to lose them, to pick them up again somewhere else. Like telephone poles seen from a moving train, suddenly they no longer parallel the tracks, they veer away, disappear, all hope is lost for another encounter. But here they come striding long-legged into view as your train makes a curve. You think now that they will march along forever. You do not see the tunnel up ahead.

For cities too, there are the good times, lean times, long times they lie low in wait for the better times. Walk the deserted streets of Krakow to see a city with hopes deferred. Then there are the times everything stops; the city has reached the end of the line.

Venice! No one sane and no one mad would let Venice die. Like Cassiopeia's Chair and the Sisters of the Pleiades, the constellation of Venice seems to have been there forever. Born in the year 421 on March 25, the legends say, at noon. Listen to its horoscope: a city built on water will grow into a republic lasting a thousand years. The Serenissima, most serene of cities. Beautiful, rich, powerful, gifted, all those conditions we tend to worship and litanize. If we cannot have them for ourselves we imagine them in our celebrities, our Superstars. Venice the Supercity. Her name has been known for forty generations. Carthage and Constantinople have come and gone, but Venice endures, though only just.

"Is Venice *dying?*" Whispering voices in startled choruses surround her in her grand bedside in the lagoons. Consumed by corrosion, corruption, drowning in the waters that launched her, she has her good days and her bad days the same as any other patient with a terminal illness. Perhaps she no longer cares to be patched up and mended. In the manner of certain elderly persons, part of her has already flown the coop into the higher realms; your great-aunt who no longer listens to what you are saying, preferring instead to concentrate on some precious memory set like a jewel in her past. Only a long history of good manners keeps her from acting the fool now.

You cannot ask a city what it wants and needs. Everyone in it would claim separate, selfish things. In the long run it is always money, love, and health, with good connections and good looks running just behind. Asking the

Venetians about Venice, you would find that they expect some larger power to determine the fate of their city—which, of course, it will do. Some leave town, others stay, until the water laps once too often at the structure of their lives. Then they too move elsewhere. Some will never leave, will risk going down like brave captains with their ship. "My parents would die if they had to leave Venice," confides a friend who is indifferent to the monuments, the art, the splendor everyone from outside Venice is concerned about salvaging. "Like fish out of water," he adds, the phrase more than usually apt. It remains to be seen whether the stone, mortar, underground tubing, and underwater pilings are in accord; whether the nearby industry can resist sacrificing tradition for progress; whether the ancient museum that is Venice will be abandoned for the quick, cheap cities across the causeway. And finally, whether the sea wants to claim her, as Poseidon did Amphitrite, once and for all and forever.

The landscape surrounding her is uncared for, untilled, unlovely, unloved. Those telephone poles seen from the train stop at the lagoon. What lies ahead looks like a badly organized fleet moored in a quiet sea. One begins to consider the inconveniences waiting at the station. There will be porters, hotel agents, folks who have a room to rent, pressing forward. Once outside there will be other porters, a bewildering selection of water ferries and private taxi boats, and then the long alleyways on foot with the *facchino* lagging behind under a mule's burden of baggage. Perhaps one would have done better to have stayed in the Alps.

By car, the backed-up summer traffic funneling into the two garages is reminiscent of an oversold carnival. Billboards loom large: Fiat, Agip, and Campari crane their necks over the grim *autorimessa.* Horns honk futilely, families fight and perspire in their lined-up cars, luggage racks are overburdened. The final drive into the garage spirals upward, around and around past the Venetians' cars to where the tourists' lot begins. Scattered about are families unloading their trunks, weary before they've seen a sight.

The arrival by plane takes you low over tiled roofs and no green spaces, past a glaring mirror of muddy water. By the time you fathom what lies below, you have passed Venice and are circling over the airstrip. Then comes the luggage wait, then the customs, then the taxis, then the arrival at the Piazzalle Roma where you converge with all the others newly arrived by train and by car. It lacks only a corps of drum majorettes to lead you one and all to the Piazza San Marco.

You cannot sneak up on Venice for a first view from country road, or sail quietly into the lagoon on a skiff. Ideally, to discover Venice, I would have you drugged and blindfolded and set down next to a side canal.

Abandon, then, the mechanics of getting there. Imagine a late autumn afternoon. You are alone with no baggage. You are not meant now to be terribly happy, for the autumnal Venice would steal it from you and not be forgiven. The unique Venetian gift out of season is a sublime melancholy. Happiness is out of the question and you were wrong to think you might find it here. Melancholy in any case has been too much maligned.

Now you find yourself moving as you do in a dream, the home-before-dark hurrying when the legs cannot keep up with the mind. The wall next to you bears a worn stenciled sign reading *Fondamenta degli Incurabili,* the Incurables' Quay, fronting a disused hospital of the same name. Someone withered sulks in the doorway as though still trying to gain admission. Far off in the lagoon a solitary boat cleaves its way across water the color of eggplant; at its helm a sailor sings to keep himself warm and less lonely. You turn the corner under an immense golden ball, the figure of Fortune skating unsteadily on top of it, pointing out the direction of the wind to no one but you.

How slowly the gondola reaches you, with barely a sound. Another passenger appears from the shadows, steps on board, and steadies himself against your shoulder as the gondola rocks, turns, heads across the Grand Canal, across water now as black as the boat itself. The methodical slicing of the oar to tug you forward is a comfort. And there, just ahead, is Byzantium.

No person, no one generation could have conceived it; nothing matches, everything leans, the elements of accident and imperfection characterize it as they do every masterpiece. You look away, study something of your own, the pattern of your shirtsleeve, the face of your watch, for reassurance just as in the bull ring the animals return to their private place, their *querencia,* when the crowd and the matador and the spectre of their approaching death is overwhelming. The Piazza seen in autumn is as eternal. Now is your chance to seize it, the surreal center of an irrational island.

When you cross the paving stones, with the solidity under your feet you try to trust that what you see will not perish before you turn the corner. Each Venetian building seems to have another mirror half wavering below it, insubstantial, changing with the colors of the sky, the tides of the Adriatic. Everything must stand on an upside-down self. Below the pavement on which you walk, a yard deeper, is yet another pavement, in a fishbone pattern, that Venetians crossed seven hundred years ago. And below that is the sea.

You overhear two elderly patrician ladies wearing their fur tippets and grandmotherly jewelry discussing the two granite columns heralding the Piazzetta. The figures way on top of the pedestals seem as unreal as the dialogue.

"It is the lion of San Marco. And it's Etruscan," says one woman with

authority.

"No, it is not. I've read that it's Persian. Or was it Chinese?" Her voice is feeble with age and indecision. "In any case, it's not a lion. It is a *chimera* with wings attached later." She nods in agreement with herself.

They continue to dispute each other, phantom voices fluttering in your ear as you try to grasp and fix in your mind the figure they discuss before it raises bronze wings and lifts into the night. In fact, the ladies' two cents' worth is all documented historical conjecture. The French took the statue away with the fall of Venice and returned it two decades later in eighty-four pieces, like a puzzle. And still no one knows its story.

The other column supports San Teodoro, the original patron saint of Venice, standing with his dragon. His head is a marble portrait of Mithridates, King of Pontus; the torso Roman, of Hadrian's time. The dragon followed fourteen centuries later from Lombardy. But what you see up there is a copy. Accustom yourself to the Venetian hide-and-seek. The original statue deteriorates in the basement of Doges' Palace, where rags are hung up to dry.

The Doges' Palace once had moats and drawbridges and towers. It has been shaped by the Gothic and Renaissance and touched by the East. It is far lower than the pavement around it, weighed down by its burden of history. No area of it is unornamented, yet it occupies its space with an inscrutable solidity. It was used to house the Doge, seat the government, and confine the imprisoned, all at the same time. Enfeebled, it now poses politely as a museum. But never mind; no museum in the world is contained in such a splendid skin as this.

It should not be discouraging that much of what you see and hear is deceptive, that layer after layer peeled away will probably not reveal the heart after all. Postcards and junk souvenirs are hawked in front of the Basilica of San Marco, itself a series of souvenirs constructed out of loot from the East; a stupendous thieves' market forming a three-dimensional icon. Gold in the mosaics catches the illumination in some mystical way, particularly the arch on the left, which happens to be the only survivor of the original façade. A canopy of pigeons obligingly unrolls swiftly across the building and disappears. It is night. The stallkeepers close up shop.

The companion piece to the church is the Campanile, the bell tower. Its present form has been achieved after centuries of restorations, earthquakes, shifts in taste. At one time it was sheathed in brass and glinted for miles around. It has served as lighthouse and lightning conductor. Galileo brought out the first telescope onto its loggia. Cages were suspended on its southern side to torture prisoners in the sun. Cannons were mounted on it in a war with the Genoese. An emperor trotted to the top of it on a horse. Finally it collapsed gracefully, in 1902, as a crowd watched from the sidelines. The

master of Venice's household, *el paron de casa,* had expired. You see a duplicate built in its place, *dov'era, com'era,* where and how it was.

Wherever the eye settles there is a story behind a story like those labels on salt containers in the grocery store showing a little girl carrying under her arm a box of salt with a little girl carrying under her arm a box of salt, smaller and smaller and less distinct as they move towards some never-never land.

A jumble of images spills out in the backward rush of that square's history. So complicated is it that you can only grasp certain views as they fly by. Napoleon closes in the far end to create what he would call the largest drawing room in Europe. Earlier, a canal runs through the center of it, the Doges' Palace is surrounded by water. Familiar sights begin to blur. The Basilica is burned down in the late tenth century. An evil Doge is murdered: "And the soul of the Duke leaving the prison house of the body sought the threshold of the realms above." Then it is quiet. Dust blows across the unpaved square. There are a few scattered huts on high posts driven into the soil and what would become the Basilica is a thatched church in the form of a Greek cross. And finally, in the farthest reaches of the imagination, a low-lying marsh reclines in the mist of a lagoon with only

the occasional cry of a tall bird among reeds. No square at all. Only the realization that no story has a true beginning anyway.

How long the Piazza San Marco has taken to accumulate! You sit drinking your espresso now that it is night and find that it is really too chilly to be outside at a caffè table. Everyone seems to have gone. The three amiable orchestras have stopped playing; the cathedral is dark; the illumination has been shut off for the long dark night. Only the amethyst glow from the street lanterns remains. Pigeons dart by urgently, now sinister, flying lower, faster. The few people crossing the Piazza shout to each other to break the silence. You get up, pay your bill to a waiter who yawns openly and disappears. When you are alone, do you notice in the corner of the square a stage manager beginning to take the scenery away?

Almost everything you can think of has been done before; in, on, under, across or on top of the Piazza San Marco. You might make love, conceive, and give birth beneath those arcades in daylight and in darkness and set no precedents. Were you to die there it would be no novelty, since there is a long list of previous deaths in the Piazza both unplanned and premeditated. In the mid-fifteen hundreds, a gentleman named Natale Veneziano hurled

himself from the top of the bell tower, beginning a vogue for that manner of suicide. Assassinations have taken place in its shadows, executions out in the open. Gallows were placed between the columns of San Marco and San Teodoro until two hundred years ago, so that the passengers disembarking from schooners would be faced with dangling corpses before they got to the church. There is also a grave somewhere under the Piazza where two erring priests were buried alive.

Bullfights were held in the square, bazaars were spread across it, oriental carpets have covered it, and an awning with stars was slung up above. Pigeons were required to spell out Coca-Cola on it, a helicopter lowered a cement saint to it and a kinetic sculpture was erected and dismantled on top of it in a day.

Earthquakes have shaken it, lightning has hit it, and it regularly floods. For eight hours it survived a bombing in the light of the full moon, the bombs all falling into the lagoon. Even Adolf Hitler had said it should be left alone. Though auctions have been held on it, *it*, itself, has never been sold. History, though, is not finished with it. Only several years ago did an American try to buy Rome's Colosseum.

Horas non numero nisi serenas, it says on the clock tower leading to the

Piazza, only happy hours. Legend has it that the clockmakers, father and son, who created the complicated mechanism, had their eyes put out so that they could never duplicate what they had achieved.

"Don't change a thing," says a lady to her guide on seeing the Piazza for the first time in a movie called *Summertime*. Later on, Katharine Hepburn would oblige two Venetian myths, first falling into a canal and later, more gently, in love. The canal would be responsible for giving the actress a chronic eye infection, but the moviegoers sighing over Venice had no idea.

"It's like, um, don't laugh, like when I made love for the first time," says a young bride when she steps into the square in a more recent film.

Love, of course, it's always that. If Venice is the Mecca for art historians, it is the Lourdes for lovers. Honeymooning couples hold hands, lovers hold hands, the narrowness of the alleys forces even friends into a physical closeness. So synonymous is Venice with love that to say one is visiting it alone seems suspect, as though one might not have correctly understood what being in Venice implies. You do not step into a brothel for a cup of bouillon.

Bright couples circle the colonnades in pinwheel colors. Even the *carabinieri*, the decorative police guards in Napoleonic costumes, stroll by in twos. The tourist alone looks very much alone in that Piazza. The vast

quadrate outdoor caffès immediately reveal the absence of tablemates; a solitary visitor drums impatient fingers in time with the music or points his swizzle stick at the chummy pigeons.

Wind up three orchestras competing across the square. The sound is that of a music school in preparation for several concerts. Music written as the score for films taking place in Venice is now played in real life, another Venetian reversal process. Celluloid images merge with authentic experience. It is the extra dimension that pushes you, no matter how unwilling, to the brink of the maudlin. You are not expected to resist. With good grace, you tilt back in your chair to be submerged by it all. The Piazza San Marco is made out of confectionary sugar and its syrupy music is just about to rise above your head. You capitulate.

The place is bathed in mauve and gold and the first star is quite clearly *there* to the east of the bell tower, and the shred of a new moon is rising just *there* above the palace roof. I remember in my adolescence being patiently taught *stella* and *luna* as I stretched suntanned limbs slouched in a caffè chair. As I mimicked those words, I thought: "Nothing will ever be more beautiful than it is at this moment," and away I floated on the magic carpet of the Piazza.

Having led you this far, Venice stops. Venice, as it happens, frowns on sex.

"But this is *VEN*ice," you say to the concierge as you pass the front desk with the girl you have discovered in all that mooning and June-ing of the Piazza. "*Un momento, prego,*" he is saying. The word Venice dies on your lips. Venice, as though it was some privileged place; Venice, as in venery, venereal, venerable. You hear him tell you that it is forbidden for men to have ladies in their rooms, for ladies to have gentlemen, for any other combination to assemble, even if they register, even if you offer to pay for the other half of the room, your lonely room with only one pathetic bed out of its superfluous two meticulously turned down for the solitary night's sleep ahead.

"What," you might ask, with mounting incredulity, "what if it happened that we were both actually staying at the hotel?"

"Then under those circumstances," he replies, commerce for the moment winning out over morality in the finest Venetian tradition, "it would be your affair." He snorts, the way they did in films of the thirties and goes over to the next client requiring his attention.

In a last desperate gesture you summon back the concierge—they prefer the French title to the more modest Italian *portiere*—and this time pull rank. After all, you are the client, it is the likes of you who keep his town from going under: "I think you may have misunderstood," you say. "I wish to get something from my room. I hardly see where there is any harm in the lady coming up to see the view of the canal. She is interested in moving to this hotel."

"I *see*," says the concierge, all smiles now that the misunderstanding has been cleared up, pleased that you have recommended his little hotel. "In that case, when you come back down I will give *the lady* your key and she may go up. I would be delighted for her to see the view."

You fly down the alleys together, lose your way, your patience, your desire. There seems no way to turn.

"Gondola!" says a man popping up from nowhere, wearing a straw hat with a crimson ribbon, divining your problem. He is sympathetic. He has dealt with these things before. He knows of bridges darker than the black of his boat. He will look to the stars, smoke a cigarette and think his thoughts. He will even sing "O Sole Mio" or "Arrivederici Roma" reasonably on key. If the concierge has the manner of an Art Deco performer, the gondolier is straight out of the *opera buffa.*

You cannot escape surveillance. You long for a stretch of beach with no footprints other than your own: Venice out there as a backdrop instead of the infernal scenery in which you find yourselves.

The outlying uninhabited islands can only be reached by private boat. Until recently St. Arian—or the Isola Bianca—was covered with human bones brought out there from the cemetery. Now the bones have been burned and the island is entirely covered with brambles higher than a kangaroo. You are cautioned not to enter; there is a high wall; the place is filled with snakes.

The low islands with no villages and no inhabitants are marshy, there is no specific point at which land begins. At the water's edge the grey mud is like quicksand.

Venice, too, falls off at the edges. Maps of the city tend to become less specific past the Arsenal and photographic inserts of the town's most popular monuments are callously printed over the less travelled streets as though they were not worth troubling about. Tourists feel ill at ease and crowds fall away as the Piazza is left behind. They cannot find their way. Beyond the Arsenal near the listless public park anxiety sets in. The area around the station produces a disturbing confusion. It does not feel like Venice. There are the cars. There is something *louche* in the air; people hang about as they do near betting windows at the racetrack. You are brutalized by billboards in a last hysterical surge of advertising. Fiat has erected a sign just opposite the canal from the railroad. Splashed across the street floor of a Gothic palace is a colossal poster of automobiles. In the water, bobbing up and down underneath, is a row of gondolas. It is uncomfortable. You wish to be in or out of Venice but not on its periphery.

When you walk back towards the center of town, your minds are no longer on the physical. It is late, the streets are empty. Down the dark alleys of Venice you hear no low moans of pleasure from behind those closed shutters.

Instead it is the sound of dishes being scraped, of yawns unstifled. The water lapping eternally against the palace walls is the sensual sound of the city, the caress tinged with sadness.

It can be considered a tease, then, the promises insinuated by those Venetian nights, like the splendid Church of the Salute which presents itself monumentally carved and ornamented facing the Grand Canal. But seen from the back it is not the great stone galleon it pretends to be: an unprepossessing provincial building is lost in the jumble of architecture surrounding it.

During the day, you drift past the palaces along the Grand Canal as though in a dream. There is a rustle, always, in the crowd on the ferries. No one takes Venice for granted. Even those who commute daily look up from their newspapers to take in the view, observe the boat life, scan certain windows of their preference. Those surfaces have been gazed upon with more love, longing, and cupidity than any other thoroughfare's flanks in the world.

"*La plus belle rue je croy qui soit en tout le monde,*" wrote de Commines in 1495.

"Man, do you believe this *street!*" says a hippie dressed in rags bought with much haggling in Afghanistan to his similarly attired girl friend. She nods.

It is impossible not to echo something already said about Venice. You find yourself thinking that the decorations on top of the cupolas of San Marco resemble children's jacks and then come upon it in Mary McCarthy's *Venice Observed.* The arches on the Basilica remind you of marble foam, and there it is, secreted in a Ruskin sentence.[1]

And round the walls of the porches there are set pillars of variegated stones, jasper and porphyry, and deep-green serpentine spotted with flakes of snow, and marbles, that half refuse and half yield to the sunshine, Cleopatra-like, "their bluest veins to kiss"—the shadow, as it steals back from them, revealing line after line of azure undulation, as a receding tide leaves the waved sand their capitals rich with interwoven tracery, rooted knots of herbage, and drifting leaves of acanthus and vine, and mystical signs, all beginning and ending in the Cross; and above them, in the broad archivolts, a continuous chain of language of life—angels, and the signs of heaven, and the labours of men, each in its appointed season upon the earth; and above these, another range of glittering pinnacles, mixed with white arches edged with scarlet flowers,—a confusion of delight, amidst which the breasts of the Greek horses are seen blazing in their breadth of golden strength, and the St. Mark's lion, lifted on a blue field covered with stars, until at last, as if in ecstasy, the crests of the arches break into a marble foam, and toss themselves far into the blue sky in flashes and wreaths of sculptured spray, as if the breakers on the Lido shore had

[1] John Ruskin, *The Stones of Venice,* Vol. II, ch. IV.

PART ONE: SPECTACLE

Sposalicio Di Vna Nobil
Dama Veneta

Procesione Con Sua Serenità
Il Giorno Del Corpus Domini

PART ONE: SPECTACLE

1. FESTIVAL OF GIOVEDI GRASSO (MAUNDY THURSDAY) ON THE PIAZZETTA

While perfumed eggs were thrown, butchers carried aloft a recently severed head of a bull in a ritual dating back to the twelfth century. In the center of the Piazzetta, an immense baroque ornament was constructed; on one of its platforms an orchestra played; fireworks were launched from another. A wire stretched from the top of the Campanile to the Doges' Palace, and a youth streaked down it to present a bunch of flowers to the Doge. The human pyramid being performed is called a *forze d'Ercole;* the small boy doing acrobatics on top was called the *crest.*

2. THE ASCENSION DAY FAIR

Bernardino Maccaruzzi designed this oval structure—collapsible in three days and reconstructible in five—winning an award to organize a fair which until then seemed to have lacked a certain Venetian grandeur. Merchants from around the world brought their goods to Venice for this event. The more expensive items were exhibited on the inside colonnades of the oval to discourage theft. Artists also brought portfolios and sculptures, and Canova, at nineteen, was among them.

3. MARRIAGE OF A NOBLEWOMAN AT THE SANTA MARIA DELLA SALUTE

Marriage preparations were traditionally elaborate. The young brides were often plucked out of convents, which were more akin to finishing schools than religious retreats. The wedding usually took place at the home of the intended husband; the girl's ballet master accompanied her into the main hall. Certain grand weddings were supplied with honor guards, seen here waiting to raise their halberds in greeting to the bride. A year following the marriage, the wife was permitted—even expected—to take on her *cicesbeo* (from the word "to whisper"), an influential and decorative male who would fortify the demands of the household.

4. THE PROCESSION ON GOOD FRIDAY

Only one square in Venice is called the Piazza. And it was under a full moon on the Piazza that this procession took place, unusual in that the Doge was not in attendance. High candles illuminated the great Venetian palaces and the façades of San Marco. Priests and patricians walked solemnly beneath a black canopy as church members accompanied them single file. In the background is the church of San Geminiano, later destroyed by Napoleon, who found it out of symmetry with the Piazza.

5. CORPUS DOMINI PROCESSION IN THE PIAZZA

Winding around the base of the Piazza, a temporary covered archway reached grandly above the Venetians as they paraded from one door of the Basilica, around the Piazza, past the clock tower, and back into the Basilica again. In the earliest days of this procession, tradition demanded that each senator and patrician walk accompanied by an impoverished person or a pilgrim as a sign of humility, but it would appear that by the eighteenth century this practice had vanished.

been frost-bound before they fell, and the sea-nymphs had inlaid them with coral and amethyst.

Every stone in Venice has been scrutinized, as we learn from reading Mr. Ruskin, who must have climbed many ladders, caught many colds in his marvelous investigation.

There is a plaque to Robert Browning who lived in the immense Plazzo Rezzonico but none visible to Whistler who also lived there later, in what was then known as sin, with his model Maude. When Byron took up residence at the Rezzonico he frequently swam the canals, his servant following along in a boat carrying his clothes. Byron inaugurated an annual swimming competition, the *coppa Byron* after winning the initial bout against an army general named Mengaldo. He proclaimed that he had remained in the water for four hours and twenty minutes. The skeptical Venetians whispered foul play, but not to Lord Byron's face.

The Rezzonico is today a museum. Its proportions are extravagant, its art collection prestigious. It is a place once cherished by visiting foreigners who came to stay for a while. Above the well-travelled gallery floors, resplendent with their Guardis, their Longhis, their Tiepolo ceilings, a terrible stillness is in the rooms. A tiny marionette theatre stands in near darkness, no audience of children to enjoy it. Lifeless wooden figures hang on the vacant stage. In a bedroom the silk bedspread is within a breath of falling to pieces. Outside the window, Venetian housetops reflect the sunlight, but a faded pattern of Roman ruins repeats itself over bed and bureau. Surely in some Roman palazzo overlooking the Forum there will be a wallpaper of Venetian Views, in a Parisian apartment a Georgian crescent will prevail on the chintz, and in Bath, the Ile St. Louis will appear on the dinner plates. There is a syndicate of scenes treasured by the Western world. Quite possibly—considering the number of paintings of it scattered around the globe—Venice heads the list. This is surely why Ruskin troubled so in trying to identify all the parts that comprised the whole, an attempt to expose, once and for all, the mechanics of a place so universally loved.

Wagner died in style at the Vendramin-Calergi palace on the Grand Canal, loved by the Venetians who considered themselves uniquely capable of understanding his brooding northern temperament. As far back as the mid-fifteen hundreds, Venice became the great center for music in Europe. Both Gabriellis served as chapel masters at San Marco, followed later by Monteverdi. Scarlatti taught at its conservatory. So often have composers been born in Venice or have settled there that history would be in debt to the city if only for the sounds that have come out of it. It is in the few touching pieces by Benedetto Marcello and the concertos of Arcangelo Corelli—the first music in that form—that the liquid quality of Venice is

revealed in music. It is a Venetian cadence close to the hearts of Vivaldi, Haydn, Handel, Mozart, and Albinoni—all of them directly influenced by Corelli.

A city slow to settle its accounts with history, the municipality only several years ago erected a tablet commemorating a visit Mozart had made to Venice two hundred years before. Probably he was called Signor Cavaliere by his hosts, having just been awarded the Golden Spur by the Pope in Rome. He was there to enjoy the carnival. He was fifteen.

Instructions were left for Stravinsky to be buried in Venice, and his funeral was a state occasion, a contrast to the burial months before of Ezra Pound, which was officially ignored. The press, film cameras, music lovers and gawkers crammed into the Greek and Russian Orthodox cemetery on the island of San Michele. The presiding archimandrite, his face and manner approximating the icons in the San Giorgio dei Greci, lifted his eyes as he recited his prayers, and it was difficult to detect whether his gaze was on a larger, more powerful diocese or a vision of the Almighty. In any case, he was trailed for his autograph for days after. Fresh flowers are placed daily on Stravinsky's grave. The custodian there is a misshapen woman whose open smile reveals carious teeth. When questioned about who had arranged for the flowers, she said "they are sent," as though some Divine power had placed the order. The tomb bears no dates, no sentiments; Stravinsky's name is written in script reminiscent of Matisse, immediately identifying his period.

Two of Venice's most popular heroes died in other lands. Casanova ended his days in Bohemia a year after the fall of the republic. His biography seems to pertain to a crowd: alchemist, mathematician, violinist, fabric manufacturer, wizard, lottery director, spy, swordsman, cook, lover: that, of course, history's favorite lover. The rustic observer of Venetian ways, the playwright "Papa" Goldoni died in Paris having written longingly of his city:

> Da Venezia lontan do mile mia
> no passa di che no me vegna in mente
> el dolce nome de la patria mia
> el lenguaza e i costumi de la zente . . .[2]

In the tradition of beloved, creative geniuses, he died penniless, far from home.

Vivaldi died in Vienna, his music slightly out of fashion in a Venice then concerned with setting new trends in style. Known as a violinist and composer who taught music to orphan girls at the Santa Maria della Pietà,

[2] "From Venice faraway two thousand miles, a day does not pass without there coming to mind the sweet name of my country, the language and customs of my people . . ."

Vivaldi was also a priest who had to relinquish the celebration of the Mass because of chronic asthma.

Of painters, the list is longest, the Venetian contribution awesome. So many canvases fill the churches, museums, schools, and palaces that they are listed like film stars on small yellow signs tacked onto the façades, miniature marquees to inform you who, in the galaxy of artists, is appearing where.

Most visitors eventually file past the Giorgione in the Accademia Gallery unless they get bogged down in the glass shops or on the gondola rides. It is suitable that such a mysterious picture should be the Venetian pride and joy. With the fanfaronade of immense canvases, of painting upon painting covering all those walls and ceilings, the one to cause a reverential hush is of sober proportions, *La Tempesta*. Everyone who sees it stands stock-still, as they do in front of the *Mona Lisa*. Like visiting heads of state behind protecting shields of plate glass, the two pictures tantalize the public. Does the Mona Lisa smile, as it has been suggested, because she alone knows she expects a child? Will the naked woman breast-feeding her baby have a liaison with the soldier in *La Tempesta?* Lightning spears the sky. We will never know what happens next. Something has been imprisoned midway to a conclusion with no explanation by the artist. The atmosphere remains with you as you go on to the other rooms in the Accademia until you reach the brilliant Carpaccios; there, the world opens up once again and fills with sunlight.

The Church of the Frari is a hodgepodge of museum, sanctuary, mausoleum, and monument. You must pay to enter. If you have come there to rest your parcels and your weary legs or are in need of a meditative moment there is an admission fee. Titian is buried there. He had been venerated as a king. The Pope received him in Rome, the reigning monarchs vied to entertain him as house guest, Charles V made him court painter at Hapsburg and Bologna. He wound up in the dictionary as the word for the color of hair he painted. When he died at ninety-nine it was of the plague, and his body was thrown onto a heap along with the other victims. Then his house was vandalized. Finally his remains were rescued and his burial at the Frari was an august occasion. Two and half centuries later Canova designed a monument to him of suitable larger-than-life proportions, a pyramid several stories high to be attached to the walls of the Frari. But Canova died before the work was completed, and it was used instead as his own tomb, finished by his pupils and paid for by his friends. His heart has been preserved inside it in a porphyry vase—Canova, who had begun his career carving butter into fanciful shapes for a patrician family's dinner table.

Among the buzzing throngs that enter the Frari, authoritative voices ring out with the artists' names, the masterpieces, the dates.

"*Ça, c'est Tintorette,*" says a Frenchman to his wife, as they gaze up at the

Assunta of Titian.

"*Non,*" she replies, clicking over the stone floors to read the inscription, then clicking back, "*c'est Titien.*"

"*Oui,*" he agrees, "*c'est comme je disais. Ça* annonce *Tintorette.*" He does not bat an eye. Hard facts are less important here than they are on the *terraferma.*

"You see those windows over there?" asks a French girl as we sail down the Grand Canal. "Desdemona's!" she announces, expecting a blond figure to manifest itself from behind the shutters, forgetting that Desdemona met her fate in Cyprus.

Looking up from the ferry railing, I stare in the direction of her pointed finger and locate three windows in the autumn gloom. I am not at all that well informed on this matter. I will try to investigate. I thought *Othello* was a made-up story, just like *Romeo and Juliet.* "And how do you explain Juliet's tomb in Verona?" she sniffs, reading my mind. "A fact is a fact." She tosses her hair, unmindful that facts and fantasies are interchangeable in this city. I admit that the windows do look sinister, though undoubtedly they are shuttered only because the owner has gone skiing in Cortina d'Impezzo.

To even things out, I point to the Palazzo Dario across the way, mentioning the murder that took place there several years ago. But Desdemona's tragedy seems more Venetian, taking precedence with my friend; dark Moorish deeds spreading across the canal more horribly than the fate of the Count of the Dario who was hit over the head in real life with a silver candelabra almost yesterday. It still crops up in newspapers, still unsolved.

Many have admired, coveted, and owned the Dario. It is the absolute Venetian palace-on-the-Grand-Canal, small enough to yearn for without feeling foolish. It was created in the calmer period of the Renaissance, designed by Lombardo with circular ornaments of marble set into its surface. It has been painted by Monet. And it leans.

The back garden is also of manageable size. You would not need a gardener. When I first came to Venice I was invited there with my mother for tea. The reflections cast by the Grand Canal onto the walls and ceilings were hypnotic. The walls were covered in a cloth printed by Fortuny, using a system so unique that its composition is kept in a Venetian vault. A large working loom stood in the solarium overlooking the garden; there was still a private gondola. But under the radiant surface it was disclosed that the foreign owners were having difficulties with an unsympathetic municipality, in the tradition of the Venetian facts and fantasies, and eventually they left and moved elsewhere. After the count was murdered, the palace was again sold. The Dario has assumed the reputation of a place of ill omen.

Later, I investigate the Othello house in Tassini, a writer who published a history in 1863 on most of the Venetian houses and streets. I learn that the Casa dell'Othello is on the Campo del Carmine. Shakespeare, he writes, confused the family name, Moro, with the man's complexion. Cristoforo Moro, Venetian aristocrat, lieutenant in Cyprus, married a certain Demonio Bianco—demon white becoming demon black. Demonio, he adds, became Desdemona for literature's sake. And then the Venetian punchline: in actual fact, it was the Guoro crest on that palace, not that of the Moro. Now the Moros, it seemed, were domiciled elsewhere. . . .

I do not tell my French friend. I cannot go through the rigmarole. She will keep on pointing out those windows anyway. Fact and illusion are of no interest to her. The next time we look up from a boat at those three windows with their Gothic arches it is warm with bright sunlight. Desdemona's plight is no longer relevant. The Palazzo Dario seems inviolate. A *cameriere* is beating the life out of a carpet from an upstairs window. We are heading for the Lido.

The hotels are closed, the cabanas are closed, there is no one on the beach. Desultory nineteenth-century streets greet us with no cheer, their houses boarded up, their trees without leaves. One small trattoria consents to serve us a plate of pasta. One lone automobile misses us as it swerves around a corner. We stand on the dark, iodic sand, looking ahead at the glinting horizon. If we were to take off from the pier and fly straight as arrows, down the long narrow passage of the Adriatic, up above Mount Olympus, we would touch down in Africa at the mouth of the Nile.

Given the dismal moods in which we found ourselves on the ferry heading back to Venice, we noted a sameness about the passengers: similar coats, similar conversations. It seemed then, that there were few strings to the Venetian bow, that variety came only with the summer and the tourists. Tourists are the Venetian entertainment.

Everyone comes through eventually; they always have. The Venetians' revenge is that they can easily reverse the zoo/spectator role, surely the dream of all caged things. They observe while being observed, throughout half of every year.

While a guide points at the Ca'd'oro, explaining in three languages that the Gothic façade was once covered with gold, Venetians can be seen jabbing each other in the ribs with delight over the plump girl in the tour wearing a floppy hat and tight shorts. In a tennis-watchers' arc of heads, they will follow with intense interest under a pouring rain the brush strokes of a British woman painting the church of the Salute, an umbrella propped over her canvas. Look at the church. Look at the canvas. Everything, everyone gets drenched.

Someone too tall and stooped, someone too low to the ground, will be noted. A horse face, a moon face, a black face, a face too pink will not pass unseen; the virago trudging by hauling her own luggage and the gent carrying his foot-long plastic replica of David destined for a curio cabinet across the seas will fall under their scrutiny. If the smile lingers too long they will suspect it, if the labored sentence in faulty Italian takes too much time they will complete it, if they are treated like servants they will not be surprised. They have long ago adjusted to that.

They will detect in their tourists fundamental truths that travelling clothes are intended to obscure. They expect everyone who visits to be a little crazy; if not crazy, then on the make; if not on the make then either they are neuter or they are scholars. They have been so used to brushing up against the famous, the frauds, the freaks, and the film stars that they profess never to be surprised. A boatman knows the inside story of a king; his father rowed Rachmaninoff; Isadora Duncan—or was it Sarah Bernhardt—left his grandfather a watch; Noël Coward taught him a song; and only last month a pair of Siamese twins hopped four-footed onto his boat. None of it is true. All of it is true.

During the off-season months the amusement lessens considerably. The tourists are few, the more earnest and academic come then, etiolated by the greyness and the winter clothes into vague shapes moving from monument to monument. They are neither original, colorful, nor amusing to the Venetians who, with relief, can relax. Gondoliers remove their straw hats, tend to drink a lot and play cards. Occasionally they will fall into their raffish ways, doing a turn to keep the act practiced. But they are humanized by cold weather. Worries shift. Children's marks at school, illnesses, relatives with whom they've been out of touch, claim their time.

A carnival diversion is set up along the quay of the Riva degli Schiavone, a provincial affair run by itinerant people who have taken jobs on their way elsewhere. On barges, large red trucks are brought in containing the generators and the bright equipment of a touring amusement park. For four months the neighborhood around the quay is altered by the noise and activity. Blinking lights illuminate the rides, outlining the swooping, turning, flying mechanisms to spread irregular patterns across the choppy water of the lagoon. Luna Park, it is called, spelled out in fast-moving bulbs.

"Does it turn?" a grandmother enquires of the carousel keeper as he sits in the fog reading a comic book.

"Certainly," he replies, glancing up, looking over at the muffled child hanging back. The child turns away and grabs his grandmother's hem, fearful of that darkened double-decker menagerie of wooden animals and chariots.

A button is pressed and the merry-go-round lights up and begins a ghostly turn. Beyond it, the moored squat tugboats with mighty names: *Furius, Strenuous, Titanus,* and *Taurus* nod slow agreement in the water, out of synchronization with the motion of the animals. His scarf wound tightly round, the lone child is lifted onto a glass-eyed horse. The concessionaire goes back to his comics; the grandmother looks up and down the broad quay, wondering why they are so alone; the child is transported around and around with no glee.

Along the midway, rifle ranges are run by pretty girls from obscure parts of Italy, stout with many sweaters. "Try a shot!" they implore, thrusting a rifle across the counter. It is like walking past the girls in Pigalle. When they are rejected they pout or shrug; but, resilient, they thrust their rifles out again to someone behind you. If you accept and manage to hit your mark, an antiquated puff of smoke accompanies the bright flash that illuminates your prize, a photograph of yourself striking the bull's-eye.

On Sundays, the carnival attracts a crowd; during the week it is forlorn, it doesn't seem possible that they can make a go of it. The red trucks remain parked along the quay, no longer noticed. In the mornings, people from the neighborhood walk briskly past the closed cartoon-decorated Fun House, past the shuttered stalls of cotton candy and the stilled Ferris wheel. I watched one afternoon a retarded person ride his Bump-Em car all alone in the rink, an entertainment provided by the long-haired pitchman who had forgotten to turn the mechanism off, so busy was he in discussing with a friend the merits of a Lancia over those of a Porche. Both of them perched in their blue jeans along the platform of the ride while the little rubber-fendered car turned, bumping now and then with an unenthusiastic thud into an imperturbed parked vehicle; then continuing on its way. Sparks flew on the wires overhead, outlining the elliptical voyage of the solitary rider. In the background, across the water, barely visible in the fog surrounding it stood Palladio's serene façade of San Giorgio Maggiore, alone on its island in the lagoon.

Part Two
SYSTEMS

"It is so!" she said, with her whole strength; and looked at them with a challenge in her eyes. She stood there, a victor in the good fight which all her life she had waged against the assaults of Reason: hump-backed, tiny, quivering with the strength of her convictions, a little prophetess admonishing and inspired.

Thomas Mann: *Buddenbrooks*

"Chi e?"

"Spazzino."

"Who?"

"Garbageman, signora."

"Ah yes, Piero, yes. It's ready."

The doorbell rings each morning; each morning it is the same exchange, a renewable surprise for the lady on the third floor to receive among her callers the fellow who hauls away her garbage. She clatters down the steps, carrying her filled garbage bag. Provided by the city, it is of a dark grey plastic printed in elegant block letters: AZIENDA MUNICIPALIZZATA/SERVIZI DI N.U./VENEZIA.

Venice the town. Population 100,000, roughly that of Beaumont, Texas. Let us leave the Piazza San Marco.

Piled into metal carts, the garbage is then heaved into scows, ferried out to a man-made isle, a *sacca*, and burned. When the garbagemen go on strike—and everyone goes on strike in Italy all the time with no remedial effect—the plastic bags form irregular pyramids along the quays. From time to time a garbage bag is lowered to the street on a rope from a window and left to dangle there like some obscure ornament. At other times garbage bags are thrown into the canals. Having put all of his energy into packaging his refuse, fatigued by the effort, the loyal citizen simply tosses it out of the window. In principle there is a fine. Three hundred and sixty-five of them were issued last year, the daily effort of dispensing the summonses apparently fatiguing the deputy as well.

The men who collect the garbage go about their business cheerfully enough. So knowledgeable are they about the rudiments of the city that when there is an empty apartment available—if such a phenomenon occurs—they are the first to know. When they do their work, there is no hurl and clatter, no defiantly leftover debris as there is on the streets of New York. Theirs is a job, not a mischance of justice.

It is impossible not to be aware of garbage in Venice. No canal is free of it. Every tourist with a camera discovers this, when, with the light falling just so on the surfaces of the palace, the gondola sailing into view from around the corner, the sky serene; there in the foreground floats part of a chair, a soiled slipper, a leafless but still tinseled Christmas tree, or a troop of empty paint cans. Then there are the less durable substances which decay and spread a greasy slick over the water. The presence of rotting thises and decaying thats and the over-all sulfuric stench of certain canals provide an earthy element to the city pulling hard against the lofty wonderland atmosphere. Detergent bubbles froth up, and creatures long dead and decomposing mingle with amputated plastic toys. No one would be sorry to have the canals cleaned up once and for all. In the mid-fifteen hundreds, there was a plan to require tenants facing the canals to excavate them biennially, but even then the idea fell through. The odor is far worse in the summer at the height of the season: *per dispetto*, say some, out of disrespect to all the sightseers poking around into private places. It could be the tides, it could be the heat, it could be because the population nearly trebles and so does the amount of waste.

When a canal is particularly shallow or is in the process of being hollowed out, when the heavier water-logged debris, the once-treasured tricycles, baby carriages, and mattresses are revealed on the floor of muck now available to public scrutiny like an open wound, everyone walks by pinching their nostrils, commenting nasally about *povera Venezia.* Poor Venice, like *povera Italia*, phrases often heard, though often with a theatrical edge of insincerity, an admonition made by parents whose beloved child has just committed an indiscretion in public. But *poor Venice* gets off scot-free, and its vapors cling in the air.

More discouraging and believable is the shrug, sigh, and the *Ah . . . si*, followed by a pause, an interjection I have heard on every social level in Venice when there is a lapse in the conversation. It is a lament that cuts like a fault deep into the human geology of the city. Venice on the brink of some disaster; Venetians acknowledging it. No where else in Italy does that *Ah . . . si*, sound so burdened.

There are a number of dichotomies in the Venetians' feelings about themselves. They are vaguely embarrassed by the deterioration of their city, yet extremely proud of living in a place so apart and unique; they are simple, provincial folk going on about their business, but you must remember that they are world-famous custodians of the earth's most precious jewel-city. Shrewd keepers of the turnstiles, they fleece the tourists; beggars on an international level, they solicit alms to pay for the crumbling museum that is their home.

On television Venice is referred to as the city of *comare*, roughly translated as neighbor or housewife, and even though Venice is on the Great City itinerary along with Paris and London, the city of housewives is

GALLERIE
POTERE
OPERAIO

just under the surface. Its exquisiteness lifted away, Venice would become a peculiar small town where everyone floats to work.

Because of this, every Venetian has developed a mild schizophrenia about the public role he plays: a contract player signing autographs on Hollywood Boulevard, who then, because of a series of misfortunes known only to himself, goes home to a modest rooming house, where he keeps a carton of milk on the window sill.

This same duality places a suspension of belief on the tourist. No one from the outside really believes that anyone in Venice has a normal day-to-day existence. They see someone down an alleyway open a door with a large key and imagine him stepping into a backstage void. Not only is the city itself on display. Anyone who publicly scrubs or carries or mends, anyone who dips an oar into water or grips a clothespin between her teeth, anyone whose remains are trundled in a coffin to a waiting barge, is photographed. Would a woman swinging her lettuce basket into a Parisian courtyard expect to find when she looked up, a team of Japanese, Nikons poised? Would she permit it? The Venetian submits; she is outnumbered almost three to one in the summer. Railing against the invasion of her privacy will accomplish nothing: tomorrow others will come with different cameras, with canvases and easels to catch her act.

The electricians, the ironmongers, bait sellers; the men who mend the nets, repair the television sets, adjust the faucets, all hold the city together. The hotels and art galleries are a lucrative decoration. Venetians rarely go near them unless they are sent to them, employed by them, or have been called in to keep them from falling apart.

No one seems inclined to feel humiliated by his work. This may be so because so few people expect to grow up to become either Rich or President. There is no Italian Dream as there is an American Dream; Venetians are not brought up on the idea of limitless possibilities. Occasionally ambition runs high, although not that high. The notion of going abroad to seek one's fortune has gone somewhat out of style. It might be Germany, it might be South America; but the United States and the large automobiles to be yearned for in it seem a set piece from another era.

Jobs are shuffled for rather than hunted down. A friend of a friend moves over, makes room; one is inserted. Venice has no employment agencies. The local newspaper, in its want ads, its *piccola pubblicità,* offers few possibilities: private persons looking for maids, hotels looking for maids; someone every now and then looking for a secretary or minor executive. Combing through the newspapers of twenty and thirty years ago the same situations crop up: maids wanted; Venice needing its houses cleaned. Everything else is managed through connections. When anyone looks for employment the Venetian grapevine twines around the problem and bears fruit somewhere along the line, even though the branches might extend as far as Milan or Rome. The call for a job goes ricocheting down alleys and across canals until it makes contact with someone who is accessible, someone who will put themselves out, someone who will make a deal. Again and again one hears *Ci metteremo d' accordo* [We'll arrange it], the phrase meant to calm and soothe, the words promising a safe port throughout Italy, even though *Ci metteremo d' accordo*, might produce unseen coral reefs or a mined harbor.

The duality of Venice as a resort and Venice as a town produces some difficult job situations. In the summer months there are many vacancies and not quite enough Venetians to fill them. Italians from upper Italy and the South, Yugoslavians somehow distantly related, cousins just back from Germany fill in. During the winter it is the Venetians and the Venetians alone trying to keep themselves busy. You will see the porter who carried your luggage from the station now doubling as florist's assistant, walking through the narrow streets bowed under a huge funeral wreath of crepe-paper-like gladioli. The bus boy of the now closed hotel carries heavy electrical equipment for his uncle's appliance store. You notice him laboriously crossing a bridge in the distance with a spastic jerk and surge; only later do you realize that he has not come down with some motor illness—he is lugging a cart behind him up the concealed steps. The once-imperious hotel managers who stood grandly in their *fracs*, issuing orders to the staff are now sitting disgruntled on benches along the quays or have left town for winter resorts like Cortina, where they wear other uniforms, have other allegiances. Most of the bartenders, aside from those who work in the hotels, remain employed. There are many bars in Venice, filing by two or three to a block, then none; then, to catch up, three or four more. You might easily imagine it to be a city of drunks until you remember that bar and caffè are synonymous, and in any case the Johnnie Walker and more ersatz Anglo-Italian whiskies gather dust on the mirrored shelves while Venetians consume milder things: grappa, hideous mixtures involving egg yolks or rhubarb or artichoke. The favorite drink is still the white or red wine and much of it comes from the hillsides of the Veneto.

What you eat in a bar depends on where you are. Near the market they might specialize in salted tripe or crude cheeses seen nowhere else. On the waterfront quays and on the islands you will find *frutti di mare*. In order to jolt these sea fruit out of their shells, you are required to hold them in your fist which you then pound down hard on the table. I remember a group of us drumming in an unregimented rhythm in a caffè, a din that did not seem to concern the other patrons, who were shouting above it all anyway. There is a great deal of shouting in the local bars, most of it in dialect. Rarely do two people sit in corners whispering confidences. Most of the clientele know each other, listen in with great interest to all conversations, and leave filled to the brim with gossip overheard.

The proprietors maintain a high level of interest in everything they hear, an accomplishment considering that there must be a great deal of duplication of information. They skillfully manage to juggle several conversations at once and only become perturbed if their clients get drunk, which they do periodically on winter weekends.

An argument will flash up out of nowhere. Unpleasant remarks are traded in among the general buzz of conversation. Suddenly someone burly pulls out a wad of money—the word money pops out of conversations with the regularity of bottles being uncorked—and someone slight is held back by a friend. Eyes all over the room swing in the direction of all those lire. No one remembers how the thing got started, but insults are now flying.

"No banks for him," says a chum of the large man. "With shoulders like iron you don't need banks." He flexes his own muscles to no one in particular.

The smaller man grumbles. The larger man shoves him and turns to leave. The crowd draws back, half hoping for a fight, readying their anecdotes. The proprietor's mother who has been napping on a stool, opens one eye, says, "Leave him alone," closes it again, and it is over.

When the money man stumbles out into the night, everyone surrounds the other man, buying him drinks, getting him to chuckle over it all, whatever it was. The big fellow will probably go on to another bar, might get into another near-fight, might run the risk of getting rolled for flashing all those bills, might fall drunk into a canal. But more likely he will go home, sleep it off, and the following day he will be seen amiably buying the smaller man a glass of wine while they both relive the excitement of the night before.

Certain bars are more elevated, less Venetian. There are student bars, tourist bars, hotel bars. And, of course, there is Harry's Bar.

You enter Harry's Bar through an interpretation of saloon doors, etched opaque glass preventing you from seeing who is inside. There is a swirl of heads. You are sized up in a flash by a croupier's glance from the cashier, the barman, the owner, and any of the remaining staff not occupied in the kitchen or the dining room upstairs. Eyes slit down for an instant; a decision is made on what, more or less, you are worth, whether you have been there before, are likely to reappear, or have made an error and do not belong. Enticing plates of expensive little sandwiches are cleverly placed along the bar; drinks are short, faultless. The lady who takes your coat does not give you a check for it. She remembers you and it. Memories are long at Harry's Bar.

You are likely to meet among the jangling bracelets and lap dogs both

DOMENICA
CHIUSO

Carni

the rich and the famous and the people who want to meet the rich and the famous, and it is a peculiar oasis, out of season, serving to remind you that Venice is, after all, attached to the Western world and its heady aspirations.

Venetians like their atmospheres reliable and well defined. A place that caters to foreigners will find very few Venetians giving it local color. A trattoria will not one evening put a moussaka or a paella on the menu. There is only one hybrid bar-caffè-trattoria-pizzeria, on the square of the Fenice, and because of its adjacence to the great opera house, it is where the musicians and theatre folk congregate. One night its clients were startled to witness the arrival of four bedraggled transvestites who had miraculously sailed into town from the provinces, their accents unmistakably from the Veneto. In a disappearing act worthy of a great magician, the headwaiter instantly whisked them out of sight to some obscure table to eat their pizzas in isolation. "But they must be foreigners!" everyone said in astonishment, forks poised mid-air.

Night life in Venice is notable by its absence. I have never seen anyone enter or leave the club advertising *il strip tease,* but the photographs in its small showcase, innocent of any prurience, are constantly if surreptitiously scrutinized by the general public. The one discotheque in town makes a lot of noise for very few customers—it happens to be situated in the building next to mine—and it is a wholesome place. The young couple who own it regularly feed a stray cat lodging in an abandoned cellar across the alley; their mother sweeps out the club in the morning; a far cry from the nocturnal syndicates operating in most cities. But it is still dimly considered a naughty place by the parents in the neighborhood, something influenced by America. Or France. Or was it England? In any case it is preferred if young people stick to billiards and pinball machines.

There is a roadhouse on a highway outside of Venice and it is frequented by people from the industrial cities. The effort in getting there spiritually, psychologically, and spatially would exhaust the Venetian conscience. Ferries stop running at a certain hour. Trains no longer arrive. The Venetian is meant to be home in bed.

Caffès are the intrinsic Venetian element of sociability. Venice began the business of coffee trading in the mid-seventeenth century, importing it from the Orient, where, four hundred years earlier, the Venetian Marco Polo first tasted spaghetti. Thus Venice is responsible for the two most successful staples of Italian gastronomy.

Italian espresso must be either a drug or a sin or both. There is no getting away from it once the habit is established. You stroll along calmly enough until suddenly, as though the body had a craving detached from the mind, you find yourself inside a caffè innocently ordering a *macchiatto*—coffee served with a foam of milk over the heavy sludge filling only the lower

half of your small cup. Among Venetians there is always a struggle about who pays for the coffees ordered, everyone wanting to make the gesture, and it is rare that each person pays for himself. A general coffee fund could eliminate the problem. But the ritual is repeated again and again throughout the day, the ordering of the coffee and the subsequent moment of gratitude or generosity and it is one of the most satisfactory ceremonies in Venice.

Espresso machines, a sweep of stainless steel and plastic, have become as sleek and elegantly designed as the Ferrari. It seems that if you wish to open a caffè in Mestre, across the lagoon from Venice, a coffee distributor will help you in deciding whether the location is favorable, will provide you at no cost with the latest coffee machine, toaster, dishwasher, and related paraphernalia of a bar along with a million lire on loan without interest to be paid back within five years if you agree to sign a contract to use only their coffee. Yes, surely it is a drug.

So delighted were the Venetians by the establishment of coffeehouses when they first appeared that they reacted by gambling less frequently, preferring to sit out of doors to watch the comings and goings of the public. A decree in 1777 required the caffès to withdraw their tables at midnight because of the noise. In 1814, Florian's, the most popular caffè in the Veneto, was closed down for the imprudent comments made there about Napoleon's victories.

Florian's is still the most elegant caffè in Venice; the one with the longest legend, probably the most expensive coffeehouse in the region. In all of Italy it has only the Caffè Greco in Rome with which to compete. Every Italian city naturally has its most distinguished caffè, the prerequisites centering around atmosphere, clientele, and a certain density of history.

These caffès become institutions on a community level with opera houses, theatres and concert halls. There is no equivalent to them in Anglo-Saxon countries, depriving the public of props and scenery for serious social promiscuity.

Florian's ceilings and walls are covered with nineteenth-century frescoes, glassed, reflecting the light from the Piazza San Marco outside. The number of grand elderly people decorously taking tea or coffee there can only be matched by Vienna's Sacher, though at Florian's there are fewer stout businessmen wearing rings on their small fingers, fewer ladies with vengeful faces. Not long ago, during the course of a Venetian winter afternoon tea, I watched at Florian's two ex-monarchs, heavily furred, mother and daughter: the one briefly Queen of Greece and the other, the ex-Queen of Yugoslavia. They gossiped with mild animation next to a beautifully dressed young French couple either just married or its equivalent who could not cease caressing each other's hands long enough to hold their teacups. Outside, it was snowing, and across the Piazza a gaunt Christmas tree, with an archaic system of pulleys, was gradually assuming a perpendicular position. The harmony was of such perfection, so timeless, that when a newsboy came in thrusting the latest headline into the air, everyone jumped.

The waiters at Florian's do not smile. They set down their trays as efficiently as nurses, the little chit is tucked discreetly underneath the crystal water carafe. It is a place that has often given me an intense, graceful pleasure.

On the first warm days the caffès of Venice spread out all over the streets and squares. You are required to circumvent areas that you might have thought were open promenades. Tables and chairs, children on rollerskates, baby carriages, and thatches of strollers are everywhere. It happens, literally, out of the blue. The winter sun sulking in the sky is suddenly, illogically, capable of warmth and brightness. Grey until now, the buildings leap into color. Small back bridges which had witnessed only the resigned wintry crisscrossings of the neighborhood now sprout dawdling lovers, young, beautiful, their magnetic field so strong that to pass them as they mumble and almost touch, one is required to brush against memories and regrets of past loves even though they might have been the last things one had wished to think about that day. Canaries are set out in cages on hooks up and down the building façades; baskets are lowered from top stories for food parcels; you bump into lunatics muttering aloud, released for those sunny hours from their rooms and relatives to jabber in the bright streets where everybody is too busy gossiping to notice or care.

The arrival of the sunshine is celebrated. Everyone in Venice seems to want to talk. The sullenness of the cold days gives way to an idiotic

garrulousness. I stepped into a caffè on the Santa Maria della Formosa to discover that some woman's dog had just lifted its leg against a table. The owner of the caffè was addressing everyone with her outrage, the woman seemed to be talking to the dog, who oafishly yawned, wagging its tail. Everyone became involved in the incident, the sun bursting across the caffè like a shot of adrenalin. "That woman's dog," someone was saying, "has been known to lift its leg against the fruitseller's stand in the Campo." Heads swiveled in the direction of the stall glittering with freshly hosed-down melons and lettuce. Someone else said, "And it barks," just to have something to say. I could not keep quiet, enjoying all this improvisation. "Ah . . . si," I said sadly, never having seen either the woman or the dog before, "that dog is the cross that poor woman must bear." The clients and owner smiled eagerly at the new, unexpected voice. I moved into the stream of sunlight. "Awhile ago, it fell into the canal and almost drowned. But . . ." I paused dramatically. Encouraging looks drew me along. "At the last moment, she saved its life. Its bladder has never been right since. She cares for it night and day." "Night and day," echoed another patron quite ready to take the embroidery into his own hands, which he did very capably, managing to turn the subject around to a recent soccer match. The woman and her dog had vanished. The floor had been mopped up. The new customers were embellishing the soccer story.

In the early morning, the area around the Rialto Bridge is turned into a vast market. Barges arrive piled high with produce, cartons are handed down, filled, carried on heads, shoulders, carried in twos, threes, haggled over even before they reach the stalls. Groups of nuns are up early buying for schools and convents; restaurant owners shrewdly eye the merchandise while, red-nosed in the cold, the nuns pinch and prod the vegetables. As the sunlight gains in the sky, neighborhood ladies line up with shopkeepers to pore over the shellfish, the chickens, the melons. Everyone laments heavily. The prices are too high. The quality is not what it once was. Everyone asks for their *sconto*, the discount automatically demanded, automatically given, both parties realizing that it was tacked onto the price, neither of them willing to admit it or eliminate it.

By the time mid-morning arrives, the marketplace is closing up, the bars swell, the market baskets are filled. Boats are piled high with goods to be delivered and traffic on the canals is at its heaviest. It seems inconceivable that floating is the only method of transport and the only way to get any object down a street is to haul it.

Venice seems to have a disproportionately large number of food stores, given its scant population. Perhaps it is the absence of supermarkets, perhaps it is because the stores are really so small that four or five shoppers form a crowd. As in the rest of Italy, one gets to know the grocer, the butcher, the news vendor, and so on. Eventually a walk down the street becomes a series of half-nods and bows, of traded cordialities and comments on the weather.

Shops are finely divided: the egg man does not sell bread, the butcher does not sell pork, and salt is only to be found at the tobacconist. I had been diligently buying my dairy products from a "little man" down the street because his shop was so amiable. The thought that I was helping in some personal way to stock his shelves and keep his kids in galoshes pleased me. One day I learned from him that it was not his shop at all, that it belonged to a syndicate of businessmen *in the Veneto*. He failed to understand either my surprise or my badly disguised disappointment. "Maybe it's just as well," he said. "I receive my salary and a pension. I have no worries." It began to sound like a testimonial learned by rote at annual dinners sponsored by the men *in the Vento*. "Besides," he concluded, "the man up the street in business for himself has to compete with *me*. My prices are lower."

Lacking the social consciousness to perceive with any accuracy the absolute merits of one system over another, I was, and have remained, disillusioned. The way in which he had scoured and polished his counter, chosen his stock, totaled his bill and presented it to me for verification before theatrically packing everything into a plastic bag (the eggs oh-so-gently wrapped into a paper cone and placed on top) seemed to pertain to his having created his own small corner of the earth: his own business.

All the small shops became suspect, their owners the vast concerns run by the faceless and nameless, the antithesis of Venetian tradition. I privately decided that it was only the shopkeepers who exhibited a photograph of a decreased relative lit by a tiny light bulb who were the actual proprietors. It is the customary way Venetians express gratitude to members of the family who began the business, and I have always respected it.

I discovered that most of the film houses, too, were owned in groups, although it seems there is a small cinema on the Lido run by its owner, an avowed Fascist who manages to insert, between films, small propaganda documentaries that are regularly whistled at and booed from start to finish.

Film theatres in Venice appear in unlikely places. On the Campo Santa Margherita, a large square referred to by guidebooks as "characteristic," stands a truncated fifteenth-century campanile which incorporates at its base a decrepit movie house specializing in horror shows. An occasional rat in the aisle has been known to add an unexpected but realistic *frisson* to the plot.

Incidentally, the Campo Santa Margherita is my favorite neighborhood

JET
POP CORN

square in Venice. It effectively combines strolling place, roller skating rink, soccer field, amusement park, fish market, vegetable market, fruit market, and gossip center with five centuries of Venetian architecture crowded on its perimeter. It also contains a small, sunny caffè inexplicably called the letter O, where you can sit for hours engrossed in card games, storytelling, watching the traffic, playing with its cat, or generally wasting time.

Movies are shown all over Venice in an indiscriminate timetable of the past thirty years. A jittery print of a post-war strife-torn Italian film is shown one day; the day following it might be a print of *Broken Blossoms*, and several days later it will be an American film, dubbed and dimly lit, of the present season. Babies are brought into the neighborhood film theatres when no relative can be located to sit at home with them. Boys howl and whistle and comment loudly when there is any prolonged kissing, and suggestions of love-making leave them doubled up with nervous laughter. Frequently spectators simply talk back to the screen when they become particularly engrossed in the plot, and you will hear someone shout quite reasonably to a cowboy that there is an Indian in the far corner of the screen.

Once you leave the center of Venice there is no logic in what will be pressed up against which, either architecturally or socially or economically. The houses of great families lean on decaying buildings half-empty and quite likely occupied by the plumber and the pensioneer. Or the plumber and the pensioneer might by some stroke of good luck live in a neglected Gothic palace snuggled against a garden any prince would yearn to overlook.

House numbers are confusing. Each quarter of Venice begins with a number 1 and goes on up until the specifically determined line that separates it from the adjacent quarter puts a stop to it. The numbers wind through the alleys, streets, and squares as though planted by a cretin and allowed to grow every which way. If you follow along in pursuit of a certain house number, you will find yourself at the edge of a canal, wondering whether the numbers have skipped across and hotfooted it along the opposite shore or whether they have turned back to sulk along a side alley. When you ask in a store, nobody knows. "You mean, you want the house across from the restaurant that specializes in fish?" Or: "Is the fellow you're looking for the one who ties up his small boat, the red one, in front of the florist?"

Neither the street numbers nor the street names seem to interest anyone but the scholars. Each street has a history. They run the gamut from the scandalous (the Riva Biasio named for a gentleman who had a sausage shop who was discovered to have mixed in *fanciulli,* or little boys, with the rest of the sausage meats, and received for his madness a trip from the jail to his shop dragged by a galloping horse, the loss of one limb after another in front of a crowd, and a final decapitation between the two columns of San Marco), to the seductive (Sottoportico del Casin where brothels used to flourish) to the simplistic (the Ponte donna Onesta, named for a conversation tradition has recorded of two men crossing the bridge arguing about the honesty of women: "Do you know who is honest, in all the lot? That one!" And one of the gentlemen pointed to a small head sculpted in stone which leaned and still leans, from the side of a building near the bridge).

I found with surprise that I, too, had no idea of the names in my immediate neighborhood. I would explain directions to my house by describing what would be seen along the route, concluding with the ultimate Venetian direction: "*Segue un po la corrente*"—Follow the stream of the crowd. Postal carriers have delivered mail to me with no address other than my name and the name of the quarter in which I lived which was frequently misspelled. I wondered how they knew. At first I was uneasy; then I was pleased by the idea. I had become part of the mechanism of Venice.

The newspaper, *Il Gazzettino* also seems to know everything that goes on in the city. It is a cheerful provincial paper and I am addicted to it, even though its political views have struck a permanent leaning far to the right of center. Its reports on Venetian daily life are absorbing; you watch, fascinated, as it lectures at its readers on the smallest detail of their behavior. Swearing is not tolerable, respect must be given one's elders, contraband cigarettes are to be avoided, gypsies in the streets will give the city a bad name, garbage men must return to work, phone booths must be placed here, not there, for the sake of the square. And the awnings of

Disegno Della
Anticha Di Venezia

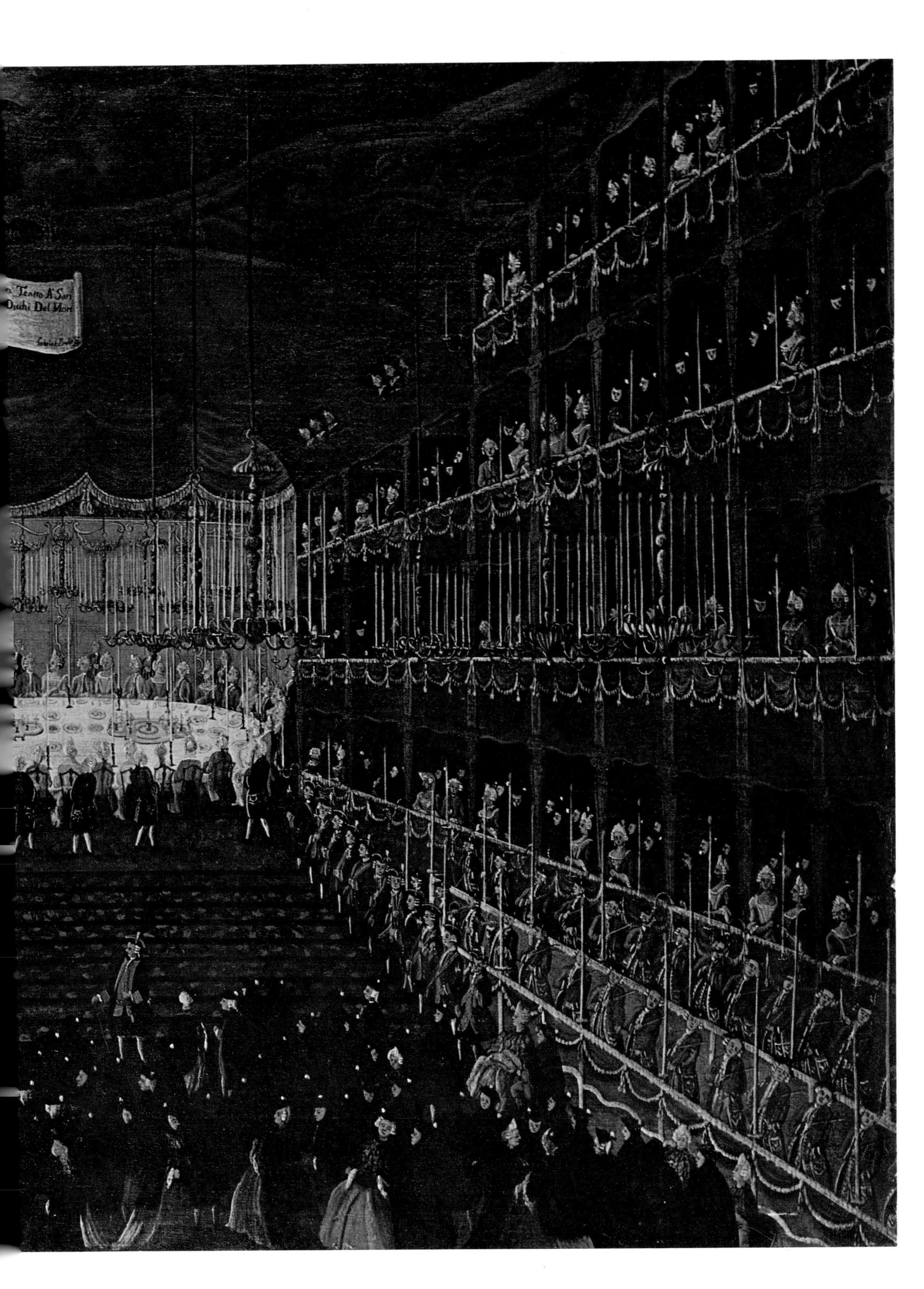
a Teatro A San
Duchi Del Nord

Passeggio Delle Signore

PART TWO: SYSTEMS

1. THE OLD ASCENSION DAY FAIR

Celebrating an annual springtime event, the Piazza was turned into a bazaar of oriental magnitude. In this painting, we see that an attempt has been made to organize what had been a haphazard open market (the Maccaruzzi design would come later) with tentlike stalls replacing the actual tents. Before this, every scrap of pavement was used as selling place, with paths no wider than two people winding throughout the maze. At night, small bonfires would warm the vendors and illuminate the merchandise.

2. CHARLATANS AND AMUSEMENTS ON THE PIAZZETTA

Minstrels, magicians, and acrobats put on their shows; puppets leaned out of tiny theatres; wild beasts were on display; exotic turbaned gentlemen hawked dates and carob nuts; a band of Commedia dell' Arte players performed for coins. And as the backdrop for this fantastic theatrical display, the Sansovino library formed the right façade, the Doges' Palace was on the left, and in the distance, beyond the columns of San Teodoro and San Marco's lion, was the Grand Canal and the island of San Giorgio Maggiore.

3. THEATRE DINNER ON THE STAGE OF THE TEATRO SAN BENEDETTO

This "ladies' banquet" was served on the stage of the theatre in honor of the archduke and duchess of Russia (who referred to themselves as "the Counts of the North"). From balconies and boxes refurbished for the event as boudoirs, an invited audience watched them dine. Musicians lined the stalls, playing violins to accompany the meal. The San Benedetto, along with another great eighteenth-century theatre, the San Samuele, was demolished needlessly in the last century. Venice retains only the lovely Fenice as its opera house.

4. PROMENADE ALONG THE ERBERIA OF THE RIALTO

The herb market just around the bend from the bridge of the Rialto still forms a part of the vast marketplace of the city. The Naranzeria (from the Spanish word for orange) is still where the citrus fruits are sold, and between the Erberia and the Naranzeria runs the forbidding Fondamenta dei Prigioni where one might see handcuffed prisoners being led into motor launches taking them from the courthouse to the jail. Strollers used to visit the markets at daybreak after a night on the town.

5. PROMENADE ALONG THE RIVA DEGLI SCHIAVONE

The closest grand promenade to the Piazza, the widest, the most sun-drenched, the Riva degli Schiavone has always attracted a crowd. In the foreground is the *ponte delle paglie*, the bridge of straw (on the same canal as the bridge of sighs) named because straw merchants unloaded their cargo there. In the center of the painting is the Palazzo Dandolo, high blue awnings on its façade. It would become, in the nineteenth century, the Hotel Danieli.

the Piazza San Marco really need to be replaced. When bicycles or junk are stored in the Palazzo Fortuny and its Gothic windows decay, *Il Gazzettino* comes to the rescue and exposes it, with photographs. When the canals are filled with flotsam, *Il Gazzettino* publishes an article: "Never has the city been this dirty. In the map of sloppiness, Venice can occupy a privileged role, first place, before Palermo, Naples, Rome . . ." The newspaper forgets that once pigs roamed the streets to clean them up and noblemen carried handkerchiefs to cover their noses.

In going through the archives of the newspaper I discovered that it used to run two editions a day and was completely incautious about its paternalism: "Mussolini," it wrote in an immense headline splashed across the front page, "has understood that the fascist state lies beyond all individual aspirations. The totalitarian aspiration of Italy is what is important." *Il Gazzettino* has tried in recent years to ride with the times, but any demonstration against the government will get small space. When a large red banner was prominently exhibited on the bridge of the Accademia, reading: NO TO FASCISM. EVERYONE IN THE PIAZZA AGAINST THE FASCIST RALLY IN ROME! the newspaper condemned the banner as abusive to the beauty of the city.

Political demonstrations in Venice are frequent, earnest and ineffective. Everyone who did go "to the Piazza" to rally against the Fascists' meeting in Rome found the square particularly festive. Large red flags waved, and music echoed out of sports arena loudspeakers. The majority of the participants were young, of college age; the men bearded, the girls with a partisan look. Slogans were chanted against the blackshirts, against Mussolini, against the then American President and any other signs of dictatorship. The atmosphere was cheerful. Baby carriages supported portable speakers. All at once the large group formed into a parade that tried unsuccessfully to surge through the narrow streets so ill fit to accommodate it. They managed, instead, a rapid walk, in columns of three or four. Sightseers and Venetians pressed against buildings to let the demonstrators pass, and shopkeepers hastily raised their shutters for the night, looking apprehensively over their shoulders. After another hour of rhetoric in the Campo Santo Stefano which consisted of the PCI, the communists, denouncing the MSI, the neo-Fascists, to shouts and cheers, the word *basta* punctuating the speeches with a decisiveness our *enough* could never manage, the group dispersed. They rolled up their flags, boarded ferries and trains and returned home to nearby towns exhilarated.

The banner over the bridge disappeared during the night.

Venice has a long list of surveillance and curtailments. In the early fifteenth century, Sumptuary Laws were put into effect designed to rein in the excesses of the population. They lasted, with various mutations, for

three hundred years. Women were fined if they were seen on the streets wearing clogs higher than ten centimeters. Originally intended to prevent mud from spattering garments, clogs became a mark of the wearer's position in society. Patrician women tottered on clogs up to two feet high, requiring them to balance themselves majestically on the heads of a pair of servants. The fashion was eliminated by decree in 1430.

In the theatre, women were required to shroud themselves in domino and hood. There is a record of two noblewomen who let their cloaks slide, baring their shoulders in the glow of oil lamps lighting the stage. They were immediately put under house arrest.

Working briefly as a spy for the Council of Ten, it was Casanova who informed them that *Coriolanus* was being presented on the stage. The Inquisitors learned that it dealt with a cruel nobility, a starving population, and a condemning Coriolanus, and had it closed. Even today, anything avant-garde goes underground or crops up briefly in some inconspicuous place. An improvisation by some students on the subject of sexual tolerance brought them a suspension ten days before graduation.

There is a tendency in Venice to remove things at random. Scenes are inexplicably cut from films, a seventeenth-century marble well is excavated from a courtyard in the Giudecca, a foreigner is given twenty-four hours to dismantle his apartment and leave town because he has given certain all-night parties the town magistrate deems suspicious. A plan for a soccer field falls through with no explanation.

In contrast to this, a bank will emerge from behind the straw matting which has concealed it while it was in construction, completely out of character with the rest of the neighborhood. A moneyed and well-connected person will "develop" the small island of Santa Christina, reshaping it and transforming it to his own purposes while the municipality looks the other way. The building code has a logic all its own. When the owners of certain Venetian palaces wish to modernize their interiors, a troop of

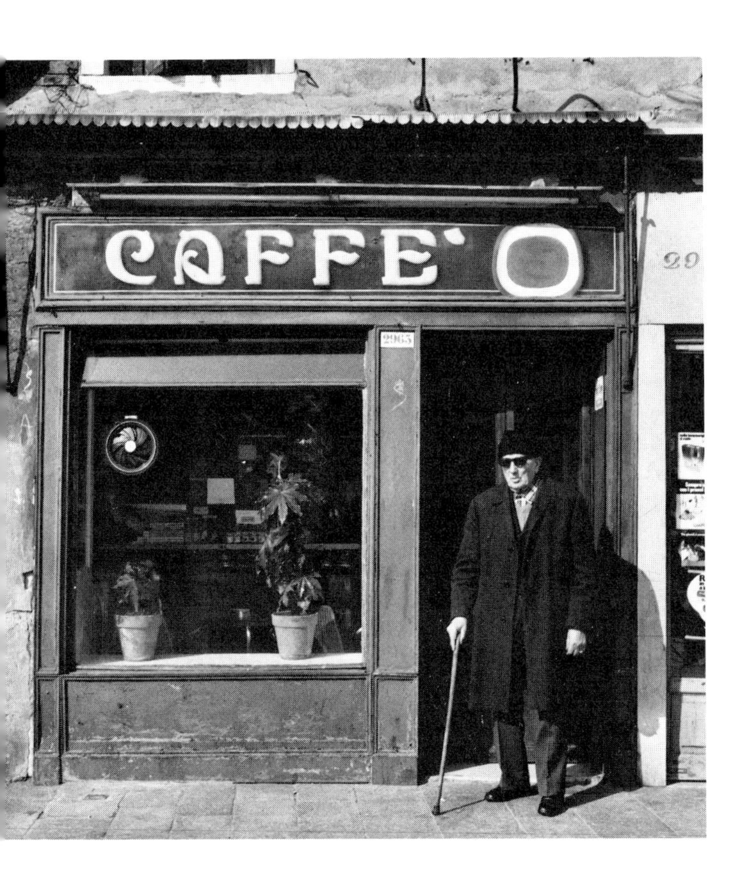

bureaucratic officials constantly tracks through the rooms to supervise every detail down to the tiles on the floor. All the good will and noble intentions in the world will not persuade them to return to their desks, where they prefer not to be seen sitting behind their typewriters pecking two-fingered with embarrassment. There is no way to speed up the process of obtaining the necessary permits for a restoration. The owners consider abandoning the project, taking their money to Switzerland, letting the place fall apart, leaving the walls to collapse as petty officials prod them.

A large number of gentlemen may be seen about the city carrying heavy dossiers. They collect and assess, hand out forms, summonses, estimates, certificates; you find them on ferries, notice them crossing squares, see them looking up at house numbers down side alleys. You try to avoid them; you make the sign of the Evil Eye against them; but they are bound to appear on your doorstep. If there is an error, if you do not belong on their lists, you must accept the desperately long voyage of trying to rectify the mistake. You will begin at the tobacconist, purchasing *carta bollata,* legal paper stamped with the seal of the government. You will buy tax stamps and affix them, take them elsewhere to be canceled. You will present in writing and verbally to interrelated offices all around town why and where and when and how it is that your name should be absent from their ledgers. Your declaration is supposed to reach someone sympathetic. At any point along the way it may bog down, enter a closed file, find its way to the top of a yellowing pile of antique documents or be stuffed

by error into a clerk's bag along with her eyeglass case to be left at home during the lunch hour and swept up with the dishes. The men with the portfolios will continue to arrive, all baleful eyes, worn suits, poised pencils, moist index fingers to turn your particular page.

The equivalent ladies resemble those women wearing tinted rimless glasses who seem to be at the helm of all private enterprise in France. Their function is to total up what is due. In Venice, behind their cashier's booths, they tend to smile somewhat more than their counterparts in Paris, but their concentration is as complete. They are distinguished. They are crafty. They are unadorned. They will take their time totaling up your bill and tell you the sum through prim lips. If they have husbands in the business they might occasionally defer to them, but more likely the husband will serve the customer with the amiability of a ventriloquist's dummy while the wife will watch over the finances and over him and over you.

When their roles are not defined, when the pair emerges as one double-headed Hydra running a shop, the results are hallucinatory. It tacks on ends of each other's sentences, makes corrections halfway through. It will cover for the other on an altered price and then reform into a dialogue of disagreement if it is so inclined. It is shrill in upstaging one another and might go off into a separated huff only to reappear within moments on another tangent altogether. After shuttering the shop, it will dine both in disagreement and harmony. Its snores, later on, will grapple and augment into eternity. It is to be avoided.

Part Three
EXTRAS

During the flight down from the window his form recomposed itself for an instant; in the air one could have seen dancing a quadruped with long whiskers, and its right foreleg seemed to be raised in imprecation. Then all found peace in a heap of livid dust.

Giuseppe di Lampedusa: *The Leopard*

So many people on the streets look as though they are related because they probably are. One begins to suspect that a certain proportion of the population might be slow-witted or slightly mad, like those enclaves in the American rural South, where villages pop up all brothers and sisters and cousins and the I.Q. average has dwindled like a river run dry. Actually there are relatively few mad people about; obviously mad, that is. There are the mutterers—but who among us does not mutter from time to time? There are the neighborhood individuals who have crossed the fragile fence of sanity and now find themselves a bit out of things. An elderly gentleman often passes on the street with a harmonica held to his crumpled mouth playing no particular tune as he hurries along, tailcoat flapping. A ruddy-faced woman sits on various protrusions of the square in front of the Accademia, depending where the sun is strong, commenting unfavorably on the passers-by, holding on her lap a plastic fuel tank, which she uses as a hot water bottle. Her garments are many and worn contiguously. When someone hands her a coin she seems as contemptuous as when someone does not. It is rumored, of course, that she is, in secret, a countess. It is difficult to find small coins to give to those who solicit them; there are fewer and fewer ten-lire pieces available. The banks, they say, do not issue them. Instead of small change you are handed a piece of gum or a *caramella* at the newsstand or the ferry booth and by the end of the day you find yourself searching for a child to deposit them into.

The absence of vehicles has affected everything in Venice. You do not worry about traffic lights telling you to stop or go; there is no danger of being struck down at every street corner. Instead, your inclination is to focus on the architecture and the people. Because of this you immediately notice when a section of Venice has been put together improperly—such as the Campo San Moisè where the eccentric and rather frivolous Church of San Moisè stands in gaudy contrast to the heavy post-war Germanic drabness of the Bauer Grünwald Hotel on the adjacent corner. You can stop mid-walk and ponder over anything that captivates your eye; nothing mobile urges you on.

One autumn night on the way to dinner I noticed a wild-eyed man in his forties intently scribbling on the white margins of a poster. So nervous and quick was he that I hesitated to look at what he was writing, certain that he was articulating some private nightmare. He turned frantically to the next poster and I went on my way. When, much later, I returned home, I discovered that all the posters from the Santa Maria dell'Giglio, across the Accademia Bridge, and on through the neighborhood of San Trovaso had been meticulously covered by his swift-moving felt tipped pen. He had written: "The post office takes your money and then waits two weeks to deliver your mail." In front of the Accademia Gallery much frequented by tourists, he had written it in English.

And I had made a detour around him, thinking him mad! The autumn leaves have fallen, winter has come, his posters have long since been covered by layer upon layer of other posters; the merits of a soup on top of those of a toothpaste over those of a trip to Yugoslavia, but sometimes, when a special delivery letter travels for two weeks before reaching Venice, when a letter from Rome never arrives at all, I think of him, wondering what, exactly, had prompted that final outburst when he cast convention aside in a city so demanding of it, bought the pen and began his labors. What letter had taken two weeks? A declaration of love received too late? The *last payment notice*, which, when unanswered, canceled forever some integral part of his life?

Venetians have been putting people with anything vastly wrong with them onto islands for centuries. Parceled out among the lagoons, the desolate stretches of low marsh have been used as hermit and leper retreats, monasteries, convents, and seminaries. The insane are kept on two islands. Until the turn of the nineteenth century, asylums were reserved only for the wellborn. The humble communities took a protective attitude towards their demented, the way they still do in remote Mediterranean villages.

The island housing the *manicomio*, the madhouse, is forlorn, its grim building looming up from flat lands. Boats make a parabolic arc around it both in metaphor and in space. Venice, seen from the island, is a distant strip of land. At night, in the emptiness of the lagoons, lit theatrically from the Piazza below, the Campanile becomes a tall, hooded figure standing terribly alone above the footlights.

There are hospitals all over Venice. Signs for them are second only to the signs pointing the way to the Piazza San Marco. Venice has maintained a reputation for being always a little miasmatic and unhealthy, not the place to seek out rosy cheeks. Both air and water can become torpid, particularly during the late summer, when the city seems imprisoned in colorless plastic. The plague in the Thomas Mann book is only an echo of earlier plagues. A certain Marquis di Stringis is remembered by history as having been

the ambassador who arrived in Venice in 1630, bringing with him along with many valises the germs of a plague that would last a year and a half and claim 100,000 victims. Earlier, in 1348, the magna mortalis eradicated three quarters of the population. The Senate decreed an official end to mourning. "Now that the storm has gone," they wrote, "there will be time for joy and gladness."

Physical deformities among Venetians are accepted with a remarkable stoicism. The clerk in the post office has a pronounced cleft palate. She deals with the public all day long, not choosing to hide in the deeper recesses of the building where the sorting and stamping takes place. The telephone operator at the intercity office has suffered a stroke. Half of her face is immobilized but this fact is not obscured by an ineffective hair style. She takes down your information with great authority. Many hands are missing digits, faces are partially burned and badly repaired. If someone has been the victim of a bad accident, Venetians do not smother him with solicitude at first and then later on treat him like the Frankenstein monster when he walks through town disfigured. They are straightforward and even humorous in their treatment of disabilities. They will call the hunchback what he is, a *gobbo*. He is long used to it. A very old, greatly gnarled woman will be referred to as the *befana*, the witch who rides on the Epiphany. She has ceased to notice the name. There is no sense of repulsion. Quirks, blemishes, and ailments are facts, curiosities, nothing more. The result is that almost everyone in Venice has a nickname.

There is an island housing a tuberculosis sanitorium, an island for infectious diseases and an island for the very old. One recent winter I followed daily in the local newspaper three separate stories of elderly people who had wandered off into the night. The woman on the island of Murano who left home wearing only her pajamas and slippers was never located; neither was the eighty-year-old gentleman who walked out of a rest home wearing a dark raincoat over a suit, with a grey hat on his head. These events were disturbing in a city unused to losing track of any of its participants. It seemed that the third person, too, was permanently lost. But he returned one morning to his clinic just as the newspaper was about to give him up. An argument with a cranky patient, he reported, is why he had left. Why such a fuss? All was forgiven. The newspaper along with its readers turned its attention elsewhere.

On a small island off the coast of Murano a group of people live in an abandoned quarry. It is referred to as the Island of Dogs because of a large pack of animals kept there to ward off intruders. I tried to visit it on a boat: in addition to my interest in its inhabitants, I had coveted some wooden molds used in glass blowing that had been left to rot in a heap at the edge of the island.

Our outboard motor aroused first one dog and then another, their barks growing into an atonal chorus echoing throughout the lagoon. The shoreline soon looked as though it had been created by Disney: every shape and size of dog crowded against each other. They bayed and yelped; they howled and bugled across the water. Soon they were followed by a ragged band of men and women emerging from behind the rocks to investigate the reason for the noise. Standing among the barking dogs, their arms folded, the residents made it quite clear that this was their adopted island, that these animals were far more ferocious than their size and manner might have led me to believe, and that they would not look kindly on the intrusion of a stranger, dog lover or not. I took their advice. I was sorry to sail away, sorry to leave those nice dogs, those gypsy faces, those wooden molds.

Surely the dogs are the happiest Venetians. No margin of sidewalk and street, no threat of honking horns, no screech of brake: their lives are unique in the world of animals. There is even a Venetian dog, appearing in Carpaccio's *St. Jerome* and again in Titian's *Presentation of the Virgin.* Elegant breeds, the Afghans and Borzois, arrive only in the summer. Aside from a preference for mongrels, Venetians seem to enjoy hunting dogs of dubious origin for those imagined more often than experienced forays into neighboring Yugoslavia for game. Among the *tout Venise,* I have noticed a number of overweight cocker spaniels. The foreign contingent seems to prefer portable decorative dogs, built low to the paving stones and bridges. I thought once that I had discovered the perfect dog for a boat; it balanced without flinching on the thinnest of rails at the point of a prow. As the boat, a scow, got closer, I realized that it was a plush velvet llama rescued from the debris.

One of my fondest memories of a Venetian winter centers around a dog

SESTIER DE DORSODURO
PAROCHIA S. TROVASO
CAMPO S. TROVASO

ROOKLYN
UNDERBERG
ORA IN 7 GUSTI
SPATEN
DIGER
CHARMS 50
ALEMAGNA
CHARMS
Picnic
miller
SPECIALITA'
BONOMELLI

with whom I was privileged to live, a great, woolly animal attracting all those who could recall that time in their childhood when they owned one, or longed for one, real or stuffed. We took her everywhere. Her ticket on the ferries was the same price as the supplement paid for a valise. She always maneuvered her way to the bow. The only part of her anatomy exposed, her nose, tested the good sea air. Restaurants accepted her with good grace, as they do in neighboring Francc and Austria, and she indulged the waiters by consuming the plates of pasta they set before her.

Venetians genuinely enjoy their dogs. One lady of my acquaintance had her dog embalmed, placing it under a large glass bell on top of her piano. It was her *last* dog, she said, in a way Browning might have admired, motioning toward the object with her little finger as she crossed her living room.

Cats act as cashier's assistants in many shops and bars, plumply decorating the counters. Street cats seem bent on some errand or other and do not stop to be stroked. When I walk into a silent courtyard to find that nothing moves, no leaf sways in the wind, no face appears in a window, I am almost always aware of the presence of some cat or other popping up like a Bedouin in the desert, dreamily appraising the scene along with me.

In the late nineteen sixties two British women arrived in Venice to do something, they said, about the cat population. Both wearing hats, Miss Mabel Raymonde Hawkins and friend were photographed on their arrival and proceeded to tell the municipality that they had come to capture the street cats. The healthy cats would be neutered. The sick cats would be put out of their misery. They are undernourished, they said, destroy them.

Venice was at that time having a problem with rats. No one took kindly to the ladies, who had planned on staying a month to follow through with their plan. The ladies did not understand, they said, why they found unsympathetic ears. They left town in a flurry. Following a slight rustle in the news, they disappeared without a trace.

Venetians do not seem particularly affectionate with their cats, at first. A Parisian friend was visiting me whom I found rather intimidated by the relative obscurity of my neighborhood. He tended to stay indoors when no excursions were planned. Finally I wrapped up some pieces of fish, suggesting he find a hungry cat nearby, hoping to combine charity with tourism. He came back quickly in a foul temper.

"Well, I found a cat," he announced. "Black and white. You remember, we passed it earlier."

"Near San Sebastiano?" I asked, trying to get back to the wonders of Venice.

"Some church or other," he said, brushing it away. "I called to it. It looked the other way. I went over to it and put the fish on the pavement."

"And?" I said, forgetting the monuments.

"A door flew open, a man came out waving his hands at me, shouting."

"What did he say?"

"I don't know. I don't understand the Italian they speak here. He pointed the way out of the square, scooped the cat up in his arms and slammed the door."

There was a pause. He looked crestfallen.

"It was no different from Paris," he said finally.

Girl friends, boy friends, family, and pets are Venetians' private property.

The largest cat, the lion, is the true symbol of Venice. Lions are to be discovered sitting on top of, set into, holding onto, falling off, and supporting many of the most noble and the most insignificant buildings in the city. There is no live lion to Venice's name, unlike Rome, where a ragged thrift-shop wolf is exhibited in a cage on the Capitoline. This wolf is not as ineffective as it appears, as an acquaintance of mine discovered during the course of one of those Roman nights. When he put a hand between the bars, he received in quick succession a bite, a ride to the hospital, several stitches, an anti-rabies injection, and an article about himself and the wolf in all the local newspapers.

But rarely has Venice seen a lion. In 1762, a docile lion passed through the city, permitting patrician ladies and gentlemen to caress it while its master collected a large fee. Dogs doing English dances accompanied it through various palatial living rooms.

An elephant was put on display in 1819 along the Riva degli Schiavone but so nervous was it made by the boats bobbing up and down that it broke its cables and went trumpeting off through the streets followed by a rattled band of soldiers. Its tour was brief. In and out of shops and stalls it thundered until, exhausted, it collapsed in a church, San Antonio alla Bragora, its rear feet caught in a tomb that had given way under its weight. After requesting and receiving permission from the archbishop, the soldiers fired upon it at dawn from a small canon hastily mounted at the doors of the church.

Venice has never possessed a zoo. Its parks are lifeless. In the Giardino Papadopoli, a few children use the swings and slides, but the concept of a park is alien to the Venetian sensibility. Venetians choose to contemplate overlooking water.

There is no way to avoid mentioning Venice's pigeons.

The legend is that in the fourteenth century, following the distribution of leaves on Palm Sunday, an original flock of pigeons were released from the loggia of the Doges' Palace with small weights on their legs. A gesture, it seems, to the poor who obliged by scrambling around on the pavement below

PART THREE: EXTRAS

Corse De Tori sopra Il

PART THREE: EXTRAS

1. THE FUNERAL OF A DOGE

The large square of SS Giovanni e Paolo incorporates the church of that name and the school of San Marco, now part of a hospital. The great equestrian statue of the fifteenth-century general Bartolomeo Colleoni dominates the center of the square, and in grave procession relatives of the Doge wearing high, peaked caps follow the bier passing in front of it. Honor guards, priests, and noblemen join the funeral rites while crowds jam the windows nearby. On the day of the funeral Venetian convents cooked beans to distribute to the poor.

2. CELEBRATION OF FEBRUARY 2 IN THE SANTA MARIA FORMOSA

A goose hangs by its feet while half-naked men run by, hopping up to grab at its neck to win points. Way in the background, a duck sits atop a greased pole as boys try to climb up to it. A game of seize-the-cat goes on at the left, and, behind that, obscured in the shadows, a seated bear is baited by a pair of dogs barking at it. A bullfight is in progress in the distance, and the remainder of the square is given over to a troop of actors. This is the celebration of the virgin's feast day.

3. VISIT OF THE NEWLY BETROTHED IN A COVERED GONDOLA

Fidanzate (or fiancées) were given to floating down the canals in covered gondolas, their hair flowing loosely about their shoulders. Their parents and prospective in-laws pored over the documents relating to the famous *doti*, or dowries, which were of great interest to everyone concerned. Matches were frequently arranged by the families involved; rarely did a youth have the opportunity to glimpse the available young ladies, though passing processions on saints' days were carefully scrutinized. Courting might take the form of lute playing beneath a maiden's window and other romantic manifestations now extinct.

4. BULL RUN AND WAGON RACE AT THE RIALTO

Long known as Venice's banking area ("What's new on the Rialto?"), some lighter events also took place there. The bridge would become a race track of sorts involving a rather tame running of the bulls. The animals were kept at discreet distances by lengths of rope held by elegantly dressed gentlemen who hurried along behind. The wagon race was run by garbage men for prizes of wine.

5. BULLFIGHT IN HONOR OF THE KING OF POLAND

Under extraordinary circumstances the Piazza was turned into a bull ring. Elaborate arches were constructed out of wood so that the bulls and bullfighters could enter and exit in style. The animals were brought to the nearest canal on boats, coaxed onto shore, and equipped with long leads. The bullfight event took three hours. Dogs were used to torment the animals by nipping at their ears. Spectators not invited had to cram the windows of the *procuratie vecchie* flanking the Piazza.

to snatch up the pigeons as they plummeted. But several pigeons strong of wing managed to reach safety in various cornices of the Piazza. From then on, these birds were considered vaguely sacred, the Church quite prepared to condemn, exonerate, or exalt according to the circumstances. They began to multiply.

There was a recent plan to rid Venice of a certain percentage of its pigeon population; a plan, undamaged by failure, certain to be suggested and rejected in the decades to come. Sick birds were to be removed, to begin with. The execution progressed no further. Butchers were accused of selling them the first day the traps were set.

Everyone had his say. Letters arrived to the newspaper in droves.

"Now that the feeding stations for the pigeons have been changed, if I were a pigeon, how would I know where to go?"

"Pigeons cannot read," answered the newspaper. "It is useless to print this information."

The pigeons, of course, will remain as long as Venice does. They will settle on your caffè table next to your cappuccino, will land on your shoulder, in your

hair, hang onto your lapel. They will deface the cornices, the heads and shoulders of real and imagined heroes. And in the winter they will fly at you like darts as the late hours toll and the dark comes on and some of them will die publicly under the colonnades and on top of back bridges.

The Italians have some special attraction/repulsion towards birds, *uccelli*, which also happens to be the slang for the male organ. They will go to great lengths to trap them and then dine on them with indifference. The skies in the Romagna and Tuscany are filled at sunset by amoebic masses of swifts so dense that they appear like ominous clouds of retribution. Birds are kept as ornaments rather than pets. Their cages are always too small.

I noticed one day a large blue and gold macaw in the window of a simple house giving on a small alley deep in shadow. The bright feathers of the bird were an unexpected touch of the exotic which made me realize that during its trade with the East, Venice must have been the host to many strange creatures brought home with the merchandise to sulk away their remaining days looking out at bleak views.

The jail is small.

Surrounded by high walls and something resembling a moat, it sits on the site of a monastery. Guards stand on the parapet spending their hours languidly watching the windows of the surrounding houses though scarce is the possibility that some unclothed female will glide by an open window. The prisoners' girl friends sometimes come to call at the walls of the prison. When they do, a shouted dialogue echoes along the lugubrious canal. Nearby is a wide, filled-in river, the *rio terra dei pensieri* (literally, the earthed river of the thoughtful), flanked by houses falling into disrepair. At the end of the street looms an immense fuel tank, one of the largest structures in Venice. Just beyond, as an extra, unexpected admonition, is the bustling railroad station, symbol of freedom and motion, scene of enthusiastic arrivals from the provinces to a big-time Venice, where everything seems possible. There is no precise record of the proportion of Venice's prisoners who arrived in just that way on the other side of the fuel tank, but I presume from following the newspaper accounts that it is high.

Crimes are rarely spectacular. Mainly, there are the thefts. Apartments broken into, gems pocketed, furs dragged across rooftops, pillowcases stuffed with family silver, paintings stripped from frames and handed down over back walls into boats. Often the thieves are inept, surprised on the parapets, falling ignominiously into the canals. Recently, a particularly acrobatic group entered a flat while the owners were spending the winter in Cortina and stole eleven paintings and a silver service for six. Then they opened the refrigerator and celebrated the robbery with several bottles of mineral water and some dry *panettone*.

Homey crimes. Kids rob a telephone vending machine, rifle a cigarette store, swipe a cassette recorder. Looking back in the newspapers of the thirties, it is the same: large photographs of political figures lucent with medals, of blackshirts marching on San Marco, surrounded by articles on skimpy thefts. Apartments broken into, handbags snatched, paintings disappearing . . .

The prisoner is put in manacles. They are not handcuffs; they are *polsi di ferro*, wrist irons. They launch an atmosphere of chain gangs and dungeons into a judiciary system filled with petty officials in shiny suits. Recently a young prisoner was permitted to visit his dying father's bedside accompanied by two policemen who carried his chains. In the area of prison reform, Italy hedges to the East and the South, ignoring it, unlike the performance record it sets for automobile design and fashion. The idea is that one can get away with almost anything but failure to do so is almost as much of a crime as the crime itself. Once caught inside the bureaucratic mechanism, you are outside the rest of the fabric of the peninsula. Earlier I mentioned the phrase *Ci metteremo d'accordo* or We'll arrange it, the words that seal the agreement, that assure everyone that everything will be all right. The other

phrase which even more significantly characterizes the system in Italy specifies a favor: *Ci penso io*, I'll take care of it for you.

Ci penso io, one hears, and so saying, the lawyer leaves, just as the contractor, the plumber, the man who was going to get the train ticket has left. A smile, a wave, a scurrying off to take care of it. At first, one sighs with relief: a burden lifted. Ah, the Mediterranean! Then one learns that the lawyer has gotten busy with a more influential client, the contractor has never before built a house, the leak turns into a flood, the train ticket is unavailable, and you are likely to spend the rest of your days in Italy hearing *Ci penso io*.

When the prisoner is sentenced it means that the system broke down. No one has been able to take care of it for him any more.

And then there is Venice's ways of dealing with death.

The gravedigger did a little dance at noon when the churchbell rang. He knew that within the hour he would be going home to lunch. Not unaware that he was being observed by me, he seemed to enjoy the clowning, as did I. Egged on by his fellow employees (picks and shovels set aside), he imitated a tango around his tractor. Row after row behind him stood the crosses.

Most Venetians are buried according to the day they die; grave after grave in a straight line that reads like a faulty calendar. Certain days there are several graves, then none. One's neighbor on the island of San Michele is that Venetian who left the world at a similar moment. Coffins remain in the ground for approximately thirteen years; then they are exhumed, in a row. The field is immediately plowed and made ready once again. Wall crypts are more permanent. Family mausoleums are forever, or so it would seem. Prices rise as they do in real estate, and religion dictates whether you will be buried

on the Island of San Michele or in the Jewish cemetery on the Lido. Certain families manage to crowd all the titles: (inherited, *Conte;* professional, *Avv.;* earned, *Gen.;* and bestowed, *Ecc.*) onto the tombstones. But most families simply place names and oval enameled photographs of the deceased in the center of the crosses and let it go at that. There are a few wooden crosses on which only the name has been painted and often it has vanished with the rains.

Sometimes the sorrow of the survivor is carved into stone. A father in the late eighteen eighties laments the simultaneous death of his unborn son and his wife and pleads for some Divine assistance in raising his five children. A spiteful mother—on a tomb outside Venice—has her revenge against a daughter-in-law: "Here lies ———, beloved son, killed in an automobile accident while being driven by his wife."

It is evident from certain gravestones that they extend the possibility of a communication link to the hereafter. Families list virtues, list griefs, list suggestions to the angels carved by the hardworking masons whose studios fill the neighborhood across the lagoons from the island.

Bordered in black, death announcements containing a pasted-on photograph are put up on walls in the neighborhood of the person who has died. People will stop, approach them with dread, and put on their spectacles.

Newspapers carry lengthy obituaries and when a noted person dies, his obituaries spread across the pages, placed by family, friends, relatives, organizations, affiliations. Funerals can be extremely large in Venice; an entire neighborhood will turn out for a once familiar face. The church bell tolls heavily: it cannot be anything but a funeral. The coffin, draped in black with a wreath, is rolled on a metal apparatus to the waiting funeral boat. Followed by private launches, the entourage sets off with the sound of great power reigned in, slowly to the island of San Michele.

One afternoon while walking down the Calle delle Erbe, I became aware of several establishments dealing in funeral arrangements. Faded photographs of various coffin styles lined the windows. Across the street were some printers' shops. "Clearly the funeral district," I thought, and as I registered the proximity of the two related businesses, I saw coming towards me, with great sorrow on her face, a woman, stumbling, assisted by two grim boys, presumably her sons. The trio cleaved its way down the narrow street and entered a shop. At the corner I came upon the Campo San Giovanni e Paolo, its Lombardoesque school of San Marco now a hospital, neatly combining practicality with tourism. Had they just left the hospital, those three? Then the arrangements; then the announcements; then the florist, all down the alleyway? Looking across the canal, I could see the island of San Michele in the last of the light, its tall cypresses bending at the tips in a soft wind. Then the cemetery?

Part Four
BOUNDARIES

She went on growing and growing, and very soon had to kneel down on the floor: in another minute there was not even room for this, and she tried the effect of lying down, with one elbow against the door, and the other arm curled round her head. Still she went on growing, and as a last resource, she put one arm out of the window, and one foot up the chimney, and said to herself, "Now I can do no more, whatever happens. What *will* become of me?"

Lewis Carroll: *Alice in Wonderland*

For a thousand years, while the rest of Europe painfully shifted boundaries and loyalties, Venice did business. In its earliest centuries, Venice was not a carnival attraction built on water. A small population of shrewd people, intensely patriotic, sent fleets out to sea whenever threatened with war, wherever in need of possessions. The rest of its time was concentrated on commerce. Venice was the aggressive merchant on the upper eastern curve of the Italian peninsula. Imagine the shape of Western Europe at the time of the Crusades: an immense Holy Roman Empire fastens onto a major portion of the Continent in the manner of those large animals which energetically manage to digest creatures even larger than themselves. Only one small corner of the Adriatic is allowed an independent breath of sea air. That it was Venice surprised no one.

No enemy penetrated Venice. No one cared to, at first; and as it grew powerful, no one knew how. No sea captain other than a Venetian could navigate those lagoons. Never laboring over allegiances, Venice immediately took sides with the powers best serving its interests. In outfitting the Crusades and sending them forth from its shores, Venice made a profit and gained some territory. There was never any pretense of religious fervor.

The republic was so small that deception was impossible. On the lagoon islands, everyone's place was clearly defined, and Venetians were quick to notice whether those places were kept.

Early in their history, the citizens of the republic would elect the Doge by a popular vote. When his actions displeased the public, he was murdered. Death was not the only alternative. Many Doges were blinded over braziers of hot coals, a system imported with enthusiasm from the Greeks. Punishment could also take a religious tone: the Doge would be required to take the monk's cowl, remaining celibate for the remainder of his days in a monastery. Doges began to leave Venice on their own. When menaced by plots on his life, Pietro Orseolo I secretly left his palace in the dead of night on the first of September 976, sailed across the lagoon to Fusina, found some horses, galloped rapidly through northern Italy, across what is now France to the Pyrenees, and withdrew into a monastery. Twenty-nine years later, he died there, and for this life of piety and devotion, he was canonized. He had been an imaginative Doge, but this did not keep him from having enemies.

The previous Doge, Candiano IV had so enraged the public by his corruption that they poured pitch on the houses near the Palace, burning a fair portion of the district and the Palace as well. They then set upon the Doge as he tried to escape with his son through a side door into the Basilica and hacked them both to death with axes. His successor, Orseolo, brought workmen from Constantinople to reconstruct the Basilica, paying for it from his private fortune. He also created the first Venetian income tax, designed to restore an immense dowry to the widow of the slain Doge, whose name was Hwalderada. Then he escaped to his monastery. Venetian ducal history is extremely florid. It is no wonder that grand opera has had such a continuing success there.

Doges learned to protect themselves. It was not only a humanitarian motive that led them to invite the more prominent citizens of the republic to share in the affairs of state. To invite is *pregare;* the Pregadi, the Invited, became the Venetian Senate.

These *invited* gentlemen of influence would naturally one day seize all the power in Venice and retain the Doge as something picturesque. He would be sat in thrones, carried around on high litters, shadowed under carved and gilded umbrellas, his form decorated with silks, satins, velvets, brocades and the *corno,* or ducal bonnet. With the fall of the republic, the last Doge would hand his hat to his servant, saying, "*Tole questo; no la dopera pui.*" Take it away, we shall not use it any more.

No individual lord would govern the land, as they did in other Italian cities. The general public was excluded from voting for any office. The Pregadi created a form of government so peculiarly Venetian that no other country would ever try to imitate it.

The system maintained by the Venetians is the following:

The Senate was composed of 160 members. They were the principal legislative body of the government and directed the foreign affairs of the republic. Ambassadors were elected here and were required to report back to the Senate on their diplomatic missions.

The Council of Ten was the essential power of Venice. Their election proceeded as follows: The Great Council elected ten men to the Council. Simultaneously, the Doge and his own councilors and chiefs of the Supreme Court would appoint ten men. From among these twenty, the Great Council would then elect ten. These men would rule for six months.

The Council of Three was elected from within the Council of Ten each month. These three Capi would receive all communications addressed to the Ten, and attend to the execution of its decrees. Both councils were feared, since they often worked in secret. Any order issued by the Ten (and carried

out by the Three) was law. There was no appeal.
The Cabinet consisted of the ministers of the state: two men to each title, acting as Secretary of War, Finance, Navy. For one week at a time, one of these six acted as Prime Minister. The purpose of the Cabinet was to sift the affairs of state and decide on their disposition.
The Six Ducal Councilors opened the Doge's correspondence and accompanied him in his official duties. If he was indisposed, they could act for him in a quorum.
The Doge presided over the Great Council, the Senate, the Ten, and in the College. His powers were limited; he was the ornament of the state.

This became one of the most successful and stable systems in the history of the world.

And so, in the early fourteenth century, with great political and social refinement and a bit of snobbery, the patrician gentlemen of Venice drew up their Golden Book. In it, they scrupulously listed only themselves and their families. Venice would be governed by a closed corporation. A marriage between one of their members and a lady from the middle class would, with a finality acceptable to any Social Register fanatic, rule out the inclusion of that lady and any of their children. Even the plague, which later in a democratic fashion removed many of Venice's most illustrious families, could not pry open the Book to admit some new names. It was only when the republic needed to finance some municipal project, like a war, that someone could buy his way in. Everything having its price is an essential fact of the Venetian ethic.

The nobles were not frivolous. They fined each other for any excesses, imprisoned each other for bribery. Sumptuary laws told them how many dinner guests they were permitted to entertain and how much embroidery was allowed on their daughters' wedding sheets. Working all year round in the Great Council, they governed the republic seven half-days a week. They were required to elect their Doge in a system so complicated that it appears to have been invented by precocious schoolboys on a rainy afternoon.

The Great Council by lot chose from among them 30
The 30 are reduced by lot to 9
The 9 vote for 40
(*with 7 or more votes each*)
The 40 are reduced by lot to 12
The 12 vote for 25
(*with at least 9 votes each*)
The 25 are reduced by lot to 9
The 9 vote for 45
(*with at least 7 votes each*)

PART FOUR: BOUNDARIES

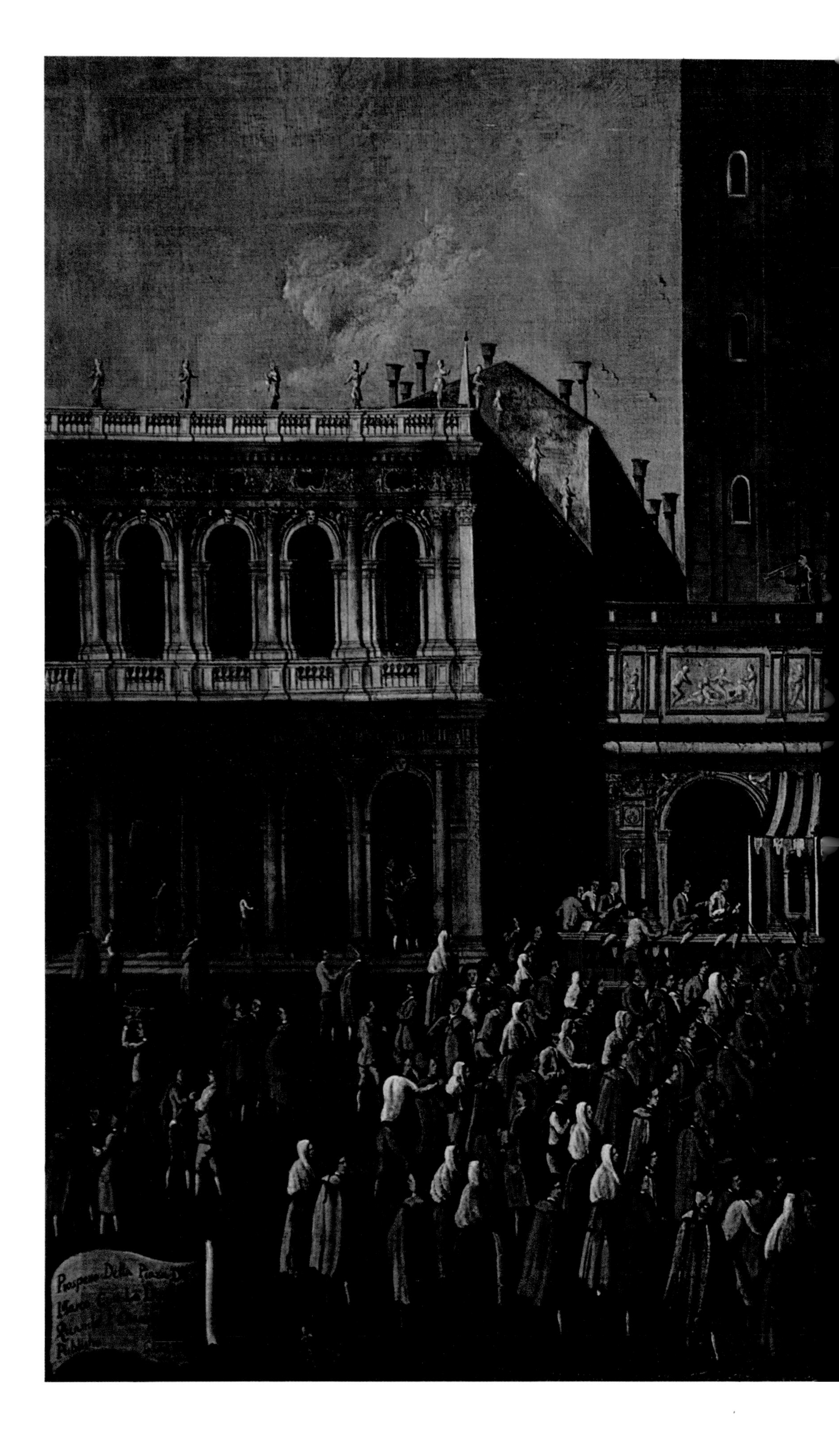

Ordine Che Tiene La
Republica Veneta Nel Dare
Di Mare

Esercizio Del Popolo Fu
Di Ven. La Battaglia
Del Ponte Co Legni

PART FOUR: BOUNDARIES

1. COUNCIL OF THE PREGADI

Membership in the Pregadi, or Senate, varied throughout the years. When the government was initially formed there were only sixty members. Rule was maintained always by the Venetian aristocracy, and *il popolo,* the people, had little to say in determining the destiny of their republic. It is interesting that they remained extremely loyal during Venice's long and complicated history. No revolutions and dissents: Venice was one of the most harmonious and patriotic republics in the history of the world. The Hall of the Senate was destroyed by fire in the sixteenth century and rebuilt on a design by Da Ponte, preserving its original Gothic form.

2. POPE PIO VI GIVING THE VENETIANS HIS BLESSINGS

Pio VI was the sixth Pope in Venetian history to visit the city. Venice was never on particularly good terms with Rome throughout its long history, and frequently the two cities acted against each other's interests. When Pio VI arrived, the Piazza was occupied with the Ascension Day Fair, and the Campo SS Giovanni e Paolo was chosen for his reception. An elaborate loggia was constructed to bring His Holiness and other dignitaries into a lofty position against the façade of the School of San Marco.

3. THE PUBLIC LOTTERY

Venice was a city of bells. The paternal gong of the Campanile dominated the various tollings from over two hundred towers in the city. Even a little "bankrupt's bell" used to ring at noon, and for a half hour, debtors were free to walk about and sun themselves with impunity. A lugubrious bell accompanied the condemned as they were led across the Bridge of Sighs to their executions. The bell announcing the lottery was a monthly ritual, along with the sound of trumpets. Seated under the canopy at the base of the Campanile, a white-wigged official would announce the winning numbers protected by a rank of military guards.

4. CONSIGNMENT OF THE SCEPTER OF COMMAND TO THE GENERAL OF THE SEA

A nobleman would be elected in time of war—and all of Venice's wars were sea battles—as townspeople gathered in front of the Basilica. Following a solemn mass and benediction, he took his command of the ships. Guns saluted, bells rang, trumpets blared, patriotism overwhelmed, and crowds followed the march to the ships moored in the harbor.

5. RITUAL FIGHTS ON THE PONTE DI SANTA FOSCA

Rivalry between factions in Venice existed since the republic began. For generations, hatreds were scrupulously maintained, often finding outlets in public games. The Castellani and Niccolotti, two clans linked by blood and neighborhood, were traditional Venetian enemies for over three hundred years. The Ponte di Santa Fosca is also known as the *ponte dei pugni,* or bridge of fists, and it is here that ritualistic battles took place. Goal marks in the form of footprints may still be seen embedded in the corners of the bridge.

The 45 are reduced by lot to	11
The 11 vote for	41
	(*with at least 9 votes each*)
The 41 *elect* by a minimum of 25 votes	the Doge

On election day, the youngest councilor entering the Basilica of San Marco was required to pray, rise from his knees, and take the first young man he met into the Doges' Palace. He would become the *ballottino*, the ballot boy: it was his duty to present the ballot box to the council and withdraw the slips of paper.

Following his election, the Doge would be presented to the public in a pulpit erected in the Piazza. Then he was carried around in a *pozzo*, or little well, throwing coins to the masses, none of whom had participated in his election. The *corno* would be placed on his head at the top of the Giant's Stairs. A banquet would then be held in the evening for the forty-one electors.

But, as unyielding as the form of government seems, and labyrinthian the method of electing a Doge, the machinery worked, and worked well, for almost five hundred years.

Not only did everyone know where he stood, but in addition, managed to peer over everyone else's shoulder. Very little of that has changed.

The Golden Book remained until Napoleon occupied Venice in 1797. He had the document publicly burned in the Piazza San Marco. Near where the flames had leaped, a Tree of Liberty was planted. There is no record of how large it grew.

Cinders of the Golden Book remain in the air of Venice, still irritating to the eye of the liberal. A family with an ancient title will probably assume that everyone in Venice knows that their name has belonged to the ruling class or a long-ago Doge. And everyone does know it, particularly the butcher and the florist who might have realized it by the *noblesse oublie* they encounter whenever they present their bills. Notable families of later centuries will generally defer to the older names, placing them in proper order at their rare dinner parties.

The newest aristocrats recklessly planted by Mussolini about forty years ago are a much heartier variety, generally taller and showier, cultivated outside of Venice in the industrial *terraferma* raised to make money.

It is appreciated if foreigners living in Venice know just who has been who in the way that they learn to distinguish a Tintoretto from a Tiepolo from a Titian.

Tourists have the advantage of not being expected to know who anybody is or was. Like cows in India they are permitted to wander around and bump into things. It is doubtful that they are ever invited inside.

The geography is simpler to learn.

Six districts were marked out on the Venetian map in 1171 and no one is going to change them now: Castello, San Marco, Santa Croce, San Polo, Cannaregio. The grudges each district holds for another have the sound of people who have lived too long together in the same sanitorium, no longer quite remembering why or when they began taking sides. The litany is a bit like this: someone is from Cannaregio? They are all thieves in Cannaregio. The San Marco people? By their proximity to the Great Piazza, they have airs and graces and tend to work in hotels. The people from Dorsoduro are respectable; they are foreigners paying too much rent, or they are a rowdy bunch (if they live on the island of the Giudecca), and some of those are thieves as well.

It is all, or almost all, nonsense, and Venetians know it. Loving categories and limitations, they enjoy the tradition. "*C'era una volta . . . ,*" you will hear, the "once upon a time" bringing forth the retelling of some ancient dispute between families. *C'era una volta,* always: Venice, the perennial fable.

Venetians have been battling each other on their small islands for fifteen hundred years. Refugees who migrated there clanned together with people from their own towns on the mainland and built hatreds for everybody else. At the time of Pepin, a certain part of the population perished fighting one another. In the pine forests that then covered the Lido their corpses were left to be devoured by sea birds. For five hundred years, two rival factions, the Castellani and the Niccolotti, from across town, sniped at each other—though never at the government. By the eighteenth century their hostility had tamed down enough to permit them to enter the cathedral by the same door. The fierceness of their ritual fights became exhibitionistic; they pummeled each other for prizes on the Ponte dei Pugni, or Bridge of Fists (which, like almost everything else in Venice, still exists by its old name), formed themselves athletically into human pyramids, and held the world's first regattas.

Today, if a man from the district of Cannaregio goes out with a girl from Castello twenty blocks away, it will not go unremarked. Were they to marry, she will always be, at heart, the wife-from-Castello. Once out of Venice, they would be ennobled by being *Veneziani.* But leaving the peninsula, they would become simply Italians from the north, a bitter pill for the citizens of a republic maintaining for centuries, and with great style, its own embassies throughout the world.

In their zeal to isolate and categorize, it would have been the Venetians who invented the ghetto. The word itself has had several interpretations until one of them was more or less agreed upon. The Hebrew word *nghedad* and the Syrian *nghetto* are both translated as congregation, or synagogue, causing etymological confusion with *gettare,* Italian for casting. This gave rise to *ghetto,* the district in which the foundries were located. It was a convenient

CAPO MADRE

neighborhood for seclusion. A document in Latin, from 1468, tells us that the foundries were enclosed in an area made accessible by only one little bridge. By 1516, the *ghetto vecchio*, contained within its limits a sizable population of Jews; no doubt a proportion of them from the 200,000 exiled from Spain several years previously. Certain historians point to Venice as a kind of haven in that exodus, a dubious position, since the little bridge was systematically raised at dusk and lowered at dawn. Ultimately, the ghetto contained the tallest buildings in Venice. Its inhabitants could not build beyond those limits, thus forcing the neighborhood to grow upward instead of out. It is a somber place made even more so by the small thatches of tourists who are herded through clucking morosely. In reality, most of its Jewish population has long ago dispersed.

Venetians still practice what could almost pass for anti-Semitism, based, it would seem, on their penchant for separating everything rather than any illusions of superiority. On the contrary, Venetians would feel a particular affinity towards their *Ebrei*, having themselves always been considered apart. Venetians' historical position as merchants to Europe is precisely that of America's turn-of-the-century Jews: They were patronized by the townspeople conveniently buying thread in "that little dry-goods shop," clients who scarcely realized that the largest department store in the county would some day belong to the thread seller.

Venetians segregate even themselves. They tend to treat each of their islands as though it had an island personality as distinctive from the others as those communities in the Caribbean. Although the difference between the residents of Murano and Burano seems inconsiderable, each island has maintained a dialect of its own. Chioggia, an island broken in two parts and bound by a bridge, has two. (People from Chioggia are gossips, brawlers. To support this theory the illustrious Goldoni is quickly mentioned; his play *Le Baruffe Chiozzotte.*)

Taking a small boat with an outboard motor through the Brenta one afternoon, a Venetian friend and I disturbed a fisherman who then gave us a stern lecture. Neither of us could understand him. "I don't know what he is saying," confided my friend as the man talked on. "They speak differently here." We were in foreign waters, five kilometers from Venice. To punctuate the man's annoyance at our disturbing his fish, he crushed an empty cigarette package, throwing it into the water. "It will end up," said my friend, claiming the right to all the refuse from alien territory, "in Venice. Everything from around Venice does." He sounded nostalgic. We started up the motor, continuing on through the canal, pioneers far from home.

Venetians retreat into their dialect as firmly as they close their shutters at night. It is their private property, a scarce commodity in a city exposing so much of itself to tourism. A waiter will take your order in Italian giving it to the chef in dialect. The nobility speak it to their servants, if they happen to have any, in a gesture designed either to merge with the people, or to keep tabs on backstairs gossip. Venetians with no education are apt to speak only the dialect and no Italian. Until a few years ago, the radio regularly broadcast a program in dialect, but it was eliminated: too quaint, no longer of the times.

At first, the dialect sounds harelipped. Foreign words from here and there are smuggled out between the teeth. *Buono* comes out as a barely uttered *bon;* a bit of Spanish wangles in and *buon giorno* is, instead, *bon di.* The word for the morning roll with coffee sounds like *corazón.* You think that you have discovered the Spanish word for heart, look again at the shape of the pastry, which is a crescent, and realize that it is the Venetian pronunciation of *croissant,* taken from the French. Certain words, like *ciapa* (take it), seem to come from the air, though you might find that, like *arsenale* (from *d'arsina* a house of industry), they come from the Arabic. Most frequently, words seem to be fundamentally Italian, like the endearment for a pal, *vecio,* as in *vecchio,* or old man. *Ostia!* heard all the time in Venice, is from *ostrica,* or oyster, and is used as an exclamation, Oyster! rather the way the English say, Good heavens!

If one was particularly inclined, as one is tempted to do, to place everything Venetian into some watery metaphor, it would not be difficult to find the splashing around of all the soft z sounds in the dialect significant:

Un lievro in mezo a do cani, un vilan in mezo a do avocati, un sorze in mezo a do gati, un mala in mezo a do dotori: chi sta pezo de lori?[1]

It is not Italian in the flowery tradition. The vowels are so often apocopated the language begins to sound unpatriotic: *L'amor no pol star sconto*[2] is *L'amore non puo rimanere nascosto.* Puccini and Verdi would have brought few tears using Venetian librettists.

Confronted with the bleeding heart dialect of the Romans or the glottal Neapolitan speech beginning somewhere in the groin, the Venetian cadence caws a bit, like Woody the Woodpecker. After a while it sounds ingenuous. In the rhythm of their speech, Venetians make no pleas.

The separation between Venice and the Continent is always there. A railroad bridge spanned the lagoon in 1846 but a road bridge was only constructed forty-odd years ago. The new highway linking Venice to Milan and Trieste is called the Tangenziale, and signs for it are posted everywhere along the small roads surrounding Venice. Tangential: as though some surreal municipal edict had found a way to express in print the Venetian relationship to the rest of Italy.

[1] A rabbit between two dogs, an outlaw between two lawyers, a mouse between two cats, an invalid between two doctors, who is in more trouble?
[2] Love cannot remain hidden.

duplo
duplo

Petrus
PIZZE
L.190.

This sense of being out of register, moored alongside rather than attached to the peninsula, is shared by Venice both geographically and spiritually with the island of Sicily. The cuff of the boot and the part near the toe. From the nearby Arab world, Sicilians consider that they have inherited an Arab feeling for passion. If so, Venice has been susceptible to the role of courtesan. She stole and copied her ornaments from the Muslim world for centuries, acquiring along with them a sense of mystery. With Sicily, she shares an isolation from the mainland even though her bridge is only three and half kilometers long.

Isolation: the concept occurs again and again, a heavy bell tolling in some weary campanile. Even the island forms of Venice illustrate its self-involvement; two fish shapes gripping each other for dear life. Streets are no wider than an open umbrella. Why? To gain space for the buildings, it is said, though I suspect that it is Venice's predilection to huddle close, to watch over each other's shoulders, to barricade in.

Venice began as a retreat. Almost fifteen hundred years ago, exiles from the mainland ran there to hide, the tenuous shore offering nothing but shallow marshes, long-legged birds, and incardine sunsets. As waves of barbarians descended on northern Italy, its refugees knew or sensed that they would not be followed into that muck. And until Napoleon, no invader ever got through. For thirteen centuries, Venice thrived on the backs of those two locked fish shapes while the mainland kept changing hands. The essence of Venice's endurance is that she was something apart, always, trading successfully with all comers, stupendously decorating herself, stashing money in her own banks, taking sides when she could, with the winners. A genuine courtesan.

Shreds of it remain. The lit-up smile vanishes when the recipient of it turns to leave. I have watched it again and again with shopkeepers: the face goes rigid, a clamshell snapped shut, only to relax and open up again for the next customer. When the dollar was suddenly devalued and the mark rose, the teller at my bank shrugged and said, "Well then, more Germans this summer. *Es war nich meine Schuld . . .*"

The three *thé dansant* orchestras on the Piazza are inclined to switch gears according to the crowd at hand. I have heard one of them obliging a group of Hadassah ladies with the "Hava Nagilla," until, spying the arrival of a Saudi-Arabian oil sheik with entourage veering around the corner from the Danieli in full sail, they broke into "In a Persian Garden" in a brave but misinformed attempt to give him his due.

Oil sheik, Shah, Maharajah, all passing figures in front of scenery even more exotic than they. Someone turbaned, kaftaned, dhotied or djellabaed does not look awkward in Venice. Drifting past the arabesques and mosaics, robed figures move with ease in a city long used to them. When country

folk arrive on the daily boat from Yugoslovia, they still wear their kerchiefs and print dresses, their coarse overalls and berets. Standing in complete bewilderment they seem as though they had been caught dreaming out in the fields. Nuns flow blackly into the Piazza and out the other end, and I am certain it is the fantasy of every ballet dancer who visits Venice to cross the vast square in a series of *glissades* and *pas jetés*, either quite alone or with a crowd on the sidelines.

Of the foreigners living in Venice there is little exoticism. It is difficult to say whether it is lethargy or courage, romanticism or monasticism or the various combinations that keep foreigners there through the long and chilly winters. It is not the usual expatriate drinking community, and there are none of the entertainments designed for the bored and the rich to be found on the amusing pages of E. F. Benson and his mythical town of leisure. There is, from time to time, a sense that the foreign contingent is a bit out of things, tending to drift away even from the community of Venice itself on an isolated raft. Tea is periodically served with the Anglican minister, and gossip is heavily traded. Venetian elements seem to remain frequently unabsorbed. Such a singular ability, for example, as the pleasure Venetians take in fashioning, through a baroque series of twists and turns, an insult into a compliment, can go unrecognized. The Venetian sense of tact is highly developed. Tactlessness (described by Theophrastus as "a painful failure in the sense of occasion,") is an imported commodity.

I recently attended, or tried to attend, a small film showing given by the British consulate on an early winter evening. Events during that season are scarce and the members of the foreign community looked inclined to stretch whatever it was and make it last. "Following the film," the invitation read, "a drink will be served."

"And where is *your* invitation?" asked the British consul, his ready diplomatic smile about to desert him as I started up the staircase.

I stammered out that I was the guest of Miss Guggenheim.

The good lady, who was at that moment struggling to remove a coat of fake fur, asked what the matter was.

Colonialism of the Great Days swept aside the good manners easily borrowed from the most modest news vendor on the corner.

"But we can't have this. Invitations are for one only. No, we simply can't. The room will fill up. And when it does, you will have to . . ."

"Leave?" I said, and did, missing the promised drink. The alien air had remained as intact and uncompromising to the surroundings as a cork on water.

The most logical explanation for the existence of a foreign colony among the lagoons is the obvious fact of Venice's extraordinary beauty and its silence. Too hot and crowded in the summer and too damp and desolate in the winter, its attractions for expatriates living there en masse are limited. Perhaps it is this reason as well—that there are so few foreigners living there—which makes it so appealing to foreigners.

I have been asked many times why I have lived in Venice, and usually I am surprised to realize that my reply sounds like a testimonial for a sea voyage on a phantasmal ship. Although the city of Venice is exceptional, it is the stillness of the waters surrounding it, the limitlessness of its lagoons, that makes living there transcend life-styles elsewhere. You are a passenger, in Venice, as well as an inhabitant.

For non-Venetians, Venice can be considered a retreat. It is doubtful that many foreigners expect to achieve professional recognition there. This is unlike Rome, where one hears of ambitions and high hopes among the *stranieri.* Many foreigners stay on in Rome for years, bewitched by the sensuous climate and perennial promise in the air. If you have not been sent to study in Venice, do not sell whatever your art is, or find that your private income has ceased to arrive, Venice tempts you with nothing. It wants you out.

Any foreigner who remains in Venice is labeled. The tradesmen attach on him something easy and manageable: he who is a leftist, she who wears those tight blouses, they who drink. The foreigners themselves reach for more obscure labels: he who was defrocked and took up a lengthy study of Palladio, and so on.

"They're very F. Scott Fitzgerald," is what we became when, after just having been married, my wife and I came to spend the winter. And so we proceeded on the small round of social events dragging along the unearned title, only occasionally longing to do something rash to justify it. We lived then on the *piano nobile* of a large, decaying palace, spending most of our time in the kitchen, where, to keep us warm, the burners and oven were permanently lit. Although they were immense, the radiators in all of the rooms would heat only the air in their immediate vicinity: that is, if one pressed up against them, one might heat a portion of one's anatomy. We shivered. We caught colds. We tried hard to believe that it was all right; that, after all, we were living in a palace in Venice. Sometimes we went outside to get warm, or warmer. We amused ourselves by the Fitzgerald myth as we sat inside our several sweaters on chairs with missing springs under lights barely strong enough to illuminate our volumes of *The Forsyte Saga.*

We visited damp churches. With Lorenzetti's guide in hand we took long walks along dank passageways. The School of San Rocca (with its Tintorettos) was closed for restorations. The Carpaccio rooms in the Accademia were shut because of lack of personnel. *Acqua alta,* the high water, lapped at the front door of our palazzo, flooding the tiny apartment

of a pretty friend of ours who lived there like a character out of Grimm, her blond hair down to her waist, spending a long winter away from a Canadian university. The pipes froze in another apartment, rousing another young American who had taken to smoking marijuana to keep his spirits up when he was not learning how to blow glass at a furnace in Murano where he also went to keep warm. On Christmas Eve we arrived in a huddled group at the Basilica of San Marco to find the doors shut and bolted. The Piazza was dark. By the time we learned the location of the one church giving a choral concert, the music was over.

F. Scott Fitzgerald did not seem to pertain to that uncompromisingly morose period. I decided—in the first of many such decisions—to leave the place forever. But the weather grew warmer, the earliest of spring flowers appeared miraculously at the flower stalls. I discovered someone with a boat and remembered again that the countryside was just across the bridge and to the north. We left Venice later, on an upward swing; the only way to leave any relationship.

The foreign intellectual community was nominally presided over by Ezra Pound, though actually he saw almost nobody. It was enough that he lived there, and this he did quietly, in a gondolier's house in back of the Salute, with his companion, Miss Rudge. Only rarely did they receive the visiting journalist, scholar, aspiring poet or celebrity seeker. A few friends were infrequently summoned to the tiny house. Its atmosphere was rustic; a large fire glowed against walls covered with the narrow painted wooden strips traditional to the lowest floors as a precaution against the dampness.

Mr. Pound sat in a large, comfortable, worn chair, a shawl wrapped around his shoulders, his great head tilted low against his chest. The quintessential Poet. Conversation in the room was agreeable, touching on poetry from time to time, though Pound would not be provoked into speaking. His eyes seem fixed at some point disconnected with us, with the room; rather he seemed focused on something remembered or experienced, though perhaps it is unfair to speculate. From time to time, as though to reassure themselves that he was, in fact, there, someone would ask him a question which would remain unanswered. Miss Rudge sat next to him, her face managing to convey that she was both alert and weary, long used to expecting some calamity for which she had been well prepared.

Everyone accepted Pound's silence, indulging his privilege to sit there in his own home unmolested. His hands moved incessantly, in the way of certain elderly people, the fingers rubbing against each other for circulation, or warmth, or reassurance.

When, finally, one of the young people asked something which got through, Pound's eyes pierced into us all. It was some banality, an anecdote one wanted to hear from his own voice. Miss Rudge repeated the question gently: "Ezra, do tell about the time Joyce left the manuscript in the taxi."

There was a long pause. "No!" he replied. "Naaoo!" A long *no*, strung together out of many accumulated no's.

Miss Rudge gave the approximation of a smile. For a fraction of a second, her mouth, so unused to smiling, turned up at the edges. It told us that she had known that story, had known him when he was able to tell it, when he was writing some of the greatest poetry of the century. And she did not choose to mind his not telling it now.

PART FIVE: LEVELS

Gioco Della Racchetta

Salla Del Novo
Redono

PART FIVE: LEVELS

1. THE LAST DAY OF THE CARNIVAL

The Venetian carnival attracted all of Europe, and since the Venetians were well aware of it, they managed to make it last six months by the time of the late eighteenth century. With the tolling of the Marangona, the biggest bell in the city, housed in the Campanile, the carnival came to an end. Harlequin and Pantalone and all the other masqueraders would now vanish from the streets. In the foreground of the painting, a mock black coffin is carried around the Piazza, signifying the death of the carnival.

2. FOOTBALL AT THE GESUITI

The game, now known as Calcio, was played most frequently by noblemen—and occasionally noblewomen—in various squares of Venice. Since the noise it produced often disturbed the tranquillity of the monasteries and convents fronting the various *campi*, it was a game that changed its playing fields regularly. The public stood about unprotected at each end of the court. The absence of a crowd indicates that it was not then, as it has now become, Italy's most popular sport.

3. A NOBLEWOMAN TAKING THE VEIL AT SAN LORENZO

San Zaccaria and San Lorenzo were the most fashionable convents of the eighteenth century. The religious aspect of them was not of major importance, since they functioned mainly as salons. Venetian women were brought up to be appealing. Courtesans in the sixteenth century numbered over eleven thousand, and they were permitted a social mobility not possible in other parts of Italy. At the ceremony here pictured, the novice receives her vows as violins play and choruses sing.

4. TENNIS GAME

Although the rackets were smaller than the ones in use today, and the tennis balls were blue and red, the game was played in the same way as it is now. Here we see a ball boy rescuing a bad shot caught in the screening. The sport was considered then, as it is now, both honorable and elegant, and it is probable that the small group of spectators behind the balustrade included the most illustrious names in Venice.

5. THE NEW RIDOTTO

Venetians had a passion for gambling. Gaming tables were so popular that they were set out on the Piazzetta between Marco and Teodoro until they became so successful that they were withdrawn, replaced immediately by sobering execution gallows. Casino is the closest term we have for *ridotto*, though it does not accurately convey the relaxed atmosphere of amiability and leisure more like that found at the intermission of an opera. Masks were particularly popular at the *ridotti*, giving a sense of mystery belied by the presence of the dogs brought companionably along.

Part Five
LEVELS

There is a kind of net that is as old as Methuselah, as soft as a cobweb and as full of holes, yet it has retained its strength to this day.

Isaac Bashevis Singer: *The Mirror*

The perpetual guest in Venice is the water. Water is the perpetual host as well. Venetians did not expect it to become the perpetual enemy.

Sheets of water greeted a Venetian at the end of every street and alley, across squares, under bridges. In creating Venice, a looking glass lay between a resident and everything he wanted to accomplish. He built his houses on it, fished for food in it, mined salt from it, and used it for battle and commerce. When not taking advantage of the water, he spent his time trying to prevent it from entering his living space. Naturally, the Venetian developed the mirror.

Think of the Chinese and *kowtow*, their word for knocking the head against the ground. Who else but the Chinese could have exported deference? How could the Venetians out in their lagoon have resisted trafficking in reflections?

Glass foundries in Murano developed the mirror as early as 1317. Eventually Venetians would be sent all over the world to wall palaces with their miracle. By the time the republic fell, other markets had taken over to provide the world with the mirror. Venice had become so absorbed in pursuing pleasure that narcissism presided. The mirror finally turned in on itself.

Carnival now lasted half the year. Venetians were obsessed by it, infatuated by their own and everyone else's image. Men and women covered themselves with jasmine oil; there were rouge pots on all the dressing tables, powder had just been discovered to cover the scars left by venereal diseases and the pox; periwigs were imported from France. In addition there was the legendary mask of the carnival. Why would anyone who did not think himself of extraordinary interest bother to go about incognito?

When the archduke and duchess of Russia visited Venice in 1782 they pretended to be disguised. Calling themselves "the Counts of the North," they toured the city, trying to make believe that no one knew who they were, even though two hundred servants in full livery accompanied them. Venetians who had not chanced to run into this odd couple on a back bridge or inside a casino were furnished with a contemporary account: "She is huge with an immense bust, a German look about her, a chipped tooth and extremely short sighted, which requires her to use a lorgnette all the time. But she seems to be a sentimental lady, and talented too, different from the grand duke who is terrible looking, awfully childish and completely unsophisticated . . ."

The local government nonetheless seemed enthralled by the Counts of the North and fêted them with banquets and balls. The teatro San Benedetto was renovated for a ladies' dinner held on the stage. Each woman was backed by her *cavalier servente*, and the theatre was hung with mirrors. An invited audience watched them dine from the boxes refurbished as boudoirs. For a while after, theatre dinners became a mania and tables were set up on stage between the acts.

Everyone gaped, gossiped, gambled. The chroniclers were much taken by how often and with what variety Venetians made love. Clothes were created out of velvets, brocades, laces, tassels, and gold threads. Venice became the refuge for "the blacklegs of Europe," the fugitives from justice who could mingle, masked and unremarked with the crowd. It is a period looked upon as Venice dancing itself to death.

Historians point stern fingers at this frivolity just before the republic came to an end in the 1790s. Its possessions were gone: in the great days over two million people had been under Venetian domination. Its unique sea route had been eliminated by competition. Its spectacular commerce had slowly deteriorated. Now Venice seemed only decorative, and foreigners came there from all over to be amused. But in fact the damage had been done long ago. Centuries before, in 1486, Diaz rounded the Cape of Good Hope thus altering forever the shape of commerce. Previously cargoes from the East travelled up the Red Sea across the Isthmus of Suez or across the Persian Gulf and on through Asia Minor: eventually they wound up in the port of Venice and from there were sent on to the rest of Europe. With the new route, Portugal would receive the ships, or Holland, or the Hanseatic countries, or England. The Mediterranean would no longer provide the necessary link, and Venice's supremacy was over.

Shortly after the discovery of the Cape route, the League of Cambrai united most of Europe against *l'insaziable cupidigia dei Veneziani e la loro sete di dominio*, the insatiable greed of the Venetians and their thirst to dominate. The League would operate until 1529, costing Venice half her fortune, exiling her from her neighbors to make it impossible to create any new frontiers. Her main concern from then on, until the pathetic dealings she had with Napoleon in 1796, two hundred and sixty-odd years later, was political survival. Her problems with physical survival would come in this century.

Venice did not go down the drain in a period of eighteenth-century madness. Her decline took just under three hundred years, roughly parallel to the time between the moment a Genoese sailor working for the Spanish stepped onto what he thought was the shore of India, and the signing of the Declaration of Independence.

Recently I tried on a carnival mask of the great days, hoping, I suppose, to recreate the experience from behind the historical lens. The mask was a fragile thing with gimlet eyes, and I found it difficult to see properly peering through those small spaces. Raising a glass to the lips became a problem because the protruding monkey mouth got in the way. A great deal of trouble, it must have been, to flirt through tiny eyes, to get drunk with a bird's beak or monkey lip hooked onto the head, to be rambunctious under cloaks, dominoes, three-cornered hats, and heavy wigs. The spirit of the rococo was ornate and cumbersome and I was glad to rip it away.

Today the carnival arrives in February and it is a kiddie celebration. Children persuade their mothers to buy or sew costumes in acetate of Mozartian ladies or American astronauts. Cowboys and Indians skate by along the sun-filled Zattere, and little Marie Antoinettes clutch hands of elder sisters in sensible suits. Only rarely are adolescents seen in costume and then only under the cover of night. Young men are apt to clomp around as Dracula and Frankenstein monsters while waiting awkwardly for boats to

take them to their parties. Their girl friends giggle, sequined and derby-hatted, holding plastic bags with spare costume parts. When the sleek hired motor launches depart with their virile *vroom,* they have more authentic flash and style than any of the costumed passengers entering them. An exception was the 1967 ball, an elaborate international affair, inserted into, rather than a consequence of, Venetian life.

The costumed Venice of one's fantasies is only to be seen, framed, on its museum walls. It is a particular disappointment in Venice because everything else has remained intact: all you have to do is squint your eyes and you can recreate a Guardi or a Bella except for the clothes. Venetians are now dressed as they are in the rest of provincial Italy, somberly, with a certain roughness of texture that marks clothing meant to last long. Nothing pretentious, nothing unpleasant, always scrubbed, suitable, and free from current trends is the Venetian wardrobe. Only the young are fascinated by the newest in clothes—*lo chic* they call it—gazing with longing into shop windows in the town's center.

Of the eighteenth-century preoccupation with style and behavior something does remain. Manners are still courtly.

An old gentleman raises his beret to an elegant couple at a water-ferry stop. To avoid a further intrusion, he leans hard against his umbrella and stares fixedly at its metal point, establishing a rapport so complete between it and himself that the couple is freed to continue their conversation without fear of offending him.

"You will offend me if you do not accept another cup of coffee," says the barman at a small caffè when he realizes he has taken away my unfinished cup. With a flourish he waves away my protestations and begins the coffee ritual once again.

People still salute the entire room when they walk into a small neighborhood shop or trattoria, whether or not they know everybody. They also wave good-by as they go out the door, a murmur and a wave, receiving a polite nod and a general murmur in return.

"Venice is an extension of one's drawing room," announces a member of the nobility as we cross the Campo della Carita. "One goes out and meets friends in the neighborhood talking to them as though one was at home. *Di essere per strada e di essere in casa,*" to be in the streets is to be at home. It sounds like something he has often said, a good excuse for his perennial inhospitality and for the inhospitality of Venice in general.

"Ah, you are staying for a while in Venice? You will surely meet a lot of congenial people," says an acquaintance on the street while preventing you from doing so by blocking a group of his friends from your view.

A girl in a restaurant favors you with a smile, which is instantly obscured by the very large menu her boy friend hurriedly requires her to consult, and then he smiles at you himself. A family insists that you must spend the evening with them, and you find that you meet, dine, and leave each other in the confines of a trattoria around the corner from their home.

There is a recurrent myth that Italians up and down the peninsula throw open their arms to you, inviting you to become part of the family while offering bowls of steaming pasta, and I suspect that this has been sponsored by certain soldiers actively involved in liberating villages after World War II. Admittedly, Naples is an exception. Foreigners entering Naples are seized upon, sold something, tangoed with, brought home to dinner, seduced by anyone not bedridden with anything contagious or terminal, and sent on their way. If somewhere in the proceedings the visitor is persuaded to relinquish the remainder of those traveller's checks, it must be remembered that they made an unsightly bulge in the pocket or purse.

In Venice the doors to visitors shut with the definitive click of a lady's handbag that says the subject is closed, the bill is paid, the affair is ended.

You are encouraged to congregate in the streets. Homes are for the family. Venetians are as inhospitable to each other as they are to outsiders.

"You see that woman over there?" asks a Venetian friend as we turn a corner.

I say that I do.

"She is Giorgio's (his best friend's) mother." He nudges me in the same way he had when we passed his oculist, his tailor. All of Venice is his as we walk through town.

His friend's mother moves by without a glance.

"Aren't you speaking?" I ask.

"She doesn't know me."

"You've been best friends since you were ten?"

He looks puzzled. "We've never been introduced."

"Never been to his home?"

"He's never been to mine either."

Perfectly normal. "And you grew up together."

"Yes. Ah, of course, he *has* met my sister." He rolls his eyes wickedly. "At school."

We walk on, and as he says hello to this person and that person along the way and notes where he was hit on the head by a small bit of sixteenth-century cornice and which boat belonged to what uncle; he gives me a running commentary on who the passing people are, what they do and what they are called by their friends and by their enemies.

"Come and meet my mother this Sunday," he says one day when I run into him at a caffè. I try to absorb this with appropriate grace. The Royal Family of Britain gives out peerage more frequently than Venetians extend these invitations.

I accept, of course.

In a Venetian household, no matter what the economic or social situation of the family, one is entertained in the *salotto,* the formal reception room of the house which a dear friend refers to as the Good Wood Room. If possible it is avoided by the family during the natural course of their home life. The room may be furnished very grandly, with pieces of eighteenth-century lacquer furniture and gilded baroque or more modestly with formica parading as wood. It might be a vast room with opalescent marble floors or a doll-sized kitchen that must treble as dining room and salon. But even if the formality of the Good Wood is not there in fact, it is there in the imagination when the entertaining is done.

You arrive on Sunday to visit your friend with the requisite pastry you have purchased prettily wrapped, tied with a string looped in such a way that the package can be hooked onto your index finger. This is a concession, I am told, to the gentlemen, on the chance that they might be obliged to carry such a package every now and then. It is not really carrying food, it seems, it is suspending it.

Everything in this particular room is larger than the room would appear to be able to accommodate. Inherited armadios from the streamlined period touch the ceiling; the dining table set in the salotto's center must have hatched and grown on the spot; there is no way that it could have been brought in through the door or the window. Everything has been polished mercilessly. As though ready to burst into the national anthem, the most humble furniture stands proudly beaming. Veneer shines like china; china shines like veneer. Tiny crystal apéritif glasses form ranks, staunch soldiers on a doily's white field atop the *terra virgine* of the credenza. Mirrors are set into the breakfront, doubling all the *soprammobile,* the "above furniture" objects Americans call knickknacks. There are therefore two vases of waxen flowers; twin Andalusian girls back up against each other in identical outfits of scarlet satin and black lace. The plaster madonna smiling pinkly reveals a sublime baldness behind her locks and halo. You see your own face look back with some surprise as you are shown the inventory of treasures handed down, handed over, handed out in the family history. Each trinket has its story. Tutankhamen's gold things were never as cherished as these.

"*Con permisso,*" you have said on entering the room, proceeding to shake hands with many generations. You had almost forgotten that your friend has a lovely child bride. She smiles timidly, one hand resting on the protrusion under her maternity blouse. This swelling is her accomplishment, her claim and justification for participating only in family duties and anecdotes, and almost never leaving the house. Purdah of the Muslim world has left its ancient relics along the Iberian and Italian peninsula.

It has all been choreographed long ago. The mother walks in, giving her hairdo two deft pokes from behind her ears. After shaking your hand, she withdraws her own, cups it into her other hand and proceeds to turn them both round and round as though drying them under a jet of hot air. She is unused to you, and you try to put her at her ease by plucking at some slim strand of the day's events or its weather. The father offers you a liqueur, the cabinet is opened, Japanese teacups and cut crystal briefly see the light of day—they will be investigated by everyone more thoroughly later—and long, curious bottles begin to emerge. The mother, now busy, now at home, raises them to a Florentine tray taken down by the husband from someplace above. The grandfather stares into the space of his own history ignoring the Strega set down on the antimacassar of his worn easy chair. He might rouse himself later, particularly if by chance politics of the thirties is touched upon. His face will brighten and he will manage to recall and recount with few teeth to block his speech how he had done the right thing under fascism, depending not at all on the success or politics of his affiliations. The family will listen with attention and respect and so will you. The mother remembers something in the kitchen, the daughter-in-law rises with a meaningful grunt to follow diligently behind. Your friend wants you to see an oil painting he has achieved in the style of Modigliani. The father is telling you about the Andalusian statuette which he now holds, evaporating her twin from the mirror's face, and you hear how, long ago, he worked on a ship that docked at Málaga.

Gradually the seams of how you behave in your society give way. The concern over where you have been, what you have done and what you are now doing, lifts. These things are of no interest here. You think of the monologues endured at smart gatherings in other cities, the opinions aired, the inside information accumulated, the climb to the summit and the ultimate conquest, like the planting of the flag at Iwo Jima, of the most clever, the best-informed, the most stylish persons at that gathering to claim it as their personal triumph. Here, you are asked to recount an excursion to Burano.

On your way home, you find yourself nodding to acquaintances, stopping to chat, wondering idly whether it would be possible to erase the tape of your life and start all over again, knowing all the while that you have a return ticket to somewhere at home in your bureau.

It is true that through the streets and especially in the *campi* there is a constant nod and bow and tip of hat. Sometimes it takes a group of idle gentlemen an hour to cross a square. They stroll, hands folded behind their coats, pause, fall into a conversational group, are joined by one or two others, once again take up their promenade until someone says something unexpected, at which point they stop again to review that bit of information. Then there is the caffè into which they must troop for a grappa, a glass of wine, or a caffè *corretto*—corrected with brandy. There they might find a game of cards in progress. And the time passes. Young people often re-enact a fast-motion edition of the same stroll. If time is short, a quick mumbled greeting en passant will do, though frequently several further sentences are exchanged as the two parties walk away from each other; phrases miraculously noted even though the heads are turned back to the direction of the fast-moving feet. It is understood that the talk will be resumed later in the day, or the day following. Since so many people are acquainted with each other in a city so small, chances are that they will leave many conversations unfinished all over town, many threads untied until the next meeting. They always seem surprised to encounter one another—surprised and pleased—even though it might be the third time paths cross that day. Among the women, the health of the entire family is investigated from the oldest surviving relative to the newest infant and the information is traded back and forth with an unfeigned, amiable interest. This is followed by the discussion of menus and food prices, and the friends disperse; slowly the group pries itself apart only to reassemble; this is repeated again until one of the women looks at her wrist watch or sees her child in the far distance about to wander towards the water, and runs off, string bag swinging, and the other women, too, gradually go their way.

The line of which sex is permitted to do what, is clearly defined. No casual interfering with the formula is tolerated. A woman does not from time to time pilot a boat, a man does not occasionally mend his socks. It is either their quirk, their hobby, or it is not done at all. I have a friend, a gondolier, who enjoys cooking fish. Throughout the neighborhood it is known that this is what he does. His daughters talk about it in school. His wife looks on with interest. The people who live in his immediate vicinity endure the small charcoal stove he sets out in front of his door on the street when he comes home with a fish he is given as a present, for the fishermen also know that he likes to prepare fish. He is indulged. His peculiarity manages to be both amusing and presentable.

In a country where bright youths burn with blazing flames only to be quickly stifled by the time they reach their early twenties, one begins to discover that there is a strong sentiment against cultivating abilities. Better to stick to the bland, unless limitless financial resources permit you to indulge yourself. Time after time, one sees young people capitulate just at the point of accomplishment. In Venice, you are respected for how well you have blended into a uniform neutrality. Barring the exceptional or the eccentric, Venetians are willing to dole out respect whenever it seems deserved. The young respect their elders, the healthy respect the disabled, the poor respect the rich and the rich respect the titled rich who respect each other. Resentment is at its lowest level in Italy and envy is rare. Although Napoleon banned titles, they have gradually returned to the shore like ancient tree stumps long ago uprooted. One hears a good deal of *conte, eccellenza,* and *commendatore* in conversations, but considering how often they are used in the rest of Italy, titles in Venice are frugally dispensed.

This is a refreshing contrast to other parts of Italy. In Rome, my portiere insisted on calling me *signorino*—comparable to master—a form of address used for the youngster of the house. One day I drove my tiny 600 Fiat out of the country and returned a week later with an old but extremely beautiful Mercedes. "*Ben tornato dottore!*" he cried. And when I drove the impractical automobile up in front of a restaurant, my position rose even higher. The beaming head waiter would usher us in, saying briskly to a waiter, "*Il tavolo per Il Conte de Combray . . .*"

The Venetians will try to call you what you are; in any case you cannot

drive up to a restaurant in an ailing Mercedes. In public there is a blanketing sameness about the social levels out in public, and this is one of the most singular facts about Venice: everyone uses the same streets, the same public transportation; neighborhoods are not particularly stratified—everyone lives where their families have lived for generations or where they have been able to tuck themselves in between layers of litigation. There is little distinction in the quality of food stores and the prices they charge. Venice, in fact, prides itself in attempting to standardize prices. The clothes shops in the center of the city cater to the tourists and the Venetians who are concerned with fashion, but chances are that the Venetian with money dresses with no particular style. The smallest door can lead to the widest garden and the largest house. An insignificant gate on an alley might belong to a palace whose other side faces the Grand Canal. Venetians are not ostentatious. It would not occur to them to carry status symbols slung over their shoulders. Vuitton handbags, Cartier bracelets, and Gucci loafers play no part in the life of a Venetian: they did that with clogs in the fifteenth century.

But there is, I suppose, what could be called a Venetian Jet Set, its members beautifully tailored and well connected. They might have just returned from seeing a few plays in the West End and plan vacations in Marrakech while dining in Harry's Bar. They sometimes extend and often extract hospitality from among their foreign counterparts. Frequently, you will discover that one of the spouses is from Naples, whose aristocracy seems to hold a special place among grand Venetians. "*Il vero gentiluomo è Napolitano*," you sometimes hear, and if the real gentleman is considered to be Neapolitan because of his charm and wit, it is probably because the Venetian tends to consider himself an austere northerner.

One sees, infrequently, an aristocratic lady of astonishing beauty, but in appearance, Venetian noblewomen generally have the look of hawks that have been to the hairdresser. Their husbands wear attitudes of perennial surprise, as though unaccustomed still, like certain British colonels, to find no colonies left. There is a *noli me tangere* look about them; they are pale, they wear clothes and have manners that seem to have accumulated no blemish throughout the years. The answer of both husband and wife to most suggestions or innovations is a simple no.

Sometimes the nobility have little left but their titles, and a complete inability to adapt to current living. A certain couple may be seen at Venetian cocktail parties of a vaguely international tone wolfing down the majority of the hors d'oeuvres. The husband will speak loftily of his past career as president of some government agency—there are 60,000 presidents of government agencies in Italy—which might enable him to use the form "eccellenza" as well as his inherited title of baron. The wife will speak largely of her contacts abroad, and in private, in the morning before it is light, she will rush off to nearby Mestre to work at a small office. Everyone in their small circle would agreeably accept the facts: that he does not work and she does, that they live frugally without servants in a large apartment which they will rent out, furnished, at a vast amount and a moment's notice. But they require a charade and it is given to them. When they are forced to reciprocate their accumulated invitations, they manage in the course of the evening to turn the subject around to the servant problem. They bewail the behavior of their elusive staff who are, it seems, either sick or incompetent.

"Claudio," says the hostess, "can never get anything right."

"Absolutely," says the husband, rising on cue. "I shall bring out the sherry myself."

When he reappears later with a small tray of ill-assorted glasses, he clucks. "What Daniela has done," he says, setting the tray down on a low table spiced with a prominent copy of *Connaissance des Arts*, "is to lock the cupboard with all the crystal. I berated her, of course, and she's gone to her bed in tears. She says she cannot find the key." He nods knowingly: the servants.

His wife sighs, he sighs, you sigh.

In contrast, there are several provincial aristocratic families filled with animation, with lands on the *terraferma* across the causeway producing salable crops.

"Come by. Ring the bell," says an energetic countess. "If no one is in, try again." It is the kind of invitation extended in summer resorts. *Senza impegno*, without obligation, the traditional Italian appointment which lets either party off the hook, if, at the last moment, something better comes along. You probably do not go by and ring the bell. You will keep meeting in the streets; either she or her husband will talk rapidly with you before dashing along on their rounds, both of them suntanned from skiing. Children will be in tow, maneuvered by nannies toward their French, English, or music lessons; accountants must be visited, architects consulted; boats must be boarded to get them to the garage where their cars are waiting. They are patrician Venice in motion, a rarity in a city so used to depending on visitors for its vitality.

There are a few elaborately rich and titled persons who maintain completely private lives. They are to be glimpsed only seldom, moving with great dignity from here to there in the manner of the actors in the Noh plays who so gradually and unobtrusively cross the rear of the stage during the performance that you are only dimly aware of their changed position as the play progresses, and by the time the curtain is lowered you are amazed to realize that they have disappeared altogether. Their social lives are the

PART SIX: CRISES

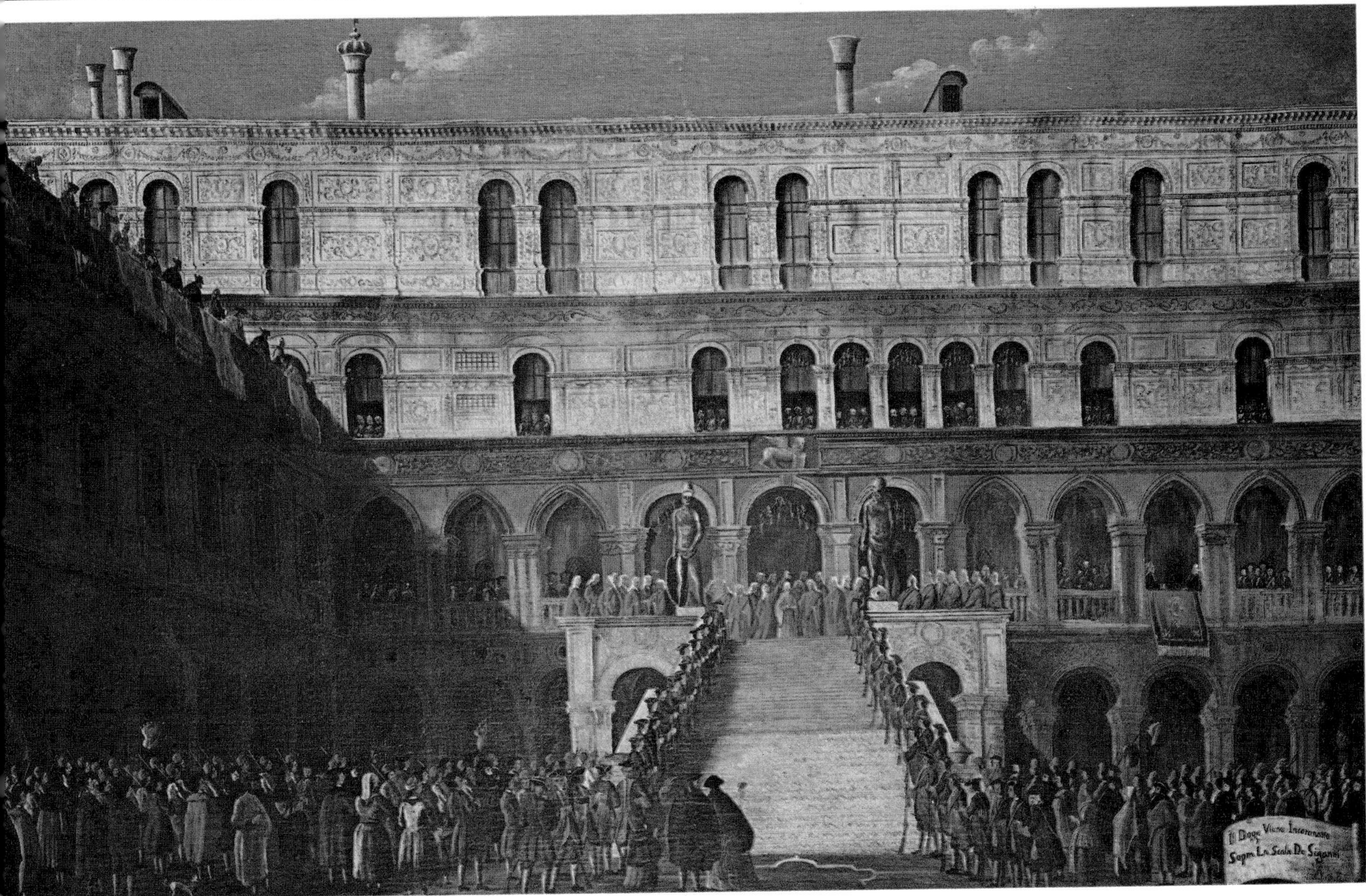

ene Portato Intorno
Di S. Marco Sparg
Sino A' Piedi Della
Siganti
Gabriel Bella F.

Del
S. Pietro Di

Anno 1310 Che Fu
Il Consilgio Di

PART SIX: CRISES

1. PRESENTATION OF THE NEW DOGE TO THE PUBLIC

A mysterious penumbra usually dominates the interior of the Basilica of San Marco but in this cheerful painting, Venetians wave white handkerchiefs as the Doge's litter is being prepared to carry him around the Piazza in triumph. Even though the election of the Doge was an event involving careful deliberation and great ceremony, the actual office had lost most of its significance. Before giving up its independence, the republic of Venice had elected 120 Doges throughout its history.

2. CORONATION ON THE GIANT'S STAIRCASE

Symbolizing maritime and commercial power, Mercury and Neptune (both of them sculptured by Sansovino) flank the two sides of the great Renaissance staircase. It was here that the Doge received the *zoia,* later known as *corno,* or "ducal bonnet," the singularly humped crown dating back to Byzantium which became the symbol of the office. Nobles and senators surrounded the Doge as he read his oath of allegiance to the state. With the words "*Accipe coronam Ducalem Ducatus Venetiarium . . .*" he was crowned.

3. THE DOGE CARRIED AROUND THE PIAZZA FOLLOWING HIS ELECTION

How triumphant it must have seemed, the Doge carried aloft in a gilded box by a herd of men, rather like a waxen *santo* in a religious celebration. With him rode several relatives and the *ballottino,* the ballot boy who had assisted during his election. Tapestries decorated the window ledges, awnings fluttered in the wind, and the masses were kept at bay on the chance that they would become too enthusiastic in scrambling for the coins thrown to them by the Doge as he was hurried by.

4. ENTRANCE OF A PATRIARCH IN SAN PIETRO DI CASTELLO

Until 1807, San Pietro di Castello was the main Venetian cathedral, the title then passing to San Marco. The bishop's mantle and stole were brought from Rome when the Venetian Senate elected a new local bishop. Wearing a heavy ermine collar, shielded from the sun's rays under a golden umbrella, the Doge accompanied him into the cathedral. The crowd had to be content to watch the spectacle from a wooden bridge, as highly decorated gondolas brought church officials in great style to the ceremony.

5. THE CONSPIRACY OF BAIAMONTE TIEPOLO

Venice has few legends of insurrection. This rare conspiracy, occurring in 1310, passed into general folklore. A group of citizens opposed a new ruling forbidding any commoner to hold office. They devised a plan to kill members of the ruling nobility, but it failed when an elderly woman threw a heavy mortar out of her window on the Merceria, the street giving onto the Piazza, killing one of the leaders. So much confusion resulted from this unexpected event that the revolt was immediately put down. The woman was given her choice of honors and rewards. Following careful deliberation, she asked that her rent not be raised for the remainder of her life.

antithesis of Newport and Palm Beach. Only God and their families know whom they entertain. They are primary constituents of the former—Venice and its Doge had always considered itself akin to Rome and its Pope—and I suspect that their families are the sole beneficiaries of their hospitality. In their immense apartments they retire early to watch television, their footsteps echoing down long, chilly corridors. Miniatures of ivory and enamel rattle in glass vitrines and the crystals on the heavy chandeliers catch fragments of light reflected from passing boats on the canals.

Often, without causing a stir, without carrying matched luggage, they leave Venice in the winter for warmer places. Their palaces are closed up soundlessly, with no obvious effort: one day you will notice that there are boards behind the shutters, that a front door has been seriously bolted.

A small staff is left behind to keep an eye on things. Wearing black uniforms with crisp collars, pale, drawn women slip out of side doors carrying many keys. They have been cautioned to maintain the furnace at a low level. They look as though they have been bred for their loyalty.

One day I watched a uniformed *cameriere* dumping a collection of paint cans, cartons, and general house reparation debris into a canal from the boat entrance of a great boarded up house. He stopped when he saw me—I

must have been wearing my ecologist's frown—and withdrew. The guilty path of garbage floated on the surface of the water like a sentence interrupted. As I turned away, he appeared again, cautiously, an actor too soon on stage, revolved abruptly and began throwing his collection in the opposite direction, secure in the knowledge that he and his palace were immune. In any case, I could not have hammered on his locked door because of the difficulty in locating it. A house known only from the water must be studied architecturally and then matched up on any of the side alleys surrounding it. Even then, such a system is not foolproof. Many Venetian buildings have changed hands so often, have been added to, have been demolished in part; sections are in litigations, wings are absorbed by neighboring buildings and incorporated into other architectural features, that no eye can identify the whole. A gate will lead to a strip of garden that scurries alongside a Gothic wall, abruptly turns, ends in a cement porter's lodge which contains, up two steps, the dwarf's door opening onto a Renaissance palace.

No matter what period, the *piano nobile* of the large palaces is always high and very grand, languidly reaching to a height it takes New York apartment buildings a frenetic four stories to attain. The actual gloom and vastness of the rooms inside them is bathysmal. If the building has the good

fortune to face the water, reflections from the canals meander on the ceilings way above. One feels like a tropical fish moving about the floor of its tank. But almost always in shadow, the lower floors are rarely infiltrated by a wedge of friendly sunshine. With lofty ceilings and reverberating walls, there seems to be no way, given our century, to make the rooms either comfortable or pleasant. Sofas and credenzas, chairs and tables and desks and grand pianos each claim a piece of territory as though waiting their turn in a giant's game of chess. The immense and gaudy Murano chandeliers hang high above, ready to cast a multiple set of eyes over the vast space. Hand-blown flowers and Moor's heads terminate in naked light bulbs which are mercifully turned off most of the time to save electricity. Patrician families are always turning off lights if by some error a servant has left even the smallest lamp to burn unnecessarily in an inactive section of the room. The best pieces of furniture huddle against walls out of reach, their surfaces less likely to receive the errant scratch, their upholstery shrivelling without love.

Some of the palaces were bought by grandparents of the present nobility intact, as wedding gifts. Throughout the years little has been added. As fortunes have declined, a proportion of the furnishings have found their way to the antique dealers, but there always seems to be something in the basement which, when repaired, will do as a surrogate. The larger palaces have been sectioned off into apartments and offices: walls go up, staircases emerge, an elevator might be inserted into a dank corner; ceilings are lowered, new terraces reach out. A typewriter pounds in an ex-storage area, a furnace rattles where once wine was stored, a Poetess from France lives just above the water where, before, gondolas reclined like beached whales. The owners often maintain the piano nobile themselves. No amount of heat can be persuaded to warm these rooms, except on the rare occasions when a cocktail party is given, which is then fueled by the gathering itself. In certain of these flats, one has the impression that the demure drinks with no ice, the scant canapés, the slightly musty guests who seem, like the furnishings, to have been taken briefly from under wraps only to be covered over once again later that evening: that given the slant of the floor and the thin carpet covering its marble surface, the whole mess might slide into a side lagoon.

"Can you divine that work?" asks Prince X, stepping back. His piano nobile is elegant still. You speak quietly in those rooms. You are required to treat them and him with a distant admiration usually reserved for ecclesiastical matters.

You try to see the painting in the long shadows, try to peel away in your mind the heavy coats of varnish. The immense portraits lining the walls wear looks of weary resignation. Too often have they been pointed out by the generations of passing owners to the occasional guest who already knows, though murmuring his praises, that they are but minor works in a city

overburdened with masterpieces.

"Piazzetta," you say. A stab in the dark. Earlier on, your "I don't know," produced such a crestfallen look that you make the extra effort.

For your trouble, you receive a patronizing look.

"No. Not eighteenth century. *Seventeenth*. Forabosco, of the great Bologna school." He savors the words, pleased, in the tradition of scholars, to impart his knowledge. Each syllable is a gift.

And on to the next. Dour faces look down on you, past you, show themselves in profiles, stare up at God. Substantial citizens once, now long dead, unremembered even by history. In Venice you have seen on the street butchers and ferry conductors who resemble portraits of admirals and doges. In America it has always been the other way around: politicians seem to look always like the man-in-the-street. The marble floor resounds with your steps as you follow obediently along. You nod to the lacquer furniture, run a hand along a piano Liszt once played, try to construct from what the Prince is saying, or rather from what he is not saying, the shape of his life. Soon, with luck, you will be offered a coffee brought in by a uniformed servant wearing white gloves. There will be a small round silver tray and on it two tiny cups and a miniature dish with sugar cubes: all of it a reliable decimal point in the complicated unfunctional logarithm of his possessions. You can never hope to solve any of it: the Prince and his family and his wife's family and their furniture, lands, ancestors, history. He recites fragments of it, shows you relics of what has been in the manner of a tour guide taking you through a place he has never ceased to respect.

When you reach the windows overlooking the canal, you find yourself smiling with real pleasure. After all, life does go on outside these sealed walls. Boats pass in a chaotic splashing parade; gulls fly. The Prince sighs heavily: his view. You sense his restlessness to move away from the windows, an expectation to have you move away as well. Will you use up too much of it with your eyes? "Ah . . . si . . ." he says, easing himself onto an uncomfortable seat in the shadows. And the coffee is summoned.

51

Part Six
CRISES

Misfortune does not lessen however much you speak of it.

Cavafy: "A Love," *The Complete Poems of Cavafy*

Municipal problems in the abstract passionately bother only the very few. One is absorbed with private problems until one feels the pinch. In Vienna and Prague during the thirties, families began to think of moving out only when the curtailments and supervisions on their own lives had become untenable. By then, of course, it was too late. People lived in Pompeii under that potential eruption, going on about their business until they were imprisoned forever in attitudes of surprise.

In Venice, everyone discusses what should be done with it all the time. Then they go off to shop for zucchini or get into boats or deliver sewing machines or turn back to sorting the mail. Outside of Venice, its problems are more *embroidered.* *"Is Venice dying?"* one is asked theatrically, and one says no or yes with equal drama depending on one's mood that day.

The existence of Venice's aquatic problems is common knowledge. Both too well known to escape notice and too poor to luxuriate in a private illness, she is not privileged to deal with her ailments alone.

When the flood hit the city in November of 1966 and left sludge a meter high in its wake, lights blacked out, street-floor shops destroyed, mouldy walls and flaking paintings, people stood around in the streets wringing their hands, carrying torches at night to find their way home, picking through the debris to salvage bits of their property. There was an urgency to the plight of the city built on the lagoons that has not been repeated. Nine years have passed since then. Anyone in the Italian government can now get his name in the newspaper by hurling arias in the Senate on the Plight of the Jewel of the Adriatic. Venice has become the damaged cross that Italy must bear. They speak in millions about repairing it and have received alarmed support from around the world. But interest is beginning to flag. Nine years is a long time to sustain a charitable concern when nothing is being done to solve the problem. Another catastrophe on the Adriatic might swamp the city with so much water that it would have to be abandoned. Less than that, a simple collapse of several monuments and a few hundred families left homeless, would probably benefit Venice with another major fund-raising effort. But the foundations and communities that have given generously to Venetian welfare would still be interested to know where the last Italian subsidy went. It seems to have drifted into an Italianate parenthesis of *ci penso io:* and whoever is taking care of it is, at the moment of this writing, out to lunch.

The specific problem of the *acqua alta,* the high water, is, simply stated, the following: ideally, when the Adriatic passes through the three openings in the Lido, the island fronting the sea, it enters the lagoon surrounding Venice, cleanses the lagoon and the canals of the city without disturbing the water level, and is taken out again by the tides. When the tides enter with too much force, spurred on by high winds and certain deep trenches (recently carved into the soil under the lagoon to permit tankers to enter the petroleum refineries in Mestre and Marghera), the lagoon swells, Venice floods, underground tubings burst, sewers overflow, and the substructure of every building is in danger of collapse because of the disturbed equilibrium. The opposite effect, the *acqua bassa,* finds the water rushing out too quickly from the canals and lagoons, exposing the underpinnings of the city, which depend on the strength of the water to hold them in place.

The industrial complex of Mestre and Marghera bears the blame. Not only has it disturbed the natural balance of sea to city by enlarging trenches in the sea base but it has pumped up springs in the immediate area for the fresh water it needs and this has caused additional sinking of the ground. The sea walls, or *murazzi,* have gradually broken down, pulled away by the currents, and have not been adequately replaced. Industrial wastes are pouring into the lagoon. Combustion gases are rotting the marble and stone.

What to do. If you have ever observed a shell game in Rome's flea market or anywhere else, you will have some idea of how quickly proposals are made and retracted and how adept each faction is at claiming your attention. The large petroleum interests will make their case seem absolutely foolproof (the economy, the number of workers gainfully employed) far faster than you can possibly manage to follow: then their argument is whisked away by the conservationists' plea, your social consciousness gives way to your concern over our monumental heritage and you hold fast to that. A parade suddenly distracts you, looming up from the political left: workers from Mestre and Marghera shouting slogans, protesting that closing down these ports will cost them their jobs. It would seem, then, that the workers on the left and the heads of the industry on the right are saying the same thing. The Save Venice Freaks are dealing in masterpieces, not life. By the time you look back, the shell game has folded up, the shabby little shark has disappeared with his buddies in a broken-down Fiat, and you are left with your puzzlement and the sound of the wind in your ears.

Your inclination is to blow a whistle and shout: stop. But your inclination is of no interest. The shell game is set up elsewhere; there is a confused murmuring, shouting, berating; groups of concerned citizens gather together in earnest conversation. Five men from Padua have developed a plan to engineer a system of locks to the sea, and pass out leaflets they print privately. Wealthy New York matrons give small dinner parties to raise money for the purchase of a palace devoted to art and memorabilia. The daughter of one of the industrial pioneers in the Veneto gives interviews aimed at the indiscriminate expansion of industry.

Meanwhile, quietly, Venetians are moving out of their city.

They pick up, pack up, pile their things into scows and find cheap, warm apartments across the causeway in the midst of the enemy's camp. They miss their views, they miss the narrowness, the beauty, the neighborliness, the water; they miss even the stink of the canals. But they do not move back to live in Venice. They complain that dirt now comes through their windows, comforting themselves for this unendurable transition by buying, of all things, an automobile. They shrug, in their new heated apartments, and tell you that after all, they are feeling a good deal less arthritic. If someone decides that he can bear it no longer, that he must return to Venice, he will never find an apartment anyway. He is now a citizen of Mestre and that is that.

When an apartment in Venice is vacated or becomes uninhabitable, it is shut: its owners seal its doors and it stays there like the walled-up closet in Poe in which only the skeleton of the past remains. It is likely that the owners are waiting for the money the government has promised Venice to come their way. They will then be subsidized for repairs. In the meanwhile, a law is still in effect which taxes anyone who cares to restore his palace. Everyone, everything stops. Wait and see, they say.

Walking the narrow streets, you look up and see many shuttered windows. "Where are the owners?" you ask the barman. "In the Veneto," he says. He, too, would like to know. He, too, has noticed all the vacancies all around him. He, too, needs an apartment.

A coffin is being wheeled from church to barge.

"Ah yes, poor Morosin is dead." A quick sign of the cross. The heavy bells toll.

"Not so poor, *cara.* Besides, he was ninety-four."

"His children will, of course, inherit his palazzo."

"*Peccato.* My son was looking for an apartment."

"So was my brother."

Sigh. Shrug. (Said together): "Ah . . . si . . . *gli eredi* . . ."

The inheritors are, in this case, four children of an average age of seventy. They will do nothing but collect the rents on the remaining apartments

RIO TERA'
DEI PENSIERI

poor Morosin modernized in 1895. They live in Verona. *Their* children, and there are many of them, in their fifties, will patiently wait to divide their share of the palace when it comes their way.

When these grandchildren inherit the palazzo, they will discover that it is not a graceful palace in Venice but rather a crumbling pile of stone with dazed tenants threading their way past rusted plumbing. The rents are absurdly low, the taxes are high, the repairs are incalculable. A rich person from Milan might come along and offer them a low price for it, hoping to fix it up, to maintain it for a while as his *palazzo a Venezia* for the odd weekend, privately considering it a potentially good investment. The offer will be immediately accepted by three grandchildren, simple folk privately wishing to use the money to buy inexpensive apartments in Padua. Two more grandchildren will say that the offer should be doubled, citing the position of the palace, its prodigious age and history, privately assuming that the rich Milanese can afford it. Four of the remaining grandchildren would prefer to hold out until money comes in from the large funds allocated to Venice which will pay for the restoration, privately hoping to become Venetian landlords. The remaining grandchildren consider it a loss of face to sell the building at all; it has been in the family for many generations: rather let it rot than sell it to an outsider. Their private hopes have long ago vanished.

Certain Venetians, unencumbered by litigious families or trenchant scruples, will rent out cubbyholes and corners of their palaces to the stray foreigners who do not wish to stay in a hotel or pensione. The rental agencies, all three in the city, have nothing to offer but cellars and shops. The newspapers advertise apartments in Mestre and villas on the Lido. It was with high hopes that I visited the luxurious palace of a Venetian lady who had, she assured me, the perfect apartment to let, a divine, she said, *garçonnière* that had just become vacant. I felt lightheaded at the prospect, for I had been drifting around the city in search of an apartment for weeks while accumulating a large bill at my charming pensione along the Zattere.

As we descended her grand staircase to the first floor and walked down the great corridor towards the Grand Canal, I became suspicious. The unused gondola entrance lay right in front of us; water lapped wildly at the stone steps; a small door appeared just as we were about to reach the canal's edge. Abruptly she turned, opening the door to brush past me and sail down what appeared to be a side corridor leading to a darkened window. A pale ray of light touched the far wall. Throwing open the shutters dramatically she pointed in triumph to the Grand Canal.

"*Ecco!*" she said, standing back.

When I realized that she had not meant I was to inhabit the canal, I glanced at what I guessed was the apartment.

"Yes, it is small," she said.
"Yes, it is narrow."
"No, there is no other room."
"No, you haven't misunderstood the price."
There was a pause while I tried to formulate the question that had been accumulating, something to do with how a Venetian would be outraged at being expected to pay a large rent for an uninhabitable hallway, put into inquisitorial form. She eliminated any such possibility.
"Look at the view!" She cried, hooking the shutters against the walls, nailing postcard Venice into place.
"Ecco!"
"Ecco!" say the Venetians, the Italians, the nations hugging the Mediterranean. *"Voilà" "Mira!"* Everyone showing you, pointing out, instructing you on the use of your senses as though, blind fool, you might have been too busy cerebrating to have taken notice. Never mind that the place is uninhabitable, that in winter there is no heating, that in the summer the sun turns the place into a pizza oven, that you may be inconvenienced by several baby carriages parked outside your door or the three-year wait for the telephone or the crack in the cement wall that permits you to see the view without going to the window.
When Venice goes sour, it does so desperately. No longer is it enough to step out of a phone booth after learning of the impossibility of placing a call because some part of the communications mechanism has gone on strike, to be soothed by the sight of a Gothic window benignly glinting its bottle-glass panes in the sun. The hammerlock grab of claustrophobia turns the island into a cage: the pokey boats, the cleft-palate dialect, polluted water, bovine looks, frivolous decoration, daily life so jeopardized by becoming within months archaic are just too absurd, given the century in which we live.
The *view* is not enough.
You arrive back in town on a late train unaccountably delayed for that last mile of track, as though the final effort of the locomotive to pull its weight was too much for it—in reality it is a semi-strike of the ticket punchers—and when, finally, you rush down the station steps in the cold night you learn that the last ferry has left. The private motor launches have long ago been meticulously tied up. It is you and Venice.
It has always been a city to strike paranoia in the heart of its residents. Until the late eighteenth century, the presence of the Three Inquisitors required everyone to keep a watchful eye over his shoulder: someone would talk, inform; someone would be thrown into the *pozzi* or under the leads; someone would vanish. The *bocche della verità*, those slot-mouthed faces of marble embedded here and there to receive anonymous accusations

had never calmed a jittery public. Today, the few remaining marble mouths are filled to the brim with candy wrappers and crushed leaflets. But their essence remains: in the narrowness of the streets, the nearness of the windows, in the fact that the system seems to break down just as you are about to rely on it. At night, whispered conversations echo mercilessly down the canals accompanied by the lapping of dark water. It is not by accident that the Venetian Othello was driven mad by nameless fears.

Alone in Venice, one notices the others who are alone as though it was some shared affliction. Sundays, the curse of solitary people, bring out the elderly in Venice, the pensioners, the leftover relatives of extinct families. There is no place to hide on a sunny day. They sit on benches and stare across water. It is a city overburdened with those who have refused to go to the mainland with the younger generation, have refused to take the tempting

twentieth-century step to big-city life, to make a stab at Milan or Rome regardless of the consequences.

The loneliness is stratified. When non-Venetian sailors are stationed in Venice, Sunday is the day they dread. Most of them cannot go home for weekends because the Armed Forces in Italy seem to send the military to the end of the peninsula opposite from their native provinces. They are marooned in the city of housewives. Venetian girls do not look kindly on sailors: they are not considered serious, they are out for a good time, they will soon be gone anyway; Venetian girls have Venetian boy friends. The sailors mope about, sit sullenly with their buddies at caffès, wish they were back in Palermo or Catania, return again and again to the Piazza San Marco, longing for some life which they were told they would find there. They were misinformed. Despite all the water, Venice is not a sailor's city. There is no whoring, no goat's climb down to a steamy port as there is in Genoa or Naples. In Venice, nothing is up or down: it is relentlessly level.

The students from out of town have no campus and no student union buildings. The two universities and one architectural institute teach students mainly from the Veneto and they disappear like migrating birds on the weekends. The Venetians themselves who study—and in Italy young people either study or work; they do not do both—usually have the money to leave town in the winter for skiing weekends. In the warmer months they plan sailing excursions. The person who has come to Venice from afar to be educated brocades a rich fantasy life while sitting alone at caffès making the cappuccino last way into the weekend afternoons.

On Sundays, Venetians come, minimally, in twos. People from the nearby villages arrive by car, boat, train, and bus. "*Che bella giornata! Andiamo a Venezia.*" The beautiful days bring them out like pilgrims, a faithful visit to the matriarch of the towns spawned about her. A family day. Everyone dresses in his Sunday best. On the ferries they take the smaller children's hands in theirs, pointing them up, way up, towards the Campanile. "*Ecco!*"

Baby carriages roll and families hang in close. Everyone is out. Roller skates score the pavements, hopscotch games are chalked in, ropes are skipped, baseball games are inaccurately constructed out of scenes remembered in movies. There is an aura of consultation among the children, among grownups, as though the week had been only a preparation for this day when everything would be resolved.

You overhear a couple with a pair of children busy with ice cream cones at a caffè. The parents are discussing the barman's wife's pregnancy as they sip hot chocolate piled high with whipped cream.

"Ah, you already have a boy and you'd like to have another? They say one boy already, two boys for sure," the barman is told.

The *they say* will reverse itself to oblige any situation.

"Ah, you already have a boy and you'd like to have a girl? They say the chances of your having a child of the opposite sex is good after the first is born."

"A child after ten years? What could be better to make you feel young?"

"A child after your wife just gave birth? How lucky! All the diapers at once."

They accommodate, they are agreeable. A girl friend older than you? A girl friend far younger? Both are perfection: either is better than the other. An elderly parent, bedridden, is better than no parent. No parent? How free from responsibility, how unencumbered. It is all desirable; everyone wishes you well. The only transgression is to leave the confines of the family, to scale the wall: up and over into the never-never land of the murky and perturbing and the unknown.

Venice cannot accommodate the eccentric, the highly opinionated or the ruthlessly creative: these people go elsewhere. They fear being mummified by the small town. Despite appearances, the city everyone is trying to save would not dream of compromising its lack of imagination.

"Make Venice into a free port," says a watchman at a boatyard, "a free city like San Marino. No tax on cigarettes or houses. A place for the rich to visit." He inhales a Nazionale. Mainly he has these tax-free cigarettes on his mind.

"The more people who leave Venice," says a shopkeeper dealing in lace, "the more pleasant for those of us who remain." He primly smooths his stock of lace-bordered napkins from Hong Kong. No longer is Burano turning out handwork for wealthy foreigners looking for tablecloths and blouses. The cleaning bills are too high. Gone are the days when Lady Alington said to Cathleen Nesbitt: "What's the world coming to? You cannot find a good glove maker any more." Tourists buy doilies for two dollars in Venice that were shipped there in bulk from the Orient. Murano sells glasses from God knows where, hoping for the odd rich customer who will order something *sur commande* at an astronomical price, an order which their own glass blowers will get around to filling sometime within the following year or two. No longer do the lovely mauve lanterns in the Piazza have panes made in Murano: it is plastic sent from Milano. If you want notepaper engraved, jewelry or cameras repaired, missing parts for this and that: all of it comes from elsewhere, it is sent away from Venice to be dealt with. Where *is* everybody? you ask, realizing that what makes a city work is the interaction of its independent people. They have begun to go away from Venice.

Lucia Munaretti has a shop the size of a stall in an Arab souk. She is elderly, but she arrives each morning to begin work cutting the silk from which she constructs her lampshades. Friends stop in to gossip, clients come and go, and everyone in the neighborhood knows her. No one will continue her small business when she retires. It will close. Carlo Piazzesi ran a small *legatoria,* a book bindery greatly esteemed throughout Italy. He is spry and energetic and he is on the far side of eighty. His one son was killed in an avalanche in 1948; his other children have become teachers. When, just recently, he chose to retire, it seems that it was an Italo-American from the Midwest who took over his business.

You walk along the narrow, empty streets and notice the beautiful iron and brass bell pulls next to doorways: then you see that they are attached to nothing at all; that the wires end in mid-air. You walk to a neighborhood trattoria along the Zattere for lunch and find it shuttered. Inquiring at the bar across the way you learn that the elderly proprietor has died. There are no relatives left. You are tempted to settle for a sandwich at the bar.

You are tempted to settle, in Venice, to watch it become a museum.

Recently, I had a discussion with a New England lady who was vitally concerned with the welfare of Venice. I listened at far greater length than I spoke, for it seemed it was she who has passed many stylish vacations there, she who was so agitated about doing the right thing for it. It was the palaces, the architectural wonders: they needed the attention, she claimed, and the yards and yards of canvases in need of restoration. As she spoke, I had an image of a fabulous Disneyland. You would enter a turnstile and find a city without inhabitants, spotted here and there with sumptuous palaces filled with great works of art. Possibly the guides would be costumed in the Ottocento period.

There have been other ideas. Venice could be covered with a dome of plastic, a sort of *Venise sous cloche* ventilated with purified air, converting it into an extraterrestrial Venice. Then there is the possibility of cementing in the canals, permanently discontinuing the problems created by the water. The buildings would stand firm in their foundations. Cars would be banned from the Piazza.

Fantastic plans for the place are not just imaginary. Consider the following possibility: tearing down certain areas of the city section by section and turning them into six story "luxury" apartments, resort areas. This is, in fact, a serious city plan devised by the municipality to attract international property speculators. The city of Venice would be divided into two zones. The A zone would be left untouched—naturally it would include the area around the Piazza. Zone B would wind around the city, centering on the poorer sections of town which, in any case, seem of slight interest to the tourists. Where the poorer people who presently live there are to be housed, has not been decided. Zone B would be destroyed.

The pending tragedy of Venice seemed solved when the Italian parliament announced in the spring of 1973 that five hundred million dollars would be

put aside to save the city. The money was raised at a low interest rate through international banks anxious to associate themselves with what would be known as the Venice loan. It had a charitable ring. The Italian government beamed with satisfaction. Law 171, it was called, of April 16. The Italian Treasury received the first installment shortly after the announcement, and kept it. Then it was reported that *all* the money was not intended to be spent on Venice anyway: a proportion of it, perhaps. In the meanwhile the loan money in the Treasury would somewhat help to stabilize the falling lira.

What everything costs and how valuable it is to the community is always relative. Americans spend eighteen million dollars a year on tooth-decay research. In India, a large proportion of the population tries to live on less than a dollar a day. Can anyone say what an investigation of healthy teeth is worth, what nourishing an Indian is worth, what Venice is worth?

In Italy, the problem of priorities is still unresolved. If everyone could agree that the city should be restored the work would have begun in earnest long ago.

Dr. Edwin Land, in discussing his newest polaroid invention, said: "If you can state a problem then you can solve it. From then on, it's just hard work." The city woven on the lagoons was created out of a similar straightforward theory. If it fails to survive, conflicting interests and a hesitating administration will be responsible. And anyone who might be implicated in such a tragedy will immediately blame the sea.

A conscientious investigation by the London *Times* presents an accurate image of how the restoration of Venice progresses.

> A scientific solution to the floods has been found. But the engineering methods of implementing it became caught up in administrative disagreement. Put as simply as possible—and nothing is simple in Italian bureaucracy—the fourth sub-committee of the Grand Committee rejected the recommendation and before the fourth sub-committee could rethink the matter the Grand Committee was dissolved. Now a new committee, the Superior Council of the Public Works Ministry has started on the problem from scratch.[1]

Everything must begin again by bringing the Venetians back. Twenty thousand people come into Venice each day to work only to return home to its periphery each evening. About a third of its working population lives elsewhere. The Mestre-Marghera industrial complex is not staffed by Venetians; it is labor from the surrounding countryside. Control of these ports is in the hands of Milan and Turin. Their directors and technical engineers may move temporarily to the community of Venice but it does not become their legal residence. Taxes go elsewhere. The losses all belong to Venice.

A city so long used to independence is now condemned to follow meekly behind the rest of Italy; a driver perpetually blocked behind someone in front of him who only has a learner's permit. The tragedy of Venice is that it cannot maneuver, conquer, or haggle over its own fate. It holds its Biennale amid great furor from the political left and right; its yearly film festival brings merchants and starlets into town for two weeks in September; it fills its hotels as best as it can during the season, often losing out to day trippers who stay inexpensively on the *terraferma*, bringing their lunches into town to eat squatted on the paving stones of the Piazza San Marco. And occasionally it is used, after bureaucratic turmoil that causes most producers to look elsewhere, as the backdrop for a film. Otherwise, it relies on bewitching everybody in the Western world by its art treasures collected long ago, and by its very existence: the last complete artifact of a time when profit was translated into grace.

After the conquest of Venice by Napoleon, it was traded back and forth to Austria, and for fifty years it barely knew its rulers. Patriotism briefly flared up under Manin, a sudden hero prepared to defend Venice in a siege against the Austrian emperor. Venetians gave their jewels, their estates,

[1] Stephen Fay and Phillip Knightley, "The Doomed City." London *Times Weekly Review*, February 10, 1974.

their furniture and their pots and pans. They bought *moneta patriottica* to support Manin's brief government; after it failed, the money was worthless: They failed, it failed. When in 1866 Vittore Emanuele entered Venice to join it to the Kingdom of Italy, it was but a small town on the Adriatic. It is still that.

Today one finds in Venice an un-Italian skepticism and stubbornness which seems to have been imported from the Austrians or South Germans just above or borrowed from the French through the Alps. "*Sconsiglio di cercare*," say the receptionists of filled hotels, of paralytic rental agencies, of artisans numbed into turning out the same salable object into eternity: they "dissuade you from looking further." It is what Parisian shopkeepers tell you: "*Ça n'existe pas*." When their particular shop does not carry what you are looking for, it is nowhere.

"Non è possibile," says a caffè owner in Venice on Sunday when you realize that you have run out of coffee beans and all the stores are closed. "I cannot sell you coffee beans. It is forbidden." You wait the length of time it usually takes in Italy; then you wait an extra minute for Venice. "How much do you want?" she asks finally.

There is a recurring sensation that Venice has already sunk spiritually into its own uneasy foundation. Independence of spirit seems to wither. Parents constantly ask their adolescent children where they are going, whom they know, why they were out. Girls from good families give up, following a succession of unsuitable boy friends and take up doing elaborate flower arrangements in the long afternoons as the years pass. Boys find that they are expected to escort their sisters, to stay at home at night with their grandparents, to relive with them the anecdotes of World War II, to stare out at the constellation of Orion and wonder when they will ever have a chance to live their own lives.

Until marriage or death they stay *colla famiglia,* a mispronunciation Freud might have enjoyed for *con la famiglia,* colla being the word for glue. Brothers remain with unmarried sisters, sisters stay with widowed father, niece with cousin, aunt with brother-in-law and his three children. Under some extraordinary circumstance one might come upon the Venetian who is the sole holder of a latchkey, who rules his own domain. I think of a friend who brought back to Venice an extremely heavy cloth coat from Russia. One winter day because of a chance rip in the lining she discovered that just underneath the rough black weave nestled a full coat of ermine. I hear you gasp. One gasps in that way when one unearths someone healthy living alone in Venice.

I have left Venice many times because it has seemed on the verge of anesthetizing me. Not long ago I found myself longing to get away, to spend a few weeks in Paris, worrying about the perils of automobile traffic and overbright conversation. I arrived at the station on a Sunday afternoon, early, and took my seat in the compartment with the usual anxiety involved in an urgent departure. Glancing out of the window, I saw a middle-aged man running down the empty platform looking up with significant concern at each compartment window. In his hand, or rather hanging from a string, was a box of Sunday pastry. In the way of many portly people, he moved gracefully, stopping, peering, hurrying on. His manner suggested the agitation of the early stages of love, in the beginning of it all, when to see that particular person in your life is all that winds you up and keeps you going. As it happened, he located her in the compartment next to mine. I found myself experiencing that recurrent Venetian sensation of witnessing a film sequence. The window adjacent to mine lowered, two hands reached out to accept the parcel, the glitter of

a woman's bracketed engagement and wedding rings caught the pale light of the Sunday sun, and the hands withdrew. They traded banalities with a vengeance, shouting them to each other to be heard over the rattle of long, empty trains shuttling on nearby tracks with an unreasonable lack of concern for their privacy. Looking carefully to his right and left, he mumbled that he was so much in love. Her hand reached out again and she caressed the air as she spoke. They would meet, he said, on the following Sunday morning at ten. She would say, in Padua, that she was going to church and then to visit a cousin. He would tell his wife the same. And they would rush to trains and boats to meet. Somewhere near the station, it would be, in the unpleasant streets with seedy hotels bearing signs in many languages. They could not walk along the quays for they would risk being seen; they could not walk in the park or across the bridges: they must have strolled only in their minds while lying on a hard bed surrounded by heavy furniture in cramped rooms with no view. Then they would walk separately to the station; he would pass a pastry shop; they would say their good-bys again on a desolate platform.

The train whistle blew, long overdue. They had run out of things to say: he with his head tilted back trying to be taller, to reach more closely into her ear; she not daring to lean out of the window. He ran a hand quickly through his grey hair; then he waved. Although he was smiling, his eyes had accumulated the worries about to be faced and his body had already turned towards the station.

"*Pensami un pocchino,*" he said. Think of me a little.

Her hands briefly grazed the fine edge of her open window and she replied without hesitation: "*Tan . . . to,*" lingering on the bridge of that brief, lovely word to promise everything.

I did not choose to watch him grow ever smaller on the platform. Leaving my compartment, I lit a cigarette and watched the ugly shoreline, my agitation at wanting to get to Paris now replaced by a sadness I attributed to these two strangers in particular and Venice in general. Tall towers stood at odd angles in the low lagoon, and here and there small birds settled on stretches of mud. Tied up like giant asparagus, the heavy wooden piles dotted the marshy water next to the train. Venice stops so thoroughly at its railway bridge. It does not drift slowly away as most cities do.

She-of-the-next-compartment was a matronly woman wearing steel-rimmed glasses tinted pink. On her lap she carried that pastry box. She was crocheting a pale scarf without looking at it, her fingers working rhythmically. I do not know what I had expected to find when I glanced inside her compartment. Given the circumstances and difficulties, I suppose I presumed it would be someone extravagant in some way, not a face in the crowd. She was truly the heart of that provincial city, stripped of all its ornamentation.

The city of housewives. It made her predicament even more unmanageable that she was so plain.

She was staring straight ahead of her; no amount of persuasion or charm could have coaxed her story from her. When she glanced up at the corridor, her gaze went through me, past me to the flatlands now revealing themselves next to our train. A wife and mother who had always done what was right: no one could detect anything that fell short of provincial expectations. But somehow she had stepped beyond the perimeter, as Persephone did one day out picking daisies: the kingdom of the underworld was opened by error.

No beams and smiles for her; no easy strolls and tips of hats.

She was on her own.

PART SEVEN: WATERS

Reggatta Delle Donne
In Canal Grande

PART SEVEN: WATERS

1. VISIT TO SAN NICOLO AFTER THE MARRIAGE OF THE SEA

The extravagant *bucintoro* was hauled into the sea each year, the Doge on board, to a place on the horizon where the Patriarch of Venice poured holy water into the sea. The Doge then dropped the *spolazio*, the ring of the republic, into the depths, saying, "We espouse thee, oh sea, in token of perpetual sovereignty." When the republic fell, the last *bucintoro* was vandalized. Stripped of all its gold, its ornaments, it was transformed by a practical administrator into a sailors' prison. Eventually the remains of it were sunk.

2. RACE AT SAN PIETRO DI CASTELLO

A very special race, with boats barely missing each other sailing in different directions. During the Quaresima, or Lenten season, these races were held each Sunday to lighten the atmosphere of the working-class district known as Castello. Situated near the Arsenal, the quarter was originally called Olivolo, named for the olive groves that had long ago flourished there. Undaunted by the chaos of the race, the vendor at the end of the bridge is doing a brisk business in fried fish.

3. WOMEN'S REGATTA IN THE GRAND CANAL

The word "regatta" was coined in Venice, where the concept of boat races seems to have thrived. Fortune, in gold, the weather vane on top of the old customs house, swung in the direction of the wind along the Grand Canal. The racing ladies are simply dressed; not so with the members of the nobility who kneel on cushions or sit back to give orders to their oarsmen as they follow the proceedings. The races were begun on various of the outlying islands, ending with victory prizes in the center of the city.

4. RACE ALONG THE GIUDECCA ON ASCENSION DAY

Venetians were restricted to the use of black boats. Visiting dignitaries and diplomats were indulged with gilded state gondolas. In this race, various boats competed; even a three-masted schooner joined in. It took place on the Ascension Day Sunday, after lunch, which might account for the apparent lack of interest along the quays of the Giudecca.

5. ENTRANCE OF HENRI III KING OF POLAND AND FRANCE IN 1574

This was the state visit of a monarch that Venice remembers as its most elaborate. "Forty young nobles were attached to the King's person" as he sailed through the triumphal arch designed by Palladio. There were hundreds of halberdiers as well; trumpeters, drummers, flagbearers, a cardinal, and the Doge. Following his throned vessel, a raft constructed to look like a sea monster, flames pouring from its jaws, contained a group of busy glass blowers stoking the coals and creating souvenirs for him: Venice giving its greatest reception.

Part Seven
WATERS

I dreamed that I stood by the water and shouted toward the bay, but the warm summer breeze carried away my cries and they did not reach their destination.

Ingmar Bergman: *Wild Strawberries*

Morning falls differently into every room. An oval of sunlight quivers, hesitates, swoops from ceiling to wall where it concentrates into a shimmering beacon. This is Venetian calligraphy. When a boat passes the window, the sunbeam goes haywire. You open up the shutters to let the rest of it in: immediately the room is bathed in a liquid honeycomb.

The water is everything. It affects the light, air, sound; it is blamed for your health when your health is poor and praised for your peace of mind when your mind is good. No limpid Xochimilco pools coated with floating gardenias, no rushing streams or sun-flecked waves. The water in and around Venice resembles a sluggish lake at best. At its worst, it's a cesspool.

The Adriatic is a sullen sea, hurling itself against no shore. You have to walk out to it at the Lido, slowly to be submerged by it, in inches. Your feet squelch into a floor of some obscene substance you would rather not investigate. When finally you are neck-high way out there, it feels more like a communal pool used by too many too often, than the sea.

In the mornings, you sense the water as a persuasive, active presence. By the time night falls it has become languid and soothing. You might be awakened just before dawn by the sound of a sea vessel; a weary shift of timber, a general resettling of elderly joints rheumatic on moist foundations. The sound is in your room, of your room. Venetian buildings are galleons, their floors are decks. During those pitch black hours before light it is rare that a boat passes on the canal next to your windows, and if it does, it is probably up to no good. Only later, when the sun begins to probe at the shutters do the first ferries pass, the first fruit and vegetable scows head towards the market, the motor launches begin their rounds of the day's more serious business. Ships' horns echo in the stillness, an occasional gull will emit its evocative sea cry, and if there is the threat of high water, the sirens go off while it is still dark.

Venice has invented its own boats. Together with friends who work on boats, I've made a short list of them. They had never spelled them, but this is how they sound: caorlina, sanpierota, topa, peata, bissona, caccio, cacciapesca, cofano, burcio, sandolo and stippone. There are boats equivalent to sports cars, boats like mule carts and boats like limousines. Truck boats, bus boats, boats requiring immense physical exertion to make them move and boats that run as the boatman guides the rudder with his knees pressed together, his hands occupied peeling a banana while he talks energetically with a friend. And with all this, he is capable of maneuvering through the traffic on the Grand Canal. These are the boats run by miracles.

And finally there is the gondola. One of these boats left the other day for Japan, flown there for an exhibition complete with gondolier wearing a straw hat with streamers, striped pullover, black trousers and velvet slippers. Gondolas have been in use since the Middle Ages. Throughout the centuries the gondola has emerged as the symbol of Venice and it is difficult to have an image of the city without the prow of that boat lurking somewhere on the mind's screen. We have seen too many Hollywood films of the thirties, watching tenors sing barcaroles while ladies with shawls sat on the edges of shores, enthralled. The form of the gondola has been pushed and prodded into every possible size and substance from little jeweled pins to styrofoam centerpieces. A gentleman from the Midwest recently hired a gondola and gondolier to grace his private lake one gaudy summer, and by the time autumn set in, the gondolier had left to pursue the American Dream on Forty-second Street, where he was available for anything but rowing his boat, which in any case, had been sold by a decorator as a planter.

Gondolas look best when they are tied up next to each other and the water is rough. In an unsteady rhythm, they knife in and out of the water like tethered stallions. Alas, they have been discredited, like the Rock of Gibraltar. They are probably an obsolete form of transportation and long ago would have gone the way of the rickshaw if sentiment had not gotten in the way. Friends of mine who work on these boats see the end in sight. Each year their number diminishes, each year there is the threat that the municipality will not have enough funds to maintain the gondoliers throughout the winter. It is strenuous work in which they take great pride. Their position is not unlike acrobats in the circus, although they face neither the risk of sudden death nor the possibility of sudden fame. Their athleticism beguiles most tourists, their uniforms are jaunty, they are quick and adept in dealing with unforeseen dangers and they constantly play to the crowd.

On a cold night in the beginning of March I heard my first *Sa-han-tan-hah Lu-hu-chee-hee-yah* coming down the Grand Canal. A cortege of gondolas softly appeared, each one lit by a small lamp, each gondolier bent forward with his oar. In their midst, a tenor gave his all to the Neapolitan favorite—there never seem to be any Venetian songs available—the boats

moved in a slow frieze against the chilly current and soon they were opposite my window. Sparks of laughter flew, a bit of chatter, a woman's voice; "Will you tell our driver not to rock this thing" and the group floated on. The season had begun.

The first purposeful groups of tourists arrive well before Easter, and they may be seen clustered about in the nippy weather like early crocuses poking through the snow. Only the very brave seem to visit in February when the weather is too cold for sightseeing or for long trips on the water.

But there is the constant sensation of sea motion, and at certain moments it would seem that Venice is supposed to move through its own lagoon. Often I have watched visitors seated in the anchored, covered *vaporetto* stops—which, it must be admitted, sway a bit with the tides—thinking that they have boarded the ferry itself. Deep in conversation, they dimly note the motion of the crowd when the actual ferry arrives; then they rise, following the disembarking passengers onto the pavement. Looking around, they become extremely agitated to find themselves at the same point in space in which they had begun their journey. There is a hurried consultation; fingers point this way and that; there are gasps: then there is the mad dash back onto the ferry stop and into the ferry itself just before it pulls away.

To fully comprehend Venice, you must observe the liquid plain outlining it. There is something it shares with Castile in Spain, *una specie*, they say, a species of austerity. The arid plain is, instead, an uninterrupted sheet of water, then, suddenly, the city rising up, crammed with tilted towers and choked streets. A wall surrounding Venice would not be inappropriate, but instead, the republic threw mighty chains across the mouth of the lagoon, cordoning itself off to resist the enemy. No one entered those waters who was not invited.

Even during the summer season, the waters are relatively uncongested, and in the winter months there are seldom any travellers to disturb the intense hush suspended over the lagoons. One freezing February day, I made a plan to visit the nearby Brenta Canal with two friends, Mirko and Sylvano, both of them boat people preparing a boatmen's holiday. Mirko was the first *capellone*—long-haired—motor launch driver in Venice. And having with some imagination and great difficulty established this precedent, he was obliged from time to time to further his reputation as a renegade. Sylvano was content to be Mirko's sidekick and he grew a moustache. I was their Foreign Friend, a prerequisite for any nonconformist; a Batman, they said, to their Robins. We all three accepted our roles with amusement.

Venetian boatmen love predicting the weather just as they relish a discussion of Venice's fate. They will stand still, let the air circulate around them; they will breathe, taste, and feel the atmosphere and then make a definite pronouncement which is usually more accurate than the weather information in the New York *Times*. Mirko appeared at my gate and said that there would be fog without question and that we had better hurry, which meant that we were to stop at only two caffès before getting to the boatyard, salute and chat with only a handful of pals, and nod to another dozen acquaintances. Had my two friends picked me up with the boat at the boat entrance to my building—I had learned to avoid skidding on its seldom used algae-covered steps—we would have been denied these interruptions. Nothing in Italy is a direct line from here to there; in Venice in particular everything ripples and slants; the buildings, the window glass, the relationships, the plans and eventually the workings of the mind.

Mirko's own boat was, and I imagine is still, being repaired. The truth is that he is never sufficiently pleased with the horsepower of its motor. He travels to and from the repair yard in a large and elegant motor launch belonging to someone else, which he pilots for a living, and there he checks on the progress of the work, admiring the other boats, larger and sleeker than his own. When he leaves, he usually has it in mind to trade in his boat for one of the others he has seen, and in this way the months pass. *My* boat only existed in my mind—the most secure mooring for it at that time, which left me free to change its style, shape, and power at will. So we were both thankful to greet Sylvano and his boat, waiting for us in a boatyard, surrounded by shrouded forms of pleasure crafts slumbering through the long winter. We tugged the boat on rollers into a harness, and a rudimentary system of winches lowered it into the water. The day got colder, the wind stronger. Finally, muffled to the eyes, we set out.

Seen from its canals, Venice has an entirely different grid. The water routes cross at right angles to the normal walking paths and yet another city is revealed. Buildings never noted from their side façades present architectural surprises. Structures are seen firmly rooted in the water, rising above the surface like robust aquatic plants. Doors, moss- and mussel-covered, undignified from years of neglect and uselessness stand waist-high in *acqua alta* or expose themselves indecently when the water is low. Fantastic collections of laundry hang way above in the air on invisible lines spanning the canals. You are dripped upon by pajamas and other many-colored and more personal garments. You are aware of legs swiftly crossing the bridges arching over you; there are machine noises and backstage sounds from low windows, and there are other people in other boats, who, sometimes with greeting, sometimes without a word and frequently with complaint, pass with wonderful dexterity in the narrow confines of the canal, while, completely disinterested in your traffic problems, the city goes on about its business up above. Walking fearlessly, Venetians have no memory of traffic, like forgotten pain.

Soon we were skimming across the Giudecca Canal, past rusting ships

left there to rot or be dismantled, past the unused docks, the stilled cranes starkly pointing downwards like giant fingers of doom. Although the horsepower of our motor was inadequate for the aspirations of my friends, I had the sensation that we were riding just above the water, slapping rhythmically against it in sadistic surges to propel us onward. Both the chilling wind and the noise of the motor were loud enough to prevent all but a shouted exchange; even then, everything had to be repeated, promoting the most innocuous banality to the stature of a soliloquy.

How flat were the marshes and how bleak they were, stretching here to the port and there to the sea. Shadows covering the water in irregular patterns turned out to be patches of mud, the only portions of the lagoon that did not reflect the steely sky above us. As the Venetian shoreline meandered off, the three of us became slightly delirious at crossing the unseen frontier, the vague longitude that separates Venice from the peninsula of Italy. Looming up ahead of us, the petroleum refineries of Mestre and Marghera traced twentieth-century outlines on the landscape.

We each savored a private and totally satisfactory rush of disloyalty: here in front of us lay The Enemy.

The intense beauty of chemical refineries cannot be denied. Possibly they look their best at night, as most cities and some inhabitants do. So awesome is the proportion of those tall towers that the little people, like us, in boats, must speed past like children skirting the ramparts of Oz. Fat vats, storage tanks with staircases spiraling alongside, indecipherable markers and numbers, miles of cables, pipes, funnels, buzzing generators, blinking lights: the whole show triumphing on its shore opposite the fabled city of the lagoons, a permanent installation of working sculpture no Biennale could ever hope for. Unapproachable behind steel screening, it is the antithesis of seductive Venice.

When finally we paused, waiting in the cold for a small lock to fill at the mouth of the canal, I went ashore to watch the water level change for our boat alone, a fair antidote for having been so minimized moments before. On the cement embankment stood an isolated rustic house. A black, leafless persimmon growing near the front door supported its globes of orange fruit like awful decorations left over from some lunatic party. A small road drifted off to a copse of mutilated poplars, pruned until their trunks looked like hedgehogs. As I looked up from the shuttered window to the trees beyond, I froze: like an army advancing across the plains, an army which would vanquish us all, strode the regimented rows of gigantic towers from the refinery. Black against the indifferent sky of winter, they reached across the horizon, going on forever. A yellowish miasma clung to the nearby ground, and as though appearing by a magician's trick, a small boy suddenly materialized, carrying a slingshot. When I greeted him, he said nothing and I tried without success to persuade him to talk. Was he dumb, I wondered, drugged into numbness by the impossibility of accommodating the rustic house to the chemical industry? It is recorded that certain overdoses create fragmentation of the star-shaped cells in the brain, the astrocytes. This child looked dazed in such a way, as though the stars had broken in his head. The colossal cracking tower breathed its flame over the fields just behind us. I had seen the flame from Venice many times, particularly in the night when it lights up the entire sky with its orange tongue. Capable of dwarfing the careful illumination of the city it becomes a curious attraction on its own, a freak show on the horizon far more visible than Geneva's *jet d'eau.*

"Do you like the flame?" I asked finally. He pivoted on his heel, took careful aim with his slingshot, pulling the elastic to send a stone flying some twenty meters in its direction. A bomb could not have stilled that tower. Then he walked slowly down the road. The lock had filled. The boat was now on our new level.

Malcontenta, the Palladian villa on the Brenta, has the morose beauty of certain plantation houses of the American South. The name and its history have a decadent southern ring; the Unhappy One, said to have been named for an aristocratic lady of the Foscari family who was banished to a solitary life along the marshy banks of the Brenta for having lived too freely in Venice. The shores of the Brenta provided Venetians of the Renaissance with country homes in the summertime. They fled there, so the chroniclers led us to believe, as soon as the carnival ended, to pursue their merrymaking into the summer months. Sumptuous villas, horse-drawn boats, parties that lasted for days in flame-lit gardens: tales of the Venetian carnival and then the post-Venetian carnival along the Brenta have always been written by the visiting nobility and epistolarian diplomats installed in Venice with the same breathless ring of today's society columnists. One reads that the gold plate was thrown into the canal at a hilarious moment of the dinner party and one knows that it was fished out by the servants as soon as the first ray of sun stole over the sleeping city.

Heavy weeping willows line the shore of Malcontenta. The lower branches mould in the water, debris collecting among them netted there by the tide. Dead leaves and plastic things—disposed plastic dies hard—hug the rotting branches. A small field mouse was trapped on a floating log, running to one end of it, stopping, peering into the water, throwing up its front paws in dismay, until it occurred to it to run to the opposite end of the log where it would repeat the process. Capturing it was no simple matter, and when finally I set it down along the ragged shore my jacket was soaked up to my shoulders and the dead leaves had begun to cling to me. It hurried off towards the great house. Birds released, animals freed, fish thrown back into the water do not turn around to say thank you.

When we had climbed the low embankment, we found our improvised visit opposed by the guardian of the place, not unreasonably. It is a private property owned by Americans who have, it seems, very carefully and unpretentiously maintained and furnished it. I have been told that Malcontenta might one day be turned into a music school. It is difficult to imagine the huge neoclassical building full of life, it is such a brooding place. Behind it is an informal and extremely beautiful park. But Malcontenta's tragedy is that it cannot look upon itself. Cement-block houses line the opposite shore; in the distance stretch the ubiquitous towers. It is the building Palladio designed to prove his worth as an architect, and it stands forlorn, confronted by the shards of contemporary architecture at its worst. Neither design nor comfort nor apparent thought has gone into those houses, a brutal gesture against the past seen again and again in a country which had created most of the world's greatest buildings.

Mirko says that he feels the weather is about to do something drastic. Sylvano brushes the leaves from my clammy jacket and mumbles something about pneumonia. I see that we will not go on to Padua, that something is brewing and we had better turn back. When we are again in the boat, the conversation takes an ominous turn, leading us into a discussion of boat tragedies in which we gleefully indulge, telling about the time this happened, that happened; boats overturned by sudden moments of treachery in the Adriatic, crossed currents, and unexpected waves: Mirko hauled up like a skinny, shivering fish as he floated towards the Gothic island of the mad; Sylvano, a few years ago, missing a ferry swept up into the air by a sudden tornado, a *tromba d'aria*, which then deposited the boat with twenty-nine passengers dead just at the ferry slip. And I, being the foreigner, mention that one of the drowned victims was someone from Spain who had remained unclaimed (and unlamented?) by any relative or friend, buried in a municipal ceremony on the island of San Michele.

A few scattered fishermen look up from small bridges as we pass. They seem unused to any activity on the canal. Only rarely does a small car drive by on the desolate road next to us. The lock is once again put into operation. "How often?" I ask. "About seven times a day," comes the reply from the man who operates it. I wonder at the odd number: one boat a day must not return. The boy with his slingshot is no longer there. The house looks abandoned. The flame above it is inexplicably extinguished. There is a morbid stillness at the mouth of the canal.

When the fog hits, it happens all at once. A giant curtain is released, immediately enveloping the island and the lagoon. Everything goes out of focus, loses color, wavers, hides. Sounds dim and muffle, conversations trail away. The moan of an infrequent boat horn lets you know you are near water. To penetrate the opaque air, ferrymen flick their headlights on and off, the beam hitting the water to bounce off in a V shape. In the thickest of fog, the ferries stop running. Everyone is left to fend for himself, to fight the shroud as best he can.

In all my experiences of sudden views, of the first glimpse, around the bend, of the Mont Saint Michel, the first step into the Sainte Chapelle, the first time, in my childhood, that a peacock opened its tailfeathers to my astonished eyes: nothing can equal the precise opposite, the sudden absence of view in Venice. Everything reduces down and loses its definition. You cannot find your way, and if you are lucky, you do not care to. It is considered a catastrophe because the normal services come to a standstill. Trains arrive, their passengers spill out in front of the station, and instead of a warm ferry ride home, they are greeted by a mystical experience.

It was, of course, dangerous to be in the middle of the lagoon when it happened. The bells of the buoys were small comfort. Gulls dipped near us and then lifted into the unknown. A horn honked portentously from somewhere in the mists; then a susurrant cleaving of water, a rolling wave, and silence. Our motor choked at the slow speed and expired. We drifted, enveloped. Now a veil would lift to disclose a weathered marker, now it would become obscured and we were left in the quiet barely able to perceive each other. Slowly and cautiously we made our way past solitary pilings; from time to time a foghorn would punctuate the silence. All at once an immense freighter loomed up in front of us, motionless. We had arrived at the island of the Giudecca: those ships moored along the quay are the stragglers, the ragged, the retired. They are brought there to await their doom. A porthole scanned us from above like the eye of God; then another porthole, then it went blank, and gradually, hugging close to the ship, we reached the planks of the quay, tied up our boat and went with relief into the nearest caffè.

The Giudecca is a place apart, although it is considered an essential element of Venice, separated from the main island by a distance only three times as wide as Rome's Tiber. Not everyone finds it as gloomy as I do, but once you form such an opinion, it sets and hardens. It is the only part of Venice in which I have been willingly offered an apartment and the only place in which I would find it impossible to live. The sun shining on the rest of Venice seems to avoid the Giudecca, the quay fronting it feels perennially cast in shadow. Is it peopled in part by a race of subhumans? But no, I am being unfair. There is something off-center, something *sinistro*, that curious word which means, among other things, left, ominous and accident. It is, then, Venice's left side. The apartment proposed to me featured chickens scrabbling in the dry earth outside the front door; slung up above them was barbed wire; the view from the window presented the occupant with the sight of the abandoned Stucki mill, all eyeless windows and bald brick, which must be the largest building in Venice and looks as though it had been imported, whole, from an industrial town in northern Germany. I understand that it has been declared a national monument, privileged to stand firm on that edge of Venice to frighten everyone for centuries.

I once had the occasion while walking through the cheerless alleys of the Giudecca in an unsuccessful attempt to alter my opinion of it, to fall into a conversation with a young woman carrying a baby in her arms. This alone is unusual in Venice, for young women with babies usually do not speak with unknown members of the opposite sex. It began pleasantly enough, but as we threaded our way through the streets towards the other side of the narrow island our conversation began to falter. It could have been that we were aware of being noticed by the old ladies peering at us in the automobile mirrors angled from their windows to the pavement; it could have been the band of kids that began to follow us banging on an oil drum to underscore their passage; it could have been the lengthening shadows, the half-breed German shepherd that snarled behind a fence, the woman with crossed eyes who ran in front of us screeching at the half-naked child who preceded her. But by the time we arrived at the opposite quay we had stopped talking. Looking at each other in fear and astonishment, we took our leave without a gesture, and fled into our separate lives.

But enough of the Giudecca. For the visitors there is a fine Palladio–Da Ponte church there, the Redentore, built in 1576 to commemorate the cessation of a plague that had claimed 70,000 lives, and in July an annual celebration is held; rafts are joined across the lagoon to the church from the mainland. In the eighteenth century, a young girl was supposed to have ice-skated across a similar route to get to her wedding when the canal unaccountably froze that winter. And finally, the Giudecca was the scene, in 1814, of communal gardens planted there to keep the Venetians from starving during a blocade by the Austrians.

On this day we were required to spend the remainder of the afternoon on the Giudecca while waiting for the fog to lift so that we could cross back over. Not even the municipal boats were running. Eventually we got quite *brilli*, that pleasant word for tipsy which has at its base the verb to glitter.

When the fog lifted sufficiently, the crowd around the ferry slip had gotten out of hand. Venetians are used to punctual service in public

transportation. Ferries do not arrive all at a clip and then none at all in the manner of New York's Fifth Avenue buses. When the ticket taker tells you a ferry will arrive in three minutes, you can rely on a ferry three minutes later. When a catastrophe causes the ferries to stop running, Venetians do not take it in their stride. The newspaper will come out the next day denouncing the measures for dealing with fog, the inadequacy of the radar systems; passengers will storm the ticket booth in anger. One would expect the Venetians to shrug it off. They have such a long list of unstable weather and sudden storms. In the thirteen hundreds an earthquake raged for fifteen days, swallowing up a thousand houses along with the bell towers, their bells tolling. A few decades later a hurricane ripped through the city carrying away three hundred people attending a fair to deposit them into the sea. Each century has seen floods and storms unequaled in the rest of Italy. The elements treat Venice as though it was simply a section of the sea slightly above the tides, which it is.

As we boarded the ferry in the crush of passengers it began to lower considerably, and the few courteous people who had stepped aside were obliged to jump down from the ferry slip into the boat. It occurred to the three of us that we would now sink like a stone to the bottom of the lagoon, adding yet another Disaster to the list previously described. The Venetian newspaper almost always has a story on some small watery event: a child falls into a canal to be rescued by a youth who stood nearby glancing at a comic book; a collision takes place between a modest *sandolo* and a fast-moving motor launch carrying a small group of opulent tourists into the water instead of the casino; a priest dies in his bathtub. But there was no getting off the ferry. We were wedged in by a crowd anxious to get home, angry with the delay, and united by the quick camaraderie induced by a calamity. Above us in his booth, the ferryman stared grimly ahead, trying to see through the fog which was still so thick that he could only gauge the shore. Soon there was a heavy thud against the dock, a cheer swelled out of the crowd, and the boat rose higher and higher as the passengers disembarked, everyone rushing to his home immediately swallowed up in the darkness.

Nothing that evening could be seen outside my windows. Every now and then the curtain of fog would lift just enough to disclose across the Grand Canal certain windows illuminated in the upper stories of the palace opposite, vague shapes that seemed to pertain more to an ocean liner in vaporous waters than a building. There was no sound at all. The thickness of the fog had insulated the air and turned it into cotton wool. No boat passed. The streets were empty. Webster defines romantic as "without a basis in fact, fanciful, fictitious, or fabulous." When I hear the word, as I often do, in relation to Venice, instead of the balmy nights, gondola rides, and glittering palaces, my memory reaches back to that evening when the city lifted entirely into the clouds.

The following day, the wooden bridge of the Accademia wove delicately into view over the canal with the quality of an unfinished Japanese print. Then it disappeared. People crossing it drifted into eternity somewhere over the water; an occasional boat would emerge in quick brush strokes only to be erased moments later.

Three bridges cross the Grand Canal and until this century there were only two. The ferry route is in a zigzag pattern and gondolas called traghettos serve as auxiliary bridges carrying the passengers back and forth at strategic points along the water. The three bridges are, in the manner in which they stitch the city together, an essential feature of Venetian life. Habits are geared to them, neighborhoods have been structured to them, and they are in complete control over the tides of the population. Any slight alteration—the closing of a bridge over the Grand Canal or the building of a new bridge—would immediately upset the balance of the city.

On the smaller islands, miniature Venices, the communities would be equally disturbed if anything new were built, but there is small hope of that: mainly, the problem is what to do with the things that have deteriorated. When you pass Murano on a boat, the island seems coated with rust. Broken walls, thrown-out plumbing, smashed windows, and mountains of broken glass surround the island. It is all the more surprising because Murano is on the direct ferry route from the airport. Visitors see it before they come upon Venice. The traditional Italian preoccupation with the *bella figura*, putting on a good face, has been abandoned. Next to the boarded-up houses, a large sign of caution reads ATTENZIONE MURO PERICOLANTE, Dangerous wall. This is an island which had once boasted its own Golden Book, its own government; it minted its own coins and was known throughout Europe for its illustrious glass factories and its *orti*, the fashionable gardens where the beau monde and the literati strolled.

In the village there are signs everywhere for glass blowing, and these ill-attended exhibitions are given by men who try to go through their ritual with some cheer in an atmosphere effectively combining mime with the sweatshop. Shops selling glass sprout like lichen on a diseased tree. Long gone are the days in the Renaissance when Murano created goblets so delicate that they were fabled to shatter if poison were present in the wine.

The remarkable artifact on the island of Murano is the Basilica of Santa Maria e Donato, country cousin to the Basilica of San Marco. Completed in 1140, it is lower than the area surrounding it, resembling the Byzantine churches in Athens which require you to take a few literal steps down from current civilization in order to enter. The postcard seller who stood out in front, an appropriately gnarled and hunchbacked gentleman, told me that he had been on that spot for forty years so that I instantly looked on him as an elementary segment of the square. The friend with whom I was visiting the island felt compelled to admonish him because his postcards cost three cents more than the usual price asked. I was pleased to see that the man had enough spunk to give him an argument while I made a mental note yet again to avoid being in the vicinity of friends whenever they did business with outdoor vendors in Italy. The cardseller had his say, there was a significant pause for his adrenalin to realign, and he stated finally, "I will die here on this square," making the sign of the cross with his panel of cards so that they shuddered and shook in their shelves. "You will die at home in a nice warm bed," said I for the usual reasons. "I do not have a nice warm bed," said he, and despite the theatricality of the reply, I responded by buying some more postcards which, along with all the other postcards I have accumulated from churches, museums, town squares, and the like, I eventually misplaced or permanently filed in the wastebasket.

When I reached the bridge and looked back on that square and the three fixtures it contained: church, campanile, cardseller, ancient and unmoving in the hazy winter afternoon, an icy wind tore down the canal and I felt my face go rigid in the cold. Imagining myself frozen into stone, to become a decoration on the bridge, I thought: "You had better hurry off soon to a twentieth-century city before you, too, become a fixed part of the scenery." Veneto-Byzantine, as the guide books say, a fragment of a civilization that has ceased to be. And when I arrived home that night, I began to make my plans.

As it turned out, the ship on which I had booked passage was withdrawn from service on the Adriatic. Venice, it seems, would no longer be a suitable port for the big Italian boats: too few passengers got on, too few got off. Genoa, the base of operation, would accept the business instead. Genoa has no pretenses. It is unbothered by historic concerns, with its monuments and grime and frescoes fast fading. Genoa is, and always has been, where money is to be made, and the Genoese are the parsimonious of Italy. Venice, with all its *manifesti* proclaiming what must be saved, is but frosting on the cake. The only public announcement I saw posted on the buildings of Genoa when last I was there was concerned with the licensing of its dogs. When the shipping line went on strike altogether, even Genoa could not make any money on it. And I was given a reprieve.

One would like to sprinkle Venice with good things, with large steamers puffing merrily into port, with small industries, small companies, small orchards, with ball parks and ballet schools, bakers and candlestick makers, and above all, one would like to infuse its population with enthusiasm, particularly its young people, who tend to sit home morosely plotting the moment in the near future when they can get out of Venice once and for all. The *terraferma* magnetizes them, signifies for them, the Twentieth Century. You talk to them about a Venice transformed and realize that your image of it looks like an animated display window at Christmas: all the little animals sawing, hammering, running up and down ladders while,

in fact, nothing gets built, the animals only repeat the empty activity again and again until the mechanism is shut off at night. Finally, in desperation you say: "But if you don't stay in Venice, there's no hope." You sound as though you are drowning. "What's in Venice?" is the answer; you have known it would be the answer and it passes like a long boat over your head.

I have mentioned that Mestre gets the Venetians, at first. It is where the nearest automobiles are. If it is not Mestre, those who leave will probably skip over the nearby cities like Padua, Verona, and Vicenza and go on to Milan or Rome, usually the true goals anyway. But Mestre and its neighbor Marghera will bog down Venetians for many generations before they get any further. The fact that these cities have little character, that they could be the newer suburbs of Mexico City or Caracas hardly matters. Most of the other cities of the world are also ugly. This is not the era of beautiful cities. Motion and disposability are on our minds. Venice meanwhile, stays still. The main concern is really to get away from the islands, out of the lagoon. And move.

An acquaintance of mine, Stefano, lives on the small island of Le Vignole, a disappointed stretch of land between Venice and the Lido that seems to attract no one. In its day, Le Vignole had been agricultural. The flood of 1966 overran all the fields, leaving behind salt deposits which killed all the vineyards and fruit orchards. The grapes never came back and were never replanted. Small fruit groves and vegetable gardens have been coaxed out of the earth by the few people who have stayed on, to serve their own needs. Most of the population has left. The barracks for soldiers that had once brought a sort of prosperity to the island have been closed for many years. There had been fourteen brothers and sisters living in a large house, now abandoned. Many of them have moved to the mainland and only sometimes manage a reunion on Le Vignole to relive old times when there was, for them, a reasonably good life. "*C'era una volta,*" Once upon a time . . .

The trip there with Stefano took about twenty minutes on the ferry. Everything we passed on the way seemed black: priests and nuns waited for the boat at the island of the dead, cranes lined the Venetian shoreline silhouetted against the sky of early spring, *gabbiani,* fish cages in dark wood hung on long ropes attached to poles stuck into the water. Soon we were to land. Garbage, mud, and stone heralded our island.

A canal splices Le Vignole in half; there is no bridge. A woman wearing a straw hat jammed on above a ruddy face rows you across in her boat for a coin. No one properly explains the absence of a footbridge. You could almost leap over the canal, it is so narrow. But the boat system is the way the canal has been crossed as far back as anyone's memory goes.

We were going out into the lagoons on Stefano's boat, and with minimal confusion we got the boat into the water, filled its tank, and accepted the companionship of Rocky, a small Venetian dog partly out of Carpaccio, so eager to join us that he hurled himself from the bank of the canal to land right on the bow. There he would remain as scout and barking horn. I looked across the land at the ruined grapevines surrounding what was once a large farmhouse. When things are left to deteriorate in Venice and its islands they do so at an alarming rate.

Low nets, high nets decorated the indigo water, serene as a lake. Periodically a jet flying to or from the Marco Polo airport soared overhead, but otherwise there was no reminder of our century. No one knows whether this estuary was inhabited before the Christian era. The barbarian invasions gradually created an island population out of fear: for hundreds of years the Marcomanni, the Goths, Alaric and finally Attila unknowingly chased people from the north to hide among the swamps. By the sixth century, the inhabitants of the island had shut out the force of the sea by using larch wood laced together to secure stones and rocks. Cassiodorus,

secretary to Theodoric the Great, in his famous letter to the maritime Tribunes had written the following:

> There lie your houses, built like sea birds' nests, half on sea and half on land, or as it were, like the Cyclades spread over the surface of the water; made not by nature but created by the industry of man. For the solidity of the earth is secured only by wattle-work; and yet you fear not to place so frail a barrier between yourselves and the sea . . .

Six hundred years later, tradition records that St. Francis of Assisi was brought to an island in the lagoons in a raging storm and when he stepped ashore, the waters calmed. There he built a hut and was visited by birds and animals. I had recently read this in some authoritative volume and thought of it when in the swamps of the lagoon, with great surprise, we came upon a boat moored among the reeds. It was no ordinary boat. A house, complete with blue shutters, was built on top of it. Both house and roof were covered in thatch. We stopped our motor, intending to drift

closer and study the strange construction, but Rocky began to bark. A more serious bark echoed his, and a gentleman wearing a peaked cap, a heavy sweater, and trousers jammed into gumboots came out with his dog on what can only be described as his veranda. He was carrying a shotgun. The fact that I was amazed was only to be expected. But with all of his hunting expeditions in a deserted lagoon he had known since childhood, Stefano dropped his jaw; then he gave a quick salute, remembering that his family credentials were respected throughout these waters.

A small chimney stuck into the roof released a puff of smoke. We stared. He stared. The dogs barked at each other from long distance. I have an instinctive respect for anyone's privacy particularly a man who has gone to such lengths to be alone. Particularly if he holds a shotgun. But I waved at him, and he waved back; quickly I made some sign to ask his permission to visit. He paused. Then, with a smile, he waved us over.

Throughout the next hour he never quite disclosed what had brought him to live all alone among the marshes but he was uniquely hospitable. In his kitchen, an open hearth stood at one end; plates and cups were arranged in orderly rows along the wall and sunlight spread across the oilcloth of his table. We tasted his pasta and his wine, and while he discussed with Stefano the merits of their rifles, I fed the chickens, my mind trying to grasp what it would be like day after day, month after month, to live in a weighted boat in the Venetian lagoon. He said, finally, that he was a sort of guardian of the waters and seemed determined to let it go at that. I could not discover whether it was a title he conferred on himself or whether it had a distant connection to the community, and it is quite possible that he no longer knew himself.

There was, in his bearing, his boat, in the sweep of the flat marshes surrounding his solitude, a distillation of the quiet of the lagoons. When he said good-by, he was solemn. His gestures were formal. When we left, we knew that we would not see him again. At the last moment he disappeared into his houseboat, returning with a bottle of wine. "For America," he said. "Take it with you to remember."

Soon we approached a low island and headed for the duck blinds where some friends were waiting throughout the day with great patience to take a shot at the rare covey of birds that might fly overhead. The mud surrounding these islands is grey and lifeless; it dries quickly and covers shoes, clothes, and dog in just the effort it takes to pull a boat onto it, and so we arrived camouflaged. A cage of ducks was disguised among the reeds to entice the flying birds to the shore; every now and then one of these ducks would oblige by emitting honking noises. We looked from them to the decoys to the sky overhead. No bird came near us; none would. The talk was of past

birds lost, of birds downed, of birds that had been seen flying fearlessly above the nearby game preserve. And in the distance stood the island of Torcello, aloof, the dying noble of the Adriatic.

There is no place in these waters as alone as Torcello. Imaginary flickers of what Venice might become are translated into substance here. Long ago it was a brave community. Torcello preceded Venice. It had its bishop, fought its wars, became rich; industry and agriculture flourished; it governed itself and sent dukes and princes to travel the world. Venice itself competed with Torcello and won. Its shores have shriveled with time: earth turning to mud turning to water in a balance so tenuous that there is no precise edge to the island. Torcello floats on the lagoon, hovering just above the waterline in an ether all its own. Late in the day the sun sets behind the campanile of its cathedral: quickly it lowers into the mists enveloping the island.

One is tempted to look away early, not wishing to see the death of the sun just there.

We speed away, strong winds in our faces as the sky darkens. The dog now snuggles in close under my windbreaker, a capitulation for one as bold as he. The motor of our small boat sounds like a roar echoing throughout the empty lagoons. As we pass the high nets strung out between the poles, I watch two lone fishermen wordlessly investigating their catch in the last light. Looking back against my will I see the sun slip like a coin into the Byzantine repository of Torcello: then it is dark. Our meandering path stretches behind us into infinity. Now nothing surrounds us but a pliable blackness merging with the stillness of the sky. And all at once we turn off to the left; small lights appear on a side canal, a sign of life: it is the farmhouse of Stefano's family. We are home. One of the brothers is outside at the dock, waiting, having heard our boat—in the way of island people—from far off. He trots down to help us tie up, greeting our arrival with a formal wave. When we detach the motor, the three of us carry it to the shed in silence.

Inside, the father is sitting in the kitchen at the big table, his beret still on his head, rubbing his hands together in anticipation of dinner. A daughter-in-law is preparing to set the table, and she smiles as we walk in the door. Stefano's mother is at the gas stove, covering the boiling pasta pot with a flourish. Under the table, a very large, very old dog, the progenitress of most of the island's dogs, pounds her tail in greeting, opening one eye with effort. Our Rocky rushes to everybody in turn and immediately goes to sleep in front of the fire.

Stefano realizes that he has left his empty game pouch in the boat, and we return outside, pick it up, and decide to walk down the path to the edge of the island.

It is not a remarkable view from there. Venice is too far away, its shapes are amorphous, everything runs together into a strip of illuminated marsh.

"It doesn't look like much from here, does it?" says Stefano.

"It looks badly defined," I say, "as though it hadn't made up its mind to be Venice."

"That's probably because it's falling apart."

"And inconvenient," say I, adding to the usual list.

There is a pause. "In Mestre, of course, it would all be fine," I continue, finishing it to the logical conclusion, knowing that he longs for the *terraferma.*

"Better," he says, and smiles. "Also, as you know, for three years I've been wanting to learn how to drive."

"You would miss the boat," I say. Then I discard the irony. I am neither a tourist nor an expatriate nor a Venetian. The only ax I have to grind is to keep everyone there and build the city back up again.

We both stare at the faintly glowing outline of Venice in the distance. I wish, then, that it would all at once come speeding towards us, its shapes disentangling themselves, faster and faster, palaces, towers, churchbells all

rushing, ringing, Vivaldi rising from the dead to compose his *Gloria* so that everyone would know again what a great city it had been, it could be.

"I think you must stay." I say this with more emotion than I imagined I would.

"I know you do."

Then he cocks an eye at me. "You really care that much."

"Yes," I say before he has finished, before he can ask me why. "It's taken so long. And nothing like it can ever happen again."

"But you live in a great modern city," he says, "it's easy for you to say."

"That's how I know," I reply, "how valuable it is."

He laughs and jabs me on the shoulder. His mother calls from the house. "*È pronto.*" The pasta is ready.

"Maybe," he sighs, "maybe I'll have to wait until my mother and father die. Then I could leave . . ." His voice trails off.

"Then," I think, "he will have grown to hate it with the dull, only mildly objectionable ache that coats everything. He will have his own family, his job, his pension to think about. He will have settled in. And he will no longer care about learning how to drive."

"Then," I say, "then you will have made peace with it," telling a small lie for the sake of the place.

We walk in the dark down the path and into the warm, bright room. I see that moment again and again in my mind; it remains suspended there: the family just about to sit down to dinner, the first drift of warm evening air ruffling the thin curtains. Soon the new leaves will make a fragile effort to embrace the wires still strung among the grapevines. Soon the birds will return from their long flight north to settle and scavenge on the dying marshes. And they will remain, this family, in its cube of light.

THE ETERNAL OLYMPICS

THE ART AND HISTORY OF SPORT

THE ETERNAL OLYMPICS

THE ART AND HISTORY OF SPORT

Edited by Nicolaos Yalouris

Introduction by Manolis Andronicos

CARATZAS BROTHERS, PUBLISHERS New Rochelle, New York 1979

PRINTED AND BOUND IN GREECE
by
EKDOTIKE HELLADOS S.A.
An affiliated company
8, Philadelphias Street, Athens

First published in the United States by
CARATZAS BROTHERS, PUBLISHERS
481 Main Street
New Rochelle, New York 10801
ISBN 0-89241-092-2
Library of Congress No. 79-51381

The Editor

NICOLAOS YALOURIS	Director of the National Archaeological Museum, Athens, and Second Vice President of the International Olympic Academy.

The other Contributors

M. ANDRONICOS	Professor of Archaeology, University of Thessalonike.
J. TH. KAKRIDIS	Professor Emeritus of Classical Philology, University of Thessalonike.
TH. KARAGHIORGA-STATHAKOPOULOU	Keeper of Classical Antiquities.
B. A. KYRKOS	Research Centre, Academy of Athens.
M. PENTAZOU	Archaeologist.
K. PALAEOLOGOS	Alternate rector of the International Olympic Academy.
J. SAKELLARAKIS	Visiting Professor of Archaeology, University of Hamburg. Curator of Prehistoric Collections, National Archaeological Museum, Athens.

Contents

The Events

Sport in the Hellenistic and Roman Periods

Introduction

In ancient Greece sport was set in the context of man's civic life as a whole, and formed an intergal part of his education. The Greek term education was a very broad one, as has been shown by the great Greek scholar Werner Jaeger: it implied the cultivation of the whole man, and could not be divided into physical and mental education, because the mind cannot exist without the body, and the body has no meaning without the mind. Socrates, the most representative intellectual figure in the ancient world, lived, drew his inspiration and taught in the gymnasia of Athens, the areas in which young men trained naked (gymnos); it was there that he admired their physical beauty and strength, and proceeded to train their minds. Sport found its supreme expression in ancient Greece in the Olympic games.

The reader should be made aware of the importance of these Games in ancient Greek society, and gain some idea of the position they occupied within its system of cultural values.

The year of the first olympiad, 776 B.C., is the first accurately attested date in Greek history, and is the starting point for the list of Olympic victors. The first historical personalities that we know of with any certainty, therefore, were the athletes who won victories in these games, and from one point of view, Greek history is thus indissolubly linked with the history of sport. The ancient Greeks, however, traced their history back to mythical times, and, in its most distant beginnings to the gods themselves, from whom the most important heroes were descended. It was only natural, therefore, that they should associate the origins of the games, especially the Olympic Games, with the ancient legends, and attribute them to the gods and heroes themselves. In doing so, they went back as far as Kronos, the progenitor of the Olympian deities, and though this connection may seem to us, and perhaps also seemed to the ancient Greeks, to be rather distant and ill-defined, the Olympic Games were indisputably closely linked with Pelops, the sacred hero of Olympia, who was worshipped in the Altis long before Zeus. It was Pelops who defeated Oinomaos in the first chariot race, and the stadium, in its earliest phase, began at his tomb, the sacred Pelopion.

It is clear from all this that games had a sacred character for the Greeks, and brought a man into contact with the gods, and this explains why they were always held under their tutelage in the most sacred sanctuaries: Olympia, Delphi, Nemea, the Isthmus. The athletic games, moreover, were only one form of competition; musical contests were held alongside them in the sanctuaries, where the theatre and the stadium were as indispensible as the altar and the temple of the god.

The spirit of competition, which was one of the decisive factors in Greek history, thus acquired a spiritual and religious depth that raised it far above the level of the simple game from which it may have originated. This natural inclination on the part of a man to test his powers and prove himself better than his neighbour was undoubtedly the initial stimulus that gave rise to the competitive spirit amongst the Greeks. The same stimulus existed amongst other peoples, however, who never developed the idea of sport, as the ancient Greeks understood it or as Baron de Coubertin envisaged it. The reason for this cannot easily be explained in the space of this introduction. It is clear, however, that the sporting ideal that found its expression in the Greek games, particularly those at Olympia, presupposed an awareness of the value of man, a belief in his freedom and his merit, a consciousness of his responsibilities and, finally, an acceptance of his democratic right to participate in public affairs. The cultivation of the sporting spirit in ancient Greece rested on the same intellectual basis as all the other cultural values of Greek civilisation, first and foremost amongst which was the freedom of the individual from any kind of despotism. The religious beliefs of the Greeks did not deprive them of freedom of action as human beings, and therefore did not relieve them of human responsibility. Social discipline and obedience to the laws was an obligation owed by free responsible citizens, and in the eyes of the ancient Greek, the Law bound gods and men, rulers and ruled alike. For a man to be able to live with this responsibility and freedom, he had to believe in himself, in his body and his mind — in short, in the supreme value of human life. Man himself was the visible image of the gods; for the gods of the Greeks possessed all the characteristics of human beings, in their ideal form. Physical perfection, for the Greeks, meant an approximation to the gods, and physical strength was an expression of this approximation; the same was true of the quality that we call "intellectual" but that the Greeks had not separated off from the whole being, at least before the fourth century B.C. The famous ideal of the *kalos kagathos* (literally: the good and beautiful man) is one that is untranslatable, and incomprehensible outside ancient Greece.

These fundamental principles of the ancient Greeks were realised in an idealised form in their public festivals. The Olympic games held a special position amongst these festivals, constituting as they did, the highest expression of the sporting spirit at a gathering of all the Greeks — which for them meant an assembly of free men from all over the world. Forgetful of the cares of daily life, of their human weaknesses, and of their frequently fatal differences, they were transported during the panhellenic (for them, world wide) suspension of hostilities, into a state of divine well-being. In the heavenly setting of Olympia man rediscovered his ideals: peace reigned throughout the world, all were free and equal, and the powerful wealthy rulers from Sicily were in no way different from the simple citizen of Athens — the god protected them all. The *Hellanodikai,* or umpires were the only people to have stone seats; everyone else sat on the Stadium embankment to watch the games, and the athletes competed naked for the victory and the crown of wild olive. Their real aspiration, however, was for something greater: fame and the respect of all the Greeks, which was the most inperishable crown of all.

It was this spirit, born in Greece and perfectly expressed in the Olympic games, that Baron de Coubertin wanted to revive: a belief in man, in his physical strength and moral worth, in democratic equality and human brotherhood, and in peace and love throughout the world. Many may perhaps believe this vision to be a chimera; but all who have enjoyed the spirit of brotherhood between athletes from all over the world that dominates the modern Olympic games, where, albeit for a brief period, the boundaries dividing peoples are forgotten; where language, race and religion raise no barriers between men; where social position, material wealth and national might are of no account; where man, stripped of all else, competes with his fellows peacefully and honourably, solely to win the glory of victory; — all who have experienced this atmosphere continue to hope and believe that the Olympic ideal will be able to inspire the whole world, not just for a few days but for all time.

Manolis Andronicos

Prehistory of the Games

Athletics in Crete
and Mycenae

Athletics
in the Geometric Period

Games and Religion

Sport in Crete and Mycenae

Introduction

According to tradition the Olympic Games were instituted in 776 B.C. This does not by any means indicate that athletic contests were held for the first time in Greece in that year. In fact, the origin of these contests is lost in the dark mists of time. The gathering of athletes from all parts of the Greek world in the earliest Olympiads would suggest that there had already existed an old tradition for such events. One must therefore seek the origins not only in the Geometric age, but long before, in the Mycenaean period, which pulsated with a primitive spirit of rivalry, as well as in the Minoan period, in the Aegean and in distant Crete, where the oldest civilization on European soil had flourished.

The earliest forms of athletic activity can be traced to the peoples of the East. In the third and more especially in the second millennium B.C., sports were common in Egypt. Wall paintings and reliefs show men wrestling or lifting weights among other exercises that can only be described as games. Various games were played with balls or with wooden staffs and knives, on land or in boats on the Nile. Both the lower and the upper classes of Egyptian society found entertainment in these games, including the great Pharaoh himself, whose exceptional prowess was often extolled for his use of the bow, his horsemanship or his sailing ability. Yet all these and other similar sports practised in the East had essentially nothing in common with the Greek athletic contests except for the natural inclination to exercise a strong healthy body. The sole purpose of such displays of athletic prowess was to entertain a spectacle-loving people rather than to serve an ideal similar to that expressed by the later Greek Olympic Games.

Sports in Minoan Crete

Athletic games and other sports took on various forms in Crete. Their purpose was to entertain spectators at public festivals. In the highly advanced stage of civilization attained in the first half of the second millennium B.C., there grew a more evolved kind of athletic training. The object of this was not only to develop slender bodies with a narrow waist, but to perform various intricate exercises that presuppose long periods of practice. As in the case of other facets of its civilization, so in athletics Crete stands between the Eastern peoples and the Egyptians on the one hand, and Mycenaean Greece on the other. One finds in Crete the first indications of the athletic spirit which was to evolve and reach a high pitch in subsequent centuries. The games that had come from Egypt and the East developed here into more exacting performances with set rules which, in addition to a show of prowess, were related closely to religious festivals and ceremonies.

Games, exercises and contests encountered in Crete include tumbling, bull-leaping, boxing, and wrestling. On many engraved Minoan seal-stones one sees the simplest form of exercise, that of tumbling, which in fact is nothing more than an acrobatic display. The tumblers were ornately dressed with splendid girdle and tasseled belt, often with feathers on their heads and bracelets round the arms. They turned somersaults and stood on their hands balancing their bodies in midair. Tumbling in Crete, as in Egypt and the East whence it originated, was performed with numerous variations, in which one or two acrobats participated with their hands placed in front or behind the body. Possibly, the tumblers also performed, as in subsequent years, spectacular gyrations and displays between swords, as the decorative theme on the gold-covered handle of a sword from Malia seems to suggest. Tumbling was far more popular in Minoan Crete than in Mycenaean Greece. Homer refers to it and associates it with the Cretan dance depicted on the shield of Achilles. And so it is perhaps not a mere coincidence that tumbling is still common in Crete today as a display of dexterous and lithe body movement in the so-called "leaping dance."

The suppleness and the technique of the tumbler led eventually to the sport of bull-leaping, a complex and dangerous game with the horned beast. Its origin and successful performance presuppose a familiarity of man with the beast, acquired through the capturing and the taming of the wild bull. In prehistoric times bull-games were common in other countries, such as Egypt, Cappadocia and even India. But these

1. The earliest form of sport in Minoan Crete consisted of simple athletic games. Seal-stone with a scene depicting somersaulting; the somersaulters place their hands firmly on the ground, lift their body into a vertical position, and execute spectacular acrobatic leaps (Oxford, Ashmolean Museum).

2. Bull-leaping was a complex and extremely dangerous development of somersaulting. On the gold signet-ring the bull-leaper is executing a difficult leap over the running bull (Oxford, Ashmolean Museum).

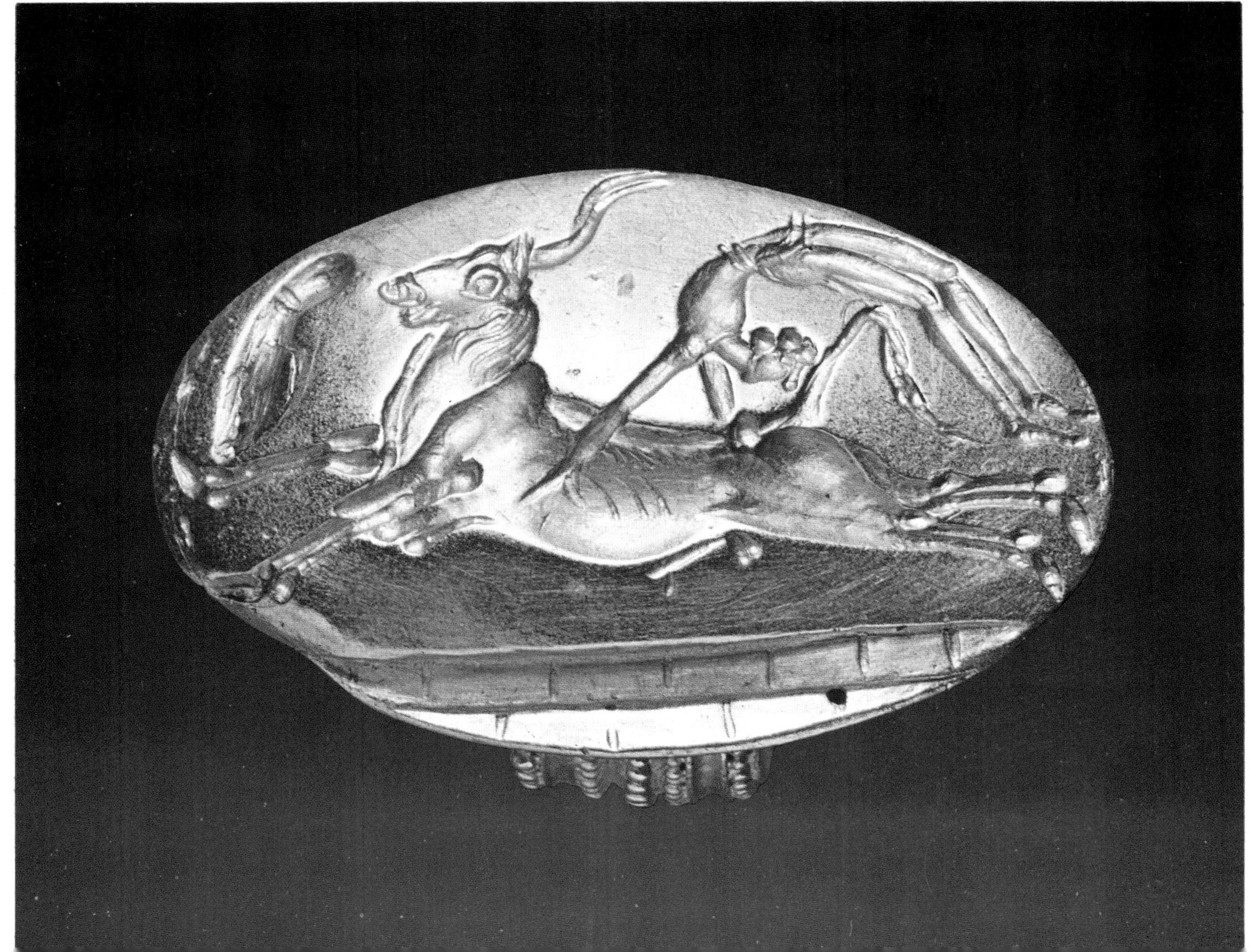

4. Reconstruction of the various stages of bull-leaping. The bull-leaper grasps the onrushing bull by the horns; the animal raises its head with a violent movement and tosses the man, who turns a somersault in the air, stands upright on the animal's back, and finally jumps down to the ground. Variations on this basic pattern are frequently seen in representations of the sport on ancient monuments (Drawing: K. Iliakis)

performances had nothing in common with the Minoan bull-leaping, and equally unrelated are the later contests of riding bull-jumpers in Thessaly and Asia Minor, not to mention the modern bullfights of Spain and Portugal.

The numerous representations of bull-leaping found in Crete permit a safe reconstruction of the successive steps involved in the sport. Initially, the athlete seized the onrushing bull by the horns. The beast, lifting its head, tossed the acrobat with mighty force upwards, as the acrobat released his hold of the horns and turned a somersault in the air to land upright on the back of the bull. Then he bounced from its back onto the ground. More than one athlete participated in the event, and often both women and men took part. The presence of more than one bull-jumper was essential in such a dangerous sport. In the final and perhaps most dangerous stage of the performance, when the acrobat leapt from the back of the running animal onto the ground, another acrobat would be near the bull to help the leaping athlete make a safe landing and avoid any injury. Accidents certainly occurred, as one well knows from surviving representations of these bull-games. For a successful performance the athlete would have to be well acquainted with the actions of the beast

3. Bull-leaping demanded great physical agility, mental preparedness, and a long period of practice in the technique. In order to carry out the difficult leap over the running bull successfully, the bull-leaper had to calculate with absolute precision his own movements as well as those of the animal, and also to act in co-ordination with his fellow athletes who would assist him as he landed on the ground. Fresco from Knossos depicting three bull-leapers at different stages of the sport (Herakleion, Archaeological Museum).

4

and be able to time his own movements to the second, in order to keep both his and the beast's movements perfectly synchronized. The coordination also required by the team of athletes would necessitate considerable physical and mental training beforehand. The striking similarity in the various Minoan representations of bull-leaping show clearly that there were established rules for the game. This certainly contradicts those who doubt the authenticity of such precise and exacting performances.

We do not know who performed these bull-games. The fine attire of the athletes, alike in both men and women, the high sandals, the decorative bands round the forehead, the necklaces, arm bracelets, anklets, the lavish coiffures, not to mention the use of special amulets with magical properties such as the sacral knot, were perhaps not mere ornamental objects, but indicative of noble birth. In all likelihood, the bull-jumpers were members of the aristocratic class.

The bull-games did not take place in the central courts of palaces, as many have supposed, but in special enclosures with provisional wooden fences near the palace, or large closed-in clearings, again near the palace, with well-structured barriers for watching the sports safely and large gates for entering and leaving the ground. Such an enclosure was uncovered to the northwest of the palace at Malia. This fact is of special significance for the history of athleticism. It is the first example of a special ground set up for the performance of a game. Undoubtedly, spectators were attracted in large numbers by such spectacular events.

It is universally believed that bull-leaping was not a mere display of agility and daring, but an exercise that was performed as part of a religious festival. The sacredness of the bull in Minoan Crete and the use of religious symbols in the performance of such acrobatics are elements that substantiate such a contention. Yet it is uncertain whether the games were followed by the sacrifice of the bull.

In the late Minoan period it would appear that bull-leaping both in Crete and in mainland Greece became less elaborate. The acrobat limited himself to jumping, from the side, over the back of the running beast. Still, the old glory of the dangerous game remained alive in the memory of many generations. The later myths of Theseus with the Minotaur and Herakles with the bull of Marathon, may have been no more than echoes of the danger-filled and long-lost sport, of the feats of some remarkable acrobats who performed as only heroes could perform.

Pugilism and wrestling were known in the Minoan period. These may well have originated in Egypt.

5. Scenes depicting field games and bull-leaping are preserved on a rhyton *from Hagia Triada. The scenes on the upper band are not clear. The one on the left is probably a wrestling match. The next band shows two running bulls, and a bull-leaper attempting the dangerous leap over the second bull. On the third band there are two pairs of boxers. The victor on the left has knocked his opponent to the ground. His stance is like that of other victors: he is holding up his left arm, slightly bent in order to protect himself, while his right arm is bent behind him as he prepares to strike a blow. On the lowest band the athletes are young boys. The defeated youth on the left has fallen to the ground, and is trying with his right hand to protect himself against further blows. The position of the second defeated youth on this same band would be more appropriate to a wrestling scene. It appears as though the winner has turned his opponent upside down with a waisthold. The sport would have been a combination of wrestling and boxing, something like the later* pankration *(Drawing: K. Iliakis). (Harakleion, Archaeological Museum).*

Representations dating from the peak years of the Minoan period, in plaster reliefs adorning the palace walls as well as in works of the minor arts, indicate the popularity of these two sports. It is certain that in Crete wrestlers wore a special kind of helmet with cheekpieces, unknown to warriors. Boxers on the other hand had their heads uncovered. In both sports the athletes wore girdles and sandals, had elaborate coiffures, and were adorned with necklaces. The actual rules of boxing and wrestling are not known. The postures of the athletes are similar with those seen in later representations. The winner, with his weight on one foot, bends the body slightly forward, raises his left hand in a defensive attitude, and clenches his right fist. The defeated contestant is depicted in various postures, in his attempt to ward off blows, or in his final defeat on his knees or haunches. The competitors are always portrayed in pairs. The lack of a third figure, which could be interpreted as judge of the contest, in the various scenes, has led some scholars to believe that the matches ended with the extermination of the loser. But this is not certain, in view of the fact that these sports, as well as the bull-games, were of a peaceful nature. Moreover, the special headgear worn by wrestlers was a protection against dangerous blows. As in the case of bull-leaping, there is a striking similarity in the various postures of the athletes, especially in the depictions of the victor of the match. It has been surmised that the winner was portrayed, much as he is in the modern ring, prancing about in triumph to show his strength. At all events, the repetition of the same scenes would indicate the existence of set rules of procedure for the matches. The use of special equipment for each of these games would also suggest a long athletic tradition. Several fragments of plaster reliefs from the royal palace of Knossos showing scenes of wrestling and boxing convey remarkably well the tautness of the muscles and the well trained bodies.

Surely, there would have been in Crete, as there were later in Mycenaean Greece, special grounds for the performance of these sports. It has been assumed that the so-called theatral areas had served this purpose. These had a flat-paved floor and tiers of steps on the sides, as the example found in the great palace. The pavement would be provisionally covered with a layer of sand. Yet, surviving scenes provide no relevant information. All that is known is that these sports were held at the same time as bull-leaping, during the festivals, at sites adorned with tall poles from which were suspended banners or flags.

Games in the Aegean Islands

Pugilism was widespread also in the Aegean islands which were directly influenced by the Minoan civilization. Evidence of this is found in a fresco dating from the middle of the second millennium B.C., uncovered in the recent excavations at Thera. The fresco shows two young children fighting with

6. Boxing was a particularly popular sport in the Aegean, as is clear from the boxing scene recently discovered in a fresco from Thera. The two young boxers — scarcely more than children — are practising, wearing a girdle and boxing-gloves. Their technique appears to be advanced, and the young age of the boxers attests the long period of practice that the sport demanded (Athens, National Archaeological Museum).

6

complete boxing equipment, much like the one depicted in Crete. Boxing gloves are not absent, but here they are worn only on the right hand. The scene is of special significance, for it reflects the advanced technique of the sport. Moreover, training from an early age would indicate that this technique required long practice.

Athletics in Mycenaean Greece

Athletics developed very rapidly in the Mycenaean period. Dominant were the competitions held in special grounds. Techniques improved, and new games — contests in the true sense of the word — such as foot-races and chariot-races, made their appearance. This development was largely due to the general character of Mycenaean society which was composed of a more warlike people.

Boxing and wrestling, as well as tumbling and bull-leaping, passed into mainland Greece from Crete. But unlike Crete, the evidence one finds here is more limited and often concise in content. Athletic events were not differentiated in Mycenaean Greece. On the contrary, it appears they were performed in similar fashion as in Crete. It is of interest to note that boxing and wrestling had become the most popular sports in the Mycenaean world. Mycenaean colonists carried these sports to Cyprus, where one encounters scenes of such events depicted on pottery of the 13th century B.C.

A Mycenaean vase from Cyprus shows two pairs of pugilists, and a schematic representation of two runners. Between the boxers two men are discerned running, with one foot behind the other and arms slightly bent. The bodies of the runners are noticeably muscular, like those of the pugilists. The athletes are nude and wear only a cover on the head which appears to be merely ornamental. This is the earliest known representation of a running contest and, therefore, the oldest evidence for the existence of this sport.

In addition to the foot-race, the Mycenaeans introduced another form of competition, namely chariot-racing. There are indications that the chariot was used in Mycenaean Greece not only for war and for the hunt, but also for athletic events. Representations on some Mycenaean funerary stelai in relief dating from the mid-16th century B.C. and on a series of vases of the 14th and 13th centuries B.C. from continental Greece, the islands and Cyprus, are apparently depicting chariot-races.

As already stated, the Mycenaean iconography of sports and games is unfortunately very limited, unlike that of Minoan Crete. In fact, all we know is the existence of a few of these, such as tumbling, bull-leaping, boxing, wrestling, running, and chariot-racing. However, by examining the Mycenaean iconographic evidence of athletic events and comparing this with the corresponding information from Crete, one can draw certain interesting conclusions for the general history of the games. It is obvious that the Mycenaeans, as in the case of other cultural manifestations, copied certain Minoan sports and at the same time rejected others. They were not sheer imitators. It is certainly typical of their tastes that they cared very little for such athletic games as tumbling and bull-leaping, but were greatly interested in boxing and wrestling which they helped to spread widely. But most important of all, they created new and exciting contests, those of running and chariot-racing, in which the competitive spirit is highly developed. Certainly in a broader sense bull-leaping could be considered (in addition to boxing and wrestling) as a competitive sport. But bull-games do not possess the element of rivalry between competitors of equal strength. Even boxing and wrestling may have aimed at the supremacy of the strongest, or expressed the enmity between two contestants. But a true athletic spirit is found primarily in chariot-racing and running, which are encountered for the first time in the Mycenaean age and are both creations of the Greeks. It is perhaps not mere accident that in the later Olympic Games the oldest contest was the foot-race and, moreover, that both the foot-race and the chariot-race remained throughout the long history of these games the most popular events with the Greeks.

Understandably, the main concern of recent research has been to seek the relation existing between the prehistoric and the historic Greek games. The lack of any written evidence from prehistoric times has forced scholars to turn to later sources relating to the prehistoric period, such as the mythical tradition and Homer's epic works. Information was also sought from other sciences, such as comparative religion and ethnology, on the games and sports of other peoples. Various theories have been advanced. It has been suggested that the games had primitive origins associated with the murder of a king, or that they are related with religious initiation rites, or with magical rites involving the sun. One theory proposes that the games began as funereal celebrations, which were established to honour some dead founder of the race. The latter theory may be nearer the truth, for it is based on Homer and the funeral games initiated by Achilles to honour the dead Patroklos, on the mythical tradition (since all the panhellenic games held in historic times were related to some mythical hero) and, lastly, on the Mycenaean monuments which are being examined for the first time for such evidence. It is indeed significant that the surviving representations of Mycenaean games are often associated with funerary monuments. In addition to the funerary stelai with their depictions of chariot-racing, all other scenes of chariot-racing, boxing, and running which have been cited, occur on kraters, i.e. vases that may have had some funerary use, since they were placed in the tombs of the departed. Significant and important from this point of view are the depictions of bull-leaping and chariot-racing, perhaps even of boxing, that accompany the representations of mourning women on a sarcophagus found in the cemetery of Tanagra, dating to the closing years of the Mycenaean period.

The Mycenaeans are not only the creators of the competitive athletic spirit. They also gave new content to the sporting events which they had learned from the Minoans and to those which they themselves had established. It may well be that they continued to hold athletic contests during religious festivals in honour of some god, but at the same time they founded funerary games with the object of honouring some dead heroes. As has been pointed out, the mythical tradition which assigns the origin of the Greek games to funerary events, the evidence supplied by Homer, as well as the prehistoric and particularly the Mycenaean discoveries in the large centres where games were held, provide irrefutable proof for the origins of athletics in the Greek world.

Athletics in the Geometric period

Introduction

Athletics and men's attitude towards competition were affected by the general reorganisation that took place in the Greek world as a result of the movements of the Greek races in the 11th century B.C. — that is, of the so-called "Dorian Invasion." The tradition which had been consolidated during the Mycenaean period, however, not only did not disappear, but continued and developed in the centuries between the end of Mycenaean times and the late Geometric age — the period of the Homeric poems. For these centuries, however, our evidence is very scanty and indirect.

The continuation and survival of the Mycenaean tradition may be traced mainly in the *Iliad* and the *Odyssey* — since both poems often reflect situations and conditions of earlier periods — and in the scenes on Geometric vases. It is only for Homeric society that we have abundant specific evidence and detailed descriptions of games.

Athletics in Homer and Hesiod

Through Homer and Hesiod, we come into contact with a society in which sport had penetrated every area of life, both public and daily. Love of competition was everywhere predominant: young men revelled in intense physical effort, and eminent leaders and heroes competed to excel, while around them a crowd — the people or the army — thrilled with enthusiasm as they followed their performance. In short, we are confronted with a society which is characterised, along with its heroic ideals, by a genuine sporting spirit.

This love of contest is diffused in both the *Iliad* and the *Odyssey*. It is encountered in the description of the games held to honour the dead Patroklos, in the games organised by the Phaiakians to entertain Odysseus in his sorrow, and in a number of other instances. All Homeric heroes yearn to distinguish themselves in the games: every hero is also an athlete who tries to surpass the others. The passion for games, and men's familiarity with them, have left their mark on the language. In simple everyday speech, expressions like "a discus' throw," or "a spear's throw," which were used to define a distance in approximate terms, are quite common. Even the poet uses an image from the field of sport in the dramatic scene of the killing of Hector, when Achilles is hunting him mercilessly around the walls of Troy: he compares the two rivals to horses running in a chariot race and trying to win some valuable prize.

The advanced technique of the sports and the detailed description of them by the poets are in a way interconnected. They presuppose a long tradition of sporting activity, and at the same time a long period during which the subject was treated by the epic language, until it obtained a suitable vocabulary. On the basis of these two factors, we may say that sport in the Helladic world had behind it centuries of trial and systematic practice.

It is not always easy to determine the chronological order in which the sports referred to in the epic poems became established — which of them, that is, belong to the earlier or later phases of the Mycenaean period, and which were introduced during the Geometric age.

Chariot racing, the most aristocratic of the games,

must be connected with the prime of the Mycenaean cities, and dates from the Mycenaean period. The same applies to wrestling, boxing and running, as we shall see in another chapter. Armed combat, the toughest of the games, was perhaps established in the same period. The other competitions referred to by Homer — archery, throwing the javelin and jumping — probably developed after the decline of the Mycenaean world. Jumping was the last event to be introduced, for it is not known in the *Iliad* but is referred to in the *Odyssey*.

The contests described in the *Iliad,* in the funeral games held in honour of Patroklos, are, in order: chariot racing, boxing, wrestling, running, armed combat, the discus, archery with a target, and the javelin. The prizes are awarded by Achilles himself: beautiful slaves skilled in some craft, horses, oxen, mules, tripods, cauldrons, cups, gold, and iron. Prizes are awarded to both victors and vanquished. We cannot tell, however, whether this meant that participation in the games was significant in itself and consequently entitled everyone to a prize, or whether it was an initiative of Achilles to give to all who took part a prize as a souvenir.

The games take place before the whole of the army, near the tomb of Patroklos and close to the sea. The atmosphere is very lively; the spectators shout and are full of enthusiasm, and utter cries of pride and encouragement to the competitors. They even make bets, like that between Idomeneus and Lokrian Ajax on which horses would come first, those of Eumelos or those of Diomedes.

The games commence with the most important and spectacular contest, the chariot race, in which five heroes take part: Eumelos, Diomedes, Menelaos, Antilochos and Meriones. At the turning-post, the most critical and dangerous point of the race, Achilles puts his old tutor, Phoenix, to watch the chariots. We get a good idea of the technique of the contest from the instructions given by old Nestor to his son, Antilochos, just before the competitors set off. He advises him to take the turn close in, leaning to the left, towards the inside, and, just as he is about to pass close by the post, to check the left horse and urge on the right, at the same time loosening the reigns of the latter. He assures him that in this way he will overcome the imperfections of his animals and win the race through his skill.

The five chariots and their riders take up a position determined by lot, and the five heroes set off impetuously, raising a cloud of dust behind them, and rush out onto the plain, shouting to urge their horses to run faster. At first they all run neck and neck, but on the last straight, when everyone is expecting Eumelos, with the best horses, to win, the yoke of his chariot breaks, and Diomedes comes first and takes first prize. Antilochos comes second, having overtaken Menelaos by a rather reckless and illegal manoeuvre at a narrow point of the course. At this point he failed to check his horses and allow Menelaos, who was in the lead, to pass through; instead, he rushed on with great speed and overtook him, compelling Menelaos to check his own horses in order to avoid a collision. As a result, Menelaos was third to the finishing post and Meriones fourth.

As Achilles is distributing the prizes, Menelaos intervenes and disputes Antilochos' beating him. But as the youth is hastily admitting his mistake, his rival relents and gives up his claim on the prize. Achilles gives a special prize to Eumelos, who had

7

7. The most important and spectacular event in the games held in honour of the dead Patroklos was the chariot race. Representation of chariot racing from the François black-figure krater. On the right is the chariot of Diomedes, and, below the horses, a tripod and a lebes, the prizes for the winners (Florence, Museo Archeologico).

8-9. Scene of a horse race. The judges can be seen at the finish, waiting to award the prizes to the winners (Paris, Musée du Louvre).

8 9

been so unlucky: a breastplate that he had won in battle.

The boxing match follows. Achilles announces the prizes, and Epeios and Euryalos stand up to take part in the contest. The athletes wear a loin-cloth, as in Crete, and have leather strips bound round their hands. Epeios quickly defeats his opponent with a blow to the face that knocks him to the ground. He himself, however, hastens to raise him, showing his good feeling.

The boxing is followed by the wrestling match, in which the opponents are Odysseus and Ajax. This sport requires greater skill than boxing, and it is for this reason that Homer represents the most important leaders taking part. The winner is the one who succeeds in throwing his opponent to the ground. The description of the contest is most interesting. The unsurpassable skill of Odysseus is matched by the indestructible strength of Ajax. At first the two come to grips and apply their powers to the attempt to throw the other to the ground. Since neither of them succeeds, however, Ajax — confident in his own strength — proposes to Odysseus that they should try to lift each other. He himself makes the first attempt. Just as he is about to lift Odysseus, however, the latter quickly succeeds in giving him a strong blow at the back of the knee, and Ajax falls to the ground on his back, with Odysseus on top of him. It is now the turn of Odysseus to try to lift Ajax, but he only succeeds in moving him a little. He then puts his knee between the legs of his opponent and the pair of them lose their balance and fall in a heap on the ground, side by side. They get up and are ready to begin again, but Achilles, seeing that they are both very good and that neither can win, announces that it is a draw and divides the prizes equally.

The running race, in which the competitors are Lokrian Ajax, Odysseus and Antilochos, arouses great interest amongst the spectators. Ajax takes the lead, but the Achaians cheer on Odysseus to exert all his strength and overtake his opponent, and in the end it is Odysseus who is the winner. The poet makes an interesting comment on the way Odysseus runs: he says that he passed Ajax because he ran more lightly, raising his hands and feet high (πόδας καὶ χεῖρας ὕπερθεν) — his movements, that is, are similar to those made by the runners in the *stadion* (sprinters) depicted on vases of the Classical period.

There follows one of the most dangerous contests, the armed combat. This is a duel in which the opponents compete dressed in full armour, and try to wound each other. Ajax and Diomedes take part in the contest; three times they rush upon each other without either of them winning, but when Diomedes is on the point of striking Ajax in the throat the spectators stop them, for fear that someone might be seriously wounded.

In the following competition, the discus, the victor is Polypoites, and his prize is the very piece of heavy unworked iron that he had thrown farther than the others.

Teukros and Meriones take part in the archery competition with a specific target. The target is a dove tied to the mast of a ship, and Achilles offers the first prize of ten double axes made of iron to whoever hits the dove, and ten single axes to the man who hits only the rope tying it to the mast. The order of participation is determined by lot. Teukros aims first, but hits the rope instead of the bird, and the dove flies free into the air. Then Meriones

10

10. Picture of a boxing match from a geometric kantharos. This was one of the oldest sports in Greece and is mentioned by Homer in the funeral games held in honour of Patroklos (Dresden, Staatliche Kunstsammlungen).

quickly takes aim and hits the bird in flight.

The final competition is the javelin, but as the leader of the army himself, Agamemnon, gets up to take part, Achilles decides to honour him by giving him the prize without the contest taking place.

Athletic games are also encountered in the *Odyssey*. Alkinoos, the king of the Phaiakians, invites a large number of people to his palace, in order to honour his guest. Those invited eat and drink and afterwards listen to Demodokos singing of the misfortunes of wily Odysseus. The king observes that his guest is moved by the song and proposes that games should be held to take Odysseus' mind off his sorrow, and:

"so that our guest can tell his own people, when he returns to his home, that in boxing, in wrestling, in chariot racing and in running, we excel all others."

They therefore leave the palace and go off to the agora, and a crowd gathers to watch the young men compete. The first contest is running, in which Klytoneos comes first, a long way ahead of the rest. Next is wrestling, in which Euryalos is the winner, followed by the victories of Amphialos in the chariot race, and Elatreus in the discus. The final contest is boxing, which is won by Laodamas, the son of Alkinoos.

After everyone has enjoyed watching the games, Laodamas decides to ask his guest, who has been following the games, if by chance he has experience in any competition and can take part himself, because he believes that, having such physical strength and such stout arms and thighs, he is sure to be practiced in some contest or other. He therefore comes forward and addresses Odysseus:

"Come, stranger, and make trial of your strength too. You look as if you have experience in games. And a man can have no greater glory than that won by his hands and feet."

Odysseus replies that he is overwhelmed by his grief and has no appetite for games, whereupon Euryalos rushes from amongst the crowd of Phaiakians and addresses the stranger with these words:

"I say that you know nothing of games, stranger. Your mind is on business and profit. You are no athlete."

The insult goes deep, and Odysseus rises in anger, seizes a discus, larger and heavier than that used by the Phaiakians and without difficulty throws it farther than anyone else. Satisfied, he turns to the Phaiakians and says:

"Reach its mark, and afterwards I will throw it even farther; and I will beat you all in wrestling and boxing and running. With Laodamas alone I will not compete, because I am his guest. Come and let us compete with the bow; it is only at running that I am not so successful — after all my misfortunes my legs no longer support me."

The Phaiakians fall silent in shame; only Alkinoos rises, wishing to calm their spirits.

"You are right, stranger. We are not good either in boxing or in wrestling. But in running and seamanship and the dance no one can match us. Let them therefore bring the lyre from my palace, so that Demodokos can play, and the Phaiakian youths and maidens can dance."

On this note, the description of the games amongst the Phaiakians comes to an end.

In the Homeric poems, games give the hero-athletes the opportunity to display their excellence, to demonstrate their desire for victory, and to take pleasure in the contest itself. However, the intense wish to win does not lead them into the use of force. The rivals are full of the sporting spirit, and demonstrate their magnanimity. When the duel between Ajax and Diomedes is on the point of becoming dangerous, the crowd intervenes and stops them. Epeios, the victor in the boxing match, hastens to raise his injured opponent Euryalos from the ground. The heroes show their courtesy and dignity in other ways too: Antilochos, who defeated Menelaos in the chariot race by a risky and illegal manoeuvre, recognises his mistake and surrenders his claim to the prize, offering it to Menelaos, as we saw. He too, however, with great magnanimity, politely rejects the gesture and forgives the thoughtlessness of the young hero, caused by his eagerness in the contest.

The ideal hero, as he appears in the Homeric poems, possesses physical and mental strength, and is intelligent and brave. This is what Peleus desires for his son, Achilles, when he instructs Phoenix to teach him "to be best in words and deeds" (μύθων τε ῥητῆρ' ἔμεναι πρηκτῆρά τε ἔργων). Homer also often portrays the leaders justifying their special position as shepherds of the people by their skill and bravery. It is only the "best men" who take part in the games, and this is why the view has often been expressed that in Homer, sport is a prerogative of the aristocracy. This is not absolutely certain, however. It may not be by chance that the army (the "people") is depicted practising throwing the javelin and the discus in book II of the *Iliad*. Furthermore, if we admit the practical advantage that certain sports, such as archery, had, it is difficult to believe that sport was entirely cut off from the soldiers and was the exclusive prerogative of their leaders.

From the Geometric period onwards, however, the sporting spirit and participation in the games is not the exclusive privilege of the "best men," as it appears in the *Odyssey*, in the Phaiakian games. The athletes who take part are not famous heroes, but figures from social life, who mainly follow pursuits connected with the sea, as their names indicate: Akroneus, Okyalos, Nauteus, Prymneus, Euryalos.

The occasion for the games differs in the two poems. In the *Iliad* it is a burial custom, and the games are connected with a religious ceremony. In the *Odyssey* they are held in honour of a guest; for the Phaiakians, the simple delight of physical effort and the pursuit of victory seem to have been the most important factors. It should be noted, also, that in these games no prizes are given; the athlete's reward is the satisfaction of coming first, an attitude that foreshadows the high athletic ideal of the Classical period.

A new element appears in the Phaiakian games: specialisation in particular events. In the *Iliad*, the heroes take part in almost all the contests, while the Phaiakians, as Alkinoos admits, are very good at running, the dance and seamanship, but are inferior in the other sports.

It is worth giving special emphasis to two points. The Homeric heroes know and appreciate the value of practice. The Phaiakians frequently stress that Odysseus appears to be practised, that he seems to know about contests, and they deduce this from his powerful build and his strong arms and legs. Odysseus himself boasts that he has competed from his youth, and that even now, after all his misfortunes, he can beat them in wrestling, boxing, archery and the discus. Even if the relevant evidence did not exist, we would arrive at the same conclusion — that is, that the developed technique and well-formulated rules of the Homeric contests presuppose a long period of familiarity and systematic practice.

The second, and more important point is the high esteem which Homeric society attached to athletics and athletes. In the *Iliad,* all the leaders of the army, even Agamemnon himself, compete. The Phaiakians are of the opinion that the most important thing for a citizen, more significant even than trade and wealth, is "what a man can achieve by his hands and feet" — that is, athletic pursuits which take a man out of the realm of the everyday and elevate him to the sphere of high ideals. "You are no athlete" (and it is the first time in the world that the word is recorded, full of expressive meaning), says Euryalos to Odysseus, and the latter regards it as a great insult, and is quick to demonstrate that the opposite is true. In the mighty Homeric world there is no place for heroes who are not athletes.

The spreading of the competitive spirit and its connection with daily life appear also in the works of Hesiod. This poet moves in a climate different from that of Homer. A large part of his work refers to the country life and to the toils and tribulations of simple men. In his poem *Works and Days,* the impetus towards work and competition is represented by two figures — the two Strifes — the one destructive and the other creative. The first seduces men into hateful war and destruction, while the second, the good one, urges them to fruitful competition and progress. In *The Shield,* where he describes the shield of Herakles, he presents two different pictures of the city: the city in time of war, and the city in time of peace. In the peaceful city, alongside scenes of the harvest and the vintage, there are sporting scenes depicting contests in wrestling, boxing and chariot racing. For the poet, the peaceful spirit of competition finds expression both in the sporting contests and in the daily strife of the farmers against nature. For him, sport is interwoven with the joys of a peaceful life.

The scanty representations of games on Geometric vases confirm the evidence supplied by the written texts. They show scenes of wrestling, boxing and chariot racing.

At the dawn of Greek history athleticism is robust and developed to a significant degree. The intense, though balanced development that was to ensue in the Classical period had begun to appear on the horizon.

The Element of Competition in Greek Mythology

The spirit of competition, which we saw developing into a genuinely athletic ideal in the Homeric poems, is equally vigorous and widespread throughout the whole of Greek mythology. And since both the descriptions in Homer and the narratives of the myths to some degree reflect the realities of daily life, we must conclude that the spirit of competition captivated the minds and hearts of the men of the period: men projected their own longing for competition onto their gods and heroes. The *Gigantomachia,* the relentless struggle between the gods and the giants, became a symbol and a model for every conflict, particularly between Greeks and barbarians.

In the myths, the gods fight amongst themselves

11

11. Although the prizes in the great Panhellenic games consisted of a simple crown, there were prizes of great value in many of the local games. On the black-figure amphora, the winner of an athletic competition is departing with his prize, a tripod, on his shoulder (Copenhagen, Nationalmuseet).

12

13

and support mortals in their conflicts; they also compete for the right to become lord and protector of a country or a city. The most famous dispute of this nature is that between Poseidon and Athena over the patronage of the city of Athens. In the same way the heroes in the myths also reveal an intensely competitive nature. They desire to be first, to outdo the others, and to realise the ideal formulated by Hippolochos to his son Glaukos: "always to be best and excel over others" (αἰὲν ἀριστεύειν καὶ ὑπείροχον ἔμμεναι ἄλλων). This disposition finds expression in all their actions, whether they are involved in an expedition as a group, as in the expedition of the Argonauts, or whether they are benefiting men by their personal feats, like Herakles or Theseus. The inclination towards competition even extends to everyday country pursuits (ploughing, reaping, vintage). The mythical Lityerses, son of king Midas, required anyone who came to his kingdom to compete with him at reaping.

The choice of a husband is frequently decided by sporting contests in the myths. Atalanta had declared that she would marry whoever defeated her in a race. She therefore competed with the aspiring suitors and defeated them all, until Hippomenes beat her and made her his wife. Ikarios gave Penelope to Odysseus after he had first beaten the other suitors in a race. Likewise, Pelops married Oinomaos' daughter Hippodameia, after his victory in the chariot race.

In other cases, trial by a contest decided the succession to the throne. Skythes, son of Herakles and Echidna, and eponymous hero of the Skythians, ascended the throne after defeating his two other brothers at archery, in accordance with the dictates of his father.

12. The mythical wrestling match between Herakles and Antaios (Paris, Musée du Louvre).

13. Atalanta defeating Peleus in the wrestling match in the games in honour of the dead king Pelias (Munich, Antikensammlungen).

An extension and consequence of the competitive spirit is the aspiration to be "the first one," which was won by competition. Gods and heroes are depicted in mythology as "first inventors" of various features of spiritual and material culture. In the Classical period, almost every contest was believed to have had a god or a hero "inventor" — someone, that is, who discovered it and gave it to mankind. It was believed, for instance, that Jason invented the pentathlon and Apollo boxing.

It was precisely this aspiration on the part of the heroes that was chanelled into athletic competitions. In the heroic period famous contests were performed, and for a long time afterwards poets spoke with reverence of both the games and the young men who took part in them. Usually they were funeral games, like those held at Thebes after the death of Oedipus, in which Mestikeus proved himself the best competitor. The funeral games for Amarynkeus at Bouprasion in Elis were also famous; Nestor, the king of Pylos — then a young man — was victorious in four contests.

The spirit of competition, the superhuman attempt to achieve a target, a feat, by great physical and mental effort, is the dominating element in Greek mythology. The mythologising turn of thought of the Greeks elevated human competitions into the sphere of the gods, and gave them the dimensions of an ideal. It was precisely this ideal that, handed down from generation to generation, lived through the athleticism of the Classical period, and continued to the present day.

Games and Religion

Games in Greece were closely connected with religious ceremonies from early times, and formed part of the worship of the gods. Much later, from the Archaic period onwards, they underwent a gradual transformation and became genuinely sporting occasions, without, however, losing their connection with religion, in that they were held in honour of a deity. At the same time, games retained their early function within the sphere of religious custom throughout the whole of antiquity, even when they had acquired an independent existence.

Games were associated with rural religious festivals connected with the fertility of the earth, or with funerary cults, and formed part of the ritual of worship. Reflections of this initial role of the games were preserved in the rural religious festivals of the Classical period, such as the *Karneia* at Sparta, in which young men from the city, who were called *Staphylodromoi* ("Grape-runners"), ran loaded down with heavy bunches of grapes (if their pursuers succeeded in catching them, it was a sign that the year would be a good one). At the *Oschophoria* in Athens, too, youths ran holding a vine-branch, and at the *Daphnephoria* at Thebes, a wand of laurel. Indications of the relationship between games and the rural festivals may be seen in the branch used to crown the victor — wild olive in the Olympic Games, pine in the Isthmian, laurel in the Pythian, and celery in the Nemean.

According to tradition, all the great Panhellenic games were established in honour of a dead hero, or to commemorate some act by a god: Pelops founded the Olympic Games in honour of Oinomaos; Apollo established the Pythian games at Delphi after he had destroyed the dragon, Python; Theseus, or Sisyphos initiated the Isthmian games at the tomb of the hero Melikertes - Palaimon; and, finally, the Nemean games were instituted by Adrastos in honour of the hero Opheltes, son of Lykourgos the king of Nemea.

The custom of honouring dead heroes with funerary games was preserved throughout the whole of antiquity. Those who were killed in the battles of Marathon, Plataia and Leuktra were so honoured. Alexander the Great also followed this tradition and organised games after each one of his victories to express his gratitude to the gods and to honour the fallen. And just as Achilles honoured his dead friend with games, so Alexander honoured his dead friend Hephaistion by organising games on a grand scale at Babylon, in which 3,000 competitors took part.

The connection of athletic games both with funerary customs and with religious festivals soliciting the fruitfulness of the earth is due to the belief of the ancients that life and death stood in a dialectical relationship to each other: the dead earth gives birth to the new shoot, and the youths involved in the competitions draw strength from the dead heroes in whose honour they are competing. The symbol of this unbroken regeneration, of the hope born from the youthful strength of the competitors, and of the vitality and joy derived from competition, was the sacred flame of Olympia which burned unceasingly, day and night, in the Prytaneion.

The dissociation of the games from religion was not absolute, and the old connection continued to underlie them. Gradually, however, as the original function of the games receded, and their specifically sporting content came to the fore, the state took on the responsibility for organising them and making them part of the process of education. The following, typical, event at Olympia constituted a milestone in this development: the stadium, which was originally included within the *temenos* was cut off from the sanctuary in the 4th century B.C., when the stoa of Echo was constructed. This symbolic act meant that the independence of the games from religion was now a fact. Nonetheless, however much the games may have been purely sporting, they were always held in honour of a deity, and it was to this deity that the winner offered his victory.

14

14. The connection of games with funeral rites is confirmed by the custom of holding funeral games to honour dead heroes. This fragment of the Sophilos vase depicts the chariot races held before the assembled Achaians in honour of Patroklos (Athens, National Archaeological Museum).

Athletics and Education

The Institution of the Games in Ancient Greece

The Role of Athletics in the Education of the Young

Panhellenic Games

The Role of Athletics in the Education of the Young

The Competitive Spirit of the Greeks

Always to be best and excel over others.

This was Peleus' famous exhortation to his son Achilles, as he was about to set off for the Trojan war, in which he was to win glory and die. This succinct aphorism, contained in the oldest poetic text in the Greek (and European) world, is an illuminating expression of the attitude and ideals not only of the Homeric heroes, but of Greeks throughout the historic course of antiquity. In the same epic poem, the *Iliad,* the warrior heroes strive every day *to be best* in the exercise of their military skills and courage. There comes a point, however, where the poet depicts not the opposing sides in the war, but the Achaians themselves competing for the "prizes in honour of Patroklos" — that is, for victory in the athletic games organised by Achilles in honour of his dead friend. It is clear that such games were a very ancient funeral custom of the Greeks, not only from this example in Homer, but also from a whole series of games connected with the burial of mythical heroes. However, the fact that, amongst all the other funeral customs, the Greeks instituted athletic games, indicates that athletics and the spirit of competition, aimed at the victory of the best man, had their roots deep in Greek society. Additional evidence is offered by the *Odyssey,* where, in the land of the Phaiakians, a peaceful, almost blissful state, the people gather to watch a full athletic display by the youths, who are competing purely for the joy of winning.

It is not difficult to follow the traces of this competitive spirit amongst the Greeks, since it is manifested in almost every aspect of life, creating a rivalry that had rich and fruitful results, though it did not always avoid excesses and dangerous, sterile confrontations.

In the games held in honour of Patroklos, the Homeric heroes take part in contests suitable for the warlike society of an army on campaign. However, in the oldest historically attested funeral games — those performed to honour the dead Amphidamas, king of Chalkis — Hesiod won the prize for his song, and so became the first man in the history of culture and art to win victory and the prize in the field of fine arts. Competition and rivalry in the sphere of art is evidenced in a most unexpected manner by a brief inscription on a vase from the last years of the 6th century B.C., the work of the vase-painter Euthymides: *Euphronios could have never painted it like this*. Euphronios was himself a great vase-painter, and a contemporary of Euthymides, and it is to him that the phrase of his fellow-artist, so full of confidence in his own superiority, is addressed. This inscription, which has survived to us, does not reflect a personal attitude of the artist but expresses a spirit of rivalry common amongst practitioners of the same art, as attested in a very vivid manner by the ancient proverb: *The potter envies the potter*. Rivalry in the artistic field, however, was not confined to people practising the same art. In one of his most notable studies, Christos Karouzos has demonstrated that during the Archaic and early Classical periods there was conscious and intense rivalry between the poets and the craftsmen working in the representational arts, and particularly sculpture, on the question of the value and superiority of their creations. Time, says Pindar, will not succeed in destroying his poetry, as it will the works of the statue-makers (see "Athletics and Poetry").

This deeply rooted spirit of competition amongst the Greeks, which supplied the stimulus to achievements of both a warlike and peaceful nature, can be seen to manifest itself not only in their personal lives; it often takes an organised form and supplies the basis for activities and creations that have broader and more significant cultural aims. It is perhaps not widely known that the commission for the creation of important works of art was often assigned after a competition, in which leading craftsmen from different parts of the Greek world took part. A later testimony informs us that Pheidias revealed his unique abilities in a competition like this; he had calculated the optical distortion that the face of the statue of Athena would suffer when it was erected on a high pedestal, and therefore changed the proportions of it, thereby winning the admiration of the judges and the prize of victory. Copies dating from the Roman period have survived of the Amazons made by famous artists of the Classical period, including Pheidias and Polykleitos, as entries in the competition at Ephesos. Finally, we have indisputable evidence for a competition of this nature in the inscription on the base of the famous Nike of Paionios: *Paionios of Mende made it, who also made the akroteria for the temple and won the contest*.

The area, however, in which the competitive turn of mind reached its highest level and undoubtedly contributed to the creation of great works of art, was in the institution of the presentation of dramatic plays at the Dionysia in Athens. The tragic poets presented their tetralogies (three tragedies around a central theme, and one satyr play) before the whole of the Athenian people and awaited the decision of the judges as to who would win the prize. The tragedians wrote their works, with this prospect in mind, and it was after such a difficult testing that the three great tragic poets emerged.

The spirit of competition and rivalry extended to every area of Greek life and gave it a particular character. Musicians and poets, philosophers and orators, painters and sculptors, competed against each other for the "excellence" that would mark them out and bring them the victory, just as athletes competed on the track for the prize of honour. This meant that there was a dialogue and a rivalry on equal terms in every sphere of social life. Such an attitude derives basically from the essentially democratic belief that every man possesses the capacity to stand up to his fellow-man and to contest, by his worth and excellence, the honour of being the best. Over and above superiority of birth or wealth, the Greeks, who believed basically in equality of political rights, valued superiority of the body or the mind, as demonstrated and realised democratically through the contest, in which everyone could take part on equal terms and display his excellence. This is shown by the way athletes from all parts of the Greek world took part in the Panhellenic games with no discrimination on social grounds or grounds of descent, other than the requirement to be a free Greek citizen. It is further attested by the way sages and artists from the most distant areas assembled in the great centres of Hellenism, where they gained fame and honour by demonstrating their worth in the intellectual and artistic spheres.

The Education of the Young

The Homeric dictum *always to be best...,* which gives epigrammatic expression to the competitive spirit of the Greeks, is attributed by the poet to Peleus, father of Achilles. Throughout the whole of antiquity, Achilles was the ideal model of the perfect youth. His premature death, coming at the moment of his greatest glory, caused the Greeks to think of him as having an idealised and unsullied beauty — the human image of divine perfection.

This mythical forerunner may represent the archetypal youth as visualised by the aristocratic society of the Archaic period. And Peleus, the select of the gods who was deemed worthy to have an immortal Nereid as his bed-fellow, was the father that every member of such a family ought to emulate. We may therefore seek in this admirable pair of father and son the exemplar of the education that the aristocratic houses gave to their children in the Archaic period. Peleus, according to legend, entrusted the upbringing of his son to the Centaur Cheiron, a strange combination of sage, trainer, physician and musician, who nourished and exercised the body of the young Achilles, so that he would become a fearless and perfect warrior; at the same time as this training, however, the famous musician also taught him music and song.

This ideal education was practised in all the Greek cities in the Archaic period: exercise of the body, along with instrumental and vocal music, which were wonderfully combined in the dance and sometimes in sport. For the ancient Greek, the human body had an over-riding value, and in order to achieve the utmost development, harmony, and effective functioning of it, he trained it determinedly, and systematically from his early childhood. He knew very well, however, that this training was not sufficient in itself to make the youth a whole man. Other powers, which we vaguely term mental, but which for the ancient Greek were bound up with his whole being — body, mind and soul — and found their expression in music and song, completed the task of giving form to a man. In these, there is one element in common with physical exercise (and perhaps in common with the whole progress of the world): rhythm. It is for this reason that the young man learned music and song alongside the exercise of his body, in precisely the same way as the legendary Achilles. This twofold, balanced education, aimed at creating a balanced being, is reflected in the transcendental world of the gods, in the form of the brightest and purest god of all: Apollo, who is "far-shooting archer" and "lyre-player" and "leader of the Muses." These were the basic principles on which the education of the young was based at this early stage of Greek history, and despite all the variations imposed by historical changes, these principles never ceased to affect education in ancient Greece.

As is readily understandable, the educational system of a society is related to the composition of, and tendencies within, this society. After the end of the Mycenaean world, ancient Greece saw the creation of a large number of city-states with differing social structures and political systems, limited in geographical scale in a way that allowed a stronger cohesion of its citizens, and with a wide variety of population types and influences. All these city-states took the basic principles we have noted as their starting-point, and each created its own "educational system," if we may so describe the upbringing they prescribed for the development of the body and mind of the young. The ancient Greeks themselves recognised that this upbringing should be related to the social and political system of each city; or, as Aristotle expresses it epigrammatically, the young should "be educated suitably to the state." Furthermore, for a great period of time and over the greatest part of the Greek world, education was aimed at producing the good citizen. As long, therefore, as aristocratic regimes were dominant in the cities, education aimed at the preservation of the supremacy of the noble families, who were also economically the strongest, by cultivating the superiority of the body and mind of their young members. They developed physical strength and endurance by a traditional system of gymnastics, which had probably derived its origins from Crete, but had been accepted and implemented throughout Greece. Alongside this, in order to inculcate in the youth obedience

15. Kylix by the painter Douris, showing a scene in an ancient school. The teacher seated on the left is playing the flute, watched by the young pupil standing in front of him. Next to them the teacher is writing, or correcting something written by the schoolboy, on a wax tablet (West Berlin, Staatliche Museen).

16. The connection between musical education and gymnastics, which had as its aim the harmonious development of body and mind, can be seen very clearly in the scene on this red-figure skyphos. The youth, who has just come from his music lesson and is still carrying his lyre, is being greeted by the trainer, who is giving him the strigil (Berkeley, University of California, Lowie Museum of Anthropology).

15

16

to the gods, love of their country and a sense of honour and duty, they taught them to recite the Homeric poems and to sing religious hymns and martial songs to the accompaniment of the *kithara*. After 700 B.C., when the new alphabet began to spread through the Greek cities, a new branch of learning — reading and writing — was added to the educational programme. This is clear from a number of early alphabets on students' tablets uncovered by archaeological excavations. The programme nonetheless varied, as has been observed, from city to city, according to its form of government. In cities based on the ancient Dorian constitution, such as Sparta, or the Cretan cities, the state saw to it that the youth had an upbringing in keeping with the military structure and its ideals. This upbringing was based on traditional gymnastic exercises and music, which was mainly choral. A similar system must have also been used in Boiotia, for a large number of famous athletes and flute-players came from there. By contrast, in eastern Greece, on the large Aegean islands like Lesbos, and in Ionia, gymnastic exercise does not seem to have played an important part in the education of the young. There the main interest for both boys and girls, was music and poetry. A balance between, and harmonious combination of all these tendencies can be found in Classical Athens, at a happy point in its history — the period which finds its expression in the sculptural masterpieces of Pheidias, and the poetic creations of the great tragedians, and which is hymned in incomparable fashion by Thucydides in Perikles' *Funeral Speech*.

Our information about how education was organised in ancient Greece is scanty, especially for the earliest periods. It seems most likely that the responsibility for the education of the children fell upon the head of the family. There is some evidence, however, to suggest that in certain cases there were laws making the education of the young obligatory. The later historian Diodorus Siculus claims that the famous law-giver Charondas made provision for the creation of public schools in the code that he drew up for Katane. Modern historians cast doubt on this evidence, and consider it more likely that this prescription formed part, not of the Archaic code of Charondas, but of the revision of it made by Protagoras for the colony of Thourioi. There is similar uncertainty surrounding the evidence for the laws of Solon connected with schools. Nevertheless, we may conclude from the evidence of the orator Aischines and of Plato, that within his legislative innovations, Solon had included the question of the education of the young, making it an obligation for the father to train his children in music (in the broad sense attached to the word by the Greeks of the Classical period) and gymnastics. There are other references, unfortunately scattered and preserved purely by chance, to fill out this incomplete picture and convince us that a basic education was considered indispensable in ancient Greece from as early as the Archaic period, and that the provision of it was not left to the whim of the parents. We learn from Plutarch that when the Athenians deserted their city in 480 B.C. and took refuge in Troizen, this city at once made sure that the small children continued their education. Herodotus recounts an accident that befell a school on Chios and resulted in the deaths of 119 children. A few years later, according to Pausanias, 60 young pupils were crushed to death in a school in Astypalaia. At the time of the Peloponnesian war, Mykalessos, a small town in Boiotia, had a fair number of schools. During the same period the Athenians punished the Mytileneans, who had revolted against them, by forbidding them to send their children to school. These scattered references, combined with other evidence, such as the institution of ostracism by Kleisthenes, which shows that almost all Athenian citizens had to be able to write the name of the man they wished to ostracise, or at least to read it if someone else wrote it for them, lead to the conclusion that at the end of the 6th century B.C., a large proportion of the Greeks could read and write. M.P. Nilsson writes that at this period there were fewer illiterates in Athens than there were in many parts of southern Europe at the end of the 19th century.

It is impossible to form a satisfactory picture of the education of the young throughout the whole of the Greek world. However, by assembling the literary and archaeological evidence, we can shed some light on the main, vital aspects of the education of the young in the two cities that constituted the poles of attraction in the ancient world, and which present us with two opposed aspects of this world: Sparta and Athens.

Education at Sparta

It is a commonplace that from the early Archaic period the Spartan education aimed at producing the perfect warrior. From this point of view, the Spartan system was a complete success. If we reflect that in all probability the Spartans never numbered more than 5,000 men (at least in the 5th century B.C.), we can appreciate even better the perfection of their military education and organisation. This permitted them not only to survive, but to be the leading military power in the Greek world, remaining undefeated until the battle of Leuktra in 371 B.C. In this battle, the military genius of Epaminondas and the heroism of Pelopidas crushed the Spartan army, whose heavy losses included even Sparta's king, Kleombrotos. The ideal of this training is summed up in the following lines by Tyrtaios:

For 'tis a fair thing for a good man to fall and die fighting in the van for his native land

and:

I could neither call a man to mind nor put him in my tale for prowess in the race or the wrestling,... nor yet though all fame were his save of warlike strength

and:

... whom he was doing nobly and abiding in the fight for country's and children sake when fierce Ares brought him low

and:

This is the prowess each man should this day aspire to, never relaxing from war.

Although this type of education may not meet with the approval of the modern age, just as it did not meet with the approval of the other Greeks, it must, nonetheless, be assessed in the historical context of the period and the state that adopted it. Viewed in this light, the Spartan system is an improvement on the attitude of the Homeric hero, who is concerned to project his own personal worth and strives to win victory and glory for himself. The Spartan subjected his own personal ambition to the group interest, and sacrificed his personal life to ensure the survival of the city — that is, the totality of the citizens. This communal life was based, however curious it may seem, on the democratic principles of a military society, in which discipline did not involve the loss of equal status before the laws and the constitution for the free citizens, the *homoioi* (equals), as the Spartans were called.

There exists evidence, however, that permits us to go beyond this assessment and arrive at a more accurate evaluation of the Spartan education and way of life. Although the ultimate aim of the system was to produce the perfect warrior, this does not mean that the Spartans in general, and the young men in particular, were confined to the intolerable, uncultured life of an army camp. Their physical training made them into good athletes, so that they won the crown of victory from the very earliest Olympiads. The first Spartan Olympic victor known to us was Akanthos, who won the *dolichos* in the 15th Olympiad (720 B.C.); and of the 81 known Olympic victors between that date and 576 B.C., 46 were Spartans, while 21 of the 36 winners in the *stadion* came from Sparta. This could not have been due only to the athletes' physical build, but certainly presupposed correct methods of training. In this light, special significance attaches to the statement of Thucydides that the Spartans were the first to introduce two innovations in the games and the training of the athletes, which constituted fundamental features of Greek athletics: the complete nakedness of the athletes in the games, and the habit of anointing the athletes' bodies with oil. There is one further peculiarity of the Spartan education, which attests the all-embracing importance the Spartans attached to physical training and gymnastics, apart from the military advantages that this training might have served. Plutarch speaks with enthusiasm of women's athletics at Sparta, which was a curious phenomenon at the period he was writing, that is the period of Roman rule. It is an obvious inference that an institution like this could not have been created at a later period, but we also possess conclusive evidence for its antiquity in the superb bronze figurines from the Lakonian workshop in the Archaic period (first half of the 6th century B.C.), which depict young Spartan girls holding up their short athletic *chiton* with one hand as they run.

Our picture of Spartan life and education would be misleading, however, if we confined ourselves exclusively to the sphere of physical exercise and military-athletic training. Although historical factors, which cannot be discussed here, narrowed the horizons of Spartan life in the 5th century B.C., it is well-known that Archaic Sparta was a brilliant cultural centre and produced incomparable works of art. The Lakonian workshops, both of pottery and bronze sculpture, competed successfully with the most important workshops in the rest of Greece. And the fear of foreigners, which led to the famous policy of *xenelasia,* or exclusion of foreigners from Sparta from the 5th century B.C. on, is a phenomenon that cannot be observed in the Archaic period. On the contrary, in the 7th and 6th centuries B.C., Sparta was a pole of attraction for large numbers of artists and poets. It is sufficient to mention the famous Ionian craftsman Bathykles, who created the most brilliant architectural achievement in Archaic Sparta, the Throne of Amyklai, as well as the "national" poet of Sparta, Tyrtaios, and Alkman.

17

18

17. The director of the palaistra. He is holding the javelins that the javelin-throwers will use and the pick for digging the soil of the jumping-pit. A discus in its case is hanging on the wall (Hamburg, Museum für Kunst und Gewerbe).

18. After they had been exercising in the palaistra or the gymnasion, the young men scraped the oil and dust from their bodies with a special implement, the strigil. The athlete pictured on the left is cleaning the remains of dust and oil from his strigil, watched by the figure on the right (Musei Vaticani).

The presence of such outstanding poets is explicable only in terms of the existence of another side to Spartan life and education. The "musical" education of the young was cultivated alongside the physical training; as in Homeric society, here too, man's mind takes form and expression through music. Music constitutes the link between intellectual and artistic activity and the training and exercise of the body, as it connects the dance with physical exercise and the song with poetry. This excellent combination appears to have been achieved by the Spartans in the early Archaic period. According to Plutarch, Sparta was a great musical centre during the Archaic period. There, the two first schools of music developed and produced their best work. The first, which was the dominant one for most of the 7th century B.C., was that of the solo instrument or voice, which is represented by Terpandros. The second, which developed at the end of the 7th to the beginning of the 6th centuries B.C., was choral-lyric music, which produced such great names as Thaletas of Gortys, Xenodamos of Kythera, Sakadas of Argos, and others. Fame has preserved the names of these men while their works have been lost. However, in the case of two others, Tyrtaios and Alkman, we know part of their work, albeit in fragmentary form, as well as their names. The fact that both of them were foreigners, who came and produced their works in and for Sparta (works intended to be sung by young men and women), does not suggest a lack of native poets, but the importance of this Dorian state for the most famous poet-musicians at that period, and the possibilities it offered for the creation of inspired works. The attraction of Archaic Sparta was due to its religious festivals. These reflected the many-faceted education of the young, which succeeded in combining together in an indivisible unity the cultivation of the body and the mind, through the rhythm of gymnastics, dancing, music and poetry. Official processions, musical and athletic competitions, choral songs and sacred dances, all formed part of the many religious ceremonies in Archaic Sparta: at the Hyakinthia, a procession of chariots with young girls and youths mounted on horses was accompanied by songs; in the sanctuary of Artemis Orthia, young boys of from ten to twelve years competed in two music contests and in a hunting-game, the *kasseratorion;* at the Karneia, the national festival of the Dorians, slender girls, the *Karyatides* (from the town of Karyai), performed the sacred dance, which has been preserved to us on an exquisite vase-painting from the 5th century B.C.; at the famous *Gymnopaidiai,* organised by Thaletas, two choirs competed against each other, one of boys and the other of married men. All these festivals had a high artistic level, which was undoubtedly owed to the combination of gymnastic and musical education of the young, and also to the inspired composers, poets and musicians. Only fragments have been preserved of the *Parthenion* by Alkman, but they are enough for us to delight in the poetic inspiration, the grace and the beauty of youth, as the chorus of girls sings with sublime fervour of the beauty of their leaders, Agido and Agesichora. To these fragments may be added the superb lyric quality of other verses by this poet, in which the poet himself, now a mature man, asks the fresh young maidens of the chorus to take him, as the halcyons take the *kerylos* (the male halcyon), on their white wings.

19. Athletes training to the accompaniment of a flute. The youth of Athens spent the biggest part of their lives in the gymnasia, where they practised jumping, the discus, the javelin. The flute-player is accompanying the movements of the athletes to ensure that they are harmonious and rythmical (Copenhagen, Nationalmuseet).

19

This atmosphere of Archaic Sparta disappeared at the end of the 6th century B.C., and its place was taken by the well-known militaristic society. Art and poetry no longer had any place in this society; along with them, however, athletics and the free exercise of the body also lost the vital position they had occupied in education, as is shown by the lack of Spartan Olympic victors, such as had so often brought glory to Archaic Sparta in the 7th and early 6th centuries B.C.

Education in Athens

The contrast between the Athenian and the Spartan education is indicated in epigrammatic form by Perikles in his famous *Funeral Speech,* as preserved by Thucydides. In opposition to the tough, military training of the Spartans, the leader of the Athenian democracy presents the free education of his own country, which yet manages to produce good citizens, capable of defending it victoriously. This education was in total harmony with the whole system of Athenian life, of which it was an inseparable and indispensable element. The contrast between the educational systems, therefore, expresses the contrast in the political and social structure of the two cities, as they had emerged historically in the period after the end of the Mycenaean world, and most intensively from the middle of the 6th century B.C. onwards. This basic difference, which was emphasised by Perikles, had been noted by the Spartan allies, the Corinthians, in their speech shortly before the beginning of the Peloponnesian war; addressing the Spartans themselves, they observed that their institutions were old-fashioned, while those of their rivals the Athenians had been modernised, and that this naturally resulted in the superiority of the latter.

It would nonetheless be a mistake to suppose that the education of the young in Athens was based on different fundamental principles, or followed a completely different programme, or that it had a content peculiar to itself. The truth of the matter is that the main body of the Athenian educational system, as of the educational system of all the Greek cities, consisted of gymnastics and music; the addition to it of a wider "grammatical" education did not change its basic nature. The essential difference between the Athenian and the Spartan systems lay in the aims of the education of the young and the character both of the physical exercise and the musical training. The difference in education in the two cities was also determined by the atmosphere in which it was practised, by the institutions that defined it, and by the social conditions that shaped it over the long period in which it was adopted. These factors were perhaps combined with the racial substructure of the Athenian people, which led to a social and political structure fundamentally different from the Dorian. Finally, the diametrically opposed historical development of Athens and Sparta, the former advancing to an increasingly broadly based and radical democracy at a time when the latter was becoming increasingly restrictive of freedom and re-inforcing its severe military organisation, was also reflected in the development of their educational systems.

At Athens, too, the education of the young during the Archaic period had a purely aristocratic character. The noble landowners of Attica lived in a society not very different from that of the Homeric poems, and the ideals that inspired them were the ideals stemming from nobility of birth and landed property. Education, therefore, had a basically aristocratic character, and was essentially to retain this character even in the period of the democracy, since education in Greece ultimately remained a matter for the private individual; it was only the basic framework of education and the responsibilities of the citizens with regard to the upbringing of the young that were defined by the state.

Literary sources and archaeological evidence are sufficient to allow us to form a clear picture of the education of the young in Athens at every stage of its history. This picture to some extent reflects the system in most of the Greek cities, if not in its entirety or in every detail, at least in its basic constituent elements and its aims. The aim of Athenian education down to the Classical period was to instil *kalokagathia,* that is to create a man who was *kalos* (beautiful) and *agathos* (virtuous, noble). It is difficult, if not impossible, to reconstruct this ideal today, for its content is the product of a whole culture and way of life, just as it is impossible to relive the ideal of the Medieval "Knight," or to grasp all the shades of the image of the "Gentleman." Modern Greece has created its own ideal, the *palikari,* whose chief attributes of bravery and magnanimity are also contained in the ancient Greek concept of *kalokagathia.* The *kalos* was the pride and joy of Athens; everyone was in love with him, young and old, men and women; his name would become symbolic and would be written on the choicest vases by the greatest craftsmen. Onetorides *kalos,* Leagros *kalos,* Euaion *kalos,* are names that occur on a number of vases, and we know that these men were of high standing: Onetorides was *archon* (chief magistrate) in 527/6 B.C., Leagros was killed while general in 465 B.C., and Euaion was the son of Aischylos. Plato gives us a lively picture of such a character, and his dazzling effect, at the beginning of the *Charmides,* the dialogue that takes its name from one of these youths. He describes him as *pankalos* (most-beautiful), and says that the moment he entered the *palaistra,* no one could look at anything else, not even the boys, *not even the youngest of them, but they all gazed at him like a statue.* This handsome human being represented the culmination of careful cultivation over a long period of time — a cultivation which remained always restricted to an aristocracy that had the free time and the material wealth to develop and continue it for many years. For education in Athens in the Classical period began in the first years of childhood, and continued beyond adolescence for all those who were able, and willing, to complete it.

Understandably, our information about the upbringing of the young at the earliest period of Athenian history is very scanty. We may conclude, however, on the basis of archaeological evidence, that music, dance and physical exercise formed the three basic elements of Athenian education from as early as the Geometric period, and that the teaching of writing was added to this tripartite system at an early point in time. Though it is purely by chance, it is still notable that the earliest surviving Greek inscription, incised on a small Geometric vase of the 8th century B.C., is the following: *He who of all the dancers dances most lightly.* It is very probable that this small vase was presented as a prize, perhaps along with others, in a dancing competition; and it is in any event certain that the epigram praises a dancer who distinguishes himself from all the others. Two splendid Attic vases, that archaeologists believe to have been painted by the same craftsman, date from a few years later: one is the *hydria* of Analatos (named from the site at which it was found), and the other is the *loutrophoros* of the Louvre. On the neck of both of them there is a picture of young men and women dancing. The first shows two half choruses, one of young men, led by the lyre-player, and one of girls; on the second, the youths and girls alternate as they dance to the music of the flute-player. There are also somewhat earlier portrayals of the dance and lyre-players, just as there are pictures of sports, such as boxing, horse racing and chariot racing — all of which demonstrate that the youths depicted are practised in music, the dance and sport. In the case of sport, we have official and significant confirmation: in the 21st and 22nd Olympiads (696 and 692 B.C.), the Athenian Pantakles won the *stadion* race, and initiated an impressive series of Athenian Olympic victors, particularly in the foot races (672 B.C. Eurybates, *stadion;* 644 B.C. Stomas, *stadion;* 640 B.C. Kylon, *diaulos;* 636 B.C. Phrynon, *pankration,* etc.).

The knowledge of writing appears to have spread quickly throughout the Greek world, and it is no coincidence that the first examples we possess of alphabets practised by pupils, copying the models of their teacher, were again found in Attica, more precisely on Mt. Hymettos. From the end of the 8th century B.C., therefore, the upbringing of the young in Athens acquires a content, which will soon present a complete and systematic programme for their education.

Every generation of Athenians was reared basically on this programme until the Classical period in the 5th century B.C., when the new ideas of the sophists and the refutation of the "ancestral constitution" changed the nature of Athenian society and, consequently, the balance of the educational system. In their early years, the children went to schools, which were kept and exploited by private individuals, to learn reading and writing, and music. Aristophanes gives us in the *Clouds* a fine description of this traditional education, which he regards with nostalgic admiration: *Then,* he says, *you never heard a sound from the boys; they all set off early from their neighbourhoods, well-behaved, and without a cloak, even if it was snowing fast, going off to the kitharistes.* There they first learned to read and write, and also the basic elements of music. An excellent picture of a scene in one of these schools is preserved on the famous *kylix* by the painter Douris (490-480 B.C.), in the Berlin Museum. On one side are depicted, from the left: the *kitharistes* (lyre-teacher), seated with the lyre in his hand, with the young pupil sitting opposite him, also holding a lyre. Next, the *grammatistes* (teacher of letters) is seated, holding in his hand the papyrus on which an epic verse is written, while the pupil stands in front of him. On the far right, the *paidagogos* (the man who accompanies the child to school), is sitting and watching what is happening. On the other side, the teacher of the flute is sitting and playing, while the young pupil stands and watches him; next is a seated teacher, writing, or perhaps correcting something written by the pupil standing in front of him; the *paidagogos* again fol-

20

21

20. Scene from a gymnasion. The two youths are practising the javelin under the supervision of the paidotribes *(on the right), who has a peg in his hand, ready to mark their throws (Paris, Petit Palais).*

21. Two boxers practising to the accompaniment of the flute. Exercise in the gymnasion and the palaistra was often accompanied by music (New York, Metropolitan Museum).

22

22. Reconstruction of an ancient gymnasion. The young men are practising running, jumping and wrestling in the open area in the centre, accompanied by the flute. The gymnasia were much-frequented places; in addition to the youths, philosophers, orators and politicians used to gather there, because this was where they found a ready audience. Music and philosophy lessons were often held in its stoas (Reconstruction: K. Iliakis).

lows events from the side. Reading and writing, then, and song and instrumental music, were the first things the youth learnt. It is perhaps worthwhile emphasising the special significance the Greeks attached to music; musical instruments and song were used to accompany the dance, which connects man with the gods, according to Plato, and distinguishes him from the animals. *The other animals have no sense of order and disorder in movement, which we call rhythm and harmony*. This means, he continues, that the man who is *achoreutos* (not trained in the dance) is uneducated, while the educated man is one who knows how to sing and dance. However, as a result of the fact that hardly any element of the music created throughout the whole of Greek civilisation has survived, we frequently forget the important role of music — and dance — in the education of the Greeks. For the rhythm and harmony that we admire so much nowhere find such clear, lively and sensitive expression as in the sphere of music and dance.

In the light of this fundamental assumption, we can better understand the importance of gymnastics and athletic training in the education of the young in Athens. The body was exercised, originally naked under the sun or the shadow of the leaves, in contests such as wrestling, boxing, the javelin, discus, running and jumping, under the supervision of the *paidotribes* (physical trainer) and to the rhythm of flute-music. The presence of the flute-player in scenes of the *palaistra,* depicted on large numbers of Attic vases, is revealing: it attests irrefutably the essential content of physical education, which was not totally different and separate from music. The aim is the same in both cases: the teaching of rhythm and harmony. Music and song, dance and exercise are aimed at a complete education that will imbue the young man with rhythm — that is to say, will make him able to achieve the harmonious functioning, both of the body and of the soul. Within a strong and agile body with harmonious proportions and rhythmic movements, there will be cultivated a psychological attitude at once vigorous and balanced, vibrant and exhuberant, but also quiet and calm; in other words, a balance of the tendencies and drives that lead a man to action or inaction. An education and training of this sort could produce the state and the citizens hymned by Perikles: the state and citizens who "love beauty without excess, and love wisdom without being weak." And if rhythm constitutes the harmonious reconciliation of the opposing tendencies in the world and in man, then we can understand the whole point of the eulogy in the *Funeral Speech*. It is nothing less than a picture of this harmony in the social, economic, political and cultural spheres as achieved by the Athenian democracy under Perikles, which had succeeded precisely in reconciling these opposing forces that threatened, through their lack of rhythm, the balance of the citizen and the state.

This is the education described by Perikles as *a free way of living* and opposed by him to the *laborious exercise* of the Spartans, and it is this that allows him to describe Athens as the *School of Greece*. It is difficult for us today to appreciate the beauty and charm of this education, after so many centuries of a divided existence that has led us to feel scorn and shame for our body, and to separate the exercise of it from musical rhythm, from song and from poetry. Anyone wanting to find a way of coming close to that

23

23. Scene from a women's race. Women's sport was a feature of the education of girls in Sparta and Crete, which later, from the 4th century B.C. onwards, spread to other Greek cities (Musei Vaticani).

atmosphere could well start by reading the introductory chapters to some of Plato's dialogues, such as the *Lysis* or the *Charmides*, and then go on to discover the countless vase-paintings inspired by scenes of the *palaistra* (wrestling-school) and the *gymnasion* (gymnastic school) — paintings like that by Euphronios (*ca.* 500 B.C.) on the *kalyx-krater* in the Berlin Museum, or that by Douris (*ca.* 480 B.C.) on the *kylix* in the Louvre. In them can be found the visual counterpart of the rhythmical movements of the discus-thrower and the jumper, the javelin-thrower and the wrestler. Other vase-paintings show handsome youths, splendidly crowned, as they are sung by Aristophanes in the *Clouds*, anointing themselves with oil, or cleaning themselves of the dust and sweat of the exercise, folding their elegant cloaks to put them on stools, or bathing themselves to refresh their weary bodies. In many of them we can see the flute-player, accompanying the athletes, or, rather, ordering their movements, by the rhythm of his music.

This free gymnastic education required suitable areas. We saw earlier that originally these could be open spaces in a place with trees, near springs, where the coolness of the shade and the presence of water would help to refresh and clean the youths after their exercise. It appears, however, that the need for an organised form of athletic training and for the existence of suitable protected areas, soon led to the construction of buildings which attracted all the well-to-do youth of Athens. The earliest such buildings included areas for exercise, and also for sitting and waiting, rooms for changing, pits for wrestling and jumping, a running track etc. We know from the ancient authors, particularly Plato, of the names of some of the wrestling-schools of his period, such as those of Sibyrtios, of Taurias, of Mikkos, and of Hippokrates, and we may conclude that there were others in various parts of Athens, especially in the suburbs. The famous *gymnasia* of the Academy, the Lyceum and the Kynosarges appear to have been founded in Athens as early as the 6th century B.C. The gymnastic schools were not private establishments, like the wrestling-schools (though these could also be public), but were founded by and belonged to the city. It is difficult to distinguish the basic difference in function between the *palaistra* and the *gymnasion;* all we may say is that a *gymnasion* had a section that was a *palaistra*, within which there were usually to be found the facilities of an independent wrestling-school. A separate chapter is devoted to the features of the *gymnasion* and *palaistra*, in the form they took at a late period in the sanctuary at Olympia. It will suffice here to refer to those parts of a *gymnasion* that were necessary for the young men to exercise. These were: 1) An open track for running practice, and also a covered track, called the *xystos*. 2) In the interior, amongst the stoas, there was an open space for practising the javelin, discus and so on. 3) The *palaistra*, a rectangular, colonnaded building with areas for training in wrestling, boxing, jumping etc. — such as the *korykeion* (room for the exercise with a punching-bag) — and other areas in which the body could be looked after — such as the *elaiothesion* (oiling-room), *konisterion* (dusting-room), *loutron* (baths) etc.

The youths of Athens spent the biggest part of their childhood and adolescence in the *gymnasia*, which were also frequented by older men. In the *gymnasia,* for example, we meet Sokrates in conversation with the young men immortalised in Plato's dialogues. The opening of the dialogue already mentioned, the *Lysis,* is typical: Sokrates is speaking: *I was making my way from the Academy straight to the Lyceum, by the road outside the town wall, — just under the wall; and when I reached the little gate that leads to the spring of Panops, I chanced there upon Hippothales, son of Hieronymos, and Ktesippos of Paiania, and some other youths with them, standing in a group together.* The group of young men invite him to go with them to the wrestling-school of Mikkos, which had just been built. *We pass our time there, he went on; not only we ourselves, but others besides, — a great many, and handsome.* It was there that the sophists found their audience, and the enlightenment of the 5th century B.C., which left its mark on the whole of Greek civilisation from that time onwards, began in the *gymnasia* of Athens. The two famous *gymnasia,* the Academy and the Lyceum, were the two great cultural centres in which Plato and Aristotle taught, thereby turning them into the two greatest philosophical schools in ancient Greece, which determined definitively the course of the philosophical thought of the whole of Europe to the present day.

The *gymnasia* underwent impressive development from the 4th century B.C. on, and especially in the Hellenistic world. Though they at all times retained their fundamental nature as places where the young men practised gymnastic exercises and competition, they increasingly acquired features connected with cultural education, such as libraries and lecture rooms. They, therefore, correctly give their name to the institution that is today called "Gymnasium" by European peoples, who have forgotten the etymology and original meaning of the word, which means the place where the young men exercise naked *(gymnos).* From the 3rd century on, there were *gymnasia* in all the Greek cities, functioning under strict rules and the close surveillance of the state. Special laws determined the programme of lessons and exercises as well as the games, the fees, the penalties, the prizes and every other detail of the working of the *gymnasia.* The basic nature of education had undergone a radical change, however, and the symmetrical and harmonious training of the body and the mind had lost its balance and its aims.

It is manifest that the kind of education, of which we have tried to give a brief picture in the preceding pages, is aimed at the creation of free citizens rather than the training of warriors. Any state, however, is obliged to attend to its military needs, even when its aim is only defence. And as we know, at many stages of its history, Athens did not confine itself simply to a defensive policy, but attempted to impose its authority far beyond the boundaries of Attica. We also know that the Athenian hoplites were numerous, and apparently good fighters. The information at our disposal allows us to form a definite picture of the military service by young men from their 18th to their 20th year, from the second half of the 4th century B.C. on, when the well-known institution of the *ephebeia* was established on a systematic basis. During these two years they were trained as hoplites, and performed guard duties on the borders of Attica. At the end of the first year of this service, they swore the famous young men's oath which has been preserved. An institution like this must have existed at a much earlier period, al-

24-25. Two reliefs from the western side of the Parthenon frieze depicting horsemen in the Panathenaic procession. The riders who took part in this, the greatest festival of the city, were the Athenian youths, raised in the gymnasia and the wrestling schools, and practised in music and athletics (In situ).

25

beit in a less defined form, and must be given its place within the whole framework of the upbringing of an Athenian citizen. It should also be added that, even though the whole educational system in Athens required considerable expenditure and was thus, in its complete form, restricted to the well-to-do classes, there was one further form of exercise and physical training that was confined to the very wealthy: exercise in horsemanship — the pride and joy, and even obsession, of aristocratic circles, satirised so delightfully by Aristophanes in his *Clouds*. To complete this picture of the aristocratic youth, mention should be made of his interest in hunting, particularly from horseback — an interest that may be reconstructed from a reading of the *Kynegetikos* by Xenophon, the typical representative of the class of big landowners.

The Panathenaia

The young men of Athens had the opportunity to demonstrate the results of their training — their ability in athletic contests, in song and in music, their beauty and prowess — in the great festival of the city, the *Panathenaia*. This festival, which must have had a very ancient origin, was celebrated in honour of the tutelary goddess of the city, Athena, on her birthday, the 28th of the month of *Hekatombaion* — that is, in the middle of summer (July-August). The festival was held every year; but

26. Panathenaic amphora from the 4th century B.C. The winners in the Panathenaic games received as their prize amphoras depicting Athena Promachos on one side, and the event in which they had been victorious on the other (Athens, National Archaeological Museum).

from 566/5 B.C., in Peisistratos' time, a four-yearly festival (held in the 3rd year of each Olympiad) was established, called the *Great Panathenaia*. Gymnic games were held at the *Panathenaia*. Peisistratos, as part of his splendid reorganisation of the festival programme, added competitions for *rhapsodoi* (reciters of epic poetry), and the first codification of the Homeric poems is attributed to this innovation. Perikles strengthened the musical competitions even more, and built his famous *Odeion,* next to the theatre of Dionysos, to hold them. He also built the most admired temple in the ancient world, the Parthenon. The games and the procession were organised by ten *athlothetai* (games-organisers) who were chosen four years previously. They were responsible for the preparation of the wonderful *peplos* (robe) which was woven over the four years by selected Athenian girls, and which always portrayed Athena in the battle of the gods and the giants. They were also responsible for ordering the Panathenaic amphoras and filling them with oil from the sacred olives of Athena. The festival began with the games on the 21st of *Hekatombaion;* the earliest contests were the chariot races, but in the Classical period these had been replaced by horse races. Six boys' and nine men's events were held over two days. The prizes for these games were the Panathenaic amphoras, depicting Athena *Promachos* on one side, and on the other, the contest in which the recipient of the amphora had been victorious. The backs of the Panathenaic amphoras thus present a full picture of the sports from 566 B.C. until the end of the ancient world. The remaining days were devoted to contests in the *pyrrhiche* (a war-dance executed in armour), and displays and contests of physical fitness. The musical competitions were of two kinds: the recitation of epic poetry, and music contests proper — that is, the singing of lyric poetry to the accompaniment of the *kithara* or the flute. These take us to the night of the 27th to 28th of *Hekatombaion,* the "sacred vigil." The torch-races and the songs helped to prepare the Athenian people, who stayed up all night waiting for the great day of the procession. The sacred procession unwound from the Dipylon gate in the Kerameikos: at its head were the *athlothetai,* followed by the *archontes* (chief magistrates), the *prytaneis* (presidents at the Assembly or the Council) and the councillors, the generals, the infantry officers, the cavalry officers, the heads of the tribes, the hoplites, the horsemen, and the charioteers. Afterwards came the sacred ship with the *peplos* spread out on its mast, so that the people could take pride in the design, with their beloved goddess. Then came the gift-bearers, followed by the sacrificial animals. The procession advanced through the Agora, ascended towards the Eleusinion, passed in front of the Areopagos, reached the Propylaia, and entered the sacred area of the Acropolis. It was this majestic procession that Pheidias sought to capture in marble in the Parthenon frieze, in order to preserve for ever an unrivalled picture of the Athenian people at its most brilliant hour. And the crowning glory of this people were its young scions that we see riding with solemn pride upon the marble slabs — the youths who had been reared in the *palaistrai* and the *gymnasia,* and trained in music and dance and gymnastic games. The Athenian state was proud of its educational system, and immortalised it in their persons through the hand of its greatest creative artist.

Panhellenic Games

Introduction

We saw in the preceding chapter the vital role played by gymnastics and exercise in Athenian education. The educational system in all the Greek cities must have been similar, judging from scattered references, and also the countless Hellenistic *gymnasia,* which must have been continuing an older tradition. We are quite well informed about the functioning of the Hellenistic *gymnasia,* partly from the literary sources, but mainly from the evidence of the inscriptions. These tell us that at the end of the school year, gymnastic and musical competitions were held in the *gymnasia;* these must have been important festivals for the whole of the city, because the names of the winners were very often inscribed on honorific *stelai* that were set up not only inside the *gymnasia* themselves, but also in other public places. It seems to have been canonical to hold games during the course of the year, and there are even cases referring to games being held every month or more frequently. We have every reason to suppose that these games were not an innovation of the Hellenistic period but continued an older tradition of the *gymnasion* programme. This means that in every Greek city, athletic games were a part of life, in which the young men had the opportunity to display their athletic and musical prowess and to compete for the honour of victory. Apart from this, however, we know that the youths from one *gymnasion* would go to neighbouring cities to take part in the games held there, and so compete with the best young men from another city. This feature will not have been confined to the Hellenistic period, nor to the pupils of a *gymnasion*. Participation in the games of another city must have been quite usual throughout the Greek world — as usual as the movement of, and competition between, artists and men of culture. We can thus understand the institution of games on a Panhellenic scale. It was only natural that the games held in areas or sanctuaries that had great renown and were centres of attraction, should go beyond the bounds of the purely local and acquire Panhellenic importance.

The most brilliant of these, "shining like the sun in the empty sky," as Pindar was to say, were the Olympic Games. Alongside them, however, there were others that also had a Panhellenic character: the Pythian games at Delphi, the Isthmian games at the Isthmus, and the Nemean games at Nemea.

The Pythian Games

The Delphic tradition has it that the founder of the Pythian games was the god of the sanctuary himself, Apollo, who instituted them after he had slain the terrible serpent there, the Python. The tradition also knew that the first contest was a musical one — the performance of a melody for the lyre as an accompaniment to epic texts praising the god — and that the first winner of it was Chrysothemis of Crete, son of the priest Karmanor, who had performed the purification of Apollo after the pollution of the murder. The earliest Pythian games were musical, then, and were held every eight years. The first reorganisation of the games is attributed to the tyrant Kleisthenes of Sikyon, and occurred after the first Sacred War. At that date (582 B.C.) a contest for the flute

27

was added, and also gymnastic games, on the model of those at Olympia; of the Olympic programme, the four-horse chariot race was not included, and in addition, there was a *dolichos* and *diaulos* for boys (the four-horse chariot race was added later). From this period, the Pythian games were held every four years, in the third year of the Olympiad and in the month of *Boukation* (August-September). At an earlier period, the athletes competed in the plain of Krisa, but towards the end of the 5th century, when the stadium was constructed above the sanctuary of Apollo, the games were held there. The prize was a crown of laurel, the tree sacred to the god.

The fact that people from all over Greece took part in the Pythian games is attested by the surviving bases of the statues of winners, by the Pythian odes of Pindar, by the victors referred to by Pausanias, and also by the imaginary chariot race, described in gripping fashion by the *paidagogos* in Sophokles' *Elektra,* in which he speaks of ten charioteers from as many different areas in Greece. The superb description by the poet shows that he had an actual chariot race in mind, with all its dramatic stages and unavoidable accidents. We may also surmise that a description like this would bring to life for the hearers races of which they had personal experience.

In the chapter "Athletics and Art" the reader will find a brief account of two famous sculptures discovered at Delphi, depicting victors in the Pythian games and dedicated to the god after the victory: the

27. The Charioteer of Delphi stood in a four-horse chariot dedicated by Polyzalos, the tyrant of Gela, after his victory in the Pythian games (Delphi, Archaeological Museum).

first is the Charioteer, dedicated by the tyrant of Gela, Polyzalos, and the second the dedication of Daochos of Thessaly.

The Pythian games had a long history, and continued to be held until the end of antiquity, with varying degrees of splendour according to the fluctuating fortunes of the Delphic sanctuary, which had many adventures and suffered hard times. Their end came, officially and decisively, with the famous edict of the emperor Theodosius in A.D. 394, which was the death warrant of the ancient Greek world.

The Isthmian Games

The Panhellenic nature of the Pythian games and the brilliance surrounding them derived from the importance and fame of the sanctuary at Delphi. However, amongst the Panhellenic games, they were not able to hold a position second in importance to the Olympic Games, for this honour was claimed by the Isthmian games which were held at the Isthmus, at the sanctuary of Poseidon. The reason for this is to be sought in their geographical location, next to the great trading centre of Corinth, and in the numerous festivals celebrated in connection with them. One tradition attributes the foundation of them to Theseus, a fact which is perhaps to be explained in terms of the interest, and mass participation, of the Athenians in them. The other tradi-

28

28. Aerial photograph of Delphi. The equestrian and athletics events were originally held outside the sanctuary in the plain of Krisa. After the construction of the stadium above the sanctuary in the second half of the 5th century B.C., the athletics events were held there.

tion, however, that their founder was Sisyphos, who instituted them as funeral games in honour of the hero Melikertes - Palaimon, is nearer the truth, for we know from literary sources and archaeological evidence alike that the games were dedicated to Poseidon and the hero Melikertes - Palaimon. The American archaeologist O. Broneer, who excavated the area, discovered the oldest temple of Poseidon (*ca.* 700 B.C.) and the site of the earliest stadium, which was on the site of the later temple of Palaimon.

The Isthmian games appear originally to have had a local character. Their reorganisation (somewhere between 582-570 B.C.) and Panhellenic nature was due to the Kypselidai, the tyrants of Corinth, which is why the Corinthians retained a hold on the organisation of them. The games were held in the stadium mentioned above until the beginning of the 4th century B.C., when a new one was built, 27 m. broad, and 600 Doric feet long. The games programme included the usual Olympic contests — running, jumping, throwing, *pentathlon, pankration* — and, particularly important, the equestrian events and the chariot races. In addition to the athletic contests, the Isthmian games also included competitions in music, recitation and painting, the last being symbolic of the place occupied by Corinth in ancient Greek painting, of which, according to tradition, it was the home country. The Isthmian games were held every two years, in the 2nd and 4th years of the Olympiad, and the prize was a crown of pine in the early period, and later a crown of celery. The importance of the Isthmian games may be deduced from the fact that while they were being held, the "Isthmian truce" was in force between the Corinthians and the rest of the Greeks, as can be inferred from Thucydides. The Isthmian games were linked with the fortunes of Corinth until that city was destroyed in 146 B.C., when the responsibility for holding them was assumed by Sikyon. Corinth resumed responsibility for the games after its reconstruction in 46 B.C. This link between Corinth and the games accounts both for their Panhellenic importance, and for the choice of Corinth as the scene of the most important gatherings of all the Greeks in history, such as the assembling of the Greeks in 480 B.C., to face the Persian menace, the summoning by Philip of a Panhellenic congress in 338/7 B.C., to decide on the question of attacking Persia, and the meeting of the Greeks two years later (336 B.C.), to proclaim Alexander leader of the expedition against the Persians; and also the "proclamation of the freedom" of the Greeks at Corinth by T. Quinctius Flamininus in 196/5 B.C.

The Nemean Games

The Panhellenic character of the Nemean (or Nemeian) games, held every two years in the valley of Nemea, between Phlious and Kleonai, seems inexplicable. The Parian Marble places the beginning of the games in 1251 B.C., while ancient tradition associated it either with the funeral games in honour of the "Seven against Thebes," or more specifically with Adrastos and Amphiaraos, or even Opheltes. Another tradition connects them with Herakles and the myth of the Nemean lion. The view that the origin of these games also must have been connected with funeral games finds support in the fact that when the *Hellanodikai* presided over them, they wore mourning dress. Ancient sources, however, give 573 B.C. as the first year of the games, and claim that the main deity of them was

Zeus, to whom a shrine, and subsequently a temple existed in the area. Prior to the Hellenistic period the Nemean games did not include musical contests, and the athletic programme was restricted to some of the games: the *stadion, dolichos, diaulos,* wrestling, *pankration, pentathlon,* and also the *hippios,* race in armour and chariot race. It is thus clear that they were the least important of the Panhellenic games, though this does not mean that they were not attended by large numbers of famous athletes.

The Panhellenic Games and Greek National Consciousness

It would be a serious omission to close this chapter without emphasising the importance of the Panhellenic games for Greek national consciousness. From a strictly academic point of view, the usage of the terms "national" and "national consciousness" is an error, or at least a historical anachronism, since it is well known that the concept of "nation," as we understand it today, cannot be referred to periods preceding the creation of the modern nations — that is, to periods earlier than modern European history. Nonetheless, if by the concept of nation we mean the awareness of the cohesive unity of a people and its difference from other peoples contemporary with it and surrounding it, then we have to accept that the ancient Greeks undoubtedly possessed this consciousness in an intense form. It found negative expression in the way they contrasted themselves with

29

29. Scene depicting a singing competition. The flute-player and singer are on a podium. In addition to singing to the flute, the musical contests in the Pythian games included singing to the kithara, and lyre- and flute-playing (New York, Metropolitan Museum).

peoples that they called "barbarians." Apart from this negative distinction, however, they had an awareness of the positive features that bound them together in a community which had close, indissoluble ties. The belief in a common racial origin, which is expressed in many ways and takes shape in the genealogical myths, being traced to the original forefather of the Greeks, Hellen, the son of Deukalion (the Noah of Greek mythology), is the first, and for the Greeks, the most important of these features. A second, equally strong, element was the common language that distinguished them from all the "barbarians," and a third was their common gods and cults, or "Common Altars" as the Greeks described them. The fortunes of history scattered the Greeks from a very early point in time to regions far removed from each other. From northern Greece, where the Macedonians remained (the "Dorian nation," as Herodotos calls it), to Crete and Africa, and from Asia Minor to the Ionian islands and later to Italy, they lived separated from each other, with their particular local character, their differences of dialect, the variations in the form of their alphabet and their culture, their special local deities and cults, their own particular interests, and very often with their differences and enmities that were on occasion fatal and unbridgeable. It would be difficult for a Macedonian, for example, in the 5th century, to feel at ease alongside a Milesian or a Syracusan, for an Athenian alongside an Akarnanian or an Epirote, for a colonist from Cyrene to feel friendship for a Perrhaibian or a Magnesian. One might claim that the distances, which were enormous for that period, the differences of geographical climate, and alien influences of all kinds would have succeeded in fragmenting the "Greek nation" into countless national groups with no link or sense of cohesion between them, but perhaps retaining the memory of a common descent in the distant past, that was rather uncertain and insignificant in terms of historical reality. This was not the case, however.

This is not the place to go into a detailed documented historical analysis. We can only remark and emphasise the importance to the ancient Greek world of the Panhellenic games, in the area of what we are calling national consciousness. That this verdict is neither arbitrary nor historically anachronistic, is demonstrated in the best possible manner by a number of ancient writers, who were aware of the importance of the "national" unity of the Greeks, and also of the value of the Panhellenic games in strengthening the centripetal spirit of which they were an expression. Isokrates, in his *Panegyrikos* writes: *Now the founders of our great festivals are justly praised for handing down to us a custom by which, having proclaimed a truce and resolved our pending quarrels, we come together in one place, where, as we make our prayers and sacrifices in common, we are reminded of the kinship which exists among us and are made to feel more kindly towards each other for the future, reviving our old friendships and establishing new ties. And neither to the common men nor to those of superior gifts is the time so spent idle and profitless, but in the concourse of the Hellenes the latter have the opportunity to display their prowess, the former to behold these contending against each other in the games; and no one lacks zest for the festival, but all find in it that which flatters their pride, the spectators when they see the athletes exert themselves for their benefit, the ath-*

letes when they reflect that all the world is come to gaze upon them.

The Panhellenic views of Isokrates are well-known, as is his famous dictum, a few paragraphs after the passage quoted, which attributes the concept of Hellenism not to any "common nature" of the Greeks, but to their common culture. *The title "Hellenes" is applied rather to those who share our culture than to those who share a common blood.* This speech was written by Isokrates to be delivered at a Panhellenic gathering at Olympia, just as his teacher Gorgias had done before 408 B.C., and just as Lysias did in his own time, when he delivered his Olympic speech before the Panhellenes assembled at Olympia in 388 B.C.

All Greeks, and only Greeks, could take part in all the Panhellenic games. This fact alone gave the games a national character and elevated them above the narrow context of the cities, giving the Greeks the opportunity to become conscious of their kinship, or what we today would call their national unity. Herodotos tells the famous story of the Macedonian king Alexandros I, who came to Olympia to compete. The Greeks, who had objections to this, claimed: *The contest is open not to barbarians but to Greeks.* Alexandros, however, demonstrated his Greek descent to the satisfaction of the *Hellanodikai,* and was able to compete in the *stadion,* where he finished with the same time as the winner.

If one refers to the list of Olympic victors, one becomes aware of the broad spectrum from which they were descended, and understands the importance for the consolidation of their national consciousness of the meeting together and competing together of all these Greeks whose fate had scattered them to the ends of the earth. It is difficult for us today to imagine the unique and moving 76th Olympiad (476 B.C.), when thousands of Greeks saw Themistokles — the victor of Salamis and the man who had defeated the Persians — as he went into the Altis. Plutarch relates how the crowds forgot the athletes and the games for the whole of the day, in order to cheer the victor of the most glorious Greek contest — that described by Aischylos as "a struggle for everything."

We have little evidence for the other Panhellenic games, and we do not know the names or cities of most of the winners. We may conclude, however, from the epinician odes of Pindar that it was customary for athletes from the most distant regions to take part in them. All are present, from the Sicilian rulers, who won the difficult equestrian competitions, and from the wealthy Cyrenians who competed with them, to the Thessalians, the Thebans, the Aiginetans and the Athenians — even distant Tenedos is glorified in the *11th Nemean Ode.*

At these Panhellenic gatherings, athletics and music delighted the hearts of the Greeks and reminded them of their ancient roots. Their wise men came to win glory and praise and to speak to them of their past and their future. Here the Greeks forgot their own particular city and all that divided them; full of elation, they lived a common life, albeit ephemeral, and began to speak of a broad motherland without borders but bounded only by the hearts of men. At Olympia, Delphi, the Isthmus and Nemea, the small countries became fused into one, which the Hellenes, without knowing its borders — for no one could draw them at that time — called by their common name, Hellas.

The Olympic Games in Ancient Greece

The Importance and Prestige of the Games

There was no religious festival and no great sanctuary in Greece that did not link worship of the gods with the holding of games. Indeed, the first competitive areas were the forecourts and surrounding areas of the temples, with the gods as the main spectators.

The Games at Olympia, however, were the most important and most ancient of all: *we may sing of no contest greater than Olympia,* says Pindar in his *1st Olympian Ode,* and continues: *just as water is the most precious of all the elements, just as gold is the most valuable of all goods, and just as the sun shines brighter than any other star, so shines Olympia, putting all other games into the shade.*

The sanctuary of Olympia became great and imposed its authority throughout the Greek world, despite its isolated position in the extreme west of the Peloponnese, between the difficult mountains of Arkadia and the inhospitable coast of the Ionian sea. It flourished far from the great centres of Greece, in the territory of Elis, which played an insignificant political and military role in the troubled history of antiquity: a triumph of the spirit over geographical and political factors. Initially being both a centre for competitions and an oracle, Olympia, as though by tacit agreement with Delphi, ultimately retained the former as its main activity, leaving the latter to Delphi. From that point until the end of antiquity, as was appropriate for two spiritual centres, there was a very close and creative cooperation and reciprocity between these two sanctuaries, and also all the others. The sanctuary of Olympia preserved as its main mission the cultivation of the spirit of competition, of contest in life, while Delphi and the Mysteries opened for man the way towards the realisation of a higher life.

Already at the dawn of history, from 776 B.C., the

30

year of the first Olympiad — some two hundred years before the establishing of the other Panhellenic games — the sanctuary of Olympia had a Panhellenic character, and its authority spread rapidly in the East and the West. Its laws and regulations were accepted throughout Greece from the early Archaic period, and continued through the whole of antiquity to be respected by individuals and states, even by the strongest in the ancient world.

The sacred truce was in force for some time before and after the Games, and all military conflict and hostilities were forbidden, as was the entry of an army or armed individuals into Elis, since its territory was recognised by the whole of Greece as sacred and inviolable (see "The Institution of the Truce"). The ancient sources make it clear, moreover, that throughout the more than one thousand years of the life of the sanctuary, there were few instances of athletes attempting to flout the severe regulations governing the Games, and that even when they did, they did not dare to refuse to conform with the prescribed penalties (see "Rules of the Competitions"). Cities and individual citizens vied with each other as to who could demonstrate more eloquently their respect for the gods of Olympia. This emerges clearly from the countless statues and other dedications in the sanctuary, as well as the "treasuries" — the temple-shaped buildings at the foot of Kronion — that large numbers of Greek cities erected in the Altis, in order to secure the favour of the gods (see "The Sanctuary of Olympia"). Every Greek city was so ambitious to claim as many Olympic victors as it could, that it passed laws and regulations designed to direct the citizens into athletics (see "Honours Conferred by the city").

Alongside the Games for men, Panhellenic games for girls were held every four years at Olympia. Greek thought gave an honoured position to women, and could not ignore them at Olympia. According to one tradition, the *Heraia,* as these games were called, were instituted in honour of Hera, by Hippodameia after her marriage with Pelops. Another tradition suggests that they were founded by the council of the sixteen venerable women of Elis who, during the 6th century B.C., undertook to bring peace to the land of the Eleans.

The competitors in the events were not concerned with improving record performances by developing one particular physical ability at the expense of the others. It is for precisely this reason that ancient evidence about the performances of the athletes is scanty and incidental. The title of "first amongst the best" was enough to ensure that the victor was covered with the greatest honour and glory. It was for the same reason that the pentathlon, which led to a balanced development of all the limbs and powers of the body, was regarded by the Greeks as the ideal contest.

The main contests at Olympia in historic times were based on mythical games which formed their divine-heroic model. The assimilation of man with the gods and heroes who founded the Games, was the main vocation of the sanctuary of Olympia, as it was of the other Greek sanctuaries. Their spiritual task was to teach that it was only through the contest that man could succeed in freeing himself from the "bestial life," in awakening and developing the inexhaustible mental and physical powers and qualities with which nature had endowed him, in becom-

30. Apollo, the central figure on the west pediment of the great temple of Zeus (Olympia, Archaeological Museum).

ing free. The Games in the sanctuary, therefore, were not simply a spectacle, but a religious ritual, especially as gymnastics and music, as Plato said, were gifts from the gods.

The Olympic victors in some way shared in the divine splendour and the timeless life of the first mythical victors, and for this reason many of them were worshipped as heroes after their death in their native cities. Victory in the Games was the highest good and the highest honour to which a mortal could attain: *only the brazen heaven is inaccessible to him,* says Pindar of the Olympic victor Phrikias of Thessaly. To Psaumis of Kamarina he writes: *Do not aim at all good things; do not try to become a god,* advising him to avoid falling into the trap of conceit. The Games laid the foundation for the ideal of noble rivalry, which was to form the basis of the education of the young in all Greek cities, and supply the motive for the cultivation and greatest possible development of the physical, spiritual and intellectual abilities of man. No other people, before or after the Greeks, ever set themselves such a target, with such single-mindedness and intenseness of purpose. And for no other people did the prize for this ideal, the crown of victory, remain so steadfastly the highest good that the gods could bestow upon a man, amongst all the treasures of the world. The element of competition was a fundamental factor in the forming of Greek culture as a whole, because it was responsible for every important achievement not only in athletics, but also in literature, in art, in politics and in every other area of life.

The sense and the need for competition, both in daily life and at the important moments for the Greeks, was so deep and direct, that *Agon* (Contest) had already assumed a concrete form by the beginning of the 5th century B.C., and a statue of him holding jumping-weights in his hands was set up in the sanctuary at Olympia. There was also a representation of him, in relief, on the gold and ivory table on which the crowns intended for the Olympic victors were laid. The coins of Peparethos (modern Skopelos), dated to 500-480 B.C., also had a picture of *Agon*.

Nike (Victory) was also a concrete, tangible figure for the Greeks. The innumerable portrayals of the goddess in works of sculpture and painting clearly reveal that she was ever-present in the thoughts and the hearts of the Greeks.

Unity and peace, which the Greek world dreamed of and strove to attain, were realised within the Greek sanctuaries, and especially the sanctuary at Olympia, which were also centres for competition. As long as the sacred truce lasted, the Greeks put aside their disputes and devoted themselves to peaceful activities under the protection of the invisibly present gods. Disruptive rivalry and mutual hostility gave way for a short time to noble and constructive competition. During this period men of wisdom and letters had the opportunity to read their works at Olympia and urge the Greeks to live in harmony (see "The Panhellenic Games and Greek National Consciousness". And this is the great contribution of the sanctuary of Olympia. Within it the Greeks became aware of their spiritual unity, over and above the particular differences separating them. Olympia did not, of course, lead Greece to political unity, but it achieved something more important: the general acceptance and crystallisation of the common features of the Greek spirit, in spite of the opposition, rivalry and fragmentation of the Greeks in their hostile, isolated cities.

The Greeks attached so much importance to these Games that even in the dark days preceding the great clash with the Persians, in 480 B.C., while Leonidas and the three hundred were falling at Thermopylai rather than forsaking their stand, the rest of the Greeks were gathered at Olympia for the 75th Olympiad, and carrying on with the Games. According to the narrative of Herodotos, this circumstance, together with the fact that the prize for victory was simply a crown of wild olive, made such an impression in the entourage of the Persian king that one of the officers called out to Mardonius: "Mardonius, what kind of men are these that you are leading us against, who compete not for gold, but simply for glory."

It was at Olympia and the other sanctuaries, then, that the heroes of Thermopylai, Marathon, Salamis, and Plataia were formed, and the victory of the Greeks over the Persians is represented as an Olympic victory, as the Olympic victory par excellence. This is why the first Olympiad after the Persian wars, in 476 B.C., was celebrated with even more brilliance than usual. At this moment, the happiest in the history of Greece and the most brilliant in the history of the sanctuary, the Greeks again assembled at Olympia, their faith in the gods and the ideal of competition between free men even greater than before. Amongst them was the prime architect of the victory, Themistokles. He was cheered in the stadium like an Olympic victor, and Plutarch tells us that the spectators had their eyes turned to him throughout the day, forgetful of the competitors.

31. The Nike by Paionios was dedicated by the Messenians and the Naupaktians. The goddess has her wings open and her dress spread out, and is descending from heaven to earth (Olympia, Archaeological Museum).

Origin and History of the Games

The beginnings of the Olympic Games are lost in remote prehistory, and connected with contests between gods and heroes. According to the ancient tradition, the gods and heroes were the first to compete here, and served as models for human beings, who continued the noble exercise until the late Roman period. It was here that Zeus humbled Kronos in wrestling, and that Apollo outran Hermes and out-boxed Ares. The obscure cult of Demeter Chamyne must also have been connected with games, which explains why her altar stood in the stadium and why her priestess was the only woman who had the right to attend the Games.

Many heroes are cited in the ancient sources as founders of the Games, amongst them Pelops, who first held the chariot race, as a thanks offering to the gods for his victory over Oinomaos; another version suggests that he instituted it as a funerary game in honour of Oinomaos, in order to be purified of his death. It was also in memory of the victory of Pelops that Hippodameia instituted the *Heraia,* the foot-race for girls, after her marriage to the victor. Idaian Herakles, who was the first to define the length of the stadium at Olympia, had his brothers, the Kouretes, race against each other, and afterwards awarded the winner a crown of wild olive. Theban Herakles, who brought the wild olive from the land of the Hyperboreans and planted it at Olympia, introduced the worship of Pelops there, according to Pindar, and instituted not only athletic events, but chariot races too. The institution of the Games is also attributed to Neleus, to Pelias, and to the kings of Elis. All these legends may be ascribed to the respective cults of the different tribes that dominated Olympia in various periods. Pisos, finally, the eponymous hero of Pisa and the main representative of the rival Pisatan tradition, is also claimed as founder of the Olympic Games.

The more rational Strabo places no faith in the mythical traditions, and believes the Games were organised by the Herakleidai after their descent and the spread of the Aitolo-dorian tribes and the Epeans to Pisa. This view of Strabo is nearer the truth, for the Games in the sanctuary at Olympia, which were originally local in character, seem to have been re-organised after the Dorian invasion, when the older cults that had existed in the sanctuary were displaced or restricted, and the worship of Olympian Zeus, as the supreme deity, was instituted. Oxylos, the leader of the Aitolo-dorian tribes that came to Elis, is said to have been the founder of these new Games, and his descendant Iphitos is said to have re-organised them. Oxylos unified the settlements around Elis and created a strong state, which extended its authority over the neighbouring statelets that composed Pisa, and took in also the sanctuary at Olympia. Lykourgos, king of Sparta, also collaborated in the renovation of the Games, as recorded in the inscription of the truce for the Olympic Games, engraved on the bronze discus whose historicity is confirmed by Aristotle. The re-organisation of the Games was connected with the sacred truce, which found Panhellenic acceptance, thanks to the intervention of the Delphic sanctuary. According to Phlegon of Tralles, Kleosthenes, the king of Pisa, also helped towards securing the general acceptance of the truce.

From 776 B.C. until the 13th Olympiad (728 B.C.), the *stadion* or single-course race was the only contest held at the sanctuary, and the Games lasted one day. New competitions gradually began to be added in the following Olympiads, but the *stadion* race con-

32. The abduction of Hippodameia by Pelops in his chariot. Tradition ascribed the origins of the chariot races to the games organised by Pelops after he had defeated Oinomaos (Arezzo, Museo Archeologico).

32

tinued to be the main event at Olympia, and right until the end it was the winner in this that gave his name to the Olympiad.

The other contests were introduced in the following order:

14th Olympiad (724 B.C.): *diaulos* (double-course race)
15th Olympiad (720 B.C.): *dolichos* (long-course race)
18th Olympiad (708 B.C.): *pentathlon* and wrestling
23rd Olympiad (688 B.C.): boxing
25th Olympiad (680 B.C.): *tethrippon* (four-horse chariot race)
33rd Olympiad (648 B.C.): horse race and *pankration* (combination of boxing and wrestling)
37th Olympiad (632 B.C.): boys' foot-race and wrestling
38th Olympiad (628 B.C.): boys' *pentathlon* (only for this Olympiad)
41st Olympiad (616 B.C.): boys' boxing
65th Olympiad (520 B.C.): race in armour
70th Olympiad (500 B.C.): *apene* (race of chariots drawn by two mules) (abandoned in the 84th Olympiad)
93rd Olympiad (408 B.C.): *synoris* (two-horse chariot race)
96th Olympiad (396 B.C.): competitions for trumpeters and heralds
99th Olympiad (384 B.C.): *tethrippon* for foals
128th Olympiad (268 B.C.): *synoris* for foals
131st Olympiad (256 B.C.): foals' race
145th Olympiad (200 B.C.): boys' *pankration*

As the number of contests increased — in the Classical period it had reached 18 — the length of the Games also successively grew from the original one day to five days.

The authority and power of Elis was considerably weakened for most of the 7th century B.C. After a series of unsuccessful clashes with its neighbours, the Dymaians in the north and the Pisatans in the south, Elis lost a good deal of the territory it had gained in previous centuries. The control of the sanctuary then (in the 26th Olympiad, i.e. 676 B.C. according to Strabo) once more reverted to Pisa which, energetically led by the kings Pantaleon and Damophon, and supported by Pheidon, tyrant of Argos, by the Arkadians and by the Messenians, dominated Elis and the sanctuary at Olympia. It is perhaps at this point, under Argive influence, that the worship of Hera makes its appearance in the Altis and the goddess acquires her temple, the earliest in the sanctuary. Similarly, it is no coincidence that it was during this century that chariot races were first introduced at Olympia, in memory of the victory in this event by the pre-Dorian, Mycenaean Pelops, over Oinomaos, king of Pisa. From this date the contests connected with this double tradition, the chariot races with the Mycenaean and the athletic events with the Dorian, continued to co-exist in the sanctuary, each of equal status.

In the early 6th century B.C., Elis recovered its strength, and underwent far-reaching cultural and political changes. The strictly oligarchic regime, which had gradually superseded the monarchy from the 9th century onwards, now became more moderate and more broadly based. The office of *Hellanodikes* ceased to be hereditary, and became elective, open to all citizens of Elis.

Having renewed its strength, Elis, in alliance with Sparta, decisively conquered Pisa in about 570 B.C., and resumed its control over the sanctuary, which it retained henceforth until the Games ceased to be held. In 364 B.C., the Arkadians attempted to reinstate Pisa; they went as far as to capture the sanc-

33. *Hera, one of the most important divinities of the sanctuary, had her own temple. The colossal limestone head of the goddess is from the cult statue of the Archaic Heraion (Olympia, Archaeological Museum).*

tuary and, along with the Pisatans, organised the Games that fell in that year. Shortly afterwards, however, they withdrew, and the control of the sanctuary reverted to the Eleans. This Olympiad was regarded as not having taken place and, as in a number of similar instances, was called an *anolympiad* (non-Olympiad).

The period beginning in 570 B.C. and lasting for the largest part of the 5th century B.C. was the happiest, most peaceful, and richest in spiritual achievement, in the history of the sanctuary and of the whole of Elis. During this period, when all the Greek cities were torn by disputes, civil wars and upheavals, Elis, protected by Zeus and the sacred truce, lived in peace and prosperity until the end of the 5th century. Even the dramatic events of the Persian wars scarcely affected life there. The following narrative from Pausanias is an allusion to the peaceful atmosphere in Elis, and the harmony that reigned among all the Elean cities. *They say that when Damophon was tyrant in Pisa, he did many evil deeds to the Eleans; when Damophon died, the people of Pisa did not want to share in the misdeeds of their tyrant, and the Eleans were desirous that the acts of violence against themselves should cease; they therefore chose from each of the sixteen cities that existed in Elis at that time, the woman who was the oldest and most respected and esteemed amongst the others, so that these sixteen women could settle their differences... And the women from these cities brought about a reconciliation between Pisa and Elis.*

The Eleans, moreover, dwelt in one of the most productive areas of Greece and had long practised agriculture and stock-raising. The fruitfulness of the land allowed the population to live throughout the whole of antiquity scattered in townships, villages

34

34. The most important god of the sanctuary, Zeus, depicted on one side of Elean staters (Athens, Numismatic Collection).

and farmsteads. Since they were self-sufficient in the provision of the basic necessities of life, they never had to devote themselves to large-scale trade or industry.

Another feature typical of Elis was that the chief concern of the state, at least until the 5th century B.C., was the organising of the Olympic Games. This is reflected in the picture of the *Agora* at Elis, which was to some extent a forecourt to the sanctuary at Olympia. It was dominated by the buildings connected with the Games: two *gymnasia* and a *palaistra,* for the standard training of the athletes from Elis and the other Greek cities who had to go into training for the Games, and finally the House and Portico of the *Hellanodikai*. Even the *bouleuterion* was housed in one of the two *gymnasia*. It is also significant that the Eleans trained their horses within the *Agora,* in a special area called the *hippodromos*.

It is thus clear that the spirit of the Games dominated the *Agora* of Elis, while other state activities were of secondary importance, and in any case the latter were largely the concern of the local authorities in a situation of wide decentralisation. However, the most important and most ancient offices of state were those connected with the sanctuary of Olympia and the Games: the *Hellanodikes,* seer, high-priest and so on.

A great change in the life of the country occurred in the last quarter of the 5th century. The Eleans ceased to remain neutral in the disputes between the other Greek cities. Active allies now of Sparta, now of Athens and now of other cities, they shared the consequences of the clashes involving their allies. From this time on, hostile armies frequently invaded and ravaged the territory of Elis, penetrating as far as the sanctuary of Olympia. Misfortune and disaster were no longer rare phenomena. Polybius attributes them to the change in the way of life of the Eleans, to their emancipation from the former benevolent protection of Zeus, and to their desertion of the sacred life they had previously lived. This change is reflected from the end of the 5th century in the architecture and also in the life and character of the sanctuary of Olympia and the spirit of the Games. The hitherto austere Dorian sanctuary is transformed into a lighter, more secular one with a large number of Ionic elements that make a sudden appearance and overwhelm it. Finally, the main sanctuary is separated off from the Games area, so that the stadium is now distant from it — a change that coincides with the appearance of professional athletics. It is precisely at this period that many philosophers, looking nostalgically back at the past and seeing the deep change that had occurred in the athletic ideal, censured a number of athletes of their time, because their main concern was the continuous, one-sided training and diet that would give them powerful muscles and enable them to reap victories as they travelled from sanctuary to sanctuary.

The dangers of this one-sided training of the body had already been pointed out by Xenophanes of Kolophon in the late 6th century B.C. He emphasised that the development of wisdom was much more important than strong arms and legs for the prosperity and order of the state. The same sage elsewhere states that an Olympic victory does not fill the city's coffers. Euripides, Aristophanes and Sokrates were later moved to the same observations, and Euripides goes so far as to say: *There are ten thousand evils in Greece, but nothing is worse than the race of athletes.*

At this same period the shrine began to become an arena for political rivalry between the cities, each of which tried by all means possible, by promises and offers to its athletes, to secure as many victories as possible. This exploitation of the Games and the sanctuary for political purposes reached its peak when Philip II and Alexander erected their family memorial, the Philippeion, within the sacred area, after the battle of Chaironeia (338 B.C.). The successors of Alexander the Great deployed the same tactics in their desire to strengthen their position in the Greek world, by offering rich gifts of money and dedications to the sanctuary. The Romans made their appearance at Olympia offering freedom and peace to the strife-torn Greek world, and sought and obtained permission to take part in the Olympic Games, thinking this would give them a more convincing excuse for interfering in Greek affairs. First, however, the Greek myths were suitably adjusted and interpreted to show that they, too, were of Greek descent.

In 146 B.C., when Greece proper became subject to the Roman state, the state of Elis also finally lost its independence and became part of the Roman province of Achaia. The sanctuary received honours and favours from many Roman officers and emperors from time to time, but only a pale reflection of its previous brilliance remained.

The Olympic Games nonetheless continued to exist for many centuries in their new form. As early as the Hellenistic period, and long before the Roman conquest of Greece, they had lost much of their religious foundation, but they made a significant contribution to the development of a new ideal, that of a broader human society which spoke, thought and lived in the Greek manner. In the 4th century B.C., Isokrates had already declared that Greeks were not those who were by nature Greeks, but those who had a common share in Greek culture.

The national unity of the Greeks, which Olympia had earlier reinforced, was now replaced by the Hellenistic *koine,* which embraced all areas of life: language, art, philosophy, science. This supra-national atmosphere, along with the internationalisation of the Games, became general in the 2nd century A.D. when the Severi extended Roman citizenship to all inhabitants of the Roman Empire. From that time, many Olympic victors have foreign names — Egyptian, Lykian, etc. It is precisely this supra-national character that survives in the modern Olympics which, as a result of the initiative of Baron de Coubertin, were organised again by the Greek state in Athens in 1896, after a break of fifteen centuries.

The Sanctuary of Olympia

Olympia, the most ancient and the most famous sanctuary in Greece, flourished in the verdant valley of the Alpheios in the western Peloponnese. Its close connections with Magna Graecia and the West find their echo in the burning desire of the river-god Alpheios for the nymph Arethousa, and his final union with her in Syracuse, at the spring named after her. The sanctuary is also closely linked with the East through Pelops, the legendary first king of the area, who, according to one tradition, came from Phrygia and gave his name to the island (Peloponnesos = island of Pelops) whereas its earlier name had been Apia.

The sanctuary extends over the south-west foot of the wooded hill of Kronion, between the plentiful waters of the Alpheios and its tributary the Kladeos, which flows into it at this point.

The area of the sanctuary and its environs was the site of a settlement that was inhabited continuously from the Early Helladic to the Late Helladic period (2.800-1100 B.C.). Evidence of this is supplied by the apsidal, rectangular and elliptical buildings, the tombs and the small finds dating from these periods that have been discovered in the area of the sanctuary and the new Museum.

The transformation of the settlement into a religious centre appears to have taken place during the late Mycenaean period, when we first have evidence for a cult there. The cult in question was that of Pelops and Hippodameia, the main hero-deities of the sanctuary. A number of figurines of horses and charioteers were discovered on the circular stone groundwork, the tomb of Pelops, which was overlain by the Pelopion of historical times. These finds attest not only the existence of a cult, but also the fact that games were already being held at this date. The games were initially of a local character, but seem gradually to have attracted the inhabitants of the cities neighbouring on Pisa, and possibly of those in more distant areas of the Peloponnese.

The cults of Kronos, Rhea, Gaia, Eileithyia, Themis and Idaian Herakles must have been introduced at quite an early period. Their shrines were situated at the southern foot of Kronion, where most of the prehistoric finds were discovered. They reveal special ties with Crete, at a time when Olympia, subject alternately to the state of Pylos (the kingdom of the Neleids) and to ancient Pisa, was a trading-post which the Cretans visited by way of the Alpheios, then navigable, and introduced some of their own cults.

In the Geometric and early Archaic periods (end of the 7th century B.C.) the Altis, the sacred grove of Olympia (the word Altis derives from the same root as *alsos,* meaning grove), was rich in plane trees, wild olives, poplars, oak and pines. It was enclosed by a low encircling wall or hedge, and had a few simple buildings: altars to the gods, and the shrines-tombs of Pelops and Hippodameia. There must also have been the single column that remained of the palace of Oinomaos, after it had been destroyed by a thunderbolt from Zeus, according to tradition; the column survived until the days of Pausanias. Some of the innumerable dedications from this period will have been hung on the branches of trees, while others will have been placed on the altars or in niches on the slopes of Kronion. The sacred wild olive will also have flourished at that time; this was the remnant of a tree cult and, according to legend, was brought by the Amphitrionid Herakles from the land of the Hyperboreans and planted in the sanctuary. The site of the stadium at this period is unknown; it probably occupied the same area as in the Archaic period.

From the early Archaic period, all the Greeks participated in the activities of the sanctuary — and not only those from Greece proper, but also those from the colonies in the Mediterranean and the Black Sea. The shrine became increasingly important, and was embellished with its first monumental buildings. These were erected gradually, some of them being connected with the cult, and other answering the continually growing and diverse organisational and administrative needs of the sanctuary. By the end of the 4th century B.C. the sanctuary had acquired its final, definitive architectural appearance. Certain additions were made in the Hellenistic and Roman periods, when a number of modifications were made in response to the historical needs and new way of life of these periods.

The Monuments

There were three main points of access to the sanctuary proper, which was separated off from the rest of the area by a *peribolos* (enclosing wall). Two of these were in the west of the wall, and one in the south. The temples and buildings connected with the cult were inside the enclosure, while the ancillary buildings — dwellings for the priests, baths, guest houses, the gymnasium, wrestling-school etc. — were outside it.

The temple of Hera stood at the foot of Kronion. Hitherto, the prevailing opinion has been that the Doric temple was built in 650 B.C., and was originally small, with only a *pronaos,* being extended in 600 B.C., when it acquired an *opisthodomos* and a row of columns around it *(pteron).* Recent research suggests, however, that the temple may have been built in a single phase and with a unified plan in 600 B.C. The Heraion, which is long and narrow and has heavy proportions, is one of the earliest examples of monumental temple construction in Greece. The lower part of the temple, which is preserved along with the enormous orthostates of the cella, is of the local shell-lime, while the upper part of the walls were of unbaked bricks, and the entablature of wood, with terracotta tiles on the roof. The apex of each of the pediments was adorned with a clay disc-shaped *akroterion.* The columns were originally made of wood, and were gradually replaced by stone ones over a period of some centuries. Each column was replaced by another one in the style of the period in question, so that the columns reflect the complete development of the Doric column, and especially the capital, from the Archaic period to Roman times. Inside the cella is preserved the base on which the stone statues of Zeus and Hera stood, though only the head of Hera has been found.

Shortly after this, the treasuries began to be built; these were small temples in the shape of the *megaron,* and were dedicated by the Greek cities, mainly of the colonies. They were erected on the natural terrace on the southern slopes of Kronion, a little higher than the Heraion. The earliest treasury (that of Sikyon, in its first phase) is almost contemporary with the Heraion, while the latest (those of Sikyon and Gela in their second phase, and those of Syracuse and Byzantium) date from the first half of the 5th century B.C. They stood in a row, one next to the

35

35. General view of the valley of Olympia, with the Alpheios in the background. This was the birthplace of the Olympic spirit, which has spread all over the world since the revival of the Olympic Games. The sacred flame is lit every 4 years in the Altis and is transported to the most distant countries in the world.

other, and formed the northern limit of the Altis. Pausanias mentions the names of ten treasuries; the ruins of fifteen small temples survive in this area, however, although only five can be identified with certainty — those of Sikyon, Selinous, Metapontion, Megara and Gela. Originally, these treasuries probably served a cult purpose, but later were used to house valuable dedications.

The Pelopion (the shrine of Pelops) was remodelled in the 6th century B.C. The wall enclosing it, which had originally been circular, now became pentagonal, and a propylon was built, which was replaced by a more monumental one in the 5th century B.C. It has recently been suggested then the Pelopion dates from the 4th century B.C., but this view does not seem to be well-founded. The earliest Prytaneion, in the corner of the Altis, belongs to the end of the 6th century B.C.; this was the headquarters of the *prytaneis,* who were officials of the sanctuary. The sacred hearth, with its continually burning fire, was kept in a special room, and official guests and victors in the Games were entertained in the northern part of the Prytaneion. The great altar of Zeus was to the south-east of the temple of Hera, but no trace of it has been preserved. It gradually acquired the shape of a mound from the ash left behind from the sacrifices and the hearth of the Prytaneion, but it was washed away by the rains after the sanctuary ceased to function. The area in front of the altar, especially the slope near the terrace on which the treasuries were built, was probably the "theatre" referred to by Xenophon. It received its name from the view it offered of the altar, the sacrifices, and the other rituals. The Archaic stadium (Stadium I), which was simple in form and had no proper embankments, ran along the terrace of the treasuries. Its narrow western end, where the finishing line was, was open and faced the great altar of Zeus. Stadium II, which took shape during the first half of the 5th century B.C., was in roughly the same position, possibly slightly further to the east; the track was on a lower level, however, and the longer sides now had regular embankments. Towards the end of the 5th century B.C. the stadium was again moved, 82 m. to the east and 7 m. to the north, and was now closed in on its narrow western side (Stadium III). Recent excavations have shown that the embankment of the narrow western side was truncated in the mid-4th century B.C., when the Stoa of Echo was built. This separated the stadium off completely from the sanctuary. The stadium, which until this period had formed part of the sacred area, since the Games had a purely religious significance, now changed both form and character, as a result of being cut off from the sanctuary, in its present position.

The Games too began to change their nature, and gradually became merely a spectacle for entertainment. The track in this new stadium is 212.54 m. long, and *ca.* 28.50 m. wide, while the starting and finishing lines are 192.28 m. apart, instead of the 186 m. of the Classical stadium. The embankments surrounding the stadium on all four sides did not have stone seats, apart from a very few for important persons: the *exedra* for the *Hellanodikai,* for exam-

36. The temple of Hera is at the foot of Kronion, at the most sacred part of the Altis. Long and narrow, and with heavy proportions, it is one of the earliest examples of monumental temple construction in Greece. The palaistra *can be seen in the background, and the Nymphaion to the right.*

36

ple, on the south embankment of the stadium, opposite the altar of Demeter Chamyne, was of stone. Otherwise, the 45,000 spectators that the stadium held sat on the ground. During the Hellenistic period, the north-west corner was connected to the sanctuary by the *Krypte,* a narrow, vaulted corridor that had a gate with Corinthian columns at the west end. Near the stadium there were a large number of wells to ensure the water supply for the thousands of visitors during the Games.

The hippodrome, which had a total length of four stades (*ca.* 780 m.), has not been excavated, and it is probable that at least part of it has been washed away by the Alpheios. It took its final form and position, to the south of and parallel to the stadium, during the late Classical period. It was at this date that a new means of operating the starting mechanism of the horse and chariot races was introduced. A small elevation in the ground to the north of the "course" of the hippodrome was converted into a regular sloping embankment for the spectators, and artificial embankments were created to the south and west by dumping soil there. To the west, the hippodrome ended at the Stoa of Agnaptos, which has also not been discovered.

The "course" in the hippodrome was elliptical in shape, and was divided along its axis by a stone or wooden partition two stades long (*ca.* 390 m.). The riders and charioteers turned both ends of this partition, which separated the "course" into two parts, and thus covered a total distance of 4 stades, or *ca.* 780 m., on each circuit.

37. The gymnasium of Olympia, built in the 2nd century B.C. In the open court inside it, the athletes practised the javelin, the discus, and running. The palaistra, *which adjoined the gymnasium, can be seen in the background.*

The southern side of the hippodrome was longer than the other. It consisted of an embankment, and there was a circular altar to Taraxippos, the Horse-scarer, at the point where there was a passage through the embankment.

Finally, the southernmost of the two *Bouleuterion* buildings was constructed after the middle of the 6th century B.C. It was rectangular, with one of its short sides in apsidal form; it was thus a continuation of the types of prehistoric building found in the Altis. During the 5th century B.C. the second, also apsidal, building was added parallel to the first, and between the two of them, a square building containing the altar of Zeus Horkios, on which the athletes swore the oath required before the Games. These three adjoining buildings were connected, possibly during the 4th century, by an Ionic stoa along the eastern side.

The sanctuary reached the height of its wealth and prosperity in the 5th century. It was then that the most important building in the Altis was erected — the great temple of Zeus, the building of which was commenced in *ca.* 470 B.C., immediately after the reorganisation of the state, and was completed in 456 B.C. The Doric peripteral temple was the work of the Elean architect Libon; it was the largest in the Peloponnese, and was considered the perfect expression, or "canon" of the Doric temple. The marble sculptures on the pediments depicted the chariot race between Oinomaos and Pelops, with Zeus in the middle, on the east side, and on the west, the battle between the Lapiths and the Centaurs during the wedding of Peirithoos and Deidameia, with Apollo in the middle. The twelve metopes, six above the entrance to the *pronaos,* and six above

38

38. The stadium of Olympia today. It dates from the middle of the 4th c. B.C., and is 192.27 m., or 600 Olympic feet, long. The spectators sat on the embankments. On the right are the traces of the exedra *of the* Hellanodikai, *and on the left the altar of Demeter Chamyne.*

39. The Krypte, *the vaulted passageway that connected the stadium to the sanctuary. It was constructed in the Hellenistic period, and was the official entrance to the stadium, through which the* Hellanodikai *and the athletes entered.*

39

that of the *opisthodomos,* portrayed the twelve labours of Herakles. These sculptures, now restored in part, are the most representative examples of Greek art of the "severe style." The central *akroterion* of the east pediment was a gilt Nike, the work of Paionios, and the side *akroteria* were gilt *lebetes.* A chryselephantine statue of Zeus sitting on a throne, by Phidias, was set up inside the cella about 430 B.C. This magnificent work is described in detail by Pausanias, but only inferior copies of it are preserved, mainly on Elean coins. The gigantic figure of the god held a chryselephantine Nike in his right hand, and his sceptre in his left. The throne and base of the statue were decorated with mythical scenes featuring gods, daemons and heroes, in gold, ebony and precious stones. A special workshop was built to the west of the temple for the making of the statue. Large numbers of tools, glass ornaments, clay moulds and other objects connected with the work of the artist have been found in and around the area of the workshop, and make it possible to assign a definite date to the statue of Zeus. Two other buildings were erected to the north of the workshop at about the same period. One of them, which is rectangular and has a peristyle court, is usually identified with the Theokoleon, which housed the *Theokoloi,* the priests of Olympia. The other, to the west of the Theokoleon is a circle inscribed in a square in plan; according to a late Hellenistic inscription found in this area it is the Heroon. The view has recently been put forward that it originally housed the baths and was only later dedicated to an anonymous hero, but there is no firm evidence for this. Still further west, towards the Kladeos, there were baths and a swimming-pool, also built during the 5th century. Towards 300 B.C., the baths were extended, and again in 100 B.C., when they were fitted with hypocausts. They were abandoned in the Roman period, when hot baths were built in many parts of the sanctuary.

The late Classical period saw Elis involved in internal discord and clashes with its neighbours. However, these difficulties did not prevent new building activity, which gave the sanctuary its final form and architectural appearance. It was now that the delicate Ionic and Corinthian styles were introduced into Olympia, where previously the dominant form had been the austere Doric, with its heavy proportions. Much use was made of white marble in the new buildings, instead of the shell-lime that had been used almost exclusively until then, and this was the token of a general change in the character of the sanctuary that was also apparent in the Games held there. For the stadium was now moved to the east of the Classical stadium, and this completed its isolation from the Altis. This separation became total, as we have seen, with the construction of the Stoa of Echo along the east side of the Altis. This stoa was also called *Heptaëchos,* because sounds re-echoed seven times in it. It was also known as *Poikile* (painted) because of the frescoes decorating its interior. It was built shortly after 350 B.C., and had two colonnades, the outer Doric, and the inner possibly Corinthian, with rooms in the interior. At this period, the sanctuary proper was separated off from the ancillary and secular buildings by a monumental *peribolos* of poros, with five gates, three in the west side and two in the south. The Metroon, the temple of Kybele, Mother of the Gods, was built at the beginning of the 4th century B.C., in front of the terrace of the treasuries. This was a Doric peripteral temple, but only the stylobate and parts of the stone entablature have survived. The Metroon was used for the cults of the Roman emperors from the period of Augustus, and many statues of them were set up inside it. The bases of 16 bronze statues of Zeus, the *Zanes* (see "The Rules of the Competitions"), have been preserved along the terrace of the treasuries, between the Metroon and the stadium. The south stoa formed the southern boundary of the sanctuary. This had two colonnades, the outer Doric and the inner Corinthian, with a wall behind it. Its façade, which faced the Alpheios, had a projection on columns in the middle of it, making the stoa T-shaped. It was built at about the same time as the Stoa of Echo, and like this, had a base and steps of marble. The south-east building belongs to the early 4th, or the late 5th century, while an altar of Artemis, dating from the early 5th century, was recently discovered near the south-east corner of the Hellenistic extension. The south-east building was demolished in the 1st century A.D. so that a peristyle villa, probably that of Nero, could be built on its foundations.

The Philippeion, the circular peripteral building south of the Prytaneion, was begun by Philip II after the battle of Chaironeia (338 B.C.), and was completed by his son, Alexander the Great. It stood on a marble stepped base, most of which is preserved, and had a row of Ionic columns around it. The wall of the circular cella was divided by Corinthian half-columns, and inside it, opposite the door, there were five statues, depicting Alexander the Great, between his parents and forefathers, on a semicircular pedestal. The statues, made of gold and ivory, were the work of Leochares. The circular type of building, which had earlier had a religious character, was now used for the first time for the cult of the heroised Macedonian dynasty. The guest house, the Leonidaion, was erected about 330 B.C., in the western part of the sanctuary, south of the workshop of Phidias; it is named after its architect, Leonidas of Naxos, who also furnished the finances for it. It had rooms on all four sides, facing inwards onto a peristyle court with Doric columns. The building was surrounded by an Ionic colonnade on the outside. The Leonidaion was initially intended for official guests and distinguished visitors, but was converted in the Roman period into a dwelling for Roman officials.

No new buildings were erected in the sanctuary proper during the Hellenistic period (3rd-1st centuries B.C.). The only work was that of preservation and repair, and occasionally of extension of the old buildings; sometimes this was on a large scale, mainly as a result of the frequent severe earthquakes. However, building activity continued in the area outside the Altis, where it was designed to produce comfortable quarters for the athletes and visitors. To the west of the Altis, near the Kladeos, in an area long used by the athletes for training, the *palaistra* (wrestling-school) was built in the 3rd century, for practice in wrestling, boxing and jumping. It was roughly square in shape, with a peristyle court, around which were covered areas with special rooms for undressing, anointing the body with oil, powdering it with dust, bathing, and also rooms with benches for teaching.

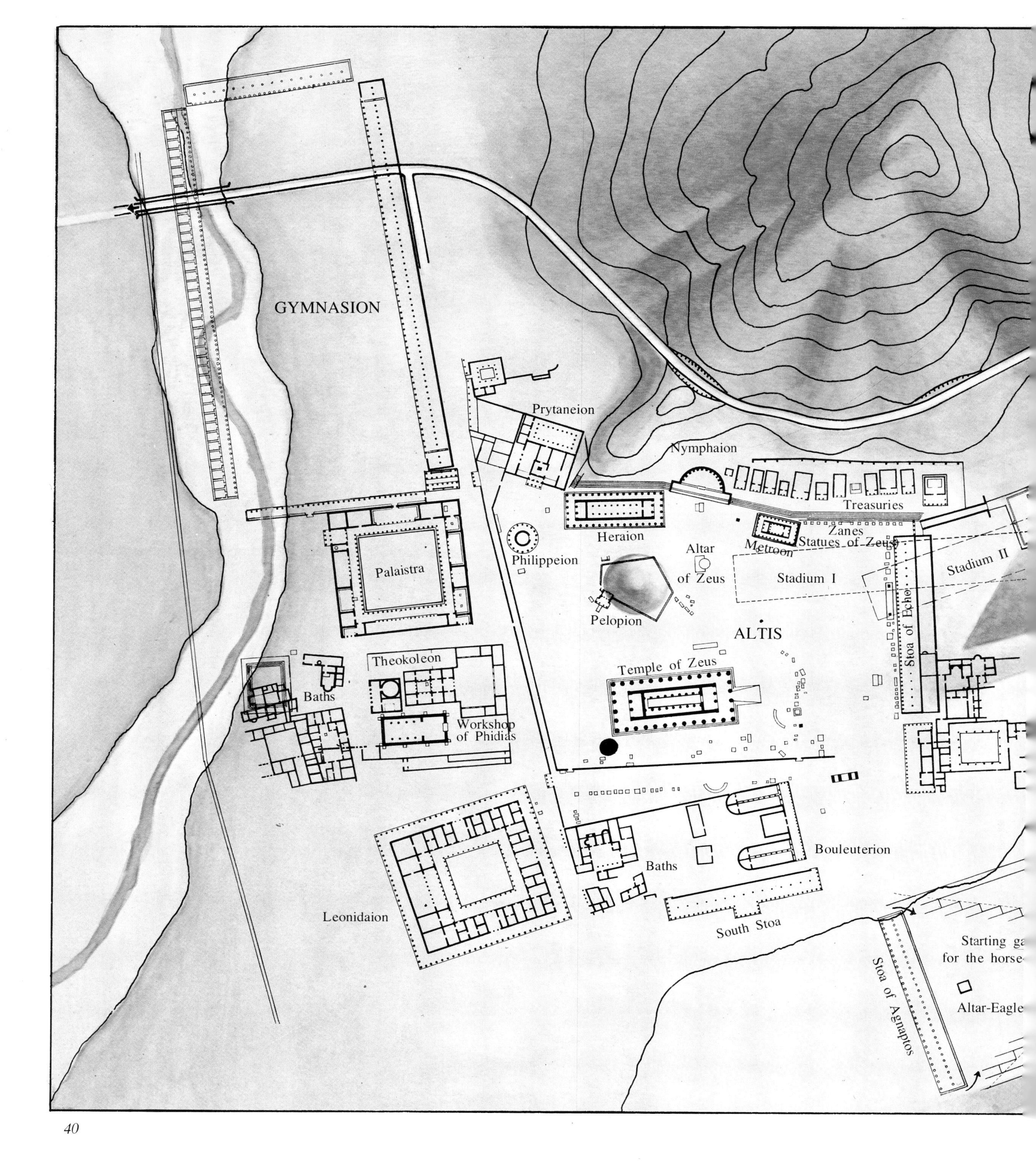
GYMNASION
Prytaneion
Nymphaion
Treasuries
Heraion
Zanes
Metroon
Statues of Zeus
Philippeion
Altar
of Zeus
Stadium I
Stadium II
Palaistra
Pelopion
ALTIS
Stoa of Echo
Theokoleon
Temple of Zeus
Baths
Workshop
of Phidias
Bouleuterion
Baths
Leonidaion
South Stoa
Stoa of Agnaptos
Altar-Eagle

40

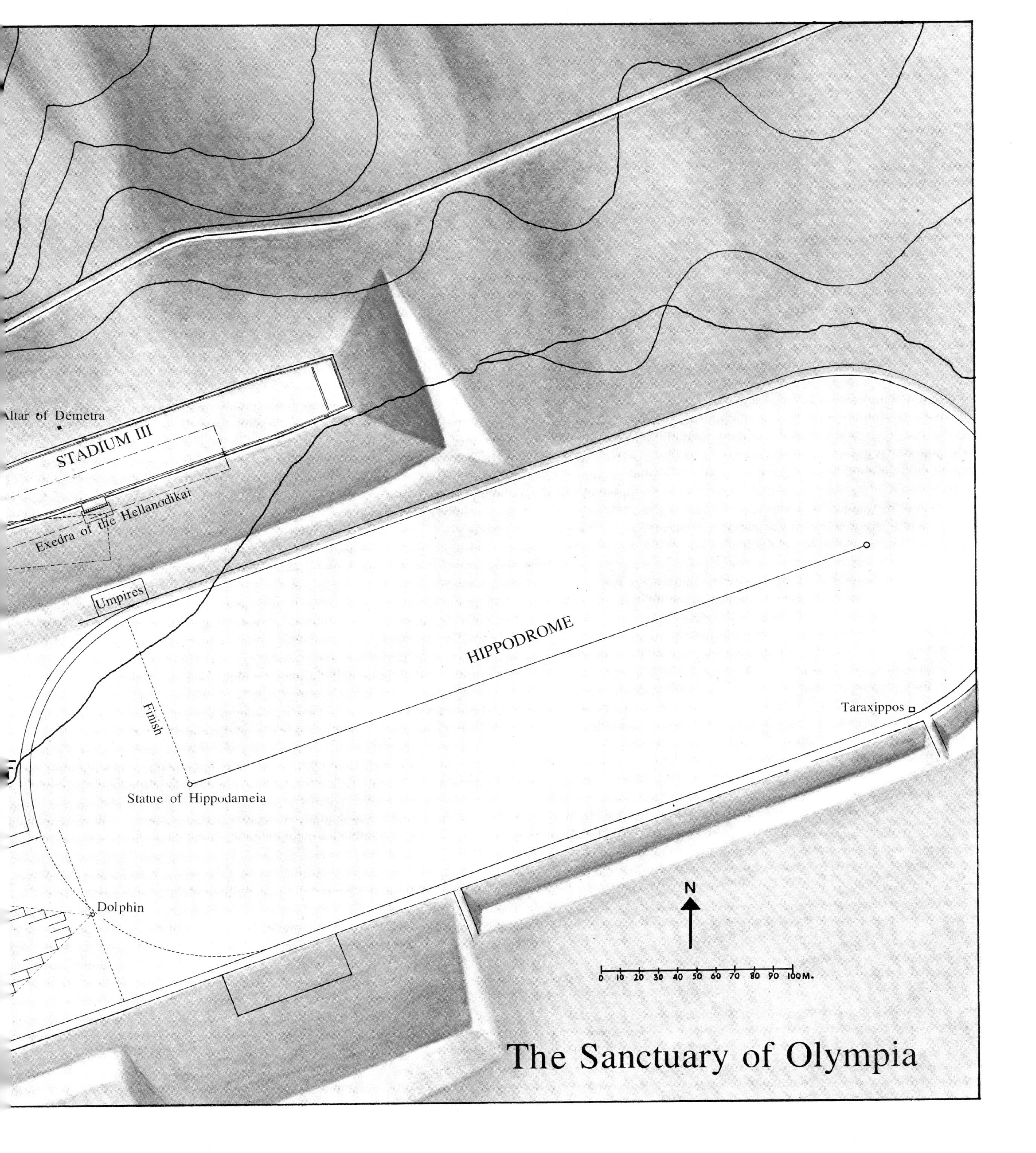

40. General plan of Olympia. The Altis, the sanctuary proper, was separated off from the rest of the area by a perimeter wall. Within it were the temples and buildings connected with the cult, while outside it were the ancillary buildings, the guest houses, the gymnasium, the palaistra, *etc. To the east, the stadium and the hippodrome (which is marked on the plan after Pausanias' description). The hill Kronion defines the northern side of the sanctuary.*

To the north of the *palaistra* and adjoining it was the *gymnasion,* a closed rectangular building with a spacious court in the centre, and stoas on all four sides. This was where the athletes trained for the events that required a lot of space, such as the javelin, discus and running. It was built in the early 2nd century B.C., though its monumental entrance, in the form of an amphiprostyle Corinthian propylon, belongs rather to the end of the 2nd century B.C.

The picture of Olympia is completed by the thousands of altars and statues of gods, deamons, and heroes, as well as of Olympic victors, kings and generals, all of them works of the most famous artists throughout antiquity. Very few of them have survived, and in many cases we have only the bases. Similar works were erected during the Roman period, most of them statues of Roman officials and emperors, which were set up not by the individuals concerned, but by cities or private citizens who wished to secure their favour. The most valuable of the earlier works were at this time transferred to the Heraion, which assumed the character of a museum.

In 146 B.C., the Roman consul Mummius, having crushed the Greeks at the Isthmus, dedicated 21 gilt shields at Olympia, which were placed on 21 metopes of the temple of Zeus. By contrast, Sulla, in 85 B.C., plundered the treasures of the sanctuary, as he did those of Epidauros and Delphi, to secure the finance needed for his war against Mithridates.

Sulla even decided to transfer the Olympic Games to Rome, and the 175th Olympiad was held there in 80 B.C. Olympia recovered from the decline that began at this date after 31 B.C., in the Augustan period. Roman emperors and officials showed their interest in the sanctuary and the Games in a variety of ways, as part of their political programme for Greece. Under Nero, the Altis was extended and a new *peribolos* was constructed, 3 m. beyond the old enclosure on the west side, and 20 m. beyond it on the south, and the simple gateways of the sanctuary were replaced by monumental entrances. At the same period, hot baths were built to the west of the Greek baths, and also to the north of the Prytaneion. Later on, yet more were added, to the north-east of the villa of Nero, and to the west of the *Bouleuterion*. A new guest house was constructed to the west of the workshop of Phidias. During this period the earlier buildings were restored or converted. Finally, Herodes Atticus built his Aqueduct in A.D. 160. The waters of a copious spring, 4 kilometres east of Olympia, were channeled into the imposing *Nymphaion,* or *Exedra*. This was semicircular in shape and had two small circular temples in front of it, one on each side; the walls were made of baked brick and faced with coloured marble. Twenty statues stood in the niches on the face of the semicircular wall, depicting Antoninus Pius and his family, and the family of Herodes Atticus. Between the two small temples, there were two cisterns on two different levels, one in front of the semicircular wall and one lower down. The water ran into the higher, semicircular cistern and from there into the lower, rectangular one, from where it was channeled to the whole of the sanctuary by a vast network of conduits.

The first serious destruction of the monuments of Olympia took place in A.D. 267, when a wall was constructed in great haste to protect the valuable treasures, and particularly the chryselephantine statue of Zeus, from the threat of the Heruli, who ultimately did not get as far as the sanctuary. The wall, formerly thought to be Byzantine, enclosed the temple of Zeus and the south part of the sanctuary as far as the south stoa. It was built with material from the other buildings both within and without the sanctuary, which were demolished for the purpose, the only exception being the temple of Hera. The sanctuary survived for a further century in this truncated form, and in an ever increasing state of decay. Some building repairs took place, mainly under Diocletian (A.D. 285-305). The life of the sanctuary came to an end in A.D. 393 with the decree of Theodosius I forbidding the functioning of heathen sanctuaries. There followed the demolishing of the Altis in A.D. 426, as a result of a decree of Theodosius II, and the destruction was completed by two major earthquakes in 522 and 551. In the 5th and 6th centuries a small settlement of Christians established itself at Olympia, and the workshop of Phidias, the only building still standing, was converted into a Christian basilica. Subsequently, the flooding of the Alpheios and the Kladeos, together with the sliding down of the sandy soil of Kronion, which had meanwhile become depilated, finally covered the whole sanctuary with a deposit 7 m. thick. The Kladeos, furthermore, changed its course and washed away many of the buildings in the west of the sanctuary.

The first efforts to discover the monuments of Olympia were those of the French "Expédition scientifique de Morée," in 1829. Systematic excavation in the sanctuary was begun by the German Archaeological Institute in 1875, and has continued to the present day.

41

41. Reconstruction of the chryselephantine cult statue of Zeus at Olympia, by Pheidias. The father of the gods was holding a Nike in his right hand and his sceptre in the left (Drawing: K. Iliakis).

The Organisation of the Games

Date and Duration of the Games. The Olympiad

The Olympic Games were held once in every four years. Like the other Panhellenic games, they had a place in the eight-year calendar. This was a period of eight years that made up the difference of 11¹/₄ days between the lunar year of 354 days and the solar year of 365¹/₄ days. The dates of the ancient festivals were calculated on the basis of the lunar month of 28 days; since this meant that the seasonal festivals were in danger of moving, and possibly falling in the winter rather than the summer, the ancients resorted to the method of intercalating a month in the lunar year three times during the eight-year period. It was on the basis of this eight-year calendar that the date of the Olympic and other great festivals was calculated. This is the explanation for the uncertainty surrounding the precise date of the Olympic Games. However, the Games were held at the first full moon following the summer solstice, and scholars nowadays agree that they took place in mid-July, from approximately the 11th to the 16th of the month.

The fact that the Olympic Games were celebrated in the middle of the summer is confirmed by the evidence of the sources, according to which both spectators and athletes suffered from the unbearable heat and the large numbers of flies and mosquitoes. Aelian tells the story of the miller from Chios who threatened his assistant (his slave) that he would take him out of the mill, where he was grinding with little enthusiasm, and send him to Olympia to follow the Games; this, he felt, would be a punishment, since it was more exhausting to roast in the hot sun watching the Games than to grind corn in the hand mill.

The number of days on which the Games were held did not remain constant throughout antiquity. Until 684 B.C. (the 24th Olympiad), there were only six competitions and the Games took place on one day only. The chariot races were introduced in the 25th Olympiad, and a second day was added. In the 37th Olympiad (632 B.C.), boys' contests were inserted into the programme, and a third day added. Later the festivals seem to have lasted five days, though there must have been fluctuations in the number of days during the centuries-long history of the Games.

The interval of time between the end of the Games and the beginning of the fifth year after, when the next Games would begin, was called an "Olympiad"; it should be noted, however, that the term Olympiad was also used to denote the Games themselves. The Olympiads formed the basis of a general dating system, replacing the various local dating systems (for example, dates were cited with reference to the eponymous archons in Athens, to the priestesses of Hera in Argos, to the Ephors in Sparta, and so on). The system had the advantage over the local chronological systems that it had a Panhellenic character and was well known and comprehensible throughout the entire Greek world.

Each Olympiad took its name from the winner in the *stadion* race, and was numbered in series with reference to the first Olympiad, which was conventionally considered to be that of 776 B.C., when the victor was Koroibos of Elis. In about 400 B.C., the Olympiads were numbered by the sophist Hippias of Elis, who probably used the archives of the sanctuary, or even oral tradition. Aristotle, and later Eratosthenes, Phlegon of Tralleis and Julius Africanus, completed the list of Olympiads, which was

42. The organisation of the Olympic Games was the task of the Eleans. They accepted the enormous responsibility for arranging the athletics events and the sacred ritual, for maintaining the competition areas, and for providing for the comfort of the huge crowds of pilgrims who inundated the sanctuary. In the picture, a youth is preparing the pit for the jumping, which formed part of the pentathlon (Munich, Antikensammlungen).

42

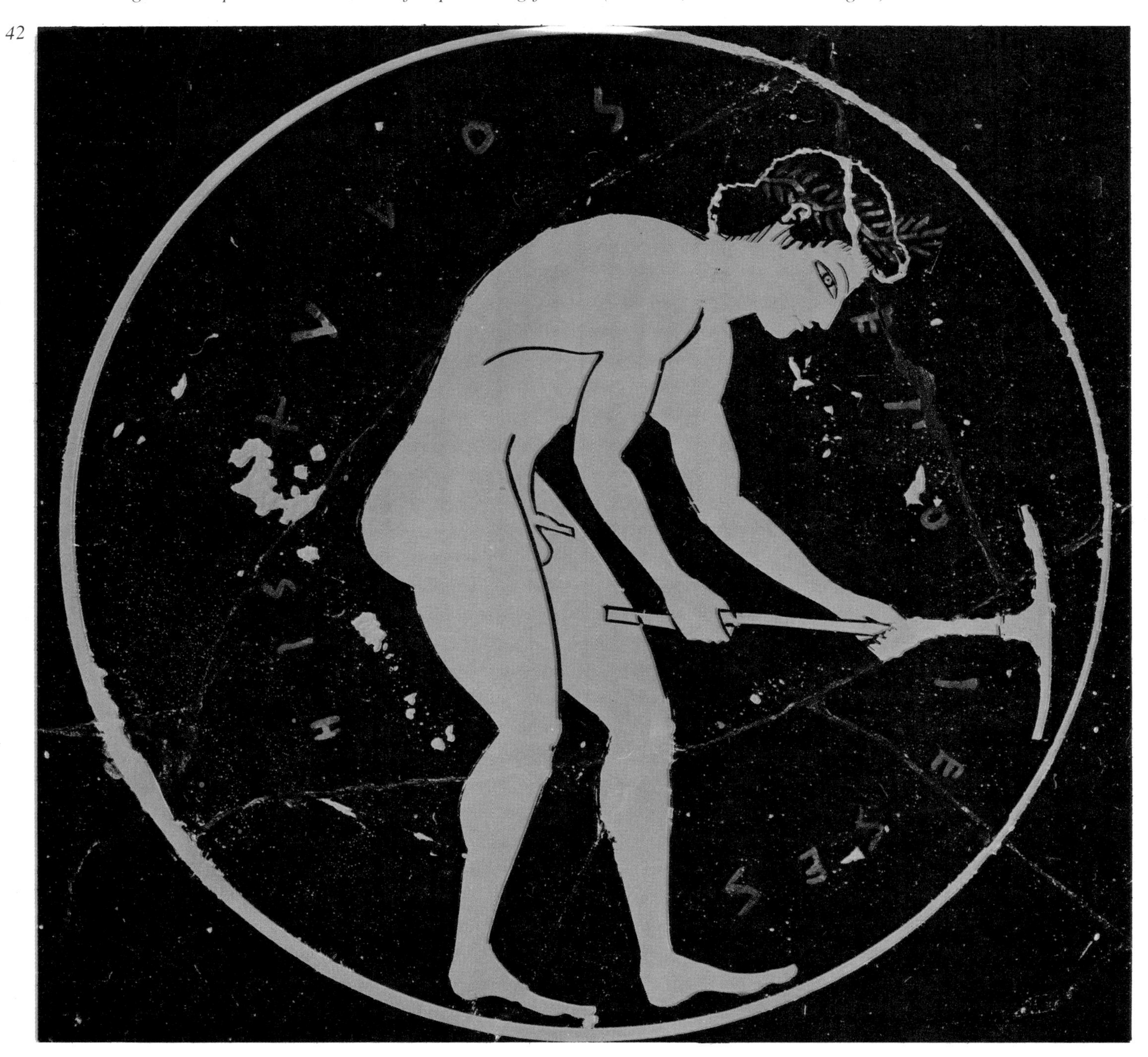

used as the basis for the ancient system of chronology from the end of the 4th century B.C.

The Institution of the Truce

The term truce (in ancient Greek *ekecheiria* which means literally "holding of hands") indicates a break in hostilities or armistice. It was an institution providing for the suspension of hostilities for a prescribed period beginning with the announcement of the Games. This institution was established as a result of the sacred treaty between three kings, Iphitos of Elis, Kleosthenes of Pisa and Lykourgos of Sparta. It is not known with any certainty how long the truce lasted, though initially it was for one month, and later three. Some claim a figure as high as ten months. During the period of the truce, the athletes, their relatives and the ordinary pilgrims could travel without fear to see the legendary Games, and afterwards return to their country in safety.

It was thanks to this institution that the sanctuary of Olympia attained great authority and fame. The Eleans, too, who kept their country free from military struggles for long periods thanks to the truce, enjoyed great prosperity, at least down to the 5th century B.C. Polybius, indeed, attributes the density of the population of Elis and the well-being of the country to the institution of the truce.

The announcement or proclamation of the Games was made by the *spondophoroi*. These were citizens of Elis, who wore crowns of olive branches and held the herald's wand in their hand, and who travelled from city to city throughout the whole Greek world, bringing the news of the sacred truce, of which they were also the guarantors.

There is no clear and precise evidence about the terms of the truce, since no ancient writer refers to it in detail, but it is possible to deduce the most important of them from the various occasions on which the truce was violated.

1. During the truce all hostilities ceased, and free access was allowed to the country of the Eleans, which was declared neutral and inviolable. Furthermore, all those who wished to follow or take part in the Games were even free to travel through territories with which their own country was at war.

2. All armed individuals or army units were strictly forbidden to enter Elis.

3. No death penalty could be carried out for the duration of the truce.

The importance of the truce was that it had been consciously recognised as a free institution and was respected by all the Greeks. This is shown by the fact that through the approximately 1,200 years of life of the Olympic Games, the violations of the truce that occurred were very few and almost insignificant.

The Spectators

Spectators came from the remotest corners of the Greek world to offer sacrifices to the gods and heroes and to follow the Games at Olympia. They set out from the peripheral areas, from the Cimmerian Bosporos and Cyrene, from Magna Graecia and the cities of Asia Minor, to enjoy the most brilliant spectacle of the ancient world. The poorest of them on foot, the richest on horseback or in carriages, they gathered in the valley of the Alpheios

43. Reconstruction of the Nymphaion at Olympia. The need for water was met from various springs and wells until Herodes Atticus finally solved the problem by constructing a large aqueduct that ended at the Nymphaion. From there, the water was supplied to all parts of the sanctuary by a system of conduits (Drawing: K. Iliakis).

43

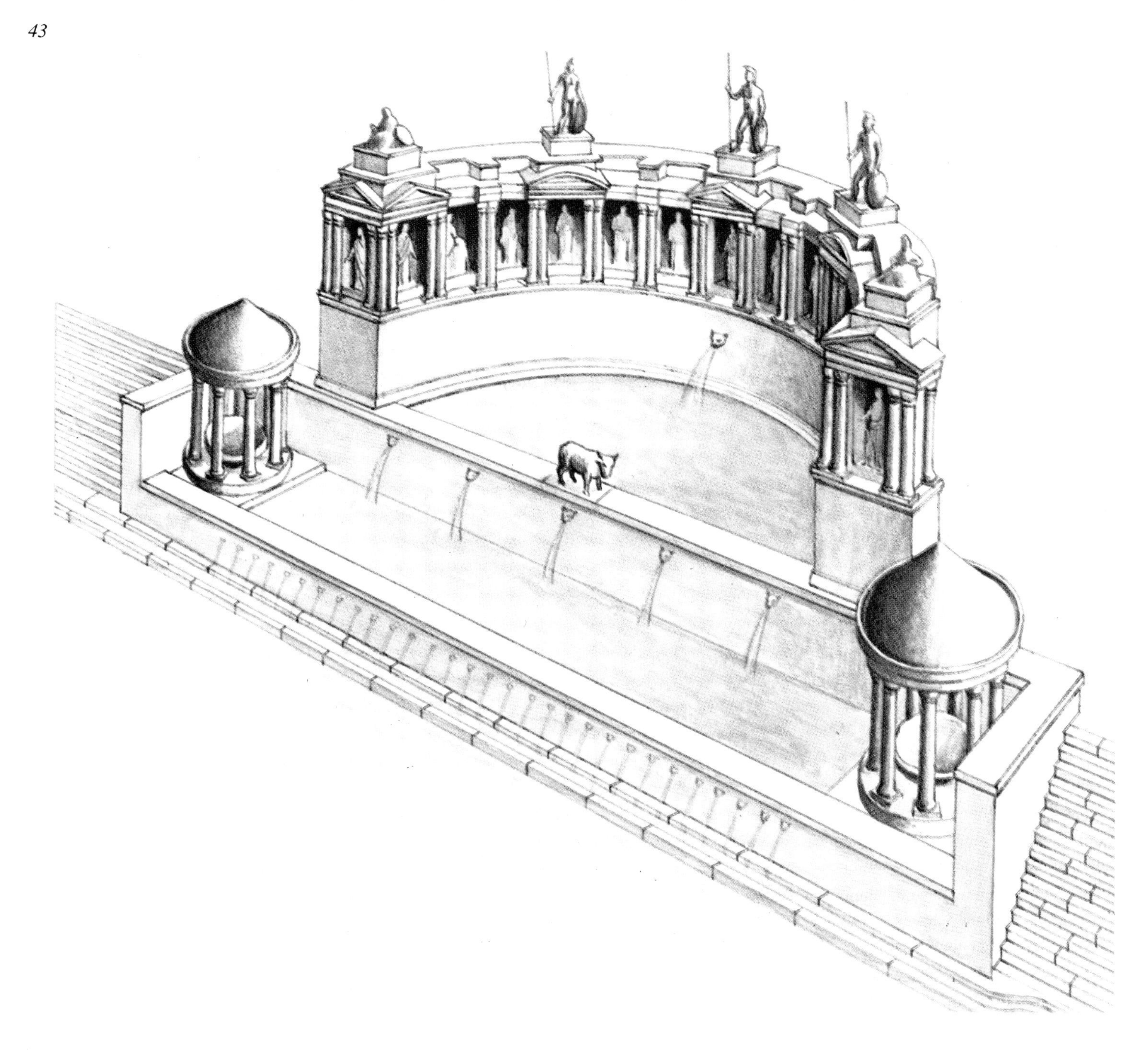

— poets, philosophers, politicians, tyrants, and also ordinary citizens and villagers. With the sole exception of married women, everyone had the right to attend the Games, including barbarians and slaves.

The Eleans, who organised the Games with great care, did not undertake to house and feed the multitudes that assembled there. It was not until the 4th century B.C. that the Leonidaion, a guest-house for distinguished visitors, was built. The crowd stayed in the open air near the rivers, pitching tents, erecting shelters of branches, or seeking protection under the trees.

However, the *theoriai,* i.e. the missions that officially represented the different cities, set up opulent tents and the shelters needed to house the horses that were to run in the chariot races and horse races. In the evenings they kindled fires, not only against the damp, but also to drive away the insects. They brought their food with them, but the water problem was a very serious one. How were the thousands of spectators following the Games to quench their thirst in the middle of summer? The need appears to have been met, to some extent at least, from the various springs and the large number of wells that were opened, particularly near the competition areas, the stadium and the hippodrome. Later on, Herodes Atticus solved the problem permanently by constructing a large aqueduct.

The Exclusion of Women

A very strict rule, that remains unexplained to this day, forbade women to enter the stadium in order to follow the Games, or even to enter the Altis during the period of the Games. The most paradoxical aspect of this rule was that it did not apply to young girls, as Pausanias unequivocally states when he is discussing the exclusion of women: *They do not prevent virgins from watching.* It is indeed strange that immature girls should be permitted to watch the rough Games, while the mothers and wives of the competitors were not. The prohibition applied only for the duration of the Games, for at other times women could enter the Altis freely.

The spectacle was attended by one woman alone, seated on an altar inside the stadium, opposite the seats of the chief judges of the Games, the *Hellanodikai.* This was the priestess of Demeter Chamyne, who received this honorary office every four years at the hands of the Eleans. Regilla, for example, the wife of Herodes Atticus, the benefactor who erected the aqueduct at Olympia, was chosen priestess of Demeter Chamyne by the Eleans, so that she could enter the stadium and follow the Games.

The penalty for women who infringed the law forbidding them entry was severe, as we are told by Pausanias: any woman who attended the Games, or even crossed the river Alpheios on the days the Games were held, would be thrown by the Eleans from the high precipitous cliffs of mount Typaion. The only woman to break the law and escape punishment was Kallipateira, the daughter of Diagoras; she was the daughter, sister and mother of Olympic victors. Diagoras had three sons, Akousilaos, Damagetos and Dorieus, and two daughters, Pherenike and Kallipateira, the former of whom had a son named Eukleus, while Kallipateira had a son Peisirodos. All six male members of the family were great Olympic victors. After the death of her husband, Kallipateira took special care to train her son. She brought him to Olympia to compete, and she entered the stadium perfectly disguised as a male trainer. When her son Peisirodos was victorious, Kallipateira lept over the trainers' enclosure, and in doing so lost her clothes, thus revealing that she was a woman. The *Hellanodikai,* however, in honour of her father, her brothers and her son, all of whom had won victories in the Olympic Games, let her free and unpunished. This incident was the occasion of an enactment decreeing that the trainers also had to be naked at the Games.

Despite the fact that women were excluded from the Games, it was possible for a woman to be proclaimed an Olympic victor. This was in the equestrian events, where the person who was crowned as victor was not the charioteer or rider, but the owner of the horse or chariot, and so there were occasions when the victor was a woman. Kyniska, the daughter of the Spartan king Archidamos, was the first woman victor, in the four-horse chariot race in 392 B.C., and she was followed by others, mainly Spartans.

The Official Missions

Alongside the countless individual pilgrims there were also the official representatives sent by the cities, the missions, or *theoriai,* as they were called. The cities attached such great importance to their missions that they made the membership of them very large, and also sent valuable gifts to the great god Zeus, to the many deities worshipped in the Altis, and to the rulers of Elis. The cities chose their most distinguished citizens to represent them; these representatives were called *theoroi* and their official leader *architheoros*.

The cities sent these missions only to the four Panhellenic games (the Pythian, Nemean, Isthmian and Olympic), and were always concerned that the part they played should be as impressive as possible. In particular, they made sure that the missions they sent to the Olympic Games were even more imposing, since these games had a special reputation throughout the Greek world, deriving from their sacred nature, the authority of the organisers, and the strictness and impartiality of the judges.

It is difficult for us today to conceive the grandeur of one of these missions, such as that sent by the wealthy tyrants of Syracuse, Hieron or Dionysios, or that of Athens during the 91th Olympiad (416 B.C.), which was financed and organised by Alkibiades, who led it, as *architheoros,* at Olympia. It was said of this mission that it was the most splendid ever sent by a Greek city, and it represented a triumph for Athens, and a personal triumph for Alkibiades. In order to celebrate the victories he had won in the chariot races, Alkibiades, as head of the mission, gave a sumptuous dinner to the host of spectators and supplied food for all the horses of the missions. Representatives of a number of cities supported Alkibiades in offering this feast. The representatives of Kyzikos gave the sacrificial animals, of Chios the hay for the animals, of Lesbos the wine, and of Ephesos the large tents for the feast. Subsequently, in his apology before the Athenian people, Alkibiades was to boast of this imposing mission, which had done so much to increase the prestige of Athens.

The Right of Participation in the Games

Participation in the Olympic Games, as in all the other Panhellenic or local games, was not open to all; there were restrictions that were very strictly observed. First and foremost, the competitors had to be Greeks; barbarians were forbidden to participate, and slaves were also not allowed to take part. After the subjection of the country by the Romans, the rule that only Greeks should participate was waived, and Romans were admitted. The first recorded Roman victor was Gaius, who won his victory in the 177th Olympiad (72 B.C.). The emperor Tiberius was victorious in the 199th Olympiad (A.D. 17), as was Nero in A.D. 65, after he had compelled his opponents to withdraw.

One rule that was strictly enforced by the Eleans was that the athletes had to go to Olympia one month before the Games began, in order to train under the supervision of the Elean judges, and also to prove that they had been in training for the previous ten months. If an athlete failed to arrive at Olympia in time, he had to justify his late arrival. During the 218th Olympiad (A.D. 93), Apollonios Rantes, an athlete from Alexandria, arrived late at Olympia, according to Pausanias, and gave as his excuse the very bad weather, that had delayed his boat. The judges accepted his excuse and put him in the draw for the boxing. Then appeared his opponent Herakleides, also from Alexandria, and proved that Rantes was lying, for he had not been delayed by bad weather at sea, but had been taking part in games in Ionia in order to make money. Whereupon the judges excluded Rantes and imposed a fine on him.

All those who were guilty of murder or robbing a temple were excluded from the Games, as were all who had violated the truce, whether they were individuals or cities. Sparta, for example, was excluded from the Games of 420 B.C. and fined 2,000 minae because she had attacked Lepreon during the period of the truce. The Spartan Lichas entered his two-horse chariot as Boiotian in order to be able to take part in the Games, and when it was victorious, he appeared in person at the victory announcement and tied the winner's ribbon round the forehead of his charioteer, to show to all that the chariot was his. His action was considered offensive, and the *Hellanodikai* ordered the rod-bearers (*rabdouchoi*) to flog him.

Every athlete registered and declared his city of origin — e.g. Athenian, Argive, Elean, Corinthian, and so on. They had the right, however, to declare themselves citizens of another city, which they could do either in order to honour the ruler of another city, with whom they had ties of friendship or obligation, or when another city offered them gifts and honours, and also, on occasion, when their own city had banished them to punish them or take revenge on them.

Astylos, the great athlete from Kroton in Southern Italy, was victorious in the *stadion* (race of a single course) in three successive Olympiads — the 73rd, 74th and 75th (488-480 B.C.). In the first of these he registered as a Krotonian, but in the other two he declared himself a Syracusan in order to honour the tyrant Hieron, with whom he had bonds of friendship. Subsequently, the Krotonians exiled him, destroyed the statue they had erected to him in the temple of Hera after his first victory, and converted his house into a prison in order to insult him.

Another athlete, Ergoteles, son of Philanor, from Knossos in Crete, was driven out of his native city by his political rivals. He took refuge in Himera in Sicily, and as a Himeran won the long-course race at Olympia, and also at the Pythian, Nemean and Isthmian games.

Dion of Kauloneia in Southern Italy, who had won the boys' *stadion* race at Olympia, was persuaded by an offer of money to declare himself a Syracusan,

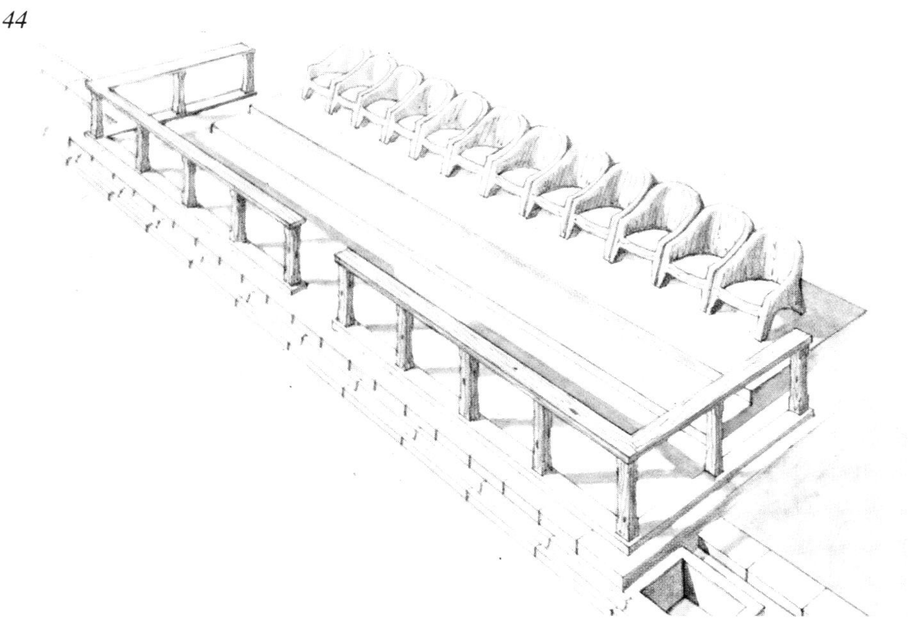

44. Reconstruction of the exedra *of the* Hellanodikai, *which was on the southern embankment of the stadium at Olympia (Drawing: K. Iliakis).*

45. The honorary seat of the Spartan Gorgos, which was found in the ancient stadium at Olympia (Olympia, Archaeological Museum).

and won many victories in the men's events for his new city.

Judges, Hellanodikai and the Staff of the Sanctuaries

In mythical times, the man who awarded the prizes was also the judge in the Games, as in the case of Herakles, Pelops, Achilles and so on. The legendary king of Elis, Iphitos, who was responsible for the major reorganisation of the Games, single-handedly supervised their conduct. It was only in the 50th Olympiad, in 584 B.C., that there were two *agonothetai,* or *Hellanodikai,* as they were known later. In the 75th Olympiad (480 B.C.), the number of *Hellanodikai* was increased to nine, of whom three supervised the equestrian competitions, three the pentathlon, and three the other events. From that time onwards, their number varied according to the fluctuating fortunes of the state of Elis. In the 103rd Olympiad (368 B.C.), there were twelve *Hellanodikai* — as many as the tribes of Elis. From the following Olympiad, however, after the war between the Eleans and the Arkadians, the *Hellanodikai* were reduced to eight, possibly because part of the territory of Elis was taken from the Eleans after their defeat in this war, and the number of constituent tribes was consequently reduced. The number of *Hellanodikai* was firmly fixed at ten from the 108th Olympiad (348 B.C.), and appears to have remained at this until the end, since this is the figure reported by Pausanias and Philostratos.

Initially the office was hereditary and held for life; but when the number of *Hellanodikai* was increased, probably after 584 B.C., they were chosen by lot from amongst the citizens of Elis.

The *Hellanodikai* held office for one Olympiad, and received training for a period of ten months. During the time they stayed in Elis, they resided in the *Hellanodikaion,* a large building in the agora of the city. There they were instructed in their duties and the regulations governing the conduct of the Games by the *nomophylakes* (observers of the laws). The last month before the Games they followed the training of the athletes, and it appears that it was at this time that they made their final selection, as we shall see in another chapter.

In memory of the royal origin of their office, the *Hellanodikai* wore purple cloaks during the Games and were responsible for the general conduct of them. They were competent to inflict financial and physical punishment, and to exclude athletes from the Games. It was also their task to award the prizes, and their verdict was respected and irrevocable. If any athlete felt that he had been the victim of an injustice, he could have recourse to the Council of the Eleans. This body sat during the Games in the *Bouleuterion* (Council-House) at Olympia, and had the power to punish a *Hellanodikes* for a mistaken decision, but did not have the right to invalidate his verdict. The case of the athlete Eupolemos, or Eupolis, from Elis, who won the *stadion* race in the 96th Olympiad (396 B.C.), is an example of this. One of the three *Hellanodikai* responsible for judging the race claimed that the winner was Leon of Ambrakia, while the other two adjudged Eupolemos to be the victor. Leon appealed to the Council, which passed a decision inflicting a fine on the *Hellanodikai*. The victory, however, still went to Eupolemos, who even erected a statue of himself in the Altis.

The Eleans, out of a desire that their Games should retain their authority and great repute in the whole of the Greek world, took great care to ensure that the rules were strictly observed and that the decisions were just and impartial; and it appears that all the Greeks shared the belief of the Eleans that their verdicts were fair. On one occasion, when Psammes, the Pharaoh of Egypt, urged the Eleans to withdraw their own judges from the Games if they wanted them to be held in an impartial manner in their own country, they categorically refused to accept his view.

In 332 B.C., during the 112th Olympiad, in which Troilos, who was himself a *Hellanodikes,* was victorious in the two-horse chariot race and the foals' chariot race, the Eleans forbade the *Hellanodikai* to compete in future chariot races and horse races, in order to preserve their authority.

The significance attached by Herodotos to the judgement of the Eleans is clear from the fact that he has recourse to it in order to demonstrate that the Macedonian king Alexandros, son of Amyntas, was a Greek. Since the Elean judges allowed him to compete in the stadium at Olympia, he argues, this proves that Alexandros was a Greek, and that his opponents, who had sought to have him excluded on the grounds that he was a barbarian, were wrong. Pindar, too, describes the judgement of the Eleans as a "pure judgement."

Another particularly important point is that the *Hellanodikai* had great freedom in the exercise of their duties. There were, of course, general rules that formed the basis of their judgements and decisions, but these rules were not binding or restrictive in their detailed application.

The *Hellanodikai* were assisted in their task by the *alytarches* and the *alytai* (special police officers), who were responsible for the smooth running of the Games, and in the execution of their decisions by the *mastigophoroi* (scourge-bearers), and the *rabdouchoi* (rod-bearers).

In addition to these officials, the sanctuary of Olympia was served during the Games by a large staff of priests and officials. Briefly, it consisted of: the *theëkolos,* the priest, the *manteis,* who gave the oracular responses, the *exegetes,* who explained to the foreigners the various features of the ritual and the Games, the *auletes,* who played the flute during the sacrifices, the *xyleus,* who was responsible for supplying the special poplar wood for the sacrifices, the *grammateus,* who announced which athletes were taking part in the Games, the *spondaules,* who gave the rhythmic accompaniment for the libations and sacrifices, the *epispondorchestai* and *hypospondorchestai,* who made sure that the treaties were observed, and the *kathemerothytes,* who carried out the daily morning sacrifices.

There was also a minor staff, consisting of the *oinochoos* (wine-pourer), the *kleidouchos* (key-holder), the cook, the head-cook, the baker, the *steganomos,* who was responsible for maintaining the buildings, the architect and the doctor.

The Prize

The only prize awarded for victory at Olympia was the *kotinos,* a crown made of branches of wild olive. According to a local legend at Elis, it was believed that the wild olive trees sprung from the olive planted by Herakles in the bare territory of Kronion; he had brought the tree from the land of the Hyperboreans, where he had gone in pursuit of the golden-horned doe sacred to Artemis. Pindar also tells this story, adding that Herakles found the treeless region round Olympia roasting in the sun and conceived the idea of transplanting olives there because they are tough trees that can stand the dry climate and the heat.

According to tradition, it was Iphitos who established the crown of wild olive as the prize, after a response from the oracle at Delphi. Phlegon records that the first athlete to be crowned with the wild olive was the Messenian Daikles, who won the *stadion* race in the 7th Olympiad (752 B.C.).

The olive branch was always cut from the same ancient wild olive tree, called the *Kallistephanos* (for making beautiful crowns), which grew to the right of the opisthodomos of the temple of Zeus. A youth, whose father and mother were both still living, cut from the tree, using gold shears, as many branches as there were contests. These he laid on a gold and ivory table in the temple of Hera — a work by the sculptor Kolotes that had representations of the competitions — and from there they were taken by the *Hellanodikai* to crown the victors.

From the time of Alexander the Great onwards, the athletes were given a palm-branch immediately after their victory, and they held this in their hand when they went to the official crowning ceremony on the fifth day.

It is also known that woollen ribbons were used as prizes and were worn around the forehead, or on other parts of the body of the victors. In the classical period, the charioteers of horsemen that had been victorious wore bands round their foreheads, while the wild olive crown was awarded to the owners of the chariots or horses.

The moral importance of the prize at Olympia was incalculable. The athletes competed with integrity, uprightness and dignity, in order to win a simple crown that was more precious than any riches, and to offer it as a gift to their household, their clan, their city, their ancestors, or their gods.

The Preparation of the Athletes

Training

The talented athletes who were going to appear at the games held in the great sanctuaries or in cities, did not have any special training. The powerful youths and trained men who won the prizes at Olympia or at the other games were undoubtedly the select few, men who had for years been improving their physical powers by a methodical cultivation and development of the human physique. This training was not limited to the gifted few, however, but was practiced by all.

In fact, Solon says, in Lucian's *Anacharsis: And we compel men to exercise their bodies not only for the games, so that they can win the prizes — for very few of them go to them — but to gain a greater good from it for the whole city, and for the men themselves.*

There is not much evidence for the way the athletes trained. It appears that the young men usually exercised their bodies by engaging in the actual sports rather than by special exercises. The sports, moreover, became more difficult as the athletes grew older. Plato advises the younger boys to run half the distance of the men, and the fact that the discuses and jumping-weights that have survived are of different sizes and weights is perhaps due to the same reason — that is, that they were intended for athletes of different physical build and age.

As we saw (see "Athletics and Education") the same *paidagogoi* who took care of the education of the young were also responsible for their physical training. Later on, however, this task was assigned to other people, who had some experience and knowledge of the subject, while methods of physical training for the young gradually developed and improved as a result of the contribution of other factors, especially of medical science.

Throughout antiquity, those concerned with training the youth employed two basic methods, the first of which was aimed at encouraging the pupil to make the greatest possible physical effort so as to achieve the best results, and the second at improving his technique and style. The most effective type of training, however, was the one that had the correct combination of these two methods to suit the particular abilities of the athlete. At the same time, one fundamental aim was that the young men's movements should be harmonious and rhythmical, and this is why vase-paintings often depict youths exercising to the accompaniment of a flute.

As time went on, special trainers appear to have emerged, who were in a position to judge the type and number of exercises that were needed for the individual athlete and the particular sport. They had detailed knowledge of how to increase the size of the muscles, and aimed at putting flesh on certain limbs, because they thought this was necessary to achieve the best performances in some events. They knew all about the rhythm and intensity of the exercises, about continuous and sporadic training, about the beneficial effects of the open air, and how performances suffered indoors. They had divided the

46. A youth practising jumping under the supervision of the paidotribes. *The training of the athletes was the task of specialists, the* paidotribai *and the* gymnastai *(Würzburg, Martin von Wagner Museum).*

athletes into physical types, according to the various events. They were able to judge whether the training schedule was progressing properly and fruitfully from the red colour and oily quality of the skin, and could also decide when the athlete was approaching, or had already arrived at the point of overwork. They were very experienced in deciding on the correct diet for each sport. They could also diagnose excessive cold or over-heating of the body during training, loosening or hardening of the muscles, contusions of the muscular fibres, muscular pain, or local tiredness of the muscles, and the way to treat all these symptoms that were not of a pathological nature. They could distinguish exhaustion or weakness that derived not from the exercises but from other, psychological causes, bad humour, depression and so on. They knew well the best ways for the athletes to relax after their daily exercises, and had a wide knowledge of breathing exercises, of the proper training for the less young athletes, and of the treatment of many conditions by gymnastics and massage. They even went to the extent of researching the family history of the athletes in case there were any hereditary diseases.

In later times, after the Roman conquest of Greece, a method of repetitive training was devised which was called the "four-part cycle" or "system". This was a periodic cycle of training that lasted four days and was continually repeated without a break. On the first day the athlete got ready for the great exertion that would ensue on the following day; on the second day he exerted his powers to the highest degree; on the third day he reduced his efforts, but without entirely losing his form; and on the fourth he tried to achieve a moderate level of performance. The description of the above system is from Philostratos, who is opposed to this kind of programmed training because, in his opinion, the trainer ought to be free to exercise the individual athlete in accordance with his psychological state, or with the weather conditions, and should not be tied to a pre-arranged schedule. The *Hellanodikai* at Elis, too, did not allow the four-day method during the months of preliminary judging, for they believed that training should not be based on a fixed programme of exercises, but on a programme determined in accordance with the particular conditions of the moment.

In modern times, the name "Interval" has been given to this repetitive system of training.

Professional Trainers

Three names have survived for people whose work it was to train athletes or attend to the physical education of the young in general: *paidotribes* (physical trainer), *gymnastes* (trainer of professional athletes) and *aleiptes* (anointer).

The earliest of these was the *paidotribes*. The *paidotribes*, as special preliminary trainer, must have made his appearance at the same time as the *palaistra* and the *gymnasion*, the athletic institutions where the youth trained in every city.

The *paidotribes* was usually a veteran athlete of some experience, who had also acquired an education in the theory of training. Judging from the famous ones that we know of, it seems that almost all of them must have had a more of less adequate gen-

47

47. An athlete using the strigil to scrape the oil, dust and sweat from his body, after exercising in the gymnasion (Vienna, Kunsthistorisches Museum).

eral education. Ikkos of Tarentum and Herodikos of Selymbria were sophists, and Ikkos was the first man to attach particular importance to the athletes' diet, which he decided in the light of the event they were training for. Pindar describes the famous Aiginetan *paidotribes* Melesias as *unconquerable in speech*.

The progress and development of athletics from the 4th century B.C. onwards resulted in the specialisation of athletes and consequently the emergence of specialist trainers, who were able to study the event and determine the training methods and diet of the athlete in accordance with his capabilities.

The *gymnastes* and the *paidotribes* co-existed and worked together for the same end. The *gymnastes* had the broader education in the art of training and determined the details of the programme, while the *paidotribes* implemented it, following the progress of the athlete and giving him practical guidance. There was no need for the latter to know the structure and functioning of the human body, for he was there simply to carry out the instructions of the *gymnastes;* his job was to teach the athletes their exercises, and the holds, and techniques of the sport.

Aristotle distinguishes the task of the *paidotribes* from that of the *gymnastes: The boys should be entrusted to a gymnastes and a paidotribes, for the former takes care of their physical constitution, and the latter their training*.

The jurisdiction of the *gymnastai* was so wide that they even followed the private lives of the athletes and intervened where they thought it necessary. There are many examples of this. The *gymnastes* Eryxias called out to the athlete Arrichion, at a critical point of his contest at Olympia: "It's better to die at Olympia than to withdraw." And, as we know, Arrichion died, and was declared winner posthumously, not because he had died but because his opponent had meanwhile withdrawn. Another *gymnastes,* Tisias, shouted to the famous boxer of the ancient world, Glaukos of Karystos, "Remember the plough-share, lad...," to remind him of his strength with the plough, that had induced Tisias to enter him for the Olympic Games. Glaukos, though still an inexperienced boxer, delivered such a powerful punch to his opponent that he knocked him out and won the match. The *gymnastes* of the great athlete Promachos exploited the youth's love for a girl, by telling him that he would only win her if he was victorious at Olympia.

Many of the athletes who won glory at Olympia honoured their *gymnastes* and *paidotribes* by setting up statues of them next to their own. And Pindar, in his odes in praise of the victories of athletes, does not omit the names of their trainers. In his *8th Olympian Ode,* he praises Melesias, the trainer of Alkimedon of Aigina who had won the boys' wrestling, and in a review of the glory won for Melesias by boy athletes, he informs us that the victory now won by Alkimedon is Melesias' thirtieth.

The *aleiptes* had an important role to play, as well as the *gymnastes* and the *paidotribes*. It was his job to anoint with oil the bodies of the boys and the men who were about to exercise. This initially simple task developed into a scientific massaging of the muscles and gradually became an integral part of good training. For as time went on, they noticed that a skilled massage of the muscles before training had beneficial effects, and also that a careful, light massage assisted the process of winding down and recovery by an athlete who had completed a long training session. Hence, the *aleiptes* became known as *iatraleiptes* (healer-anointer).

48

48. Three athletes getting ready for exercise in the wrestling school. Their names are given in the inscriptions on the vase. On the left, Tranion is massaging the sole of Hippomedon's foot, while the latter is leaning on his staff and resting his left hand on Tranion's head. Hegesias is pouring oil from an aryballos into his hand in preparation for anointing his body. Lykon, the athlete on the right, is carefully taking off his cloak, and is about to hand it to the small boy on the right. The clothes of the other athletes are neatly folded on the stool (diphros). Tranion and Hippomedon are wearing crowns of oak, while Lykon's crown is of wild olive (W. Berlin, Staatliche Museen).

49

50

49. The aleiptes *massaging the muscles of a youth under the eye of the trainer. The scientific massage of the muscles was an essential part of good training (Rome, Villa Giulia).*

50. Young men washing themselves after exercise. In the gymnasia a special area called the loutron *was set aside for the young athletes to cleanse their bodies and refresh themselves after exercise (London, British Museum).*

Rules of the Competition

Introduction

The Eleans made great efforts to retain and sharpen the interest of all the Greeks in the Games, and they achieved this by strict observance of the rules of the competitions and their impartial verdicts. For there were rules in force, like the conventions of today, which were unwritten, but which the Eleans were careful to preserve with religious devotion. It was for this reason that they assembled the *Hellanodikai* for ten months in order to train them. It had been demonstrated that all the Greeks religiously respected and observed the rules, and Pindar describes the regulations that applied in the Olympic Games as "Laws of Zeus."

Age of the Competitors

One task of the Elean judges in the competitions, was to investigate closely the age of the aspiring competitors, in order to separate out the boys. The very young were singled out and excluded even from the boys' games, while those who were past the age of children were classified as adults, and could compete in the men's games if they wished. Those who competed immediately after they had passed the age of childhood took part in the Games as "men from boys." There was no intermediate category, such as that of "the beardless" attested in other games. On one occasion at Olympia, a boy from Athens was almost excluded from the Games because he was a very big and tough competitor. In the 78th Olympiad (468 B.C.), Pherias of Aigina was considered too young and was excluded from the Games. In the following Olympiad, however (464 B.C.), he was admitted into the boys' events and won the wrestling. Nikasylos of Rhodes, on the other hand, an 18-year-old youth, was excluded by the Eleans from the boys' wrestling, but took part in the men's category and won the event. It appears therefore, that the right of the *Hellanodikai* at Olympia to allocate the athletes to age groups, and either to accept or to reject them, was unrestricted. They decided in which category any youth of between 12 and 18 years was to compete, on the basis of his appearance.

The *Hellanodikai* gave similar attention to the question of separating the horses from the foals; usually they were assisted in this by former Olympic victors, who took an oath before the Council that they would separate the foals from the horses honestly.

Withdrawal of a Competitor

Once a competitor had been admitted into the Games, he could not withdraw or resign. This ruling was intended to apply to an athlete who had been selected and had been drawn to compete in an event involving pairs of competitors.

Sarapion of Alexandria, who entered the *pankration* in the 201st Olympiad (A.D. 25), became afraid of his opponents, and secretly left Olympia the day before the Games. He was fined for this, and it seems that up till the time of Pausanias (2nd century A.D.) he was the only athlete punished for such a reason.

Ephedros (The Bye)

Among the regulations of the contests, there was one that seems inexplicable and foreign to the way we view sporting competition today: this was the rule of the *ephedreia* (the "bye"). In events where the athletes were drawn to compete in pairs, such as the wrestling, boxing, *pankration,* and perhaps also the *pentathlon,* it would occasionally happen that one competitor would be left over, without an opponent. He was not excluded, as one might imagine, but, quite the reverse, was the lucky man in the draw, for he would compete with the ultimate winner. He was called the *ephedros* (the man waiting), and was lucky in that he would meet in the final, when he himself was fresh, an opponent who would come to it tired from his previous matches.

An example of a competition which took place with an *ephedros* is recorded on an inscription preserved at Olympia:

P(ublius) Cornelius Ariston, son of Eirenaios, of Ephesos, a boy pankratiast, victor in the 207th Olympiad (A.D. 49), *to Olympian Zeus...*

I won the crown in the boys' pankration at Olympia, without being drawn as ephedros,
having competed thrice with my opponents.

Ariston competed three times to win the Olympic crown. There were seven opponents, divided into three pairs for the first round, with one *ephedros;* in the second round the three victors and the *ephedros* competed in two pairs, and in the third and final round the victory was contested by the two winners remaining in the competition. Ariston won, and was proud of the fact that he had done so without having had the luck to be drawn as *ephedros.*

"Akoniti" (The Uncontested Victory)

It is not only the rule concerning the *ephedros* that seems strange and inexplicable in terms of modern sporting ideas and practice. There was another rule in force both at Olympia and at the other great games that gives cause for perplexity. It was possible for an athlete to be proclaimed victor without competing; the victory was described as *akoniti* — that is to say, without competition, without falling into the dust *(konis)* on the ground. The Suda gives the following definition: *akoniti:* without dust, without struggle ... not getting dusty.

Philostratos, stating that the Eleans recognised an *akoniti* victory only in the wrestling competition, gives us the required explanation. *It is for this reason, then, that the Eleans, though they consider it inappropriate to award the crown of victory akoniti to the pankratiast or the boxer, recognise an akoniti victor in the wrestling. And the reason that the rules make this prescription is clear to me. For in the light competitions, the athletes only perform part of the competition in their training, whereas in the heavy competitions, the athlete is trained by the Eleans in the burning heat of the summer, and in the dust of the wrestling pit, which is baked by the sun, and is obliged to undergo the exhausting training. And the wrestler competes even when training, whereas the boxer and the pankratiast perform only a part of the contest, and they wear light gloves when they hit each other so that they are not injured; but the wrestling event is no different in the preliminary contests, and so the Eleans, judging correctly, award the akoniti victory in this contest alone, should the situation arise.* In spite of what Philostratos says, however, we know of occasions at Olympia when athletes were crowned *akoniti* in the boxing and the *pankration.* The episode involving Theagenes of Thasos and the boxer Euthymos of Italian Lokroi is well known. In the 75th Olympiad (480 B.C.),

Theagenes, who had entered for the *pankration,* wanted to compete in the boxing too; he defeated Euthymos, but was too tired to compete in the *pankration,* and therefore withdrew, in the belief that his opponent Dromeus of Mantinea, would not be awarded the crown for the *pankration,* since the law stated that it was only in the wrestling that an *akoniti* victor was recognised. The *Hellanodikai* judged that Theagenes had not observed the rules and gave the *akoniti* victory to Dromeus. Theagenes was also fined two talents, one for the god and one for Euthymos, who had been wronged. He paid off his fine to Euthymos by not competing in the boxing contest at the two following Olympiads, and thus allowing Euthymos to win. It is said that Dromeus was the first *akoniti* victor in the Olympic Games.

The so-called *hiera* (sacred) victory was somewhat similar to the *akoniti* victory. When a competition ended indecisively (that is, when it was a draw, the victory being awarded to no one), the victory crown was offered to the god in the sanctuary. A base is preserved at Olympia, dating from the early 2nd century A.D., the inscription on which states that the pankratiast Rufus (Tiberius Claudius), a *hieronikes* (winner of the sacred victory), fought until the stars filled the heavens, and was thus neither victorious nor vanquished, the contest ending without a decision. He nonetheless set up a statue of himself since he was honoured for his physical strength and endurance.

Gymnic Competitions

The athletes taking part in all the competitions had to be naked. It is not absolutely certain from what date this custom prevailed, or who imposed it first, for the ancient sources are confused on the point. Pausanias makes reference to Orsippos of Megara, who won the *stadion* race in the 15th Olympiad (720 B.C.). His loin-cloth fell off during the race, but he continued to run and won the contest. Pausanias himself voices the suspicion that the loin-cloth did not fall off by accident, but that Orsippos let it fall deliberately in order to run unimpeded. Julius Africanus states that the first man to run naked was the Spartan Akanthos. Thucydides, however, observes that *not many years have elapsed since the athletes at Olympia ceased to wear loin-cloths around their private parts.* The explanation may be that it was only the runners who abandoned the loin-cloth from the 15th Olympiad, while the competitors in the other events did so at a later date.

Later (in 388 B.C.), after the already related incident involving Kallipateira, the daughter of Diagoras, it was decreed that the trainers also should enter the stadium naked during the Games. Philostratos believes that the Eleans compelled the trainers to go naked because they wanted them to be well-made and strong, living examples to their athletes, and strong enough *to endure and to be burnt* — that is, able to withstand the great heat at Olympia.

Violations of the Rules. Penalties

Throughout the long history of the Olympic Games the rules were seldom broken. On a very few occasions we hear of penalties imposed on an athlete who had caused the death of his opponent by an illegal hold or blow. Amongst the few examples of this is that of the boxer Diognetos of Crete, who

51

51. One of the earliest inscriptions connected with sport. It refers to the 4 victories of Aristis, *son of Pheidon, from Kleonai, in the Nemean games (Nemea, Museum).*

52. The rules were rarely broken in the Olympic Games. On the few occasions that this happened, fines were inflicted on the guilty party, and the money was used to erect statues of Zeus, called Zanes. *The figure shows the bases on which these statues were placed in front of the entrance to the stadium at Olympia.*

52

killed his opponent Herakles during the course of the contest; the *Hellanodikai* denied him the olive branch and drove him from Olympia.

The penalties were of three kinds: a fine, exclusion from the Games, and corporal punishment. The penalties were imposed by the *Hellanodikai,* and executed by the *alytarches* and the *alytai* and by the *rabdouchoi,* as Thucydides calls them.

Flogging was one of the lighter penalties; it was imposed for minor infringements, and most usually carried out during the Games.

The money from the fines imposed on those who broke the rules went in part to the treasury of the god, that is to the sanctuary, and in part to the wronged opponent, if there was one, as in the incident already referred to involving Theagenes of Thasos. Another case was that involving the fine imposed on the Spartans for the capture of the two small towns, Lepreon and Phyrkon, during the truce. The Eleans fined the Spartans two minae per soldier, and since the Spartan soldiers had numbered 1,000, the sum due was 2,000 minae. The Spartans pleaded as excuse that they had not been aware that the truce had been announced. The Eleans then proposed that Lepreon should be returned to them, and that they should in turn abandon their claim to their share of the fine, so that only the god's share would be paid. When the Spartans refused to give way, the Eleans excluded them from the Games, and it was at this stage that they agreed to evacuate Lepreon and pay the god's share of the fine.

It is certain that the fines were invariably paid by those who violated the rules, for they knew that the sanctions were severe. If, indeed, the athlete did not have the means to pay, the responsibility was undertaken by his city, to avoid exclusion from the Games. The Delphic oracle also aided the Eleans and strengthened their hand in compelling the cities to pay the fines.

The revenue from the fines was used to make statues of Zeus, which were called *Zanes.* The statues stood in the Altis, after the *Metroon* and at the foot of the *exedra* of the treasuries. Six of them were first erected during the 98th Olympiad with the fines paid by the Thessalian Eupolos, and the boxers he had bribed, Agenor of Arkadia, Prytanis of Kyzikos and Phormion of Halikarnassos.

After Eupolos, writes Pausanias, *they say that the Athenian Kallippos, who had taken part in the pentathlon, bought off his potential opponents with money, and this happened during the 112th Olympiad. After a fine had been imposed by the Eleans on Kallippos and his opponents, the Athenians sent Hypereides to persuade the Eleans to absolve them of the penalty. When the Eleans refused, the Athenians treated them very haughtily, and did not pay the money, or take part in the Olympic Games, until the god of Delphi told them that he would not give oracles to the Athenians under any circumstances unless they paid the fine to the Eleans. When they had therefore paid it, statues of Zeus were made, six on this occasion also.*

Elegiac verses were engraved on the statues emphasising that an Olympic victory should not be won by money and underhand means, but by fleetness of foot and strength of body.

The Preliminary Selection

Philostratos, in his *Life of Apollonios* writes that *When the season for the Olympic Games arrives, the*

Eleans train the athletes for thirty days in Elis; and when they have gathered them together (and trained them and examined their general condition), they say to them: if you have trained as much as is necessary for the Olympic Games, and have not done anything base or mean, go and compete with courage, but if you are not well-trained, as we have said, then depart from here wherever you wish.

Pausanias also speaks clearly of this obligation upon the athletes to stay in Elis, and justifies it in terms of the Eleans teaching them all they should know about the Olympic Games during the course of the month. He then says there were three gymnasia at Elis: the *Xystos,* which had a special area in which the runners and contestants in the pentathlon competed for "practice" — that is, where they trained; and a special area for "competition between the runners"— that is, where they competed for selection. There was also another area called the *plethrion,* where the *Hellanodikai* met together and had the athletes compete by age in the wrestling. The second gymnasium, which was smaller, was called the *Tetragonon* (from its square shape); normally, the athletes practised wrestling and boxing there, the boxers wearing soft gloves so as not to be injured seriously. The third gymnasium was called *Maltho,* and was intended for the training of youths.

It is therefore probable that the Eleans selected the athletes who were suitable — those, that is, who had trained carefully and seemed worthy to compete in the stadium at Olympia — while at the same time they excluded those who had not had satisfactory training. They were also concerned to present in the stadium well-trained athletes who would offer a perfect spectacle.

Pindar gives us an example of these trial games; in his *8th Olympian* and *8th Pythian odes* he states that Alkimedon and Aristomenes, respectively, each competed with four rivals in the boys' wrestling before they got to the final. We may say, therefore, that these preliminary competitions at Elis had the same purpose as the eliminating heats in the modern games: to bring into the stadium to contest the great victory the best trained and most worthy athletes.

The trainers were obliged to follow the training of their athletes. This is made clear by Philostratos: *There* (in Elis), *the method of preliminary training and the kind of exercises are decided by others, and it is not the trainer, but the Hellanodikes who, entirely on his own initiative and without being bound in any way, organises everything, in accord with the particular circumstances pertaining from time to time. And the Hellanodikes has the whip at his disposal, not only for the athlete, but also for the trainer, and he uses it in case of any contravention of his orders; and all have to conform with the orders of the Hellanodikai, since those who violate them may be immediately excluded from the games.*

The institution of the preliminary games, however, must have had a wider application and significance than the mere preliminary selection of the athletes.

The preparation for the Games was a mental as well as a physical trial. At Elis, every athlete followed a prescribed programme of work and diet, and during the course of their preparation there, the Games officials judged the competitors on terms of character and morale, strength, endurance and perseverance, ability and technique, and singled out those they thought fit to appear in the stadium before the Panhellenic public and offer a spectacle worthy of the history and reputation of Olympia.

An Olympiad

First Day

It is possible, on the basis of the ancient texts and the archaeological discoveries, to reconstruct the programme of the Games hypothetically, and to describe them with relative accuracy. Neither the length of the Games, nor the order of the competitions remained unchanged throughout antiquity. The description that follows is of the noisy sanctuary, the happy crowd and the festive atmosphere of an Olympiad in the 4th century B.C., when most of the events had been included in the programme, and the Olympic Games retained all their authority and splendour.

Around the Altis, the stadium and the hippodrome, and also further afield, on the hills and slopes as far as the banks of the Alpheios, the whole countryside has been full of a noisy throng for days now: athletes, trainers, philosophers, politicians, former Olympic victors, official missions, and ordinary spectators. Compatriots talk in groups beneath the trees where they have spent the night, or outside the tents, both improvised and luxurious. The whole countryside echoes with voices, songs and laughter. The whole region round Olympia is in a state of commotion. The great day is dawning.

Two days earlier, the official procession set out from Elis, headed by the *Hellanodikai* and other officials, and followed the Sacred Way — the road that linked Elis with the sanctuary at Olympia. It stopped at the spring Piera, where a sacrifice and purification ceremony took place. Those taking part in the procession spent the night at Letrinoi, and at dawn of the following day, they entered the valley of Olympia in festive mood.

Meanwhile the noisy crowd is jostling in the Altis, where the official procession has already begun to appear, with the rulers of Elis, the priests, the *Hellanodikai,* dressed in purple, the judges, the official guests, the athletes, the charioteers, the trainers, and the boy athletes, accompanied by their fathers and brothers.

The ceremony begins with the registering of the athletes, and the official oath, which they swear at the *Bouleuterion* (Council-House) in front of the statue of Zeus Horkios. Fearsome and threatening, the god raises his two hands holding the thunderbolts. The base of the statue is engraved with inscriptions and elegiac verses for oath-breakers and all those who dare break the law. A boar is sacrificed in front of the statue, and the competitors swear that they have trained for the last ten months, in accordance with the rules, and that they will not perpetrate any "evil deed," that is, infringement of the rules, during the Games. Every violation of the regulations, and also the pursuit of victory by underhand means, is described as an "evil deed." Then the athletes, their fathers and brothers, and their trainers, take an oath on the genital organs of the boar. Lastly, the judges who will assist the *Hellanodikai* in allocating the athletes to their age groups, and in separating the foals from the horses, swear that they will judge justly and will keep their decisions secret.

Next the registering of the men, the boys and those participating in the equestrian events, takes place in the *Bouleuterion* — the declaration of the athletes in the various events, as we would say today. This is followed by the draw for those contests that are performed in pairs. In the afternoon one may see on a whited board outside the *Bouleuterion,* the notice bearing the names of the athletes who have entered, and the competitions that will be held.

On the same day (from 396 B.C. onwards), the

contests for trumpeters and heralds are held, and the winners will offer their services for the Olympiad. The contests are held in front of the altar near the entrance to the stadium. The trumpeters compete first and then the heralds, the winners being those whose trumpet or voice carries farthest. These men will have the honour of calling out the names of the athletes, and blowing the trumpet throughout the Games.

The official ceremonies of the opening day are now over. The missions from the cities sacrifice to their own patron gods and ask them to give the victories to their own cities. The horse-breeders offer a greater number of sacrifices, not only because they are the wealthiest men, but because the competitions involving horses are dangerous and the help of the gods essential. There were altars to Poseidon Hippios, Hera Hippia, Ares Hippios, Athena Hippia, the Dioskouroi, Aphrodite, Pan, Tyche and Taraxippos. The last-named is feared by all, for he is a fearsome deity of the hippodrome, who disturbs the horses at the turning post at the bend in the track, where most of the accidents occur. It is for this reason that an altar was erected at the turning post in the hippodrome at Olympia, on which the charioteers made sacrifices to appease this fierce god.

Then, the crowd scatters throughout the Altis, to visit and admire the temples, shrines and altars, to look at the treasuries of the cities and their works of art, to recall the achievements of former Olympic victors as they gaze in wonder at their statues, to read inscriptions and elegiac verses, and to hear authors and poets reciting their works. Until late into the night the pilgrims will sit around the fires that have been lit by all the tents and discuss and pass the time making forecasts for the Games that will begin in the morning, while the athletes will relax under the stern gaze of their trainers.

Second Day

As the sun rises, the stadium is packed with people. In front of the low division that separates the track from the mound on which the spectators are sitting, the rod-bearers pace to and fro to impose order. The *Hellanodikai* holding palm-branches in their hands enter the stadium from a special entrance in the south-east side of it. The oldest of them goes in front "with slow, measured step," followed by the others. Next come the boy competitors, and the procession closes with the special Games police. The *Hellanodikai* cross the track, cheered on by the vast crowd, now on its feet, and reach roughly the middle of the stadium, where special seats have been set for them. Opposite to them, on a small altar, sits the priestess of Demeter Chamyne. The athletes also take the positions allocated to them.

The head of the *Hellanodikai* now rises to his feet and raises the palm-branch high, the trumpeter blows his trumpet, and immediately afterwards, the herald proclames the opening of the Games.

Immediately after, the herald calls on the entrants for the *stadion* race to come forward. Solemn and handsome, the boys run in front of the starting point on the east side of the stadium. The *Hellanodikes* responsible for overseeing the race has already taken up his position, and next to him stands the chief of the special police and some of the rod-bearers, each holding in his hands a bundle of scourges made of slim willow wands.

The judge holds out the urn to all the athletes, who take a sherd from it bearing the letter determining their turn. Then the judge collects the lots, arranges the runners in the order that has fallen to them, summons the starter and then withdraws, with the scourge-bearers, behind the line. At the signal, the runners dash quickly towards the finish, while the spectators follow the race with bated breath. The winner returns to the starting point to wait for the final. As soon as the preliminary heats are over, the winners line up again at the start, and soon run in the final. The winner returns exhuberantly to the start, while the crowd cheers him and throws flowers and laurel leaves. The noise of the crowd and the cheers are silenced by the voice of the herald announcing the name of the winner; and while the *Hellanodikes* is giving him the palm, his fellow-countrymen rush up, overcome with joy, lift him on their shoulders, and carry him round amongst the spectators.

The boys' wrestling competition now begins. The young athletes wrestle in pairs, and the shouts of the crowd each time a competitor succeeds in making a decisive hold carry beyond the Alpheios. The wrestling matches last for some time, until out of all the pairs there remain the two wrestlers who will compete for the great prize.

After the wrestling, the same procedure is observed for the boxing competition and the *pankration*. Meanwhile, the sun has already risen high in the sky, and the heat bakes and scorches. The spectators suffer, because they are following the Games without cover, as the rules prescribe. The sweat streams from the bodies of the athletes, the holds become difficult, and blows slide off.

The boys' games end late in the day with the setting of the sun, and the crowd, no longer able to hold itself back, floods onto the track, lifts the winners onto its shoulders, and carries them to the tents with cheers and shouts of joy and songs of triumph, and there they celebrate the victories until late into the night.

Third Day

The great day of the Olympiad dawns. This is the day for which the crowds have set out from the ends of the earth, and have suffered the indescribable hardships and toils of their long and difficult journey — weeks and months, by land and by sea — until they arrived at holy Olympia. They will soon see the spectacular equestrian competitions, and the day will close with the *pentathlon,* in which the most famous athletes in the Greek world will take part.

Even before the stars have faded from the sky, the great area of the hippodrome is inundated by spectators wanting to see the dramatic equestrian competitions. The events are held in the following order: four-horse chariot race; races for fully grown horses; race of chariots drawn by a pair of mules; trotting competitions, or races for mares; two-horse chariot race; four-horse chariot race for foals; two-horse chariot race for foals; and foals' races.

The richly decorated chariots take up their positions, each in its special bay at the starting post, and the great contest begins. Each circuit of the stadium is four stades (*ca.* 1,770 metres), and the chariots will have to complete ten circuits. With great skill, the charioteers attempt to take the inside of the track, to take the bends tightly, to avoid a collision with other chariots, and to avoid chariots which have crashed and are now lying in the competition area. They also try to pass close to other chariots, so that they can bring the axle of their own chariot into

53. Model of the sanctuary at Olympia. During the Games the crowds assembled in the Altis and surrounding areas.

53

contact with the other and overturn it, thus eliminating a rival. They have to hold onto the chariot with all their strength, for there is always the danger that they will be thrown out at a sharp turn.

The great chariot race offers the crowd a gripping spectacle, and all the excitement attendant upon the successive changes in the position of the chariots during the course of the race. The same interest is shown by the crowds in the remaining equestrian contests.

It is now past mid-day, and the competitions in the hippodrome are over. From all sides, the crowds flock to the stadium for the *pentathlon,* the most difficult contest in the Olympiad. The competitors are many, strong and agile, with bodies that glisten under the mid-day sun. And there are five events: the jump, the discus, the *stadion* race, the javelin and the wrestling. A hard contest will follow, until the last two athletes remain on the track; these will contest the victory in the wrestling, the winner of which will be the ultimate victor in the *pentathlon* (see "Pentathlon").

The sacred ceremonies in honour of Pélops, the legendary founder of the chariot races, were probably performed in the evening of this day and a black ram was sacrificed on his tomb, the *Pelopion.*

Fourth Day

This day, which coincides with the full moon, is the holiest day of all. The morning commences with the main offering, the hecatomb from the Eleans to Zeus, the great deity of Olympia. The festive procession that set out from the Gymnasion or the Prytaneion, and which is heading for the altar of Zeus, is composed of the official delegates from the cities, the priests, the athletes, the embassies with their splendid gifts and dedications, and the animals that will be sacrificed. The 100 oxen that make up the hecatomb will be slaughtered in front of the altar, but only their thighs will be burnt. Along with the official offering by the Eleans, sacrifices will also be made by the embassies from the other cities, and by private individuals. After the sacrifices, the running, wrestling, boxing and *pankration* contests will be held.

The first event is the *stadion* race. At the herald's summons, the *stadiodromoi* approach the starting point and take up their positions. When the signal is given, they dash forward and the stadium echoes to the cries of encouragement of the spectators. Then, the voice of the herald silences the cries. The name and city of the winner is now on everyone's lips, and the victor departs, showered with flowers and leaves from the crowd.

At the end of the stadium, at the point where the runners in the single-course race recently finished, the *diaulodromoi* (double-course runners) are now lining up. They will run until they reach the other end, turn round the posts opposite them, and return to the start, which is now also the finish. Next the *dolichodromoi* (long-course runners) will run in a similar fashion; they will run a number of times from the start to the finish, each time turning round the post at the start and finish.

The heat is becoming increasingly intense in the stadium as the herald calls forth the wrestlers. The crowds jostle on the two sides of the stadium near the pit. Three *Hellanodikai* oversee the event, and the rod-bearers surround the wrestlers sitting around the pit. The athletes are divided into pairs by lot. As the contests start, pandemonium breaks loose in the stadium. Cheers and shouts of encouragement intermingle with laughter and jeers. The pairs wrestle

54. The Greeks personified the spirit of competition and created a deity, Agon *(Contest). On this tetradrachm from the island of Peparethos (Skopelos),* Agon *is depicted with wings and with two crowns in his hands (London, British Museum).*

55. The longed-for Victory, which rewarded the long period of effort by the athlete, is here depicted on coins from Elis. A winged Victory is running towards the left, probably holding a crown in her right hand (Athens, Numismatic Collection).

54 55

and the losers depart, new pairs are matched, and in the end the two best come to grips for the final victory.

Immediately afterwards, the boxing competition starts, with the same procedure of drawing lots. The tireless crowd sings the praises of the winners and mocks the unlucky ones, while it suffers for its defeated athletes. All this is repeated during the *pankration*.

The Olympiad closes with the race in armour. The runners are competing naked, as in other events, but carry a spear, shield and helmet. With the race in armour, the last event of the Olympiad, the truce will come to an end — symbolically of course; in practice, it will continue for a period of time long enough for the athletes and spectators to return to their homes.

Fifth Day

The Olympiad began with the worship of the gods, and it will end with sacrifices and thanks to the gods. The victorious athletes gather at the temple of Zeus with their palm-branches in their hands; the herald calls out the name and the city of the victors one by one, and the oldest of the *Hellanodikai* crowns them.

At mid-day, the Eleans give a banquet for the winners of all the contests in the Prytaneion, and in the evening great feasts are given by the representatives of the cities or by wealthy sports-lovers who wish to honour the winners.

Until far into the night, the quiet valley of Olympia echoes with songs and merry-making, hymns and paeans, wishes and congratulations.

The Olympiad is over.

Honours conferred on the Victors

The Olympic Victory

The ancient Greeks believed that victory at Olympia was owed to the favour of the gods. The victor was their chosen, whom they helped to win the legendary prize, and whose name would remain on men's lips even after the thread of his life had been cut. And this fame, which would make him live for ever in human memory, was his highest reward.

For the victors, the day on which the prizes were awarded was the crowning moment of their whole life — the moment they had been looking forward to eagerly during the long, hard hours of training. As the sun's first rays fell on the sacred Altis, the victors set out, their hearts filled with pride, for the temple of Zeus, where the official crowning would take place. Around their head was tied a red woollen band, and they held a palm-branch in their right hand. They had received these distinctive symbols from the hand of the *Hellanodikes* immediately after their victory, while the herald was calling out their name, and the name of their father and city, and the crowd, carried away with enthusiasm, was cheering their performance. These symbols that marked out the victors were connected with very ancient cults and traditions. The band of wool, which was very commonly found in religious practice, was usually used to adorn sacred objects. Its power was intensified by the red colour and was transmitted to the man who wore it. The palm-branch was directly connected with Theseus: as he was returning from Crete he organised games on Delos in honour of Apollo and the victors were crowned with a palm-branch.

Adorned with these symbols of their victory, the chosen few proceeded to the temple, while the crowds showered them with leaves and flowers. This *phyllobolia* (throwing of leaves) was connected with the very ancient vegetation cult in which the games had their roots. Within the temple the crowns of wild olive lay ready on the gold and ivory table made by the sculptor Kolotes. Three of its sides were decorated with figures of gods carved in relief; on the front were Hera, Zeus, the Mother of the gods, Hermes, Apollo and Artemis, while one side had representations of Asklepios and Hygeia, and the other of Pluto, Dionysos, Persephone and Nymphs; on the rear was a series of depictions of the Olympic competitions. The bronze tripod, on which the crowns had been placed in former times, was always kept in the *prodomos* of the temple of Zeus.

The victors assembled in front of the temple of Zeus, while all around, their relations and friends and a large crowd jostled for position to follow the ceremony. One by one the Olympic victors went up to the *pronaos* and were crowned with the precious prize. This ritual signified a mystic communion between deity and man, and the crown always represented a transference of the powers that are active in the growth of vegetation to the man who was being crowned. The victor was accounted a favourite of the gods, for it was only thanks to their help that he was able to win his victory.

It appears from most of the sources that the victors

56. A victorious athlete. He is holding branches and leaves in his hands and has woollen bands tied round his arm and thigh (Leningrad, Hermitage Museum).

56

were crowned at the end of the games, but a few isolated references leave us to understand that they were crowned immediately after their victory. Since these two versions cannot be reconciled, we may suppose that some time during the long history of the Olympic Games a change occurred in the procedure of the festival.

It is not sure whether a sacrifice of thanksgiving was offered on the altar of Zeus after the crowning ceremony, but the festival certainly closed with a celebratory banquet given by the Eleans in their Prytaneion in honour of the victors. And as night fell over the Altis, the general rejoicing reached a crescendo, and the songs of the victors and their companions filled the valley of the Alpheios.

The following morning, everyone set out on the homeward journey. The victors, however, would always be remembered at Olympia, for the Eleans took care that the names of all the winners at the Games were entered in the archives, while the winner of the *stadion* race, the representative type of the ancient athlete, had the unique honour of giving his name to the Olympiad. This honour perhaps fell to the winner of the *stadion* race, because for many years this was the only event in the Olympic Games.

Honours Conferred by the City

Victory in the Olympic Games caused the fame of the victor to spread to the ends of the Greek world. The name of his city was indissolubly linked to his own name, so that this, too, became known throughout the Greek world. The return home of an Olympic victor was therefore greeted with delirious enthusiasm. Standing in an imposing four-horse chariot, he entered the city, but not through the gate: part of the wall was demolished specially for his entry. In earlier times, when it was believed that the victor was comparable with a deity, the significance of this custom was that he was entering the city not as a man, but as a god, and therefore needed a special gate. Later, the meaning behind the custom changed: as men began to rely on their own powers for success, they no longer needed the intervention or assistance of a god, and the opening in the wall came to signify that the city which had given birth to such a strong fellow had no need of fortifications.

During the later period, the honour conferred upon the victors continually increased, even to the point of excess, especially in the rich cities of the West. An example of this excess may be seen in the welcome reserved for Exainetos of Akragas, who was twice proclaimed winner of the *stadion* race, in 416 and 412 B.C. After his second victory he entered Akragas in a four-horse chariot, accompanied by three hundred of the most important citizens riding in chariots pulled by two white horses. The reception given to an Olympic victor was like that reserved for a general returning from a victorious campaign, for the Olympic victory was valued by the Greeks as highly as victory in battle. As Pindar says:

But he who in contests or in war achieves the delicate glory is magnified to be given the supreme prize, splendor of speech from citizen and stranger.

The festive entry into the city was followed by the triumphal procession of the victor within it, while the assembled crowds showered him with flowers and leaves. The victor went first to the great central square and from there to the temple of the patron deity of the city, to whom he offered a sacrifice and dedicated his crown, in the same way that soldiers returning victorious from a campaign dedicated their spoils to the god. This was followed by a great celebratory banquet, to which the ruler of the city, or the victor himself, if he were wealthy, invited a huge number of people — on occasion, the whole city.

These honours, however, paled into insignificance for the Olympic victors, when compared with the immortality which their fame ensured them and of which the simple crown of olive was the guarantee. It is not surprising, therefore, that kings and rulers strove with all their might, alongside ordinary men, to win the crown of honour which would guarantee to them the right to perpetuate their name by erecting a statue of themselves in the sacred Altis. An inscription accompanying the statue included the name of the victor, his father's name and the name of his city, and often also the contest in which he had been proclaimed victor. Thanks to this inscription he would become famous not only in his own lifetime, but also throughout the centuries that followed, as long as the crowds continued to flock to Olympia. The inscriptions were normally carved on the stone base of the statue, most usually on the upper horizontal surface of it, or on the vertical side that was most immediately seen. Some of the inscriptions were incised on bronze plaques fastened to the base, but there were also instances where the text was inscribed on the work itself, on the thigh of a statue, on the chariot or on the horse. When the text of the inscription gradually deteriorated with the passage of time, the victor's descendants or the authorities at Olympia had it restored or renewed. The victors attempted by all possible means to draw the attention of the spectators to their own statue, and often they commissioned a poet to write the text in verse, in order to avoid simple prose, or it may have been both in prose and verse; occasionally, too, the epigram was accompanied by a relief. Olympic victors had the right to set up a statue of themselves in their city as well as at Olympia, and this accounts for the fact that whole series of statues adorned the official areas of the Greek cities, such as temples, theatres, the *agora, gymnasia* and so on (see "Athletics and Art").

The honours conferred upon the victor were sometimes of a material nature. In Athens, Solon passed a law offering a prize of five hundred drachmas to an Olympic victor (see "Athletics and Education"). The great value of a prize like this can easily be appreciated, when one reflects that a sheep or a *medimnos* of cereals cost one drachma and that the *pentakosiomedimnoi* (men whose land yielded 500 *medimnoi* per annum) were the wealthiest economic class. There is also evidence for still greater prizes: Dio Chrysostom claims that some cities gave to Olympic victors five talents, the enormous size of which can be seen from the fact that Solon had fixed the value of the Attic talent at 6,000 drachmas.

The privileges and distinctions varied from city to city. One of the most important of them was the right to dine for life in the Prytaneion at public expense, a privilege which put the Olympic victors on the same level as the most important office-bearers, citizens and benefactors of the city. They had a seat of honour at the public games, along with the officials, priests, distinguished generals and foreign ambassadors. From the middle of the 5th century B.C., they were probably given exemption from taxation. Their names were also inscribed on stelai that were set up in public places, though we cannot claim with any

57

58

57. A winner in the boys' section, standing on a pedestal. In front of him is an older man, the umpire, or his paidotribes *(Baltimore, The Johns Hopkins University).*

58. The agonothetes *tying a band around the head of a young victor, who is holding branches and leaves in his hands (Munich, Antikensammlungen).*

certainty that this privilege was invariably accorded them.

In the Hellenistic and Roman periods there are cases where not only his city of origin, but other cities too, honoured an Olympic victor by giving him citizenship and an honorary seat on the council. In the Imperial period in particular, it was not uncommon for even boy victors to become members of the council. Some times the victors were honorary citizens of so many cities that only the most important of them were recorded in the inscription on their statue, the others being simply alluded to in a phrase such as "and citizen and councillor of many other cities." At Sparta, the Olympic victors enjoyed the highest privilege, that of being included in the *Homoioi* (the Equals), which entitled them in war to fight at the side of the king. In many places the fact that a man was an Olympic victor was one of the basic reasons for his being appointed general, or leader of a colony.

The immortality of the victor was also ensured by the means of the *epinician* (victory ode), which the victors commissioned a poet to write for them (see "Athletics and Poetry"). Many other Olympic victors, however, were immortalised because myths, legends and traditions were woven around their achievements.

Finally, rulers and kings struck coins to immortalise their victories in equestrian contests. Anaxilaos, the tyrant of Rhegion, who won a chariot race probably in the 75th Olympiad (480 B.C.), struck a silver tetradrachm with a picture of a chariot. Philip II of Macedon commemorated his victory in the horse race at the 106th Olympiad (356 B.C.) by striking a silver tetradrachm with a head of Zeus crowned

59

60

61

62

with laurel on the obverse, and a picture of the victorious rider, holding a palm-branch in his hand, on the reverse. He also celebrated his victory in the chariot race at Olympia in 352 or 348 B.C. by issuing a gold stater depicting on its obverse the head of Apollo wearing a laurel crown, and on the reverse a two-horse chariot and charioteer. In the Imperial period, cities are known to have made the Olympic victory of one of their citizens the occasion for an issue of coinage.

One of the rarest and greatest honours for mortals in antiquity was heroisation, that is, worship of them as heroes after their death. Instances are recorded in the 6th and 5th centuries B.C. of Olympic victors being heroised; it is believed, however, that this was due not to their Olympic victory alone, but also to other accomplishments and personal qualities. Finally, many athletes also made reference to their victory at Olympia on the grave stele that stood over their mortal remains, striving at this final moment of their lives to ensure their survival through the centuries.

59-60. Rulers, kings and tyrants immortalised their victories by stricking coins. Philip II of Macedon struck a silver tetradrachm to commemorate his victory in the horse race of 356 B.C. It depicts the winning rider and the horse. On the other side of the coin the head of Zeus (Athens, Numismatic Collection).

61. King Philip II of Macedon struck a gold stater with a picture of a two-horse chariot, in memory of his victory in the chariot race (Athens, Numismatic Collection).

62. Tetradrachm from Syracuse, with a four-horse chariot. The charioteer is nearing the finish, and Victory is running to meet him with the crown in her hand (London, British Museum).

Athletics in Poetry and Art

Athletics and Poetry

In 485 B.C. Pytheas, a youth from Aigina, was victorious in the *pankration* at the Nemean games, and his relations asked Pindar, the Theban choral poet, to write an epinician for him. When the poet demanded a fee of 3,000 drachmas, however, they said that they preferred to order a bronze statue of the youth for the same price. Later they changed their minds and gave the commission to Pindar, who took the opportunity to defend his art at the beginning of this ode:

I am no maker of images, not one to fashion idols standing quiet
on pedestals. Take ship of burden rather, or boat, delight of my song
forth from Aigina, scattering the news
that Lampon's son, Pytheas the strong,
has won the garland of success at Nemea, pankratiast,
showing not yet on his cheeks the summer
of life to bring soft blossoming.

It is Pindar's belief that of the two art forms, sculpture and poetry, it is the latter which is more suitable for furthering the renown of the victor. For the statue would remain immobile in the sanctuary of Zeus at Nemea, or wherever it was erected, and the only people who would learn about the victor and his prowess would be those who chanced to pass by and read the inscription on it. Whereas Pindar's ode, from the first time it is heard at the celebration on Aigina, will be taken up and sung in every corner of the Greek world.

The honours bestowed on the victor in the games by his country were many, as we saw: he was given an official reception on his return home, high offices, public maintenance in the Prytaneion, etc. He also had the right, a little later, to organise at his own expense a celebration in some shrine of his country, or in his home, at which a choir of his friends and contemporaries, after making the indispensable sacrifices to the gods, sang, to the accompaniment of a flute and lyre, the victory ode written and set to music by a famous poet.

Naturally the epinician, however much it may have been a poem of the occasion, was not forgotten immediately afterwards. Earlier we saw Pindar, in the introduction to his ode for Pytheas, estimating that it would immediately spread throughout the Greek world. The family of the poet too, undoubtedly took care to preserve it later, as an enduring testimony to its own glory. They could sing it at some family celebration in the years to come. It is even reported of the *7th Olympian Ode* by Pindar, written in 464 B.C. for the famous boxer Diagoras of Ialysos, that the Rhodians had it incised in letters of gold on a plaque dedicated in the sanctuary of Lindian Athena, since it recorded the mythical history of their island. Finally, we may be sure that the poet himself kept copies of the poems he wrote.

Since man cannot live forever, he has a great desire to ensure that his memory, at least, is kept alive for as long as possible. And of all the honours received by the victor, only two could keep his name alive throughout time: the statue and the epinician. Whoever was not wealthy enough to pay for both was obliged to make a choice. And although the dissemination of his name over a wide area was best secured by the epinician, as Pindar had correctly observed, when it is a question of its enduring through time, our first thoughts turn to the statue of marble or of bronze: this would certainly have greater resistance to destruction than a song written on papyrus, however carefully the relations of the victor might treasure it. And yet what remains today of the countless statues of athletes that adorned the great sanctuaries? As the poet Simonides accurately predicted, the marble has crumbled and the bronze melted, not only as a result of natural disasters, earthquakes, fires etc., but also at the hands of men. In contrast, roughly sixty victory odes from the 5th century B.C. have had the good fortune to survive to the present day, and have thus demonstrated the accuracy of Pindar's belief that the word survives longer than deeds in this life.

It is a matter of great regret that so many works of ancient plastic art, carved in many cases by great artists, have been lost forever; it is very gratifying, however, that so many literary works of art have escaped destruction, to proclaim the prowess of Greek athletes through the centuries. And it is the word which, by its nature, possesses greater resources of expression with which to glorify their skill. The word is much more moving than a statue, however expressive this may be, since it can go into details, make comparisons and appreciations, and so on. For this reason it is the victory ode, first and foremost, that transports us into the happy atmosphere of a victory celebration; it also helps us to understand that the Greeks viewed a victor at the Panhellenic competitions as manifesting his moral character through his athletic achievement, bringing honour to his family and his country, and glorifying the gods who had helped him to his victory.

It is an unshakeable belief of the Greeks that the deed, however significant it may be, has need of the word: otherwise it cannot receive recognition and justification. So, victory in the games too, as a successful deed, "thirsts" for song if it is not to be cast on one side and quickly forgotten. The same belief appears clearly in a sacred myth treated by Pindar: at the great celebration held on Olympos on the day that Zeus married Hera, after he had defeated the Titans and restored order in the world, he observed that the other gods were silent, as though they were not completely satisfied. When he asked them what else they wanted, they requested him to create some other divinities, whose sole duty it would be to sing of the mighty deeds of Zeus and of the order he had imposed on the world. The great god agreed with them and fathered the Muses, whose mother, significantly, was Mnemosyne (Memory). Even the deed of Zeus, then, needed to become word in the mouths of the Muses; otherwise it would have fallen into oblivion.

The same belief finds further expression in the *Iliad,* in the fear of Helen (a fear that was at the same time an unvoiced hope), that Zeus had ordained that she and Paris would become *aoidimoi* (from ἀείδω, to sing) — in other words, that they would become a song on the lips of generations to come. And in fact, without the immortal words of Homer, who today would know of Helen, whose beauty occasioned a bloody war lasting ten years? The same belief, finally, is shown by Isokrates when he writes that after mature reflection he considers that the best way to preserve his work, after a life of eighty years, was to entrust it to words, rather than to bronze dedications.

Thus, roughly fifty victors at the great games ensured their immortality by becoming *aoidimoi* — worthy, that is, to be sung by a poet. Most of them were sung by Pindar, and fewer by Bacchylides, while a few fragments only of the victory odes by Simonides have come down to us. Pindar and Bacchylides were active during the first fifty years of the 5th century B.C., and Simonides a generation earlier. Immediately afterwards, this poetic genre declined. It is only reported to have been subsequently used by the tragedian Euripides, who sang the praises of Alkibiades when in 416 B.C., he gained three victories in the chariot races at the same Olympic Games. Kallimachos in the 3rd century, wrote a victory ode for one Sosibios, who had won victories with his chariot at the Nemean and the Isthmian games.

Our knowledge of the nature of the victory ode is thus based on Simonides, and to a much greater extent on Bacchylides and Pindar. Despite the differences manifested by these three choral poets, we can gain some understanding, from the features common to their victory odes, of the reason why a victory in the games brought such great honour to the victor, his family and his country — honour that was qualitatively different from that attaching to a modern victor in international sporting competitions.

First of all the athletes were not professionals; they were individuals, mature men and youths who, at least in the 5th century B.C., generally belonged to aristocratic families that looked upon athletic competition as one of their prerogatives, and who expected the poet to glorify in his victory ode the social and political ideals of the aristocracy (and this is particularly true of Pindar who was himself conservative). Nor should it be forgotten that even in democratic Athens, the aristocratic houses retained their magnificence undiminished. To these athletes, who were private individuals, must be added the tyrants of Sicily, Hieron of Syracuse and Theron of Akragas, who themselves competed for the victory at Olympia and Delphi, by preference in the expensive chariot races, out of a desire to spread their fame to, and retain their close ties with Greece, the mother-country. Pindar also wrote two victory odes for Arkesilaos IV, king of Cyrene, who had come first with his chariot at Delphi in 462 B.C.

It is characteristic that the writer of a victory ode is not concerned to report the details of the course of the contest. We are never told who the victor's rivals were. And in no victory ode will we find anything to parallel the wonderfully graphic description by Sophokles, in the *Elektra,* of the chariot races at Delphi, where Orestes had supposedly met his death; for in this ode, the physical competition is merely the occasion for displaying the φυά of the competitor, the natural qualities which distinguish him both physically and mentally, and which are inherited from his ancestors and at the same time bestowed upon him by the gods. The personal worth of a man even from a humble family, which democratic Athens so readily recognised, has no place here. In the foreground is the divine power which is nurtured in the noble families by their very nature.

The exacting training inflicted by the athlete on his body gains its meaning from the fact that it serves a world of values firmly constructed and governed by the gods. All the parts of the victory ode: the praising of the victor and his ancestors, the numerous maxims, and even the personal statements of the poet about his own obligations towards the victory — all these are designed to relate the achievement of the athlete to the context of this world. Above all, the mythical narrative, indispensable in any reason-

63. *Bronze statuette of a Kouros from the Acropolis. It depicts an athlete who was holding a javelin, or jumping-weights. Ancient artists often used athletes as their models (Athens, National Archaeological Museum).*

63

ably long ode, by referring to the history of the gods and of the sanctuaries where the games took place, and even of the victor's mythical ancestors, and by comparing the feat of the mortal with the feat of an ancient hero, unites gods, heroes and noble houses in an indivisible whole. Thus the athlete who is at the time the last link in a line that traces its descent from gods and heroes, passes under the protection of the gods who had made him "noble and good" (καλὸς κἀγαθός), that is, who had endowed him with the youth and the strength, and above all the moral character, to prove himself worthy of victory.

We spoke above of the great desire of man for some form of immortality; human nature seeks as far as possible to exist forever and to be immortal, according to a statement of Plato. It should be added that for the ancient Greek the desire was even more intense, since his religion — apart from the Eleusinian and Orphic sects — did not hold out to him the promise of an after life.

The only form of immortality for common mortals was therefore to leave descendants behind them, for it is only in this way that a human being survives — that is, "by the being that is growing old and departing leaving behind it another young being similar to itself. By this device, whatever is to die gains a share in immortality, whether we are talking about the body or anything else." The victors at the games, however, had the additional advantage that their name and their achievement would be preserved in the memory of the generations to follow — by the statue they had erected, and above all by the victory ode which perpetuated their glory.

In 446 B.C., shortly before he died, Pindar composed his *8th Pythian Ode* in honour of the pankratiast Aristomenes of Aigina. His experience, after seventy years of life, had taught him how vain human affairs were:

We are things of a day. What are we? What are we not? The shadow of a dream
is man, no more.

He continues, however:

But when brightness comes, and God gives it, there is a shining of light on men, and their life is sweet.

The victors in the games were also ephemeral; but the brightness sent by Zeus had covered them, and their life became sweet, and the shining light accompanies them to this day.

Athletics and art

If art is expressive of the characteristic features of a society, then we must conclude in studying the history of ancient Greek art that, for ancient Greeks, athleticism constituted a second religion. "Even if the words 'gymnastics' and 'athletics' had not been handed down to us in the written tradition, we would have to recognise this exceptional and unique flowering of athleticism as it is mirrored in the representational art" (Ernst Buschor). Although judgements like these today sound like exaggerated rhetorical devices, an objective study of this art affirms their truth and accuracy. One could formulate yet another of these judgements by way of introduction: in no other art of the ancient or modern world does sport have the position that it occupied in ancient Greek art.

Indeed, if we were to look for sporting subjects in modern European art we would discover, possibly with some surprise, that they are almost non-existent. This contrast is sufficient in itself to shed light on the investigation, and permit us to arrive at a correct evaluation of the importance of physical exercise and athletics in Greek society. One vital and unique element in Greek art, especially plastic art, is nudity. The basic subject of Greek plastic art from the early Archaic period on is the naked youth, the *Kouros*, a figure that depicts both god and man in the same manner. This nudity, of course, does not reflect the reality of daily life, but neither is it an idealised abstract form of the human figure. It is a real picture of the young man when he is training, that is to say, when he is exercising his body naked. Sport and nudity are inseparable concepts in ancient Greece; and the place where the youths train is called *gymnasium,* just as the training itself is called *gymnastics,* concepts that all derive from the same root as γυμνός, meaning naked. So Greek art depicts not only athletes, but also gods and heroes, naked, and gives them the appearance of athletic youths at the moment of their youthfull prime and beauty. This idealised picture of man, created in the workshops of Greece and handed on to inspire the wonder of the centuries, is not a divine vision of its creators; it is the artistic realisation of the figure of the naked youth, who is training completely nude and exercising his body so as to bring it to the greatest possible perfection. Rodin had his young models move naked about his garden so that he could study the functioning and expression of the human body, but this facility to watch and study was permanently available to Greek artists in the place where the young men were exercising. It is for this reason that the great historian of Greek art, Ernst Buschor, is well justified when he writes: "One

64. The Doryphoros by Polykleitos portrayed the perfect athlete, and this is why it was called Canon *(Munich, Glyptothek).*

could say, with some exaggeration, that for a time Greek art depicts only athletes.'' We have only to compare the small bronze Apollo of Deinagoras in the Berlin Museum with the slightly later athlete in the National Archaeological Museum in Athens, to become convinced that the god could be about to take part in the same sport, particularly since he is holding in his right hand the *aryballos*, the vase that is typically associated with athletes. The importance of sport in Greek art, and the close relation between the two becomes even clearer when we note that throughout the whole of the Archaic period and until the end of the 5th century B.C., only victorious athletes had the right to erect statues of themselves in a sanctuary or in their city. During this period the number of other human statues that were erected was very small, and the circumstances completely exceptional.

All of this means that if we wished to trace the sequence of athletic scenes or representations of athletes in ancient Greek art, it would essentially be necessary to write a history of this art viewed simply from a different stand-point. It is enough to note that in the field of Attic vase-painting alone there are 1,571 representations of sporting scenes, without taking into account the figures of victorious athletes or the depictions of horsemen that are very frequently connected with equestrian competitions. As regards statues of athletes, we know that when the famous 2nd century A.D. traveller Pausanias visited Olympia, at least 230 of these statues were preserved in the Altis. We may, however, cast a quick glance over the ancient Greek world, from Archaic times to the late Hellenistic period, and take note of a number of outstanding works which combine in their form the demands of the art and the athletic models of their age.

The earliest work of plastic art connected with athletics is a landmark in the history of Greek art, and is the creation of a great Athenian artist just before the middle of the 6th century B.C. This is the famous *Rampin Horseman,* discovered on the Acropolis of Athens. The crown of oak leaves on his head shows that the statue depicted a victor in the Pythian games — possibly one of the sons of Peisistratos, as archaeologists have suggested. Whoever he may have been, it is significant that, in order to thank the goddess who helped him to his victory, he set up in her sanctuary this mounted statue of himself — the earliest mounted figure in Greek art. Another masterpiece from the hand of the same artist is the fragment of a grave stele of an athlete, on which the very fine head of the youth is preserved, standing out before the circular discus, which he is holding high, ready to throw it in the contest. The head of the *Diskophoros,* which is almost contemporary with the horseman, attests the way in which Attic art was inspired by athleticism and acted in its service, immortalising the young athletes in either dedicatory or funerary works, and with both figures in the round and figures carved in relief. A typical example is to be seen in another, slightly later Attic funerary stele (550-540 B.C.) depicting a boxer, as is clear from the leather straps on his raised left hand. Again the artist has advanced beyond the bounds of Archaic art and has given us a ''portrait,'' as this is to be understood at such an early period.

All three works of Attic plastic art are earlier than, or roughly contemporary with the first statues of athletes erected at Olympia — that of Praxidamas of Aigina, victor in the boxing in 544 B.C., and that of Rexibios of Opus who won the pankration in 536 B.C., as Pausanias informs us. However, although the canons of Archaic art allowed the artist to depict the young athlete at the peak of his physical strength and beauty, they did not permit him to give expression to the vital element of the contest, the tension and movement of the body when it was extended to the utmost in the attempt to gain the victory. This picture of the striving athlete, which will give plastic form to the unique moment when all the powers of the human body are concentrated and tensed to the extreme in order to produce the great performance demanded by the contest, will be portrayed in Greek sculpture in the short period from 480-450 B.C., to which the name "severe style," or perhaps better "early classical," is given. The *Diskobolos* of Myron (450 B.C.), which was famous in antiquity, may be regarded as the crowning achievement of this vision. It is not easy to conceive the dynamism and artistic quality of the bronze original, which has perished, but we can form a satisfactory idea of it from the Roman copies that have come down to us, especially from the best one which is now in the National Museum in Rome. It is easy for anyone who is not initiated into the language of art, and particularly of ancient Greek art, to make the mistake of imagining that Myron does no more in his work than give us a "snapshot" ("instantané") from the discus contest. An error like this (which has been made by many, including specialists) may be attributed to the fact that the great sculptor has achieved a totally "convincing" picture of a discus-thrower, which succeeds, with solidity and power and with a

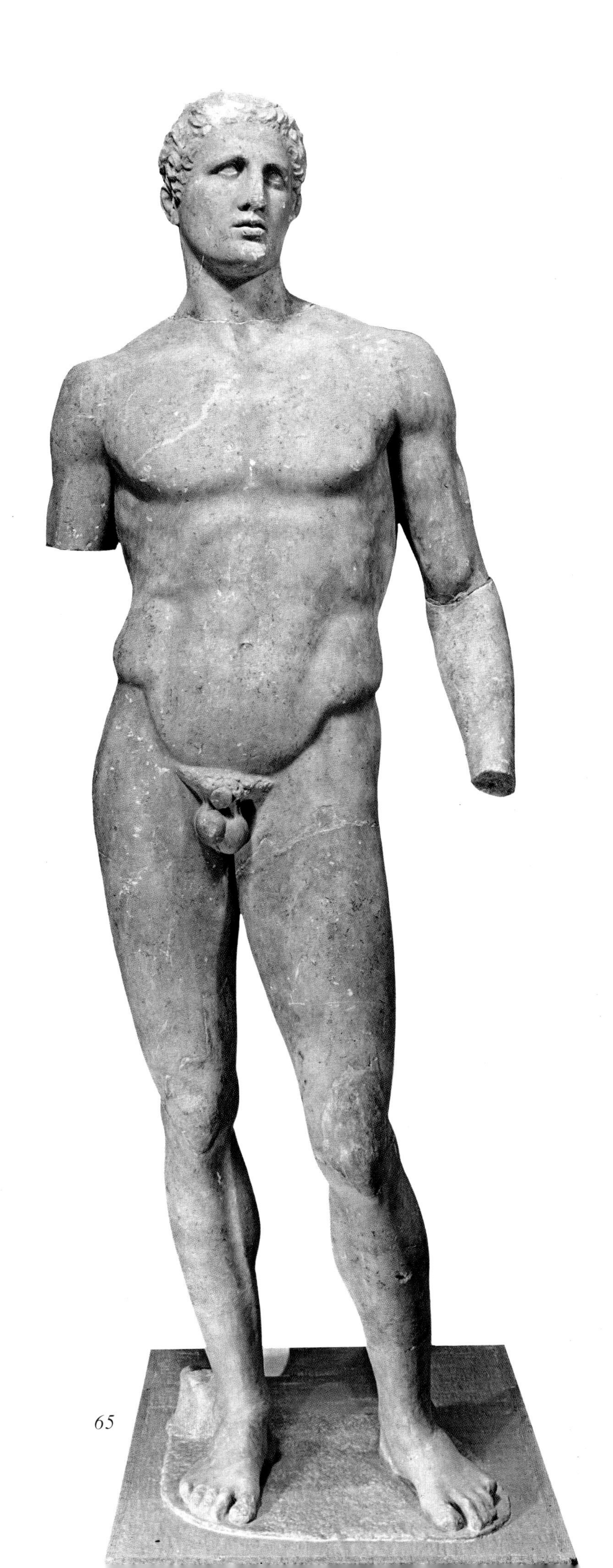

65. Agias was a famous athlete of the 5th century B.C. who won many victories in the pankration. The statue by Lysippos bearing his name, with its compact body, bent elbows and tired head, represents the artistic beliefs of the last years of the 4th century B.C. (Delphi, Archaeological Museum).

65

wonderful timeless tectonic structure, in giving expression to the whole contest, in a condensed and clearly comprehensible form. In a word, we could say that the "momentary" has been made "eternal," and the "movement" has been captured in an "unmoving" balance, without losing the vital and vibrant elements either of the movement or of the changeless moment.

Even during this phase, however, and much more so during the Classical period that followed it, Greek art recognised that sculpture in the round — i.e. the statue — was not a suitable medium for rendering a detailed narrative, but demanded the greatest economy of expression, an epigrammatic formulation of the essentials, and the creation of a figure that includes "potentially" all the component elements in such a way as to go beyond the transient and coincidental features and depict that which overcomes the mortal nature of man. A unique and unrivalled example of this attitude can be seen in the Charioteer of Delphi (470 B.C.), which portrays the victorious athlete standing in his chariot immediately after his triumphant victory. It is a rare original work, which retains its plastic vigour and freshness intact, and speaks for hundreds of other lost masterpieces that depicted the athlete shortly before or after the contest and his victory.

The *Doryphoros* by Polykleitos (440 B.C.) was called the *Canon* and remained the ideal canon of the trained youthful body. Archaeologists have demonstrated that the youth portrayed in the statue is Achilles, but this does not mean that the figure, which has a perfect form according to the classical standards, does not represent the complete and perfect type of the athlete. Polykleitos and his workshop, which continued to be active for many years in Argos, attempted to render the three-dimensional harmony and the plastic dynamism of the perfect athletic figure, in all its tectonic solidity. Another of his works, the *Anadoumenos,* completes the picture formed by the *Doryphoros* by depicting the athlete at the moment that he is tying the band around his head.

The tradition of Polykleitos was continued and renewed in the 4th century B.C. by Lysippos of Sikyon. In his exceptionally fine work the *Apoxyomenos* (— the athlete who is cleansing his body of the dust and sweat of the contest —) he brings to art the new type of athlete, who is much more slender, lithe and sinewy than his predecessor. A splendid dedication set up in the sanctuary of Delphi by Daochos of Thessaly, who was his country's representative in the Delphic Amphiktyony from 338 to 334 B.C., probably comes from Lysippos' workshop. On a large base, which has been preserved, Daochos himself, his son, and his ancestors, five generations in all, stood in front of the statue of Apollo. Only a few remains of these statues have survived, but one of them, the best preserved, portrays Agias, the great-grandfather of Daochos, who was a famous athlete of the middle of the 5th century B.C. and won the pankration in the Olympic Games, was five times victorious in the Nemean games, three times in the Pythian and five times in the Isthmian. It is this legendary figure that is depicted in the athletic youth who today stands in the Museum at Delphi with his strong sturdy body, bent arms, and tired head. The tectonic structure of the naked athletic body with its many expressive counter-balancing movements, its well-formed masses and vigorous proportions, illustrates the artistic beliefs of the last years of the 4th century B.C.

During this century Greek art made progress in an area that had until then lain outside its objectives, and created the plastic portrait in the sense that we attach to the word today. It attempted, that is to say, to render the personal features of the man it was portraying; it was no longer satisfied with the "type" of the figure, even though it was differentiated, but sought to depict the individual with his own particular features. This was a fact of special importance for the artists who created statues of athletes, for henceforth these statues would be genuine portraits of the victors and would immortalise specific individuals. Chance has preserved to us the bronze head of one of these portrait-statues which was discovered at Olympia and is today housed at the National Archaeological Museum in Athens. The boxer depicted is probably the famous athlete Satyros, and the portrait was probably made by the Athenian sculptor Silanion about 330 B.C. This portrait remains faithful to the "type" up to a point, but succeeds in rendering the personal features of the particular individual, and above all in reproducing the face of the combative athlete with the rough features surrounded by the thick hair, beard and moustache. This tendency grew steadily in Hellenistic art, and at times exceptionally intense realistic works were achieved. Naturally enough this tendency in art found ready subject matter in the field of athletics, where the extreme tension of the athlete striving for victory, now reinforced by the new conception of the athletic ideal, offered rich material for the realistic expressionism of the Hellenistic baroque. An excellent example of this art is the bronze statue of the "jockey" discovered along with the famous Poseidon in the sea off Artemision, which has now been restored and delights the visitor to the National Archaeological Museum in Athens. The young rider seems minute on the horse, which is galloping with loose rein. The figure of the child, with his face contracted in his state of high tension — an unparalleled example of the Hellenistic realism — competes with the striking formation of both the body and the head of the animal. This glorious monument to equestrian sport, which was a favourite subject of the Greek artist from as early as the Geometric period, was worked in the middle of the 2nd century B.C.

The reader will discover elsewhere in this book the direction taken by the athletic ideal at the end of the ancient Greek world. The contests became increasingly tough and inhuman, and the competitors further and further removed from their original beauty. Like any other sphere of human activity, athleticism is an expression of the society in which it is created and comes to maturity; and art, in its turn, mirrors as faithfully as possible the powers that compose and give expression to this world. So the famous boxer in the National Museum in Rome, a work by the Athenian artist Apollonios, who was active in the middle of the 1st century B.C., puts an end to the series of athletes portrayed by Greek art in a most striking fashion. The boxer with the inhumanly tough and mis-shapen features is resting his limbs that are fearsome with their great physique and overgrown power, after the fatal contest, which is made even tougher by the terrible "gloves" that reinforce his physical strength and remove the last humane element from the contest.

Greek athletics, which flowered in the great panhellenic sanctuaries, will now give way to the combats of gladiators who will shed their blood in the Roman arenas. And art will depict them without the beauty of the naked athlete, and without the love for the youthful body that inspired it to create the Apollonian figures of mortals and gods during the course of the six centuries before Christ.

The Events

Running

Introduction

Running is man's most common form of physical exercise, and the easiest and most improvised way in which competition can take place. This type of contest will undoubtedly be as old as the most primitive human society. The distinction achieved by the winner, and also by the other competitors in proportion to their success, is so direct and vivid as to give birth spontaneously to the idea of rivalry without any specific practical purpose — the idea, that is, of athletic competition.

Running was of special importance throughout the whole of antiquity. Xenophanes, the founder of the Eleatic philosophical school, considered swiftness of foot to be the most highly prized quality a man could possess.

Achilles is described by Homer as "fleet-footed" because the poet regards this as the most important of the physical endowments. The significance attaching to competition can also be seen from the fact that the famous Gortyn inscription divides the citizens on the basis of the competence at running, into *dromeis* (runners) and *apodromoi* (people too young ot too old to run), and these formed two different social classes.

It is in no way surprising, therefore, that the ancient Greeks thought of their gods and the heroes of mythology as devoting themselves to a contest so spectacular and so familiar as running.

The original invention of the contest is attributed by various sources to different mythical figures: to Idaean Herakles and the Daktyloi, figures belonging to the legends on the creation of the world; to Endymion and his sons; to the suitors of Atalanta; to the hero Herakles, famous for his labours (see "The Element of Competition in Greek Mythology"). The lack of clarity surrounding the "first inventor" and the place of origin of the sport of running indicates precisely that its origin was so old that the question could not be settled in a definitive and generally acceptable manner.

Running as a sport attracted the attention of a number of writers, who dealt with it either theoretically, within the framework of their views on the exercise and upbringing of citizens, such as Plato in the *Laws,* or from the point of view of the techniques of the sport, such as Philostratos in his *Gymnastikos*.

The runners always ran barefoot. In the earliest times they wore a kind of loin-cloth, but later they abandoned this. Tradition has it that the first man to discard it and run naked was Orsippos of Megara, a winner in the 15th Olympiad (720 B.C.).

Initially the runners must have come from amongst the young men whose natural abilities and daily tasks, such as pasturing animals or hunting, gave them a predisposition for the sport. As time went on, however, preparation for the games became increasingly systematic. Methodical training took place under the supervision of the boys' trainer, involving a careful diet, the proper massages, daily exercises in walking, running, the techniques of starting, breathing and turning, and the tactics of the sport generally. In addition, the runners were taught to compete honourably: not to impede their rivals by pushing them, knocking them down or holding them back, not to cut obliquely across the track, and above all, not to resort to bribery or the casting of magic spells. This training did not take place simply when games were being held, but was a permanent feature of the education of the youth.

The Competition Area

For the running contest, all that was needed was a level area long enough to allow the runners to reach their top speed in comfort, and broad enough for a large number of athletes to take part: that is, a long, level, rectangular space. This space was defined as being 600 feet long, and was called a stade, or *stadion,* which gave its name to the distance, the event (the *stadion* race), and finally the place, whether natural or man-made, in which the games were held (the stadium).

When the games were institutionalised and held on a regular basis in the presence of spectators, the need arose to locate the competition area next to hills or natural slopes, from which the judges of the contests and the public could follow the events. The stadia were therefore built on the slopes of a hill (Olympia, Delphi, Delos, Priene), in small valleys between two hills (Athens, the Isthmus, Epidauros, Messene, Miletos), or in a natural hollow in the side of a hill (Sikyon). These natural areas that had suitable configurations provided room for a large number of people. They were inadequate, however, for the occasions when a very large crowd of spectators attended, and it proved necessary to extend

66. Bronze figurine of a runner. The athlete is probably depicted at the start, despite the fact that his stance is unorthodox. Both arms are held out, the body is slightly inclined forwards and the left leg is advanced a short distance (Olympia, Archaeological Museum).

67

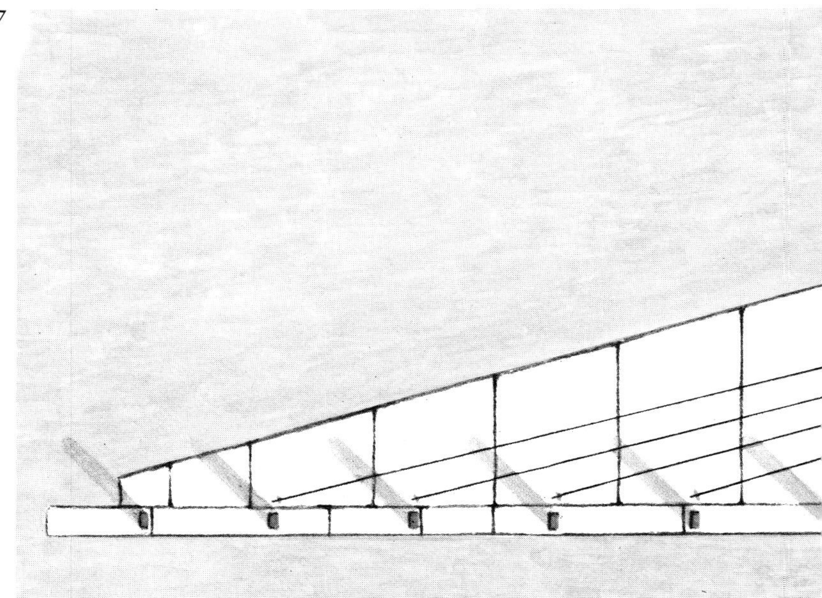

68

67-68. Plan and reconstruction of the starting mechanism in the stadium at the shrine of Poseidon at the Isthmus. It is an isosceles triangle in shape, the base of which was the starting line. At the apex of the triangle is a circular pit in which the starter stood. There are hollows along the starting line that received the upright posts which divided it into 17 positions. The athletes stood behind horizontal movable bars resting on the posts. These bars were tied with cords that went down to the bottom of the upright posts, through staples and along furrows that brought them together at the starter's pit. In the reconstruction, the starter pulls all the threads with a jerk, the bars suddenly fall and the runners all start together (Reconstruction: K. Iliakis).

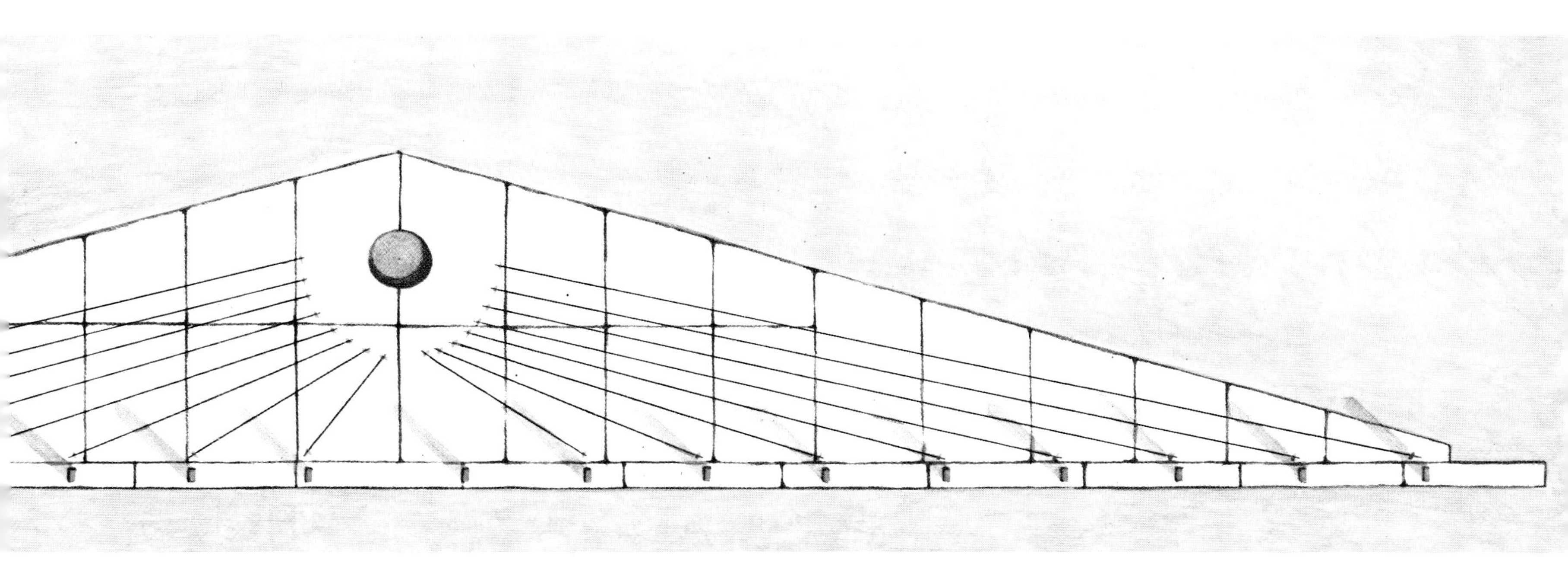

them by constructing embankments on the flat sides of the track. At Olympia, for example, when the stadium was moved to the east during the 4th century B.C., artificial slopes were built opposite the hill of Kronion to enclose the other three sides, and the stadium ultimately held about 45,000 spectators.

Initially there were no seats on the embankments of the stadium, whether the latter were artificial or natural, and the public sat on the ground, apart from a few specially privileged people, such as Gorgos, an official representative of the Eleans at Sparta, who had permanent seats marked by inscribed stone slabs. At Olympia this arrangement, with no seats for the spectators, continued right till the end, the only exceptions being the seat of the priestess of Demeter Chamyne on the north side of the stadium, a few rows of seats in front of it for people of some importance, and the *exedra* of the *Hellanodikai* opposite. In the other stadia, however, rows of seats began to be built, possibly under the influence of theatre architecture; they were divided horizontally and vertically into sections, which facilitated the arrival and, more importantly, the departure of the spectators. The stadia in Athens, at the Isthmus and a number of cities in Asia Minor acquired marble seats, and those of Delphi, Delos and Rhodes stone seats, while at Epidauros seats were built only on the two sides of the stadium near the finish. During the Roman period they began to build monumental entrances to the stadia, and the narrow side at the far end became semicircular in shape, though the track itself, where all the events took place, remained rectangular; conduits were built around it to lead off the rain-water and drain the track.

The distance the runners had to cover differed from stadium to stadium, since the *pous* (foot), the basic measure of distance, differed from place to place. The 600 feet represented a distance of 192.28 metres at Olympia; 191.39 at Priene; 184.96 at Athens; 181.30 at Epidauros; 177.55 at Delphi; and 177.36 at Miletos. The runners at Delphi thus had to cover 14.73 metres less than at Olympia, but this fact had no real importance in an age when the stop-watch was unknown and times were not recorded. The overall length of the track was greater than a stade (600 feet), since it also included the additional distance needed by the runners to slow down after the end of the race (modern rules require 15 metres). This additional distance measured 15.14 m. at the eastern end of the stadium at Epidauros; at Olympia, it measured 10.50 m. at the western end and a mere 9.50 m. at the eastern end of the stadium.

The start. At first the start, and the finish, were marked simply by lines scratched in the earth. The lines naturally had to be renewed every so often, involving the danger that they might be moved to the advantage of some interested party, as is shown by the prohibition of this ("do not move the line"). Because of this, permanent starting-lines were constructed from the 5th century B.C. onwards. Somewhat later, these starting-lines were fitted in places with a quite complicated starting system operated by a cord or fine rope, the existence of which is attested by an inscription from Delos and confirmed by the excavations at the Isthmus.

The starting-lines generally had the same form as the one that survives at Olympia, which is particularly clear: a row of long and narrow stone slabs with two continuous parallel grooves in them, 0.18 m. apart, in which the runners put their feet at the start. There are hollows in the slabs at intervals of 1.25 m., to hold the posts that separated the positions of the runners. At Olympia the starting-lines have positions for 20 runners; at Delphi for 17 or 18; at Miletos for 12; at Epidauros for 11; at Priene and at Didyma for 6. The stadia at the Isthmus and on Delos have only one groove on the starting-line. At Corinth, where 16 positions for runners were provided, the continuous grooves are replaced by two separate depressions in each position, one in front for the left foot and one for the right foot 0.63 m. behind it — much further apart, that is, than at other stadia. Traces of the *hysplex,* a narrow bar or a rope that was used to give the starting signal, have been preserved in the stadium in the sanctuary of Poseidon at the Isthmus; it was in operation from the beginning of the 4th century B.C. until the destruction of the stadium by the Romans in 146 B.C. The starting arrangement had the shape of an isosceles triangle the base of which was the starting-line. At the apex of the triangle was a circular pit about 1 m. deep and 0.53 m. in diameter, in which the *aphetes* (starter) stood. The starting-line had hollows in it to hold vertical posts, rectangular in section, which divided it into 17 positions. From each vertical post runs a narrow groove, and all of them meet at the starter's pit, and are bridged by bronze staples. This evidence permits us to reconstruct the way in which the *hysplex* worked with absolute certainty: there were movable pieces of wood resting horizontally on the vertical posts that separated the positions, and the runners stood behind them. The horizontal bars had cords connected to them, which passed through the upright post, ran down it and through the staples and along the grooves to the starter, who held all the cords together in his hands. A sudden jerk caused all the horizontal bars to fall, and opened the way for the runners, who thus all started together. This method of starting a race is verified indirectly by the ancient sources: Lucian speaks of the *hysplex* falling, and an anonymous epigrammatist claims that the *hysplex* made a noise at the start of the race.

The Holding of the Event

The start. The ancient runners had a standard method of starting, of which the various surviving representations depict only a single stage, which is clearly a preparatory one. But if all the relevant information from written sources, representations, and excavations is brought together, a number of clear observations may be made: 1. The herald called the names of those taking part. 2. The position of each one at the starting-line was determined by lot. 3. The athletes lined up at the starting-line with their feet close together. 4. They set off together at some word of command, though it is not known precisely what this was. Anyone who started before the word of command had some punishment inflicted on him, apparently corporal. The stance adopted by the runners at the start can be deduced more specifically from a number of statuettes, vase-paintings and from

69

70

69. A runner in the stadion *race (a sprint) running with his legs apart in a long stride, his body slightly inclined forwards and his arms swinging vigorously, with the palms open (Bologna, Museo Civico).*

70. Scene of a men's stadion *race. The five men are running waving their arms vigorously back and forth to increase their speed, having their legs wide apart in a great stride (New York, Metropolitan Museum).*

the construction of the starting arrangements: both feet rested on the starting-line with the toes in the grooves, or the hollows that corresponded to them, one foot slightly in front of the other (it is only at Corinth that the distance between the two feet is equal to a whole pace). The knee of the front leg is bent and the heel raised from the ground, so that all the weight of the body is supported on the toes, while the rear leg is extended backwards with the sole completely in contact with the ground. The body leans forward and the head is raised, while the arms are stretched forward, almost horizontally, with the palms turned down. In the race in armour, the stance is the same except that only the right arm is stretched forward since the left is holding the shield. This stance, particularly when considered in connection with the horizontal bar of the *hysplex,* which was located roughly at chest-height, demonstrates that the ancient runners started from a standing position, and not from a crouched position supported on fingers and toes, as in today's races.

The turn. In races that covered a distance of more than one stade, the athletes were obliged to make a turn and come back to the start, as many times as was necessitated by the length of the race, which was always, as we shall see, a multiple of a stade. The turning-point *(kampter* as it is called in the sources) was naturally located on the line at the other end, opposite the starting-line, or on the starting-line itself, if the race involved several laps. As a number of vase-paintings show, it had the form of a small column or post, and was quite probably one of the posts that separated the positions at the start. It is not certain precisely how the turn was executed. Four main possibilities have been proposed. According to the first, each runner ran in his own lane and made the turn as soon as he reached the opposite line. The second suggests that they turned the post to the left or the right of them and ran the return length in the lane next to them, but this would inevitably have led to collisions between a runner who had just made the turn and one who had not yet reached it. The third view is that all the runners turned round the same centrally placed post, in which case those who had drawn outside positions would have to cover a slightly greater distance (at Olympia, the difference is no greater than 0.51 m.); this would account for the custom of drawing for positions before the race. However, collisions will certainly have occurred at the critical point of the turning-post, because the runners would arrive there at roughly the same time. The fourth view is perhaps the most probable, therefore: this envisages each runner having exclusive use of two lanes, and consequently assumes that only every second position was occupied at the start.

Preliminary heats. The number of positions varied from stadium to stadium, but the number of competitors was normally in excess of them, and the runners were therefore divided into groups by lot (groups of four according to one source, but they were probably larger), the winners of each group running in the final. A victory in a preliminary heat appears to have been an honour in itself, and the eventual winner took pride in having twice come first.

71. Scene of a stadion *race. The runner in the lead is turning his head to see if the other runners are catching him (Paris, Louvre).*

72. A runner spurting in an attempt to pass an athlete who is now tired and does not have the strength to accelerate (Bologna, Museo Civico).

71

72

73. Fragment of a panathenaic amphora with a scene of a runner in the diaulos. *On the right is the inscription* diaulodromo eimi *(I am for the diaulos runner). The* diaulos *was a sprint race (Athens, National Archaeological Museum).*

74. Scene of a middle distance race (the hippios?). The runners have an open stride, their arms swing less than in the stadion, *and their body is more upright (Northampton, Castle Ashby).*

75. Scene of runners in the dolichos. *Their stride is short, their arms hardly swing at all and are held at waist-level, and the body is completely upright. The* dolichos *was a long-distance race (London, British Museum).*

73

Types of Foot-race

The stadion. The *stadion,* a single length of the track, was the oldest event, and indeed the only event at the first 13 Olympiads. From the 37th Olympiad on (632 B.C.), boys competed in this event as well as men. This was the sprint event, par excellence, and produced the swiftest athlete. Philostratos, basing himself on the experiences of centuries, enumerates the natural qualities that a *stadiodromos* (*stadion* runner) had to possess: he had to be somewhat taller than average, but not much, otherwise he would lack stability. His legs had to be in proportion to his shoulders and his thorax narrow, but with robust lungs. The knees had to be agile, the legs straight, the body sturdy but not very muscular, because greatly developed muscles gave a man weight and reduced his speed; and the arms should be longer than average. Philostratos justifies the last point by claiming that sprinters move their arms vigorously back and forth to increase their speed, an observation that is certainly accurate and needs no further development. It had already been made by the vase-painters who depicted sprinters with their arms outstretched at shoulder-level or head-level, their palms open, the body leaning slightly forward in an extension of the line of the rear leg, and the legs wide apart in a great stride.

The diaulos. This was also a sprint, covering two lengths of the track — a distance of 1,200 feet, which varied from 355-385 metres according to the length of the stadium. As an Olympic event it is first recorded in the 14th Olympiad (724 B.C.), when it was added to the *stadion* which had till then been the

74

75

only event. Naturally enough, the technique of this race did not differ from that of the *stadion,* though the double distance, covered in the same style, was a greater test of the breathing and endurance of the athletes. Philostratos therefore requires runners in the *diaulos* also to be slight, but more strongly built than runners in the *stadion*. Because they ran two lengths, they started from what was the finishing-line in the *stadion* (the west end at Olympia), so that the finish would be at the same end for both events and the runners would have the margin they needed in which to stop.

Hippios. This was a middle-distance race held in the ancient stadia. It was included in the programme at the Isthmian, Nemean and Panathenaic games, but it was never introduced into the programme of the Olympic Games. It covered 4 stades (that is, 710-740 metres) and was apparently the same distance as that of the horse races, which explains its name (*hippos* = horse). Philostratos merely alludes to it in connection with the race in armour, and gives no details. It is doubtful whether there are any representations of it in art, and difficult in any case to recognise; it is conceivable that it is portrayed on some of the Panathenaic amphoras, where the runners have an open stride, and their body slightly bent forward, but their arms bent at the elbows at waist-height.

The dolichos. This was a long-distance race, the longest of all, and was held after the *stadion* and the *diaulos*. The first reference we have to it is in the 15th Olympiad (720 B.C.), when the first winner was the Spartan Akanthos. The length of the *dolichos* varies in the sources, and probably also varied at the different games and at different periods, ranging from 7 to 24 stades. For the most part however, it was defined as 20 stades, or 3,550 - 3,850 metres. According to the ancients, the *dolichos* was inspired by the performances of the *dromokerykes* or *hemerodromoi,* who were professional messengers who carried messages and instructions over great distances, particularly during times of war; most of them were Arkadians, famous for their speed and endurance. This view is perhaps a little far-fetched, but it is not impossible that it has some foundation in fact.

The *dolichos* demanded a different physical build from the sprint races. The *dolichodromos* (*dolichos* runner), says Philostratos, must have strong shoulders and a strong neck, like the pentathletes, but slender, light legs, like the *stadiodromoi*. One might add that the *dolichos* had a tendency to produce particularly muscular legs, for it was on them that the result depended. Vase-paintings depicting *dolichos* runners show the familiar, natural running style in long-distance races: the torso is upright, the arms bent at the elbows and held close to the body at waist-height, the palms clenched, and the stride short, with both knees bent and the forward leg only a short distance in front. The runners used this style for the biggest part of the distance, but over the final metres they tried to develop the speed of the *stadion* runners and adopted their movements.

The race in armour. The race in armour, between athletes carrying a bronze defensive panoply, was only introduced into the Olympic Games at a late date, being attested from the 65th Olympiad on (520 B.C.). It was the last event and was held on the afternoon of the fourth day of the Games. The distance involved was small (examples of 4 stades are

76

76. Bronze figurine of a runner in the race in armour, portrayed at the start. The race in armour was the same length as the diaulos *(Tübingen, Archäologisches Institut der Universität).*

cited, but it was normally 2 stades, i.e. the length of the *diaulos,* and the runners covered it wearing a helmet and greaves and carrying a shield. About the middle of the 5th century, possibly in 478 B.C., the greaves were abandoned, as was the helmet after the 4th century, but the shield was retained as long as the event was held.

This type of race, in which the athlete had to carry weights and have his left arm encumbered by the large round shield, required a special kind of physique, which combined strong well-developed muscles, a sure sense of balance, flexibility and lightness of foot. Philostratos recommends that a man who runs in the race in armour should have a long torso, broad shoulders, and knees that do not project so that the shield does not impede his running. These features can also be seen in the vase-paintings, particularly in those of the 4th century B.C., in which the human form is rendered in a less idealised, more realistic manner.

In spite of the heavy, awkward equipment carried by the athletes, the race in armour was a sprint, and the depictions of it show all the hallmarks of the *stadion* and the *diaulos:* the runners have a broad stride and are on the tips of their toes, while the right arm moves vigorously to and fro, followed by the left, as far as the shield permits this.

The variety of helmet shapes and of the emblems painted on the shields demonstrate that the athletes used their own personal armour, not only in training but also in most of the games. Pausanias states, however, that at Olympia 25 bronze shields were kept in the temple of Zeus, to be given to the runners to carry during the race in armour.

77. Scene of a runner in the race in armour at the start. The competitors wore a helmet and greaves and carried a shield (Paris, Louvre).

The race in armour was a very spectacular event, and this may explain why it was such a favourite subject amongst vase-painters, and so frequent a theme in the visual arts.

The Heraia. The Heraia, a series of races for girls, were held every four years in honour of Hera. They took place in the stadium at Olympia, but were completely independent of the Olympic Games. According to mythology, they were founded by Hippodameia and 16 other Elean women. The legend is clearly a subsequent aetiological explanation, but it demonstrates the great antiquity of these games, as well as their origins in the worship of Hera and their connection with the group of 16 venerable women who, in historical times, were entrusted with the tasks of weaving the goddess' *peplos,* organising primeval ritual dances, and directing the games.

The girls were divided into three categories according to their age — children, adolescents, and young women — and competed over a distance of 500 feet (160 m.) or 5/6 of the *stadion;* they ran with their hair unbound, and wearing a short *chiton* which left their right shoulder uncovered to the breast. The prize for the winners consisted of a crown of olive, a portion of the cow that was sacrificed to Hera, and the right to set up a portrait of themselves. The Heraia were not the only women's races in antiquity; there were others, all of them connected with religious ceremonial (at Sparta, for example, and at Cyrene), but those at Olympia were the most celebrated.

Performances. We know nothing of the performances achieved by runners in antiquity, since they had no means of measuring the times. The ancient Greeks, moreover, had no particular desire to know the time it had taken an athlete to run the *diaulos* or the *dolichos;* they were content to know who came first, who was the winner who would wear the crown of olive. When a particularly wonderful or striking performance was achieved, it was referred to by the authors, and we can draw our own conclusions about the speed and endurance of ancient runners from the information they give us.

Ageas, a *dolichodromos* from Argos, took part in and won the *dolichos* in the 113th Olympiad (328 B.C.). This was in the morning; immediately after the event, he set off and ran all day, arriving at Argos in the evening to announce his great victory. He was thus able to run approximately 110 kilometres in one day.

The *hemerodromos* (one who ran all day, messenger) Pheidippides ran from Athens to Sparta in two days to seek Spartan help for the Athenians in the Persian wars. He may have been an exceptionally talented messenger. The group achievement that followed is even more amazing, however. 2,000 Spartans in full armour covered the same distance in three days. The distance from Sparta to Athens is 230 kilometres.

Euchidas went from Plataia to Delphi to fetch the "pure fire," and returned on the same day before the sun set. He therefore ran a total of approximately 180 kilometres, and it was perhaps because of this that when he had handed over the burning torch, the unfortunate athlete collapsed and died.

This scanty evidence allows us to see the amazing endurance of the athletes of the period. We can also form some idea of their speed, however.

Lucian, in his *Timon,* alludes to an athlete who claims: *As soon as the hysplex fell, I had already been announced victor, because you would have thought I covered the stadion in one step, with some of the spectators not having had the time even to see me.*

The following epigram refers to the Spartan *stadion* runner Ladas: *Ladas either jumped or flew over the stadion, his speed was phenomenal, and impossible to relate.*

It was also said of Polymestor of Miletos, who won the boys' *stadion* in the 46th Olympiad (596 B.C.) that one day, while grazing his goats he gave chase to a hare and caught it alive.

We can judge the great strength, speed, endurance and generally exceptional abilities of the athletes in ancient times from the instances of competitors who won victories in four, five or six successive Olympiads, or from athletes who were crowned for victories in two or three events in the same Olympiad. Phanas of Pellene won the *stadion,* the *diaulos* and the race in armour in the 67th Olympiad (512 B.C.). Leonidas of Rhodes also recorded a great achievement. In four successive Olympiads (154th-157th, 164 B.C.-152 B.C.) he won three races: the *stadion,* the *diaulos* and the race in armour, and thus won 12 Olympic crowns within 12 years. Hermogenes of Xanthos also won three events in the 215th Olympiad (A.D. 81) — the *stadion, diaulos* and race in armour; in the 216th Olympiad he won the *diaulos* and the race in armour, and won three events again in the 217th Olympiad (A.D. 89). His fellow-countrymen called him "the horse." The feat of the athlete Polites of Keramos in Asia Minor was more impressive, however; in the 212th Olympiad (A.D. 69), he won the three races, *stadion, diaulos* and *dolichos,* within a short space of time.

78. Bronze figurine depicting a female Spartan athlete in a sprint. The Heraia, *the women's races at Olympia, were not held at the same time as the Olympic Games (London, British Museum).*

78

ANCIENT RACES

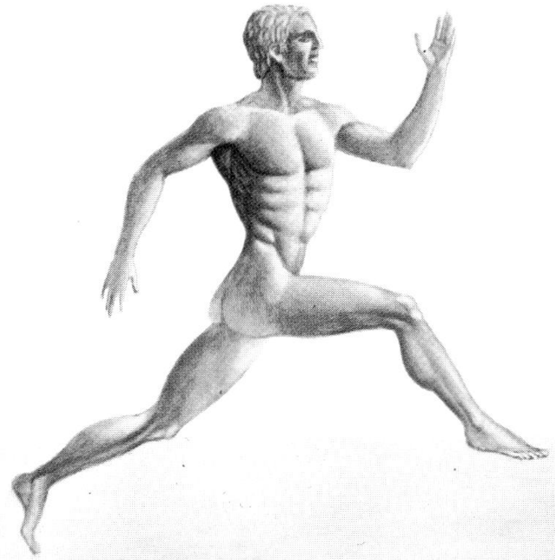

ANCIENT NAME	DISTANCE OF ANCIENT RACE	CORRESPONDING MODERN RACE
stadion	1 stade =600 ancient feet =192.27 m. (Olympia)	200 m.
diaulos	2 stades =1,200 ancient feet	400 m.

ANCIENT NAME	DISTANCE OF ANCIENT RACE	CORRESPONDING MODERN RACE
hippios	4 stades	800 m.

ANCIENT NAME	DISTANCE OF ANCIENT RACE	CORRESPONDING MODERN RACE
dolichos	7 to 24 stades	2,000 m.

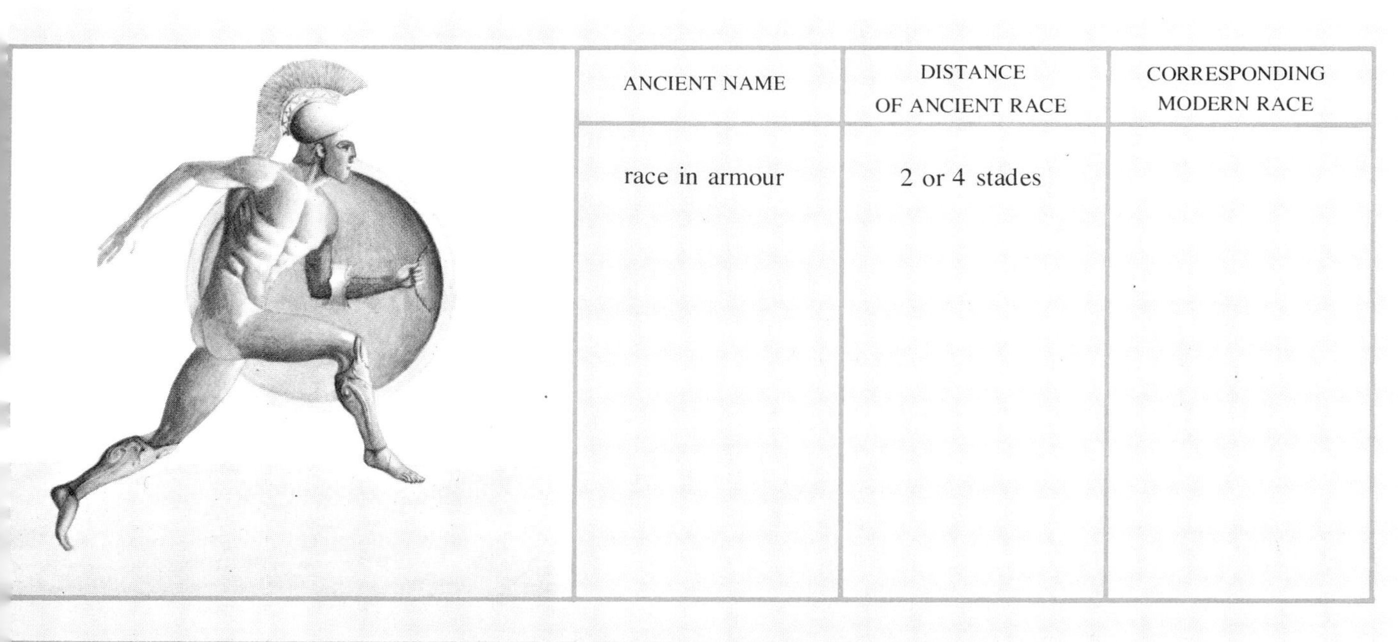

ANCIENT NAME	DISTANCE OF ANCIENT RACE	CORRESPONDING MODERN RACE
race in armour	2 or 4 stades	

ANCIENT NAME	DISTANCE OF ANCIENT RACE	CORRESPONDING MODERN RACE
torch-race	2,500 m. (Athens)	relay race

ANCIENT NAME	DISTANCE OF ANCIENT RACE	CORRESPONDING MODERN RACE
Heraia	5/6 of a stade =500 ancient feet. (Olympia)	women's 200 m.

79. Table of races, with the corresponding modern event.

Jumping

Introduction

Jumping, like running, was one of the simplest sports and arose spontaneously and naturally out of a man's need to leap over a natural obstacle, such as a ditch. It appears for the first time as a sport in its own right in the *Odyssey,* in the Phaiakian games, and is referred to in mythology, in the games held by the Argonauts on Lemnos, where the winners were Zetes and Kalaïs.

In the Classical period, jumping — invariably in the form of the long jump — always formed part of the *pentathlon.* It is only mentioned as an independent event in a dedicatory inscription engraved on a jumping-weight from Eleusis. However, Eleusis was a long way from the centres of athletic activity, and the event should be regarded as an isolated instance. As a *pentathlon* event, jumping improved and advanced technically, chiefly as the result of two innovations, both of which assisted the jumper: the use of jumping-weights, which the athlete held in each hand and which helped him to achieve a greater distance, and the accompaniment of his efforts by the music of the flute, which helped him to perform graceful and rhythmic movements.

The Competition Area: the Pit

Jumping was practised in the *skamma,* a rectangular pit 50 feet long, which was dug out and filled with soft soil. In his *5th Nemean Ode* in praise of Pytheas of Aigina, Pindar writes: *Let them dig me a long pit for leaping. The spring in my knees is light.* Each time an athlete was getting ready to jump, the soil was smoothed over to erase the marks of the previous jumper, so that the new marks could easily be distinguished.

On one side of the rectangular pit there was a fixed point, the *bater,* which all the athletes hit before they jumped. This was also the point from which the length of the jump was measured. A small marker *(semeion)* was inserted at the point where each athlete's feet hit the soil after his jump, so that his performance could be distinguished; this can clearly be seen in a number of vase-paintings. The length of the jump, that is, the distance from the jumping board to the marker, was measured with a wooden rod, the *kanon.*

Some of the athletes, like the legendary Phayllos, managed to jump more than the length of the pit and landed outside it: this gave rise to the proverbial expression, "to jump beyond the pit."

The Use of Jumping-weights. Weight-training

The *halteres,* or jumping-weights, were stone or lead weights that the athletes held in each hand while they were jumping, to help balance their body so that they could achieve a better result. The weight of them must have varied, for weights have been discovered of 1.610, 1.480, 2.018, or even 4.629 kilograms (though the last appears to have been a dedication). This difference in weight is due to the

80. Scene of a jumper engraved on a bronze discus. Jumping did not constitute an independent event, but formed part of the pentathlon in the great Panhellenic games, though there was a separate prize for jumping in local games and in the games in honour of Patroklos (London, British Museum).

80

81. Successive stages in the jump. The jumper gained impetus by running and swinging the jumping-weights. When he arrived at the take-off board, he waved the weights vigorously up and down and projected his body forwards. At the highest point of the jump he was doubled up, with his legs and arms almost parallel. As soon as his body began to fall, the jumper powerfully brought his arms backwards and used the weights as counter thrusts to propel his body forwards. Just before he hit the ground he dropped the weights behind him and landed on the soil with his feet together (Reconstruction: K. Iliakis).

82. The two types of jumping-weight, the "long" and the "spherical." The jumpers used the weights to try to get better results (Drawing: K. Iliakis).

83. The stone jumping-weight of Akmatidas of Sparta, who won the pentathlon according to the inscription on it. It weighs 4.629 kg. and was probably a dedication (Olympia, Archaeological Museum).

81

82

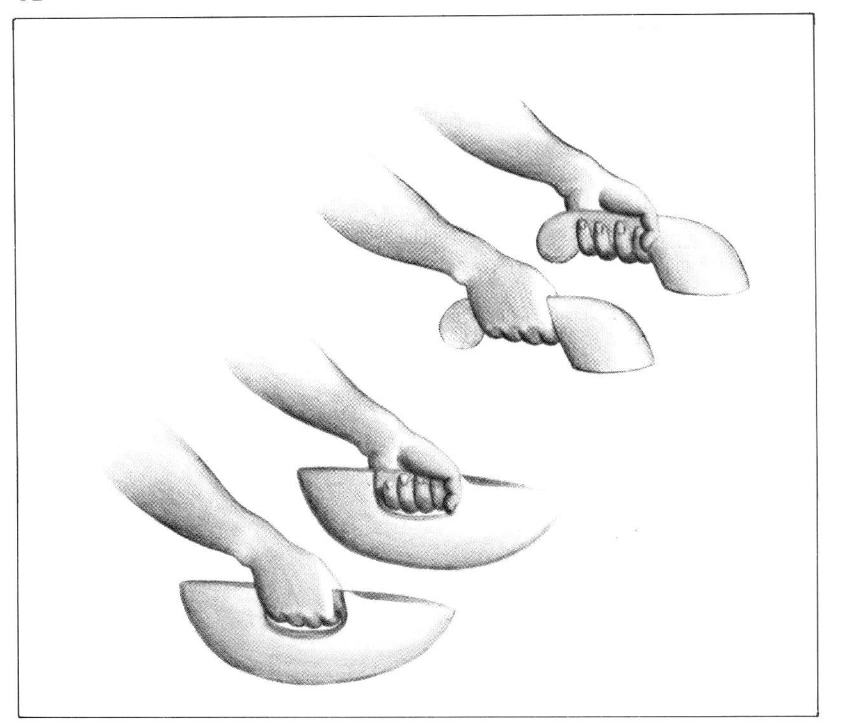

83

84

fact that the jumpers used weights suited to their physical build: the more strongly built the athlete, the heavier the weights he used.

The simplest form of weight was a solid rectangular piece of stone or metal, with a shallow depression towards the middle of the four long sides, so that the jumper could grip it. This was the shape of the weight used by Epainetos of Eleusis, referred to above. In the Archaic and Classical period there were two basic types of weight, the elongated and the round. The former had the shape of an irregular semicircle with a recess on the under side so as to provide a grip. The round ones normally consisted of a solid hemispherical piece usually of stone, having a hollow for the jumper to insert his fingers.

There were other types of jumping-weight, however, such as the elliptical. The use of the weights was not compulsory. It seems, however, that the jumpers usually used them, because they were a great help, as we shall see below. Philostratos says that the *halteres* are an invention of the pentathletes for the jump, from which they derive their name; the weights guide the hands of the athletes and make their pace steady and sure.

The pentathletes did not use the weights simply for the jumping events, but also to exercise their hands, fingers and arms with suitable movements. This usage of the weights was called weight-training *(halterobolia)*. Scenes of weight-training from the *gymnasia* are frequent in vase-paintings.

84. A jumper swinging his weights up and down and preparing to begin his run-up (Paris, Louvre).

The Jump

The details and rules of the event are not known with any certainty. The literary sources do not tell us, for example, whether the athletes had a run-up before the jump to gain impetus, or not, though in the vase-paintings they usually do. There is, however, a vase-painting of the 4th century B.C., that depicts an athlete preparing to jump from a standing position and without weights. This type of jump appears to have been rare, and was probably only used in practice.

The modern long jumper sets off at great speed and reaches maximum acceleration at the point that he hurls his body above the pit. The methods of the ancient jumper were different. His forward movement was produced both by his run-up, which was short, but powerful, and by the swinging of the weights. As he arrived at the take-off point, the athlete swung the weights vigorously backwards and forwards. At the point of hurling his body, he stretched his hands with the weights in front of him, and at the highest point of his trajectory, his body was doubled up, with feet and hands parallel. As soon as he began to fall, however, the jumper brought his arms forcefully downwards and backwards and used the weights as counter-thrusts to propel his body forward. Just before he landed, he jettisoned the weights behind him to retain the momentum he had gained from the sudden downward movement of the arms (the weights would have acted as a brake on his body), and came down on the soil with his feet together. The role played by the

85

86

weights and the significant way they aided the athlete is clear from this description.

In modern times a number of attempts have been made by jumpers to use the weights, and have brought encouraging results. These experiments have been of a sporadic nature, however, and the use of weights has so far not become general.

The Types of Jump

It is not known whether the type of jump used by the ancient pentathletes was a simple long jump, or a triple jump. The lack of knowledge on this point has given rise to much discussion and created disputes and conflicting opinions amongst modern scholars, who attempt to put forward hypotheses to support their views. The conflict of opinion stems from the epigram relating to the performances of the athlete Phayllos of Kroton: "Phayllos jumped 55 feet and threw the discus 95." Phayllos was an exceptional athlete, an almost legendary figure, who was victorious three times in the Pythian games, twice in the *pentathlon* and once in the *stadion*. His great fame throughout the ancient world was due not only to his qualities as an athlete, but also to the courage he showed during the battle of Salamis. A similar performance is recorded by Julius Africanus in connection with the winner in the 29th Olympiad (664 B.C.), Chionis of Sparta, "who jumped 52 feet." These jumps were of 16.28 m. and 16.31 m.; but it is not physically possible for a man to jump 16-17 metres, however swift his run-up, and however strongly and firmly he hits the take-off point. Many modern scholars have therefore supposed that the jump in the *pentathlon* was a triple, not a simple jump. This view is supported by a number of written sources, the most important of which is a scholion by Themistios on Aristotle's *Physics,* which says that the jumpers moved continuously like horses when they were competing — an observation that would not make sense if the jump was a simple one. A further argument is that the tradition of the triple jump survived into the Middle Ages and modern times in Greece, mainly in Cyprus, where the term *trapedeso* (to jump thrice) occurs in the medieval period.

However, a whole series of arguments have been deployed against the views expressed above. Some of them are as follows: Philostratos nowhere records that there were two types of jump. There is no word in Greek for "triple jump." None of the scenes of jumping on vases depicts a multiple jump. And, finally, it would be difficult to use the jumping-weights effectively in the triple jump. There is also another, simple, explanation of the superhuman jumps by Phayllos and Chionis. A host of stories and anecdotes were told about the great athletes and their achievements in sport and in life in general. As time went by, these stories became increasingly exaggerated, and superhuman abilities were attributed to many famous athletes. This is probably the explanation behind the fantastic jumps of Phayllos and Chionis. It is also one more proof of the respect and admiration that the ancient Greeks felt towards their athletes.

85. A long jumper with his weights during the run-up (Heidelberg, Archäologisches Institut der Universität).

86. The jumper with his weights at the moment of take off (Paris, Louvre).

87

87, 88. Athletes portrayed during the long jump (Basle, Antikenmuseum. Boston, Museum of Fine Arts).

88

There is evidence for a type of jump similar to the modern pole-vault. It appears always to have been a jump over horses. On a red-figure cylix, a youth is depicted getting ready to leap over some horses with the aid of a pole. It is probable that an event of this nature existed, for there is a scene on a Panathenaic amphora showing athletes leaping or performing other exercises over horses, before an audience. The fact that the scene is depicted on a Panathenaic amphora lends support to this hypothesis for, as we know, they always had representations of the event for which they were offered as a prize. The amphora

89

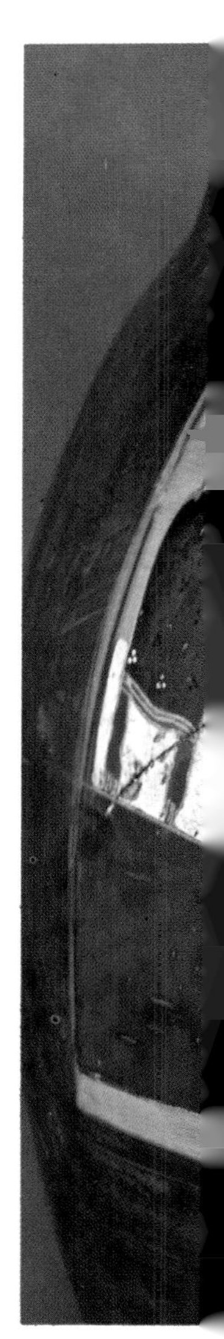

also has the interesting inscription "Well done, the acrobat." We are faced with the very word used to describe the athletes who executed acrobatic leaps over bulls in Crete. It is probable therefore that this type of jumping continued the tradition of Cretan somersaulting.

89. The jumper before landing. Behind him can be seen the marks of other jumpers (London, British Museum).

90. Public display of acrobatics, including en event resembling the pole-vault. The jumper (on the right) is preparing to leap over the horse with the aid of the pole (Paris, Bibliothèque Nationale).

90

The Discus

Origin and Mythology

Throwing the discus was one of the competitions that did not have any direct connection with either military exercises or farm work, and it does not appear to have derived from either of these. It nonetheless had a long tradition in the Greek world. The earliest evidence we have for it is in Homer, who relates that it formed part of the games organised by Achilles in honour of the dead Patroklos.

In Greek mythology, the discus is connected with accidents and killings. Apollo accidentally killed his friend Hyakinthos with the discus, when the Zephyr blew it off its course. Another tragic incident related in mythology involves Perseus, who unwittingly killed his grandfather, Akrisios. And Oxylos, the founding father of Elis, is said to have left his country because he had killed his brother Thermios with the discus, again by accident.

The Discus

The discus called for rhythm, precision and power, and was an event particularly well-liked by the Greeks; subsequently it formed part of the pentathlon.

Archaeological finds and a range of vase-paintings make it clear that the discus was originally made of stone, and later of iron, lead or bronze. In Homer the bronze discus, which was either cast or hammered, was called *solos;* this was a weight which was tied with a leather strap and thrown in the same way as the hammer today, the thrower turning it around and around. Like its modern counterpart, the discus was circular with two convex curves in section, and a large circumference. The examples that have been discovered range from 17 to 32 cm. in diameter, and weigh from 1.3 to 6.6 kilos. The most likely probability is that a particular weight was prescribed for the discus at the different games , but that this varied from city to city. The competitors must all have thrown the same discus at the games, because it was only in this way that they could have competed on equal terms, and that the decision could have been fair and impartial. An obscure phrase in Philostratos has led some scholars to conclude that there was a special Olympic discus for the Olympic Games, but there is no certainty on this point. A lighter discus was used, naturally enough, in boys' contests.

Engraved scenes are commonly found on ancient discuses, sometimes depicting athletes, such as javelin-throwers, jumpers etc., and often purely decorative in character, with dolphins, birds, and so on. Inscriptions and poems were also incised on discuses, and one that has survived has a merry poem by Anakreon on it. Similarly it was the custom in early times for agreements and treaties to be inscribed on discuses; according to Pausanias and Plutarch, the agreement about the Olympic truce was inscribed on a discus.

The Event

The way in which the discus was thrown in antiquity will not have been very different from that of today, since the movements a man has to make in order to throw an object like the discus a long way are dictated by nature itself. Many of these movements can be seen in the vase-paintings. The statue of the *Diskobolos* (discus-thrower) by Myron, however, has created some confusion and has given rise

91

91. A discus thrower. The discus was an event requiring rhythm, accuracy and power. In the Classical period it formed part of the pentathlon (Munich, Antikensammlungen).

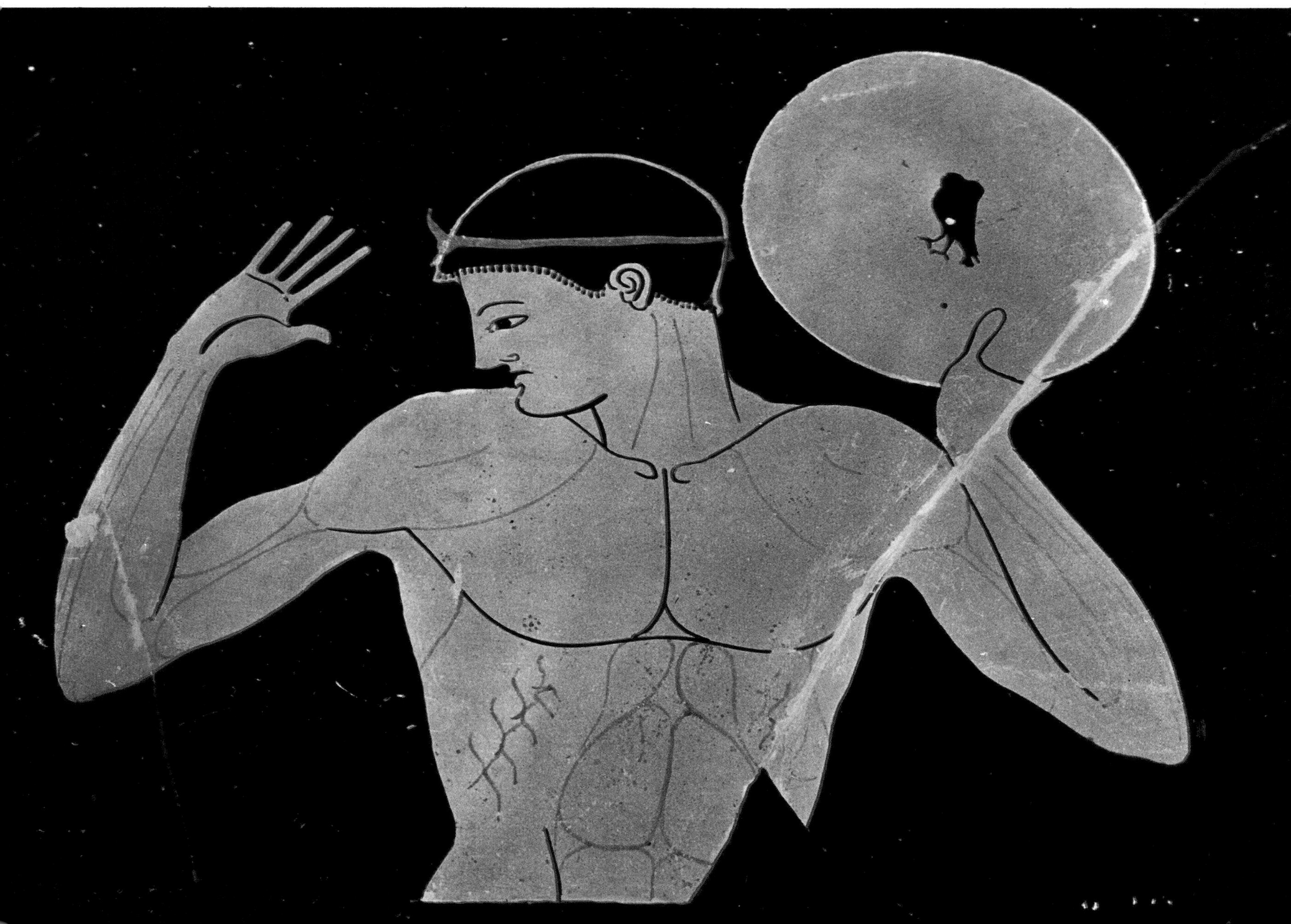

to a number of misguided theories, because the statue portrays a single fleeting stage of the whole series of movements. This has led many scholars to a mistaken interpretation of the stance of the statue, and to a theory that describes the throwing of the discus in ancient times in terms of a series of unnatural and forced movements, which have even been named "the Greek discus."

In order to throw the discus a good way, the athlete would use one hand to hold the discus high and support it with the other; he would then swing it vigorously down and forwards or from the side and behind forwards. It is only in this way that the muscles of the shoulder and shoulder blades, and of the chest and ribs, can be brought into play in the throw. The throwing of the discus may be described as follows: the right-handed discus-thrower stood with his left leg forward and the weight of his body on the right foot. He held the discus in his right hand and swung it up and down a few times, supporting it with his left hand when it was above his head. As it came down and behind him, he turned his body slightly to the right. After a few preliminary swings, he bent his knees a little more when the discus was at the end of its backward arc (for the last preliminary swing), tensed his knees and, transferring his weight from his right foot to his left, front foot, he threw the discus upwards and forwards, with a vigorous accelerating swing. This was the last stage in the throw, for we do not know if it was preceded by a run-up or a turn, as in the modern throw.

The whole of the procedure in throwing the discus, with its free, rhythmical preliminary movements, the concentration, the sudden turn, the backward swing of the discus, and finally the throw itself, in which all the physical powers were involved, made a picture of incomparable plastic beauty.

Myron, in his *Diskobolos,* is depicting a fleeting movement from the throwing of the discus (probably during the final forward swing), and not a complicated, composite rule as to how the discus should be thrown, that would have prescribed what stance the athlete should adopt, how much he should bend his knees, how much he should turn his body and head, how high he should lift his hand, and how many steps he should take before throwing the discus. Nor was there any need to restrict the freedom of the competitors to avoid accidents. Not a single instance of an accident involving either injury or death, to a competitor or a spectator, is referred to in the ancient authors, because the spectators sat on the embankments. Accidents might occur during training, when spectators and athletes were not careful enough when walking in the areas where the discus was being thrown. Philostratos, in his *Eikones,* in the passage narrating of the death of Hyakinthos, gives a description of throwing the discus which tallies with the stance of the statue by Myron.

The performances of the discus-throwers were marked with small wooden pegs, and were measured with rods. We know from ancient evidence that the famous athlete Phayllos threw the discus a distance of 95 feet, and another athlete, Phlegyas, is reported to have thrown the discus from one bank of the Alpheios to the other. We may say, in conclusion, that the ancient technique of throwing the discus was similar to that used today in the freestyle discus, whether or not the thrower made a turn before releasing it.

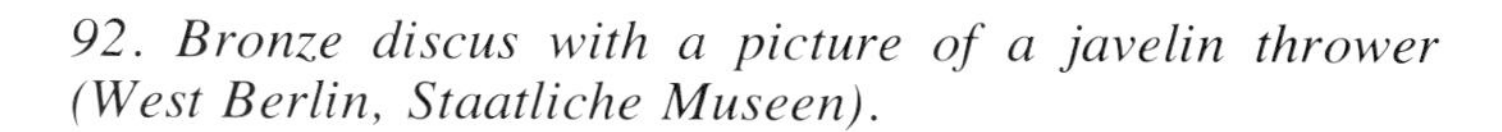

92. Bronze discus with a picture of a javelin thrower (West Berlin, Staatliche Museen).

93. The bronze discus dedicated to Olympian Zeus by Publius Asklepiades, the winner of the pentathlon in A.D. 241 (Olympia, Archaeological Museum).

94. Bronze statuette of a youth preparing to throw a weight (the solos, *similar to the modern shot) (Bologna, Museo Civico).*

94

95

96

97

95. The discus thrower during the initial swing (Musei Vaticani).

96, 97. The final swing before the release of the discus (Rome, Villa Giulia. Würzburg, Martin von Wagner Museum).

98

98. Throwing the discus. The stance of the discus thrower is an artistic representation by the vase painter and has no connection with the stance adopted in reality (Naples, Museo Archeologico Nazionale).

99. The Diskobolos of Myron. The statue depicts a fleeting moment in the action of the thrower (Rome, Museo Nazionale Romano).

The Javelin

Introduction

The javelin was one of the athletic games directly connected with daily life, and undoubtedly derived from its use in war and hunting.

According to Pindar, the winner of the javelin in the games organised by Herakles at Olympia was Phrastor. Achilles also included a javelin competition, with a very valuable prize, in the games held in honour of Patroklos (see "Athletics in the Geometric Period"). It further appears that the Achaian soldiers passed their leisure time competing to see who could throw the javelin or the discus farthest, or who could aim most accurately. The *Iliad* tells us that the soldiers of Achilles "rejoiced in throwing the discus and javelin and in archery," near the sea-shore.

As an athletic event, the javelin had two forms: throwing the javelin for distance or throwing it at a predetermined target. The former was basically the predominant form, and was included amongst the light events, constituting one of the *pentathlon* events in the Panhellenic games. There are scattered pieces of evidence indicating its existence as an event in its own right (e.g. at Kea).

Types of Javelin

The javelin used by athletes was a wooden pole, roughly as long as a man's height, with one end pointed, and lighter than that used by warriors. This form of javelin, which was used in the *pentathlon,* was called *apotomeus,* and it is doubtful whether it had the iron or bronze head with which the military javelin was provided. Both javelins with a head and javelins with a pointed end are found in vase-paintings. In target practice, a javelin with pointed head was necessary so that it could be stuck in the target. The accidental killing of a youth by a javelin in a *gymnasion,* referred to by Antiphon, was probably caused by the head of an athletic javelin being used by the athletes during practice.

When the javelin did not have an attached head, a blunt ferule was attached to the end of it so that its centre of gravity would be towards the front, which gave it a steady and accurate flight. When the centre of gravity was towards the back, on the other hand, the throw gained in length, but the javelin's flight was not stable and there was a risk that it would deviate from its path.

The basic difference between the ancient and the modern javelin is the use of the thong, a leather strap that formed a loop, and which the ancient athletes attached at the centre of gravity of the javelin. Javelins for use in war and in hunting also had thongs, but in these cases they were permanently attached, while in the case of the athletic javelin, each athlete tied the thong where it helped him the most, depending on his ability and the lenght of his fingers.

The Event

The javelin was thrown from a fixed point which, judging from a number of vase - paintings was very probably the starting-line of the stadium. The distance from the end of the track to this line was ade-

100. Bronze discus with an engraved picture of a man throwing the javelin. Javelin throwing for distance (as opposed to target javelin) formed part of the pentathlon (W. Berlin, Staatliche Museen).

101

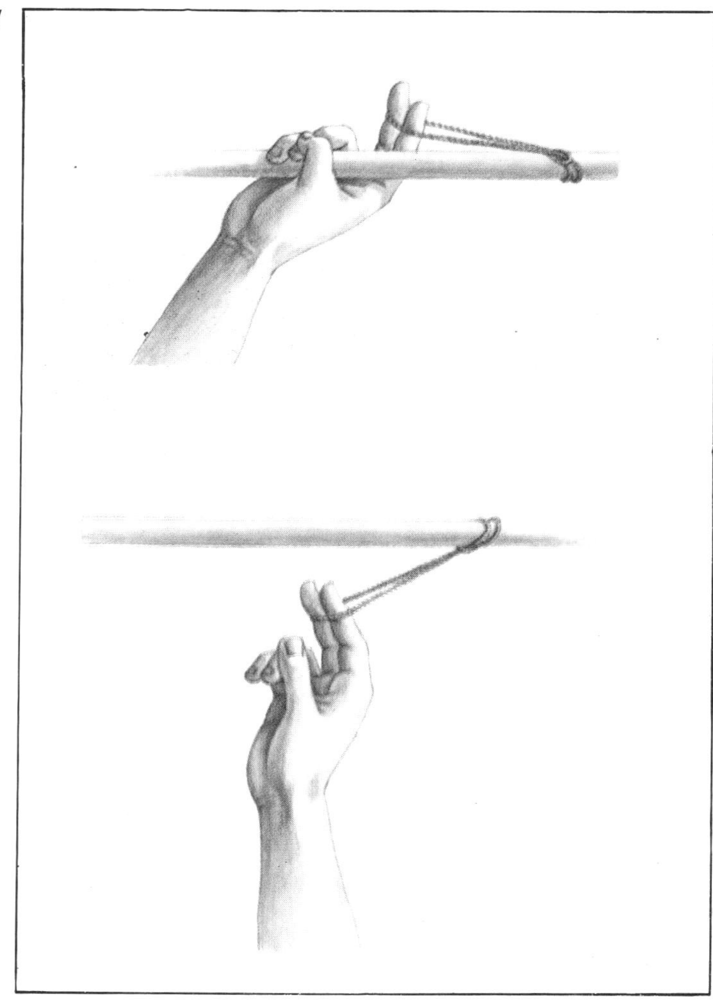

101. The thong was a leather strap that formed a loop and was attached at the centre of gravity of the javelin. The athletes inserted one or two fingers in the loop, which helped the throw to achieve greater distance and stability (Drawing: K. Iliakis).

102. The javelin thrower took a short run-up before the throw, holding the javelin horizontal next to his head (Munich, Antikensammlungen).

103. A javelin thrower in the final stage before the throw (East Berlin, Staatliche Museen).

quate for the few steps that the athlete needed to take before making his throw. The javelin had to fall within an area strictly defined on three sides, and the throw was invalid if it fell outside this area. The athlete tied the thong as tight as he could, tested it several times, and then put his index finger, or the index and middle fingers, into the loop. Before beginning his run-up, he pushed the javelin back with his left hand to tighten the thong and make it grip the fingers of his right hand. Then, holding the javelin horizontally, close to his head, with the point of it inclined slightly downwards, he turned his body in the direction of the throw and started his run-up. A few paces before the starting-line, he stretched his right arm backwards and turned his body and head to the right; at the same time he crossed his right foot in front of the left, and drew his left arm backwards to help the turn. He then bent his knees slightly and stretched his left leg out in front of him to break his impetus. Remaining behind the line, he hurled the javelin over his head from this final position. This is the throwing style used by all javelin-throwers today.

The thong assisted the throw in two ways: it increased the power of it because it made the grip more secure, and secondly it gave it a rotating motion about its axis that stabilised the javelin in flight and so helped it to achieve a greater distance.

The thong was fastened to the javelin in such a way as to remain attached to it when it was thrown. This is demonstrated by the fact that the fingers were loosely inserted into the noose, so that they could release the javelin as it was thrown.

Target Javelin

Throwing the javelin at a target, usually from horseback, was one of the basic exercises taught to

102

103

104

the Athenian *epheboi*. Plato and Xenophon speak of horsemen throwing the javelin while riding and recommend this as a very useful form of exercise.

Throwing the javelin at a target from horseback was one of the events in the Panathenaic games. A Panathenaic amphora depicts riders (probably *epheboi*) aiming their javelins at the centre of a circular target (a shield?) suspended on high.

As the horse was galloping, its rider had, at a certain point, or a certain distance, to throw the javelin and hit the target. The horse's movement affected the steadiness of the rider's hand, and limited his control over his movements. At the appropriate moment, then, he had to achieve complete co-ordination between the rhythm of the horse's gallop and the movement of his hand which was about to throw the javelin, while at the same time keeping his attention focussed on the target. All this demanded a lot of practice and the combination of many qualities — a sure eye, a steady and strong hand, and the flexibility of a competent horseman.

Javelin-throwing from horseback was particularly respected at Argos, where it was the main athletic competition during the festival of the Heraia. This contest was called "the shield," or "the bronze event," after the shield-target which was also given as a prize to the winner, along with a crown of myrtle. According to the aetiological myth attaching to the foundation of these games, like all the great games, the first shield to be awarded as a prize was the shield of Danaos himself, and the first winner was Abas, the son of Lynkeus, the legendary founder of the Heraia. This competition achieved great fame in antiquity, as is shown by proverbial expressions like "You are worthy of the shield at Argos," or "He is proud as though he has won the shield at Argos."

104. A javelin thrower during the run-up (Paris, Louvre).

105. Scene of mounted target javelin. The target for the riders is a shield hung up high. The rider had, at the appropriate moment, to achieve complete co-ordination between his throwing hand and the rhythm of the horse's gallop, in order to hit the target (London, British Museum).

105

Wrestling

Mythology and History

Philostratos claims that the whole earth rejoiced at the invention of wrestling. *Palaistra, the daughter of Hermes* he writes, *who spent her adolescent years in the forests of Arkadia, invented wrestling, and the whole earth rejoices at the discovery, for the iron weapons of war will be flung far away from the hands of men, and the stadia will gain sweeter glory than the military camps, and men will compete naked.*

The same author emphasises the usefulness of wrestling in war by claiming that the military achievement at Marathon was almost a wrestling contest, and that the Spartans at Thermopylai fell unarmed upon the enemy with their bare hands, after their spears and swords had broken in fighting. Plutarch attributes the victory at Leuktra to the supremacy in wrestling enjoyed by the Thebans and the Boiotians generally, at that period.

The art of wrestling was believed to have been invented by Theseus, when he wrestled with and killed Kerkyon, for, as Pausanias says, *prior to this, they used only size and might in wrestling,* that is, before Theseus, the qualities needed by a good wrestler were strength and a great build. The Academic philosopher Polemon attributes the discovery of wrestling to Phorbas of Athens, the trainer of Theseus, while the historian Istros believed that Theseus was taught wrestling by the goddess Athena herself. Other "inventors" claimed for the sport include Hermes and Peleus, who wrestled with Atalanta in the funeral games in honour of Pelias, and Herakles, who defeated the giant Antaios, Acheloös and Triton in wrestling contests. Wrestling is the oldest and most widespread sport in the world, and is the earliest form of fighting without weapons. It was therefore directly connected with war, both in Greek mythology and in the traditional legends of other peoples. The first detailed description of wrestling is in Homer, in the games held in honour of Patroklos (see "Athletics in the Geometric Period").

Forms of Wrestling

Wrestling called for a combination of skill, agility and strength. It formed part of the pentathlon, and was also an independent event, at the Panhellenic games. There were two forms of wrestling: "upright" wrestling *(orthia pale, orthopale,* or *stadaia pale)* and "rolling" or "ground" wrestling *(alindesis,* or *kylisis,* or *kato pale).* In the first, all the wrestler had to do was throw his opponent to the ground, whereas in the second, a fall was not enough; the contest continued until one of the two competitors was compelled to admit defeat and writhdraw. In this respect the event was similar to the pankration, except that the wrestler did not hit his opponent, but merely applied a hold. An athlete only withdrew when he was so completely exhausted that all further resistance was impossible. He would then raise his hand with the index finger or the index and middle fingers extended, so that the umpire could see him. Using the second form, i.e. ground wrestling, Antaios, the son of Poseidon, is said to have thrown his opponents to the ground,

106. An athlete raises his hands and prepares to come to grips with his opponent (Munich, Antikensammlungen).

fallen on them with his enormous weight, and killed them. Herakles realised that Antaios was invincible as long as he was in contact with earth, for Earth was his mother; so he seized him by the waist and lifted him, thus separating him from his mother, and then threw him to the ground.

There were separate areas in the *palaistra* for the two kinds of wrestling. Upright wrestling took place in the sand in the pit, while ground wrestling was normally held on wet soil. The mud stuck to the bodies of the competitors, which made them slippery and holds therefore difficult. In upright wrestling, the upper part of the body (head, neck, shoulders, arms, chest and waist) was exercised, while in ground wrestling, it was the lower part (waist, thighs, knees and, naturally, arms also).

The Event

In order to gain the victory in upright wrestling, a man had to throw his opponent to the ground three times, in which case he was called *triakter*. For competitions in the stadium, a minimum of five and maximum of eight pairs of wrestlers were selected. Each competitor drew from a helmet a lot, on which was marked a letter indicating his opponent. The Scholiast on Pindar writes of Alkimedon or Alkidamas: *He beat four boys and made them return home in grief, because he had deprived them of victory; and they, silent in defeat, set out secretly, on hidden ways and paths, and not by the public roads.*

The initial stance of the wrestler was similar to that of today. The athlete stood with his legs open and bent at the knees, ready to take advantage of any opportunity his opponent offered him. This stance was called *systasis* or *parathesis* (square-on stance, or side-ways stance).

The various holds and tricks used by the athletes during the contest had a large number of names, according to the part of the body to which the hold was applied. Some of them were: *hamma* (clinch, from the word "knot"); *anchein* (strangle-hold); *ankyrizein* (hook, or trip); *rassein* (throw to the ground); *drattein, helkein* (pull); *trachelizein* (neck-hold); *dialambanein* (waist-hold); *perisphingein* (squeeze the opponent with both arms). A frequent and impressive hold was the *mesolabe* (waist-hold), in which the wrestler lifted his opponent from the ground, making it easier to throw him. There was also the hold called *anabastasai eis hypsos* (holding on high) which was comparable with the modern "flying mare."

It is not known for certain whether leg-holds (which were frequently used in the pankration) were forbidden. Plato, in a passage in the *Laws* where he is comparing wrestling with the pankration, makes no mention of leg-holds in connection with the former, and they are not depicted in the vase-paintings. This does not mean they were forbidden, however, for the term *hyposkelizein* (to trip) is at-

107. Beginning of a wrestling match. The wrestlers are locked in one of the opening holds (Leningrad, Hermitage).

108. Scene showing Theseus wrestling with Kerkyon. Theseus (on the left) is gripping his opponent by the side and trying to throw him (London, British Museum).

109. Wrestling match. The competitor on the right is attempting to apply a waist-hold (W. Berlin, Staatliche Museen).

109

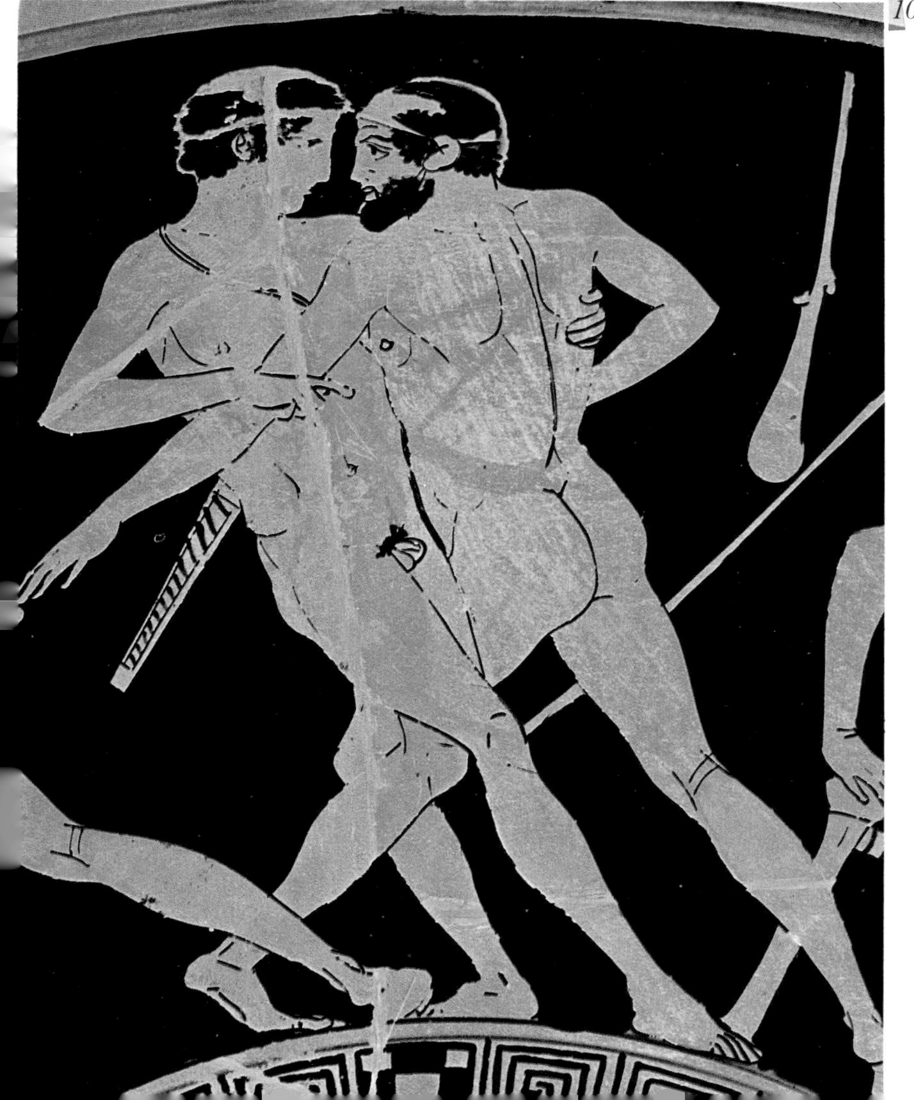

110

111

112

110. The man on the right is successfully applying the neck-hold (trachelizein), *and his opponent has lost his balance and is falling (Turin, Museo di Antichità).*

111. Wrestling match (Musei Vaticani).

112. The wrestler on the left has succeeded in lifting his opponent with a waist-hold (W. Berlin, Staatliche Museen).

114

tested for wrestling matches (it was more frequent in the pankration).

In order to achieve a fall, a competitor had to throw his opponent to the ground and either remain standing himself or fall on top of him. If any part of the body touched the ground, even only a knee, it was accounted a fall against a wrestler. It was not necessary to pin an opponent's back to the ground, as in modern wrestling, because in that case the contest would continue on the ground and would cease to be upright wrestling. We have, on the contrary, evidence that if both men fell on their sides at the same time, they rose and began again, without a fall being recorded, *because there was a rule that when they fell together it was reckoned that neither had thrown the other, and they set them up again and made them begin the match from the hold they had before they fell.*

The Qualities of a Good Wrestler

According to Philostratos, the wrestler should have a good height and a well-proportioned body in

113

113. "Ram" position. The two wrestlers are pushing each other with their heads, each trying to upset the balance of the other (Athens, National Archaeological Museum).

114. Wrestling match, in bronze. The man on the left is pulling his opponent's arms backwards, making him lose his balance, and has almost thrown him (Munich, Antikensammlungen).

all respects. The neck should not be long, but nor should it be buried in the shoulders; the shoulders should be stout, and the arms and wrists strong; the chest should be broad, but should not stick out too much; the ribs should be strong enough to resist the pressure applied by the opponent; the stomach should be flat, for a swelling stomach constituted useless weight; the hips should be supple and flexible; the thighs should be compact and the legs, shins, ankles and soles strong enough for the wrestler to stand on the ground like an immovable column. This description means that the good wrestler should resemble the statuettes of Herakles which are "godlike" and a joy to behold, with their well-proportioned bodies and long neck, like proud stallions.

Rules of Wrestling

Wrestling had certain rules that had to be observed by the competitors. These rules were said to have been drawn up by Orikadmos, an early athlete from Sicily. We can summarise the main prohibitions in wrestling from extracts from ancient texts. Blows were not allowed, since these were the basic feature of boxing. Holds on the male organs were forbidden, as was biting and wrestling outside the area of the pit. When the opponents went outside the pit, the umpires stopped the contest and brought them back to the centre of the pit, where they were obliged to resume with the same hold as when the contest was interrupted.

Leontiskos of Messene in Sicily used to win by breaking his opponent's fingers, a technique that brought him one victory in the Pythian games and two at Olympia. He appears to have used *akrocheirismos,* that is holds applied only to the fingers, which allowed him to sprain his opponents' fingers. This technique was used both in wrestling and in the pankration. Philostratos gives us the following description of wrestling, in his *Eikones: One of them seized his opponent from behind and hugged him so tight as almost to strangle him, gripping his body with his legs; the other did not raise his hand in submission, however, but broke the hold of the arm that was strangling him by dislocating one finger, which you would have thought he had torn from the others with tremendous force. All this incurred the displeasure of the spectators*. The victories of Leontiskos are to be explained by the fact that dislocating the fingers and strangle-holds were not forbidden.

The heavy events, which included wrestling, produced men of psychological strength, physical endurance of iron, and an indomitable spirit, for the victor in wrestling needed to have will-power, strength and endurance. The wrestlers contested the victory stubbornly, but respected the rules, as is shown by the very small number of cases in which they were broken. This was natural enough, for it was the clean victory that won the praise of the spectators.

It is certain therefore that as in the other heavy events — boxing and the pankration — there were no restrictions in force to protect the life and limbs of the competitors. Plutarch calls wrestling "the most skillful and cunning of sports," and many wrestlers had a facility for particular wrestling tricks and holds. Counter-holds were used against attacking holds to defend against and neutralise the attacker. Hence, the art of wrestling developed to a high level. Particular wrestling methods were used in different cities, and Thessalian, Sicilian and Spartan wrestling were all well known. The Sicilians were very crafty in their wrestling and did not have the reputation of being honourable athletes. The Spartans, on the other hand, tried to prevail by virtue of their strength, rather than by techniques and tricks. The epigram written for a Spartan wrestler runs as follows: *Others use tricks; but I win by strength, as befits the sons of Spartans.* The athletes of Argos were famous for their wrestling skill, and this gave rise to the proverb "Argive, not Libyan wrestling." The spectators at the games had all passed through the *gymnasia* and the wrestling-schools; they therefore knew all the details of the sport and were able to appreciate and applaud a good, skilled wrestler. Kratinos, a boy from Aigeira in Achaia was much admired at Olympia for his great wrestling skill, and was in consequence granted the right to set up in the Altis a statue of himself and also of his *paidotribes*.

115. The beginning of the hold called anabastasai eis hypsos *(hold on high). The wrestler on the left is gripping his opponent by the waist, and is preparing to turn him over and throw him onto his head (Boston, Museum of Fine Arts).*

115

Famous Wrestlers

Names of wrestlers who won fame from their victories at Olympia and in the other sacred games are referred to in the historians. In addition to Milon of Kroton, about whom we shall speak later (see "Famous athletes of Ancient Greece"), there was Timasitheos of Kroton, who defeated Milon when he contested his sixth Olympic crown; the Spartan Hipposthenes who won six Olympic victories; his son Etoimokles, who won five; Amesinas of Barka who trained by wrestling with a bull; Aristodemos of Elis, to whom no opponent ever succeeded in applying a waist-hold; and Isidoros of Alexandria, who, according to Phlegon of Tralles, "never fell."

116

117

116. The sequel to the preceding move. The wrestler on the right turns his opponent over, all resistance by the latter being vain (London, British Museum).

117. The lower wrestler is using his hip to throw his opponent (tour de hanches) (London, British Museum).

118. The last stage of the hold called anabastasai eis hypsos *(hold on high). The defeated wrestler falls onto his head (Florence, Museo Archeologico).*

118

The Pentathlon

The pentathlon was a combination of the two types of event that existed in the ancient world: the light and the heavy. Of the light events, it included jumping, running (the *stadion*) and the javelin, while the heavy events were represented by the discus and wrestling. Running and wrestling, as we have seen, were also held as separate events in the Panhellenic games, while jumping, the discus and the javelin were not autonomous sports with a prize awarded for them, but merely events within the pentathlon.

According to mythology, the pentathlon was invented by Jason. Before this, jumping, the discus and the javelin had been separate events with their own prize. Philostratos tells the following story about the origin of the pentathlon: "At the time of the Argo's journey, Telamon was the best man in the discus, Lynkeus in the javelin, and the two sons of Boreas, Zetes and Kalaïs, at running and jumping. Peleus was second in all these, but could beat everyone at wrestling. When Jason wanted to award the prizes, therefore, he combined the five events out of a desire to honour his friend Peleus, to whom he gave the victory; in this way he created the pentathlon."

The pentathlon was first included in the Olympic Games in the 18th Olympiad, in 708 B.C. A boys' pentathlon was held only in the 38th Olympiad, in 628 B.C., and on no other occasion. There was a boys' division in the pentathlon at other games, however (e.g. the Panathenaia), and an intermediate youths' division.

According to Aristotle, *The pentathletes are the best, because they are naturally endowed with both strength and speed.* The ancient Greeks did in fact look on the pentathlon as a major event, since competitors in it had to possess a combination of all the qualities and physical and psychological endowments that an athlete needed — such as speed, strength, skill and endurance — and these are not usually found in combination in the competitors in each individual sport.

The question of the order in which the events were held in the pentathlon has provoked much discussion and controversy amongst modern scholars. The ancient texts make it clear that wrestling was the final event, and there is no doubt on this point. There are therefore a large number of possible hypotheses concerning the order in which the other four events were held. Probably the pentathlon began with the jumping, went on to the discus, running and javelin, and ended with the wrestling, as a result of which the ultimate winner emerged.

Despite the efforts of scholars, the problem of how the winner of the pentathlon was decided remains unsolved. It is almost inconceivable that the same athlete could have won all five events. The view has therefore been put forward that it was enough for a competitor to win at least three of the events (of which one had to be the wrestling), to be declared winner of the pentathlon. The term *triakter* (winner in three events), and a number of relevant ancient texts, point in this direction. Pausanias refers to the case of Tisamenos of Elis and his contest with Hieronymos of Andros. Tisamenos won in running and jumping, while Hieronymos took the javelin, discus, and wrestling, and won the victor's crown.

Many other hypotheses have been suggested as to the way the pentathlon was held and how the winner was decided, all of them based on the principle of drawing lots in pairs. They remain hypotheses, however, and none of them gains any absolute confirmation from the ancient texts.

119

119. Athletes competing in the pentathlon: jumping, throwing the javelin, throwing the discus, and a second man throwing the javelin. The pentathlon also included the stadion *race and wrestling (London, British Museum).*

Boxing

Origin and Mythology

Boxing is one of the oldest sports. An early form of it is known on Crete in the Minoan period (see "Prehistory of the Games"), and the depth of its foundations in Greek prehistory are attested by the Thera fresco of the two young boxers.

We first meet boxing as a contest in the Homeric poems, where it was one of the games in honour of the dead Patroklos, in which the winner was Epeios; it was also one of the games on the island of the Phaiakians (see "Athletics in Homer").

According to mythology, Apollo was the inventor of boxing. The claim was also made for Herakles, Theseus, and others, but Apollo remained the main patron of the sport. He killed Phorbas, a boxer who lived in Phokis and who compelled travellers to Delphi to compete with him. No one escaped, until the god defeated him and inflicted upon him the same fate he had reserved for others.

The model boxing match in ancient mythology was the contest between Polydeukes and Amykos, the king of the Bebrykes, who lived in Bithynia on the Black Sea. The latter used to compel all strangers travelling through his country to box with him, and killed them in the course of the contest. When the Argonauts came to his country, he challenged the best amongst them to box with him, and Polydeukes courageously accepted the challenge. It was a very tough fight. The barbarian kept hitting on the blind side and Polydeukes avoided his blows with agile swerves and feints. In the end his skill and ability neutralised his opponent. He did not kill him, but forced him to swear that in future he would leave travellers passing through his country unmolested.

Himantes (Thongs)

The boxers wrapped *himantes,* or straps of soft ox-hide, round their hands to strengthen their wrists and steady the fingers.

In Homer, the thongs were simple straps of fine ox-leather, and this type, called *meilichai* or *strophia,* seems to have been worn by boxers until the 5th century B.C. They were wrapped around the first knuckles of the fingers, ran diagonally across the palm and back of the hand, leaving the thumb uncovered, and were tied round the wrist or higher up the forearm.

The form of thongs gradually evolved. To make the blows more effective, straps of harder leather were added around the knuckles of the fingers, and the thong was padded inside with wool. According to Plato, these thongs were called *sphairai* (balls).

It was a complicated and time-consuming business to wind on these *himantes.* From the 4th century B.C., the boxers ceased to bind them on their hands on every occasion, and wore instead a kind of glove, formed of ready-wound leather straps. These were called *oxeis himantes* (sharp thongs), and they, too, left the finger-tips free, had applied straps of hard leather to strengthen them and an inner layer of wool

120. Bronze statue of a boxer. He is shown seated, his face disfigured by punches, and he is wearing himantes oxeis *(sharp thongs) (Rome, Museo Nazionale Romano).*

1055

to protect the hand, and were secured by leather straps in the middle of the forearm. This type of "glove" was used by boxers in Greece until the end of the 2nd century A.D.

In the Roman period, the boxers used the *caestus*, a boxing glove reinforced with iron and lead. Punches from this glove must have been very hard and dangerous. The *caestus* was an entirely Roman invention that transformed the Greek art of boxing into an inhuman and deadly contest.

Every change in the form of the *himantes* brought with it important changes in the technique of the sport. Some researchers even divide Greek boxing into periods, based on the type of *himantes* worn by the boxers. At the time when the thongs were soft, boxing required agility, adroitness, flexibility and a good technique. With the introduction of the "sharp thongs," however, the blows became harder, and the boxers paid more attention to defence, with the result that the contest became heavier and slower,

121

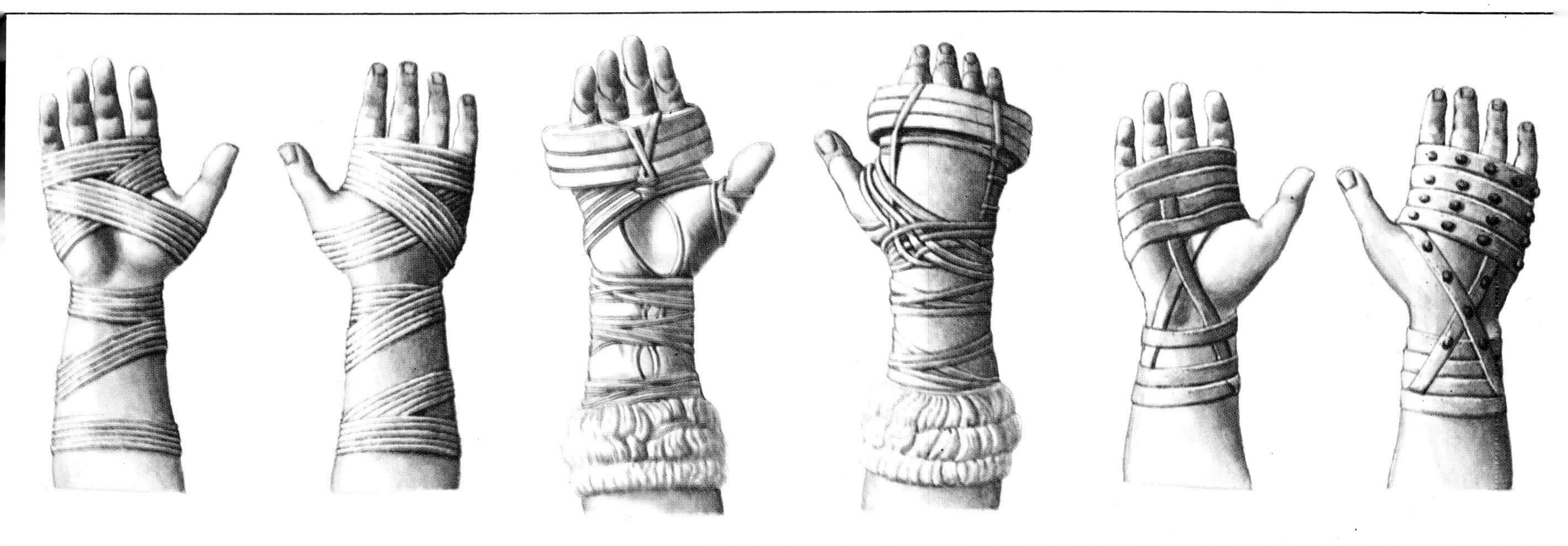

121. The himantes *were originally straps of fine hide, which were tied around the wrist and helped to steady the finger joints. These were called* meilichai *(soft) (left). After the 4th century B.C. the boxers wore a kind of glove made of ready wrapped* himantes, *called* oxeis himantes *(sharp thongs). They were reinforced by the addition of straps of hard leather, and they were also secured with leather straps around the arm (centre). In the Roman period, boxers used a boxing glove reinforced with iron and lead, called the* caestus *(right) (Drawing: K. Iliakis).*

122. A boxer binding the himantes *around his wrist (Vienna, Kunsthistorisches Museum).*

122

123

124

and rested more on brute force than on skill.

The Event

Ancient boxing differed in a number of ways from modern. First and foremost, it is not known what was the form of the area in which the contest was held. It was undoubtedly a space that was marked off in some way, though not like the modern ring. There was, moreover, no time limit on the duration of the contest. The opponents fought until one of them withdrew, by raising one or two fingers to show that he admitted defeat, or fell to the ground senseless. Sometimes the referee, after joint consultation with the two contestants, allowed them to break off the fight for an interval of time to regain their strength. Finally, classification of the boxers by weights was unknown. Indeed, since they had to fight with whoever fell to them by lot, a heavier contestant would be at an advantage and stand a better chance of winning.

The stance of the boxer at the beginning of the fight can be seen in the vase-paintings. His body is upright, his left leg advanced and slightly bent. The left arm, normally used for defence, is held out in front of him, while the right is bent and held close to the body, with the fist clenched, ready to hit the opponent the moment the chance arose. The Greeks seem to have preferred blows to the head, as being more effective.

The style of boxing changed from the 4th century B.C., when the "sharp thongs" became the prevalent form. Attacking moves were restricted and the pace became slower. The sport now required less skill and agility and more powers of endurance, so that it was the heavyweight boxers that took part in the Panhellenic games.

The position of the boxer in relation to the sun was of importance in boxing. A contestant who managed frequently to manoeuvre his opponent into positions facing the sun gained an advantage, for the other man would be blinded by it and it would be impossible for him to distinguish clearly the movements of his adversary.

When a contest continued even for a long time, the two opponents might seek to have the system of the *klimax* applied. In this, each of them in turn stood motionless and received a blow from his opponent without making the slightest attempt to avoid it. The order of delivering the blow was determined by lot, and it is obvious that whoever had the first turn to strike was in a much more favourable position. In the end, the man who held out longest against the blows was declared the winner. It was a very tough method, and it appears that recourse was had to it only in exceptional circumstances. Apart from other

123. Boxing match. Blood is running from the nose of one of the boxers, as a result of the punches he has received (London, British Museum).

124. Boxing. The man on the left is preparing to throw a punch at his opponent, who is trying to defend himself with his elbow (Paris, Louvre).

considerations, it could lead to the death of one of the two opponents, as in the case of the boxer Kreugas, who was killed by Damoxenos in the Nemean games. For the training methods and special exercises for boxers see the chapter "Exercises and Games."

Rules of Boxing

We do not know today the precise nature of the rules of boxing in antiquity. The rules of the sport were submitted for the approval of the Eleans by the boxer Onomastos of Smyrna, who won the event when it was first held at Olympia, in the 23rd Olympiad (688 B.C.). They forbade: holds — which were the basic feature of wrestling —, blows to the genital organs, the reinforcing of the thongs with extra layers of straps, and the use of pig-skin straps. The referees examined the thongs before every contest to ascertain whether they conformed to the rules.

Despite all this, injuries to boxers were frequent and sometimes so severe as to be fatal. Boxers who were responsible for the death of their opponent included Kleomedes of Astypalaia, who subsequently went mad, and Diognetos of Crete. Fatal blows of course were not very frequent, but misshapen boxers' faces were more common, with flattened noses from a fracture of the nose-bone, torn ears, etc. Some boxers even received names alluding to these features, such as Otothladias ("Cauliflower ears") etc.

In order to avoid injury during training, the boxers wore ear-protectors called *amphotides* or *epotides*. They consisted of two circular pieces of thick leather that covered the ears and were fastened with thin straps over the head and under the jaw. Occasionally they were made of metal. However, it was not permitted to wear them at the games, and injuries during the contest were therefore inevitable.

The Qualities of the Good Boxer

According to Philostratos, the good boxer should have long and powerful arms, strong shoulders and a high neck. His wrists should be steely and flexible, because strong wrists produce hard punches. Men with thick shins are not suited for boxing, since they are not agile. A large stomach is a handicap for a boxer, for it prevents him from being supple in his movements.

The boxer should also possess persistence, patience, endurance, psychological character, great will-power and strength, in order to withstand the pain, the blows and injuries. These qualities could only be achieved by continual and intense training.

Famous Boxers

Dio Chrysostom refers with admiration to the boxer Melankomas from Karia in Asia Minor, who won many victories without striking his opponent. Diagoras of Rhodes was idolised as the most famous boxer in Greece, because he was "a fair fighter" who never swayed to avoid his opponents but always met them face to face (see "Famous Athletes in Ancient Greece"). Julius Africanus mentions Kleoxenos of Alexandria, who was never injured, although he had won victories at all four sacred games. Pausanias writes of Hippomachos of Elis, who fought at Olympia, that he met and defeated three opponents *without receiving a single cut or mark on his body*.

One of the most famous boxers in the ancient world, renowned for his skill, was Glaukos of Karys-

125. The boxer on the right is landing a punch on his opponent, reminiscent of the straight left. Both boxers are wearing the type of himantes *called* sphairai *(balls) (London, British Museum).*

125

126

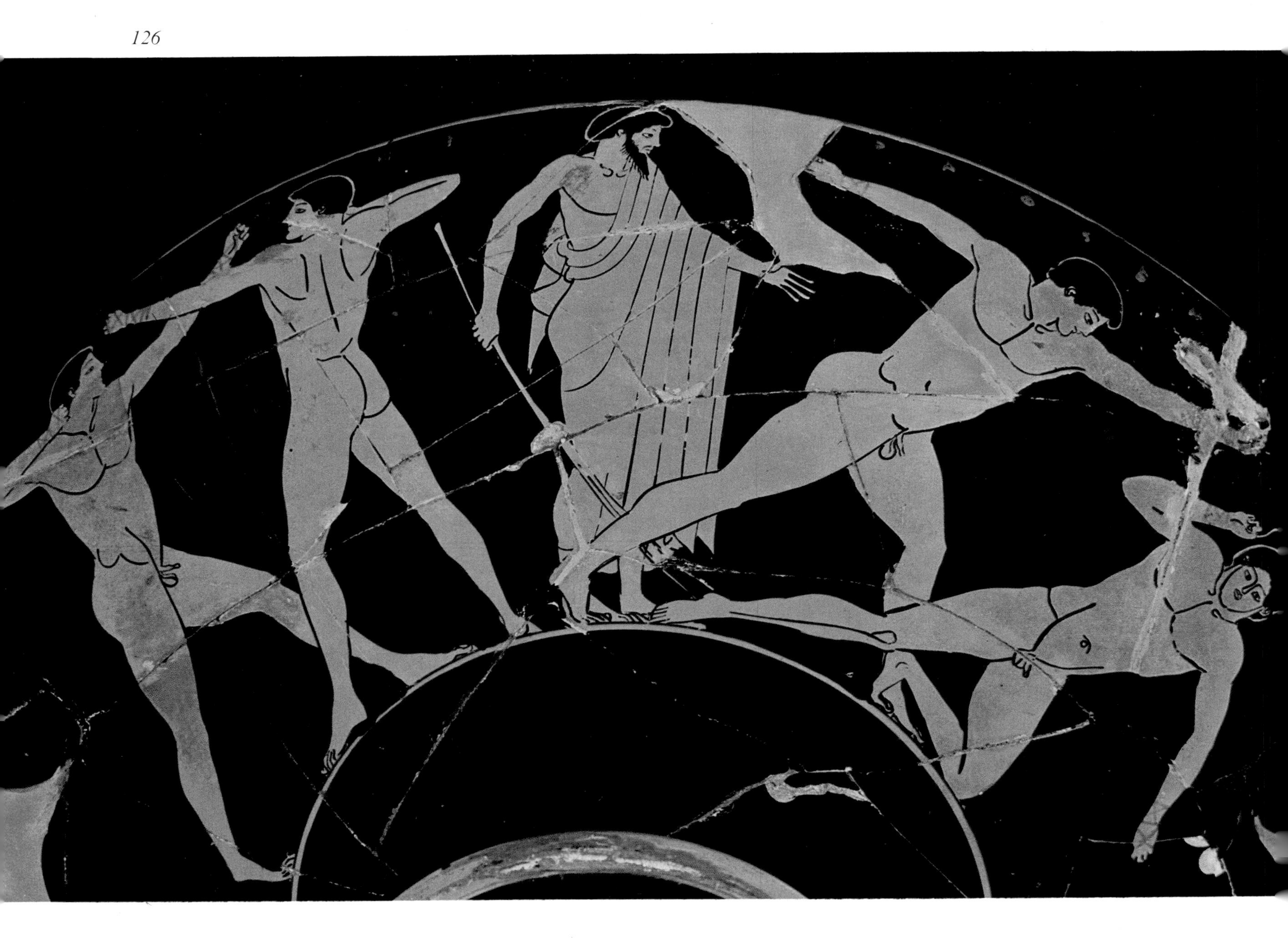

126. Two scenes of boxing matches. On the left the boxers exchange blows. On the right the boxer who is standing has knocked his opponent to the ground and the latter is raising his index finger in the signal for submission. In the centre, the referee is proclaiming the game at the end (London, British Museum).

tos. He won at Olympia, twice at the Pythian games, eight times each at the Nemean and Isthmian, and at many other games. A poet wrote of him: *Not even Polydeukes could stand against him, nor the son of Alkmene wielding his iron club in his hands.*

Moschos of Kolophon was a famous boy boxer, and the only one to win at all four great games. We may also mention Daïppos of Kroton; Kleitomachos of Thebes, who won two victories; Tisandros of Sicily, three; Thaliarchos of Elis, two; Euthymos of Lokris, three; Theagenes of Thasos, who won countless victories at many games; Eukles of Rhodes; Alkainetos of Lepreon and his son Hellanikos; and Agesidamos of Lokris, in the boys' category.

It was not only glory that surrounded the boxers, however. The disfiguring suffered by their faces as a result of the blows they received provoked a host of ironical and derisory remarks, and even satirical poems and epigrams. We can see from the few preserved satirical texts just how caustic was the sarcasm poured on the vanquished at Olympia. A few verses from these poems follow.

After twenty years when, safe and sound,
Odysseus returned to his fatherland,
His dog Argos knew him as soon as he saw him.
But you, Stratophon, who fought for four hours,
Are unrecognisable to the city, far less the dogs.
And if you were to see your face in the mirror,
You'd shout "I'm not Stratophon," I swear it.

Your head has become a sieve, Apollophanes
Like a worm-eaten piece of paper filled with a million holes,
Holes made by ants, straight and skew.
But box fearlessly on, and even if you get any more cuts
Than you have now, you can't suffer any more.

127

127. End of a boxing match. The defeated boxer is submitting by raising his index finger in admission of defeat (Athens, National Archaeological Museum).

The Pankration

Description

The Greeks believed that all the events were founded or invented by a god or a hero; and they thought that the pankration was founded by the great hero and civiliser of Attica, Theseus, who combined wrestling and boxing together in order to be able to defeat the fierce Minotaur in the labyrinth. Aristotle claims that the techniques of the pankration were given form by Leukaros of Akarnania, and Pausanias informs us that Herakles is said to have won victories in wrestling and the pankration.

The pankration probably evolved out of the primitive way of fighting used by a man when he came to grips with an enemy, whether the latter was a human being or an animal. It is not one of the games described by Homer, nor, unlike boxing, is it one of those held by the Argonauts on Lemnos.

As an event, the pankration was a combination of wrestling and boxing, and is described as such in the scholia on Plato: *a contest combining imperfect wrestling with imperfect boxing.* Philostratos considers it the best and most manly event at Olympia, and also an excellent exercise in training warriors. The same author, writing in the *Eikones,* tells us that waist-holds were allowed in the pankration, as well as holding the ankles, twisting the hands and hitting, and that the only things forbidden were "biting and gouging" — that is, a competitor was not allowed to bite his opponent, or to put his fingers in his opponent's eye, nose or mouth. These things, he continues, are permitted by the Spartans in training, for they regard it as good practice for warfare. We may therefore deduce that the Spartan pankration was different from that of the Eleans and the rest of the Greeks.

The Rules and Techniques of the Event

The pankration, like the other events, had its rules and prohibitions. As mentioned above, it seems that all the holds used in wrestling were allowed, and all the blows used in boxing (though with bare hands), and that the only things forbidden were the use of the nails and teeth against the opponent. The pankration was thus the most dangerous and the toughest of all the events. Injury to the competitors was unavoidable, since they sought to win by all possible means, heedless of the danger to the body, and even to the life, of their opponents.

The sport had two forms: *kato pankration,* in which the contest continued after the opponents fell to the ground, and *ano,* or *orthostanden pankration,* in which the opponents had to remain standing. The blows delivered in the pankration were less painful than those in boxing, for, as we have seen, the pankratiasts did not wear thongs on their hands; in the pankration, however, the fighter could hold his opponent with one hand and hit him with the other, which was not allowed in boxing. The man who was the first to fall to the ground was in a difficult position, for his opponent was able to fall on top of him and immobilise him with his legs, leaving his hands free to strike him or apply a strangle-hold. The fighter who fell often turned on his back so as to try to use his arms and legs to protect himself, and indeed, when the competitors were slightly built they often deliberately fell on to their back. This device was called *hyptiasmos* (back fall), and was used by Melissos of Thebes to win the event at the Isthmian games. Pindar, who sings his praises, draws a wonderful comparison with a fox trying to ward off a swooping eagle: *The athlete who falls on his back stretches out his arms in front of him and draws up*

128. Pankratiasts in action. The contest, which is taking place on the ground, is kato pankration *(Florence, Galleria degli Uffizi).*

129

his feet, kicking powerfully, just like the fox who, when the hook-clawed wild eagle rushes on him, turns on his back to defend himself. The *apopnigmos,* or strangle-hold, was frequently applied as follows: the pankratiast jumped on his opponent's back and squeezed his body, applying the hold known today in freestyle wrestling as "the scissors." At the same time he put his arm around the opponent's neck, under his jaw, and with the help of the other hand, applied pressure. This hold was called *klimakizein* (the ladder-trick). A tall, long-limbed athlete would naturally use punches to assert himself, while a smaller, thick-set man would prefer wrestling holds. Kicking played an important part in the pankration. The kick to the stomach was called *gastrizein* (the stomach-trick). The hold by which a fighter held the foot of his opponent as tightly as he could to make him lose his balance was called *apopternizein* (the heel-trick).

The *kato pankration* was the form used in the games, while *orthostanden,* the lighter and safer form, was used in training or in preliminary contests. Though the pankration was a very hard, tough, and almost unhuman event, it aroused strong emotions in the spectators, which are understandable, when one reflects on the indomitable physical and psychologi-

130

129. Pankration. The competitors did not wear gloves, but it was permitted to hold one's opponent with one hand and hit him with the other (London, British Museum).

130. A forbidden hold in the pankration. One competitor is trying to gouge out his opponent's eye with his finger, which was strictly forbidden (London, British Museum).

131. Leg-holds were permitted in the pankration. The fighter on the left is lifting and pulling his opponent's leg in order to throw him (New York, Metropolitan Museum).

132. Pankration. The competitor on the left is knocking down his opponent with a direct punch (Paris, Louvre).

131

132

cal powers that were required in the men competing for victory. A vivid imagination is needed to visualise the titanic struggles at Olympia, Delphi, the Isthmus, Nemea, and throughout the rest of Greece. Plutarch narrates a typical incident involving Alkibiades, from which the tough nature of the Spartan pankration emerges. He was once competing in the *gymnasion* at Athens, and bit his opponent. The latter was furious, and shouted contemptuously "You are biting, Alkibiades, just like a woman!" The clever, sharp-witted Athenian, who had trained at Sparta where biting was allowed, flung back at him "No! Just like a lion!"

Qualities Needed by the Pankratiast

All that has been said of the boxer and the wrestler holds good for the pankratiast. According to Philostratos, the perfect pankratiasts were those whose physical build was such that one might describe men suited for the event as being the best wrestlers amongst the boxers and the best boxers amongst the wrestlers. Psychological qualities, like courage and endurance, played an equally important role, however. Pindar, in his *4th Isthmian Ode*, praises Melissos of Thebes: *His courage in the contest is like that of the wild lions, and his cunning and craft like that of the fox; he does not have the great build of Orion, and he does not take the eye, to look at, but in the contest he has unbeatable power; he is a man, small of build, but with an indomitable spirit.*

Famous Pankratiasts

Lygdamis of Syracuse was a pankratiast of renown. He became the first man to wear the crown of victory in the pankration, when the event was first held, in the 33rd Olympiad (648 B.C.), and owed his fame to his great physique.

Other famous pankratiasts were Dorieus, the son of Diagoras, and his nephew Eukleus, son of Pherenike. Sostratos of Sikyon, the *akrochersites* (wrestler who broke his opponent's fingers), was no less famous. He would squeeze and bend his opponents' fingers, and would not let them go until they were compelled to yield. He won a total of twelve victories in the Nemean and Isthmian games, two in the Pythian, and three at Olympia.

Many men achieved fame by winning victories in two, and sometimes three of the heavy events in the same Olympiad. Kleitomachos of Thebes won three crowns in the Isthmian games, for wrestling, boxing and the pankration. The same athlete, and Theagenes, were the only two ever to win the boxing and pankration at Olympia. A more difficult feat was to win the wrestling and the pankration in the same Olympiad. Apart from the demigod Herakles, who was counted the first to do this, it was achieved by seven famous athletes: Kapros of Elis, Aristomenes of Rhodes, Protophanes of Magnesia, Straton of Alexandria, Marion of Alexandria, Aristeus of Maiandria, and Nikostratos of Cilicia. Finally, the famous Arrichion of Phigaleia became immortal in the history of the games. In his despairing attempts to loosen a terrible hold which was almost strangling him, he seized the foot of his opponent, and with the last drop of strength remaining, he crushed it and dislocated the ankle. His opponent, unable to bear the pain, raised his hand in the signal for a withdrawal, while Arrichion expired at the same moment. He won the victory, not because he died, but because his opponent gave up.

133. The dramatic moment when a pankratiast gives up the fight. The defeated competitor raises his finger in admission of defeat (Boston, Museum of Fine Arts).

133

Equestrian Events

Tradition

The patron deity of equestrian competitions was Poseidon, who was for this reason called *Hippios*. It was Poseidon who sired the famous horse Areion, with which Herakles defeated Kyknos, the son of Ares, in a horse race at Troizen.

According to tradition, the earliest chariot race was that between Pelops and Oinomaos, the king of Pisa. Homer includes the chariot race amongst the games organised by Achilles in honour of Patroklos, the competitors being Antilochos, Eumelos, Menelaos, Meriones and Diomedes. Finally, Herakles, with his companion Iolaos as his charioteer, was victor at Olympia, when he first instituted the Games.

The Hippodrome

Down to the Classical period the hippodrome was a wide, level, open space with two pillars at the ends, one marking the start and the finish, and the other the turning-post. The distance from one pillar to the other appears to have differed from place to place, in accord with the configuration of the terrain. No hippodromes have survived, and we are therefore limited by the information concerning that of Olympia, given by Pausanias. The hippodrome at Corinth and in other parts of Greece were similar to it.

The course itself was divided along its axis by a partition of stone or wood, called the *embolon*, round which the horses and chariots ran, covering a distance of four stades on each complete circuit. The most impressive feature of the hippodrome at Olympia was the *hippaphesis* — that is, the starting-gate for the chariot and horse races. The chariots and the horses did not stand in a straight line, but one to the side of and behind the other, so that the *hippaphesis* formed the shape of a triangle resembling the prow of a ship with its peak pointed in the direction that the horses would run. There was a bronze dolphin attached to a high rod, almost at the end of the peak. Along each of the long sides of the triangle, which were over 400 feet long, stalls were constructed, open above and to the front, into which the chariots or the horses were led, after lots had been drawn. Before the event started, a rope, called the *hysplex* was stretched in front of each stall to fence it in. For each Olympiad an altar of unbaked bricks, plastered on the outside, was constructed roughly in the middle of the prow. The starting mechanism was placed inside the altar, and a bronze eagle with its wings completely extended stood upon it. When the trumpet sounded for the start of the contest, the starter set in motion the mechanism inside the altar and the eagle rose up so that the spectators could see it, while at the same moment the dolphin fell to the ground. Simultaneously, the ropes fencing in the horses of the two last chariots, one at each end of the base of the triangle, fell and the horses set off. As soon as they drew level with the horses of the chariots immediately in front of them, the ropes of these latter fell and they set off, too. This was repeated until the ropes had fallen for the last two chariots, which were in front at the apex of the triangle. At this point all the chariots were in motion, and they were all in a line. It was now up to each charioteer to demonstrate his skill, and his horses to exhibit their power. Everybody would try to be first

134. The bronze Jockey of Artemision. The young rider is riding bareback (Athens, National Archaeological Museum).

134

135

136

to the turning-post, get round it quickly and take the inner side of the race-course, which was the shortest.

This starting method was devised by Kleoitas, who was so proud of it that he made reference to it in the epigram on a statue made by him in Athens: *Kleoitas, son of Aristokles, made me — he who first invented the starting-gate for the horses at Olympia.* Aristeides is said subsequently to have introduced some innovation into the starting mechanism.

Chariot Races

These events which, as we have seen, had their roots in the warlike life of the Achaians, preserved their aristocratic nature in the historical period. The race-course became an area for demonstrating one's wealth and political power, and some of the most distinguished men in Greek history competed in the most spectacular event, the race of four-horse chariots.

The chariot races held in the Olympic Games were, in chronological order of their introduction: the *tethrippon* (four-horse chariot) (680 B.C. onwards); the *apene,* a chariot pulled by two mules (500 B.C. onwards); the *synoris,* a chariot pulled by a pair of horses (408 B.C. onwards); the *tethrippon* for foals (384 B.C. onwards); and the *synoris* for foals (268 B.C. onwards).

135. Chariot racing: the tethrippon *(four-horse chariot). The charioteer, wearing a white* chiton, *is standing in the light two-wheel chariot and driving carefully as the tethrippon nears the turn (London, British Museum).*

136. Front view of the tethrippon. *The two inside horses were called* zygioi *(yoked), and the two outer horses* seiraphoroi *(trace-horses) (Munich, Antikensammlungen).*

The *apene* made its appearance in the 70th Olympiad (500 B.C.), but it does not seem to have aroused much interest amongst the spectators, perhaps because the stubbornness of the mules hindered the smooth running of the race, or perhaps because these animals were not highly thought of. It was therefore dropped in the 84th Olympiad (444 B.C.).

The chariot was a small wooden vehicle, wide enough to hold two standing men and open at the back; it rested on an axle, to the ends of which were fastened two strong wooden wheels. In the four-horse chariot, the horses were yoked together in a single line. The two in the middle were called *zygioi* (yoke-horses), and the two on the outside *seiraphoroi* (trace-horses). The strongest and liveliest horse was normally yoked on the right-hand side, and called *dexioseiron* (right-hand trace-horse). This position was given to the strongest, fastest animal, so that in would be easy to make the turns. The horses were branded with a hot iron on the hoofs or thighs, either with the archaic letter *koppa,* in which case they were called *koppaties,* or with the letter *sigma,* when they were called *samphores* ("bearing *san*", an archaic name for *sigma).* The horses were also given other names, deriving from individual features, such as Boukephalas (ox-head), Alexander the Great's war-horse, which was named after the shape of its head. The war-chariot carried two men, the charioteer and the warrior, who was called *paraibates* or *kataibates* because he might dismount and remount during the course of the battle; but both the four-horse and the two-horse chariots used in the races only carried the charioteer. In Homeric times the chariot was driven by the owner himself, but in the contests of the historical period, the charioteer was a specialist in the technique of chariot racing, who undertook to drive the chariot, or ride, on behalf of the owner of the horses. The victory and the glory went to the owner, who received the crown, while the only prize awarded to the charioteer, or rider, was a woollen band, which the owner tied round his forehead; the winning horses were also crowned in this fashion. Thus children, women, and even cities were occasionally declared Olympic victors. Kyniska, the daughter of the Spartan king Archidamos and sister of Agesilaos II, won the four-horse chariot, and according to Pausanias, her ambition to win an Olympic victory led her to become the first woman to raise horses. Belestiche of Macedonia was a victor in the 128th Olympiad (268 B.C.), and a number of other women, particularly from Sparta, also won victories. The children of Pheidolas were victors, as was Aesop, son of Timon. In the 75th Olympiad (480 B.C.), Argos was declared winner in the horse race *(keles)*. Argos also won the four-horse chariot in the 77th Olympiad (472 B.C.), and Thebes won this event in the 90th (420 B.C.).

During the chariot races every charioteer was concerned, as we have seen, to take the inside of the hippodrome so as to cover the shortest distance. In order to do this, he had to be able to run close to the inside of the track and round the turning-post, without his speed causing him to overshoot towards the outside of the track. All the charioteers strove to achieve this, and this is why accidents, collisions and upsets in the order of the chariots always occurred at this dangerous turn. However, this was also the point that revealed the skill and technique of the good charioteer, as well as the strength and speed of the horses. Much can be learned about the technique that the good charioteer needed to master, from the advice given by the wise old Nestor to his son Antilochos before the start of the chariot race in the games for Patroklos outside Troy, and from the passage in Sophokles' *Elektra,* where the messenger is describing the supposed death of Orestes. A good charioteer had to drive the chariot without swerving, which was not easy, given that there were four horses of varying strength. The charioteer who knew how to use the whip and hold the reins securely would not run the risk of colliding with another chariot, of falling out of the chariot as it passed the turning-post, or of veering wide of the post.

It was a great disaster if the charioteer dropped the whip, or if his axle became locked with that of another chariot. Sophokles, in the *Elektra,* relates graphically how, when two of the chariots collided, it was impossible for those close behind to swerve round them: *and then one fell upon the other, and one collided with the other, and the Krissa hippodrome was filled with wrecked chariots.*

The famous charioteer Antikeris of Cyrene demonstrated his skill to Plato by driving his chariot several times round the Academy in the furrow left by his wheels on the first circuit.

All of this demonstrates how great a role was played in the contest by the charioteer, and how difficult was his task. Good charioteers were accordingly much sought after, and they are frequently praised by Pindar. It is reported that Karrotos, the charioteer of Arkesilaos, king of Cyrene, competed with forty others, whose chariots collided during the course of the race, and finished with his own chariot totally unscathed, to win the victory. Other notable charioteers included Phintis, who drove for Agesias of Syracuse, the Athenian Nikomachos, for Xenokrates of Akragas, Chromios, for Hieron, the tyrant of Syracuse, and many others, who won not only great glory, but also great wealth.

137

137. Picture of the apene, *a chariot pulled by two mules (London, British Museum).*

138

Very little is known of the rules of the chariot races and the horse races. It is certain that the competitors had to keep their chariots or horses on a straight course and not swerve in front of the others, which was only allowed if they were well ahead, so that there was no danger of a collision. It is equally certain that the Eleans passed a law forbidding the *Hellanodikai* to enter their own chariots or horses in the Games. This decision was taken after the *Hellanodikes* Troilos won the *synoris* for horses and the *tethrippon* for foals, in the 102nd and 103rd Olympiads (372 and 368 B.C.) and set up a statue of himself at Olympia. The distance covered by the chariots is not known, and it appears that it was not definitely fixed; most probably it differed according to the size of the race-course. The perimeter of the

138. Reconstruction of the hippodrome at Olympia. On the left can be seen the stoa of Agnaptos, and the hippaphesis, *or starting-gate. The complicated starting system, devised by Kleoitas, enabled all the chariots and horses to start at the same time (Reconstruction: K. Iliakis).*

race-course at Olympia was eight stades (1,538 m.), and it was one stade and four *plethra* (320 m.) broad. The *tethrippon* for horses completed twelve circuits of the race-course, as may be deduced from Pindar, who calls this race *dodekadromos* (of twelve courses), and the horses' race *dodekagnamptos* (of twelve bends), from the fact that they had to turn the post twelve times. The *synoris* for horses, and the *tethrippon* for foals ran eight circuits, and the *synoris* for foals three. Bearing in mind that the chariots ran along the inside of the course, we should subtract at least 4 kilometres from the total perimeter, and conclude that the *tethrippon* for horses covered approximately 14,000 m., the *tethrippon* for foals and the *synoris* for horses 9,000 m., and the *synoris* for foals 3,500 m.

Horse Races

The following horse races were held at Olympia: the *keles,* a race for fully grown horses with a rider, in which they covered six circuits of the race-course (648 B.C. onwards); the *kalpe* (trot), or race for mares (496 B.C. onwards); and a race for foals (256 B.C. onwards). The *kalpe* was a curious event, and it is not known how many circuits of the race-course it involved; all that we do know about it, is that on the last lap the rider dismounted and, still holding the reins, ran alongside the mare to the finish. This event was first included at Olympia in the 71st Olympiad (496 B.C.), and was dropped in the 84th (444 B.C.), along with the *apene.*

39
40

We do not even know with any certainty whether the rider rode bareback or used a saddle-cloth. Xenophon, in his *Peri Hippikes* gives instructions about the way the rider should sit on the bare back of the horse or on the saddle-cloth. One possibility is that the saddle-cloth was used only by warriors and that in the races the rider rode bareback, without cloth, saddle or stirrups, as he is shown in the surviving representations of horse races. The Greeks were very fond of horses and knew a great deal about how to look after and breed them.

As we have noted, they gave the horses names, many of which have survived. In addition to the famous winged horses, Areion, the son of Poseidon, and Parthenia and Eripha, the mares of Marmax, the suitor of Hippodameia who was murdered by Oinomaos, we know the names of the horses of Kleosthenes of Epidamnos, who was victorious in the 66th Olympiad (516 B.C.). They were called Phoinix, Korax, Knakias, and Samos, and formed part of the bronze statue of the victor's chariot at Olympia. At Athens there was a special tomb for the horses of Kimon, son of Stesichoros, because they had won three times in succession at Olympia. The horses of Euagoras of Sparta were also famous for having gained three successive Olympic victories. Aura, the mare of Pheidolas of Corinth was equally renowned. During the race at Olympia she threw her rider, but did not stop and, when she heard the trumpet sound for the last lap, she accelerated powerfully and won.

The importance of a victory in the chariot or horse races, and the glory won by the owners, charioteers and riders, was no less than that attaching to the athletic games. Many people reared horses and retained charioteers in order to win the crown of victory at Olympia — men like the tyrants Gelon and Hieron of Syracuse, Arkesilaos of Cyrene, Periandros of Corinth, Aratos, the leader of the Achaian League, Ptolemy, son of Lagos, Demaratos, king of Sparta, and so on. The Alkmaionid family had a long tradition of horse-rearing and won one victory at Olympia, five in the Isthmian games and two in the Pythian; and Alkibiades entered seven chariots in the Olympic Games and took first, second and fourth place.

139. Horse racing. The riders are naked as they gallop furiously along on their horses (London, British Museum).

140. A herald announcing the victory in a horse race. He is followed by the victor, on horseback, and, behind him, a young man with the tripod that was the prize for the event (London, British Museum).

Other Sports and Games

Local Sports

It was a natural consequence of the splendour and influence enjoyed in the ancient world by Olympia and the games held there, that the individual events, in the form they developed with the passage of time, should also spread throughout the Greek world and constitute a major part of the programme in the various local games.

Certainly from the 4th century B.C., the by now standard Olympic events were customarily held in all the cities and sanctuaries that traditionally celebrated festivals including athletic and equestrian competitions. The kinds of sport that found their way into the festival programmes differed from place to place, as did the relative importance attached to them, because the precise nature of these "provincial" games was ultimately decided by different local religious, political and social factors; running and the pentathlon, however, were never left out of any of them. The individual nature of these local games found its expression in variations of the established Olympic events and in other sports that were unknown at Olympia.

Archery

Achilles included an archery contest amongst the games in honour of the dead Patroklos, and the best of the Achaian archers competed with a moving target, a dove, as in hunting (see "Athletics in the Geometric Period"). This event did not survive into historical times, however, but died out along with the other aristocratic traditions of the heroic Homeric society. The bow, moreover, was not greatly valued by the Greeks as a weapon of war. The military units of archers, along with the other light-armed troops, might on occasion be effective in action, but they always remained auxiliary forces, consisting of professional mercenaries, usually from Crete or Skythia. It was only from the 4th century B.C. onwards that the bow gained in importance, as did all offensive long-range weapons. Archery then became part of the training programme for the *epheboi*. Games were also organised in this connection on Kea, in Sestos, and at the Pamboiotian festival at Koroneia, which were more of a military display in character. The bow was always useful in hunting, of course, and as an exercise, archery had beneficial effects on the physical development, especially of the young. Plato recommends that children of both sexes should practise archery, with both hands, from the age of six. He also proposed that competitions should be organised between mounted archers (the specialised military bodies had names meaning "horse archers"), but it is not known whether they ever actually took place in Athens or elsewhere.

Armed Combat

Hoplomachia (armed combat) was the name used by the ancients to describe a duel between two opponents wearing heavy armour — that is, a shield, breastplate, helmet, greaves, spear and sword. Normally, the spear was used along with a small round shield, in which case the duel was described as "with small shield and spear", and sometimes the sword was used with a large rectangular shield *(thyreos),* when it was a duel "with large shield and sword". The two types of contest were known respectively as *hoplomachia* and *thyreomachia*. They were held in the Hellenistic period, when a number

141. Coin from Thebes showing Herakles fitting the string of the bow to the shaft. Archery did not establish itself as a sport in the great Panhellenic games in ancient Greece (London, British Museum).

141

142. Scene of armed combat, a duel between opponents in heavy armour — shield, breastplate, helmet, greaves, and spear. The armed combat was basically a demonstration of skill in the use of hand to hand weapons, flexibility, and physical endurance (Madrid, Museo Arqueologico Nacional).

142

of cities, Athens amongst them, instituted prizes for armed combat between men, youths and even boys. The precise nature of the rules for these armed duels is not known. The competition seems essentially to have been a demonstration of skill in the use of hand-to-hand weapons, flexibility and physical endurance, if one bears in mind the weight of the defensive armour worn by the competitors. The event itself was a formal imitation of the methods of genuine warfare. These duels were simply mock fights, and bore no relation to the bloody armed combats of the Roman amphitheatre, even though on purely external evidence they could be regarded as their forerunners, and even though on occasion unfortunate accidents will have occurred.

Bearing all this in mind, we may conclude that armed combat as an event must, like archery, have been connected with the changes in military tactics and the nature of the upbringing of the young that occurred after the beginning of the 4th century B.C. Professional teachers of armed combat at this period held a prominent position in the *gymnasia,* and began to be highly paid for teaching armed combat as an art.

In earlier times the citizens of the Greek states had looked down on this specialised practice in the technique of weaponry as useless, because, to their way of thinking, superiority in battle was secured by other qualities, and also because in practical terms, the mode of operation of the *phalanx* of hoplites left little room for individual confrontation. Naturally everyone who served as a hoplite always practised the use of the weapons; but this practice was never valued as a sport in itself, with the educational importance attached to athletic games. Men who had been reared on the competitive spirit of these athletic games, and had made a name for themselves in the *palaistra,* were best equipped to take part in armed combat and to distinguish themselves in war. Eurybates of Argos, who excelled in the war between Athens and Aigina *practising single-combat* is known also to have been a famous pentathlete. Nor did armed combat as an event ever find a place in public festivals for the same reason, with the possible exception of a few special cases, such as funeral games.

In this case, the duel between armed warriors assumed the character of a celebratory — almost ritual — reconstruction of a real scene of hand-to-hand fighting, in honour either of a single distinguished dead warrior, or of those who had died in a war. As such, the event goes back to periods when individual confrontations and single-combat between warriors — usually between the leaders of the sides engaged — was the normal pattern of military tactics on the field of battle. Games like these were known in the Geometric period, both in the exceptional circumstance of the burial of a distinguished warrior, and within the context of hero-worship, in places where the traditions surrounding the death of a local hero were conducive to the establishment of games at regular intervals. In the minds of the people who organised them, these games were initially simply a commemorative repetition of the first funeral rites in honour of the hero. Plutarch asserts that armed combat was practised at an early date at Olympia *(in Pisa),* and his claim is indirectly confirmed by what we know of the worship of Pelops at Olympia, and the nature of the Olympic Games during the early stages of their history.

Equestrian Events

There was a widespread series of variations of the

standard Olympic equestrian competitions, which may be classified as a combination of horse racing and human racing plus general horsemanship. This last was made much more testing by the addition of an acrobatic exercise, which was the main feature of the event: the competitor dismounted from the horse (or chariot) while it was galloping, ran alongside it without losing speed, and remounted again before the race ended.

A similar horse racing event, the *kalpe* (trotting-race) made its appearance, as we have seen, amongst the equestrian events at Olympia, but only for the short period between 496 and 444 B.C. From that date, variations of the *kalpe,* having the general name "mounting competitions," survived in a number of cities in the Greek world, and were very popular, especially in horse-raising areas, such as Thessaly, Cyrene, Southern Italy and Sicily. In these contests, however, horses were used instead of mares, and unlike the *kalpe,* in which the competitors simply had to dismount once and finish the race running alongside the horse, the riders were obliged to remount again to continue the race. It is possible, indeed, that they had to dismount and remount several times, without letting go of the reins or losing speed.

The critical and dangerous point of the event was, of course, the moment at which the competitor jumped to the ground. The rider turned, swung one leg over the horse's neck, and sat facing towards the side. Then he allowed himself to slide down, either with both legs together, or with one bent (the one towards the horse's head) and the other stretched ready to hit the ground. He held the reins with one hand and steadied himself firmly on the back of the animal with the other, to make it easier to throw himself forwards and upwards when he jumped. There were no stirrups in horse-riding, and the riders therefore practised mounting and dismounting from either side.

In another variation of the sport, the rider was armed. Sometimes naked and sometimes wearing a short mantle and a conical helmet, he held a round shield and a javelin in his left hand during the competition. This equipment was not that actually used by the cavalrymen of the period, nor was it the heavy weaponry carried by the runners in the race in armour; its purpose was to make the whole acrobatic manoeuvre even more difficult, and was at the same time a reminder of the military origins of the event. The shield in particular went back to the period before the Persian Wars, when the aristocratic class of horsemen went to the field of battle mounted, but wearing the heavy armour of the hoplites, and usually leading a second, reserve horse with its groom. They were obliged to dismount in order to fight, to run and remount if they had to flee or pursue the enemy, and they could even change horses without touching the ground. The extent of the admiration felt for performances like this in the aristocratic society of that period can be gauged from the excellent Homeric description of the rider who had harnessed four horses and rode *without stopping, but leaping from one to the other and frequently changing as they sped along.*

The dismounting event proper *(apobates),* however, involved the use of the chariot. The roots of this event, too, are to be found in the methods of warfare in the Geometric period. The nobles rode to the field of battle fully armed in their chariots, and had to dismount from them to fight, and to remount, often at a run while the horses were already moving, either to move from one point of the fray to another, or to pursue an opponent, or to take flight themselves. After the end of the 8th century, this use of the war chariot became a distant memory, and the practice of "dismounting" survived only in the chariot competitions at a number of festivals, mainly in Attica and Boiotia.

There were two people in the chariot: the man who had to jump down from the chariot, run and manage to get back into it again before the race was over; and the man who held the reins and had to drive the chariot in such a way as to assist the movements of the other. He would tighten the reins to check the speed of the horses at the point when the "dismounter" was getting ready to jump to the ground. The latter wore the same armour as the warriors in the chariots of old, or sometimes only a helmet and shield, and gripped the rail of the chariot firmly with his right hand. Bending his right leg and stretching his left out of the chariot, so that it was almost touching the ground, he flung the full weight of his body backwards, to counteract the forward impetus given to it by the movement of the chariot. In this way he was able to remain upright the moment he hit the ground, and avoided the risk of falling forward, as a result of the physical law of inertia. The greater the speed of the chariot, the more he had to lean his body backwards. There was the further problem of the weight of the shield, which pulled him into the oblique stance, strongly turned to the left, that we see in all representations of this moment. As the left foot touched the ground, he let go of the chariot rail with his right hand, and ran along immediately behind the chariot, without dropping behind. This meant that, on the one hand, he did not run the risk of being run down from the side by the chariots of his opponents (his own chariot would open a path for him), and on the other, he would be able to remount easily, because the chariot was open only at the rear. The act of remounting was easier, and is for this reason depicted only rarely in ancient art. All that was needed was a slight leap forward, because, since he was running, his body already had the forward impetus that would be needed in the chariot. It is possible that the wheels of the chariots used in these competitions had a special form, to make the dismounting and remounting easier. The ancient lexicographers speak of "descent wheels" *(apobatikoi trochoi),* and though it is not clear from representations of the event how these differed from normal wheels, it was almost certainly a question of the axle passing underneath the chariot.

The value that the ancient Greeks placed on this event emerges clearly from a passage of the *Erotikos,* a speech falsely attributed to Demosthenes, where it is described as the most respected and the best of the events.

The event owed its splendour in large part to the Panathenaia, where it occupied a prominent position as a national event. According to the Athenian tradition, the equestrian events in the Panathenaia were the first to be held in Greece, and it was Erichthonios himself who had established the dismounting competition, driving a chariot with a warrior standing by him. The Parthenon frieze has a number of scenes of armed youths jumping either into or down from chariots.

Team Events

There was one category of competitions, namely the team events, that were only held in local games. The most widespread of these was the torch-race.

This event was known as *lampadedromia* and by various other names, all of them deriving from the word *lampas* (torch). Throughout its whole history, it remained first and foremost a religious ceremony, its ritual aspect taking precedence over its competitive character. The event had to serve a purpose — the carrying of the sacred fire from one point to another without extinguishing it. The fact that it had to be transported swiftly to preserve its purity and power resulted in competition for swiftness, and a purely ritual act developed into a sporting event. The purpose always remained of prime importance, however, and it was this that distinguished the torch-race from purely athletic exercises such as the foot-races. It was for this reason that the event was not included in the Panhellenic games, and even in the areas where it was practised, it always remained outside the stadium and distinctly separated off from the purely athletic events; at Samos it was included amongst the musical competitions, while at Thespiai it had the significant name "sacred" torch-race.

143

143. The main hallmark of the torch-race was the swift passing of the lit torch from one runner to the next. The torch-bearer holds the torch up as he nears the next runner, who stretches out his hand towards the torch so as not to break the impetus (Paris, Louvre).

The torch-race was one of the light events, and was practised by all age-groups, mainly youths and adults, but sometimes boys as well, as is known on Delos, for example, or in the festivals of the Theseia and Anthesteria at Athens. In the sanctuary of Brauronian Artemis in Attica, there was even a torch-race for young girls.

The end of the torch-race was always an altar, that of the patron deity of the city or the god in whose honour the festival was being held, and the winner had to light the fire for the sacrifice with his torch. This, the most important stage of the event, is the one usually depicted in ancient works. There was usually also an altar at the starting-point, like the altar of Prometheus in the Academy in Athens.

The city magistrate, under whose general direction, supervision and presidency the event took place, was the *archon basileus,* who was responsible for religious matters, aided in his task by other officials, the *hieropoioi* and *agonothetai*. The costs of equipping and training the runners was met by a

144

144. The torch-race was at once a religious ritual and a team race. The torch-bearers had to carry the holy fire from one point to another. The finish was the altar of the god in whose honour the race was being held. In the picture a member of the victorious team is wearing the diadem of spear-shaped leaves usually worn by the torch-bearers, and is holding the holy torch. On the right is a priest standing by an altar, and a winged Victory, who is leading a victor, may be seen on the left (London, British Museum).

special levy which initially the state demanded from the *gymnasiarchoi,* the officials who superintended the *gymnasion;* later, however, from the 3rd century B.C., the *gymnasiarchia* ceased to be voluntary and became a regular office of state, and the costs were met henceforth by the *lampadarchai* (superintendents of the torch-race).

When the torch-race was held as an official event, the competitors were *epheboi* from the different tribes of a city. Each tribe appointed a man to take charge of the event *(gymnasiarchos* or *lampadarches)* and he chose a team of youths from his own tribe, out of the *gymnasia* and wrestling schools, and then fed them, equipped them and subjected them to intensive training. The numbers in each team varied from one place to another; teams of 48, 40 and even 10 are mentioned. The distances to be covered also varied. In the Panathenaia, if the starting point was in the Academy and the finish on the Acropolis, the distance will have been over 2,500 m. — a genuine long- distance race, as it is described in the inscriptions. At Delphi, the distance from the *gymnasion* to the great altar in the temple of Apollo, which was run by torch-bearers of the Eumeneioi, was 1,500 m., and at Epidauros, it was about 800 m. from the altar of Asklepios to the altar of Apollo Maleatas.

The runners from each of the competing teams spread out along the whole length of the course and took up positions in a row at intervals, exactly as in the modern relay race. In the Panathenaia, where there were 40 runners from each tribe and the total distance was 2,500 m., each man would have to run about 60 m. If, as seems most probable, only five of the ten tribes competed each year, then five rows of runners will have been drawn up alongside each other, and they will have run in five parallel courses. The first five runners lit their torches, and the starting-gate was probably used as in the normal athletic races, the trumpeter having first sounded the signal. The chief hallmark of the competition, as in the modern relay-race, was the "relay" of runners and the quick hand-on of the lighted torch from one to the other. There is a series of very fine paintings on red-figure vases from the 5th century B.C. that give us graphic scenes of this "relay" of runners in the rows of competitors drawn up alongside each other: the torch-bearer appears to be running with the great speed praised in the texts of the ancient authors, towards the next man, holding on high the flaming torch of his team. As he draws near, the latter keeps his gaze firmly turned towards him and holds his hand out towards the torch, having already begun to run, so as to save time and not break the impetus of the first runner. Naturally enough, it was important that the torch should not fall at the handover and should not go out before the end of the race. Interest intensified as the last man from each team set off on the final leg of the race, making every effort to be first at the altar, where the *archon basileus* awaited the winner, and to light the fire from his own torch and win the victory for his tribe and his *gymnasiarchos.*

Later, from the Helenistic period onwards, it seems that another type of torch-race established itself, both in Athens and elsewhere, which did not involve the "relay" of runners. In this, the runners competed as individuals, and the winner was the first one to arrive at the altar with his torch still burning.

The runners in the torch-race were naked. On their head they carried a radiate crown, a device of religious significance and purpose which, like the torch itself, was unknown in athletic events. The crown consisted of a series of lance-shaped, or, more appropriately in this instance, flame-shaped pieces of bone or wood, sometimes all of the same length and sometimes of two different lengths alternately, set upright on a metallic or leather crown. The crown, or band, on which the name of the competing tribe was often written, was tied at the back, and had two small tongues at the temples to help it to fit better and prevent it from slipping during the race.

An important variation of the event, which was also very widespread, was the torch-race on horseback. The sport had its origins in Thrace from where it was introduced into Athens, or more accurately into Piraeus, along with the worship of Artemis Bendis, at the time of the Athenian alliances with the Thracian tribal leaders Sitalkes (429 B.C.) and Kotys (380 B.C.). The idea was a novel one, and the nocturnal horse race with lighted torches held a special fascination for the Athenians, as can be seen from Plato's *Republic*.

The chief hallmark of the mounted torch-race was also the "relay." The torch passed from rider to rider, with no interruption of the speed of the horses vying with each other — clearly a more difficult and more spectacular procedure than the torch-race on foot. The distances to be covered were in this case certainly greater, but the number of competitors in each team may have been smaller.

We need not spend much more time on the category of team events. For the activities that usually belonged to it were competitions only in the sense that they involved rivalry for a prize in some particular facility, and athletic only in the sense that they were based on physical movements, and therefore demanded the exercise of bodily powers that presupposed a physical education. For the rest, they were exercises that were not always, and not exclusively athletic. The *pyrrhiche,* for example, which came from the Dorian states to Athens during the 6th century and entered the programme of the Panathenaia as an event for which a prize was awarded, was a group dance with weapons, whose movements imitated the real movements of warfare in a co-ordinated rhythmic form. It was, as a consequence, inseparable from the music that accompanied it, and was a musical and gymnastic demonstration involving co-ordination and precision of movement. Another competition known at Athens was the *anthippasia,* a mock cavalry battle which required a special military training. The *anthippasia* was a depiction of mounted warfare, just as the *pyrrhiche* was to some extent a depiction of the armed combat. Two opposed groups of cavalry made a charge against each other and after they had crossed, wheeled to repeat the attack on a new front. They crossed again and again at an ever-increasing rate, until in the end they formed a single *phalanx*. The competition took place every year in the Athenian hippodrome purely as a military exercise. It was for political and strategic reasons, rather than any interest in the display as a contest, that the *anthippasia* was included in the Panathenaic games, as early as the middle of the 4th century B.C., though it did not form part of the equestrian events of the festival.

Exercises and Games

In addition to the athletic competitions familiar in the games, other sports took place in the *gymnasia* and the wrestling-schools, that might more accurately be described as exercises, as indeed they are called in the ancient texts. These were athletic exercises whose aim was either physical development, well-being and strength in general (educational training), or more specifically the training of athletes for particular events (athletic training). The variety of postures and movements depicted on vases is indicative of the wide range of these exercises. We also know the names of many of them from the written sources, though it is not always easy to reconstruct them in the imagination or recognise them with any certainty in ancient representations.

Two exercises suitable for training the arms were *cheironomia* and *skiamachia* (shadow-boxing and shadow-fighting). In these the athlete practised the movements of boxing, in the case of the first (see "Boxing") and of the armed combat in the case of the second, without an opponent. Related to the *skiamachia* as a gymnastic exercise was the *pyrrhiche,* which the boys were taught in the wrestling-school by the drill officer. The *pyrrhiche* is better known, however, in its rhythmic, orchestrated form. The exercise of *pitylizein* (regular swinging of the arms as with oars) falls into the same category; this involved imitating the movement of rowing with the arms, again without using the oars themselves. *Halterobolia,* or weight-training (see "Jumping") was an excellent exercise for developing the arm muscles, and the various bends and stretches executed with the weights in the hands also developed the muscles of the body.

The legs were exercised by *anatrochasmos,* or running backwards, and *peritrochasmos,* or running in a circle. This type of exercises also included *ekplethrizein,* or running a *plethron* (about 31 m.) forwards and backwards alternately, reducing the length on each occasion until it became zero. There were many jumping exercises, such as *aphalmos,* which consisted of scissor jumps.

The boxers and pankratiasts used the *koryx,* or punch-bag, in special training; this was a sack filled with sand and suspended so that it swung at shoulder height. On this they practised different combinations of punches *(korykomachia),* just as modern boxers do. Other exercises used in training for the heavy events were *akrocheiria,* where two opponents wrestled holding each other only by the hands, and *pyx atremizein,* a test of endurance which involved standing motionless with the arms stretched out either in front or above.

Another common way in which competitors in heavy events developed their physical strength was weight-lifting, or throwing the weight. The weights usually consisted of unworked stones. In one picture of this exercise, in a vase-painting, the massive, almost spherical stone that the athlete is raising from the ground with both hands, has a diameter four times as great as that of his head, while in another, in which a youth is lifting two unworked stones, one in each hand, either stone has a diameter almost one and a half times that of his head.

In passing, it should be noted that weight-lifting never became an official event in antiquity. It found favour as a popular spectacle, however, since it was a means of demonstrating physical strength that easily aroused men's inclination to compete, and that equally easily met with a response from the wide public at the popular festivals, thanks to the original techniques and devices used by the weight-lifters. From time to time isolated performances occurred in this sphere that gradually passed into legend as

145

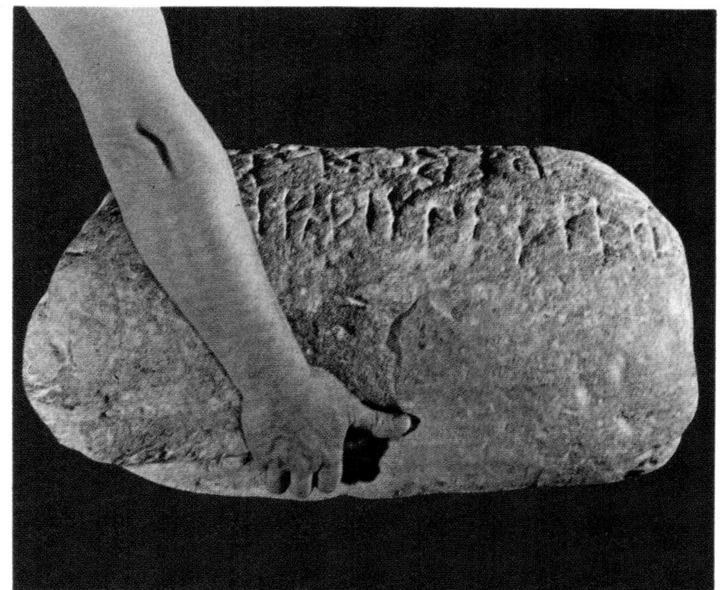

145. Weight-lifting was not included on the official programme at Olympia. It was mainly used as a training method by the competitors in the heavy events. However, a stone weighing 143.5 kg. was discovered at Olympia, where it was dedicated by the athlete Bybon, who boasts in the inscription on it that he had lifted it above his head with one hand (Olympia, Archaeological Museum).

146. Weight-lifting scene. A youth is lifting two unworked stones, one in each hand (Würzburg, Martin von Wagner Museum).

146

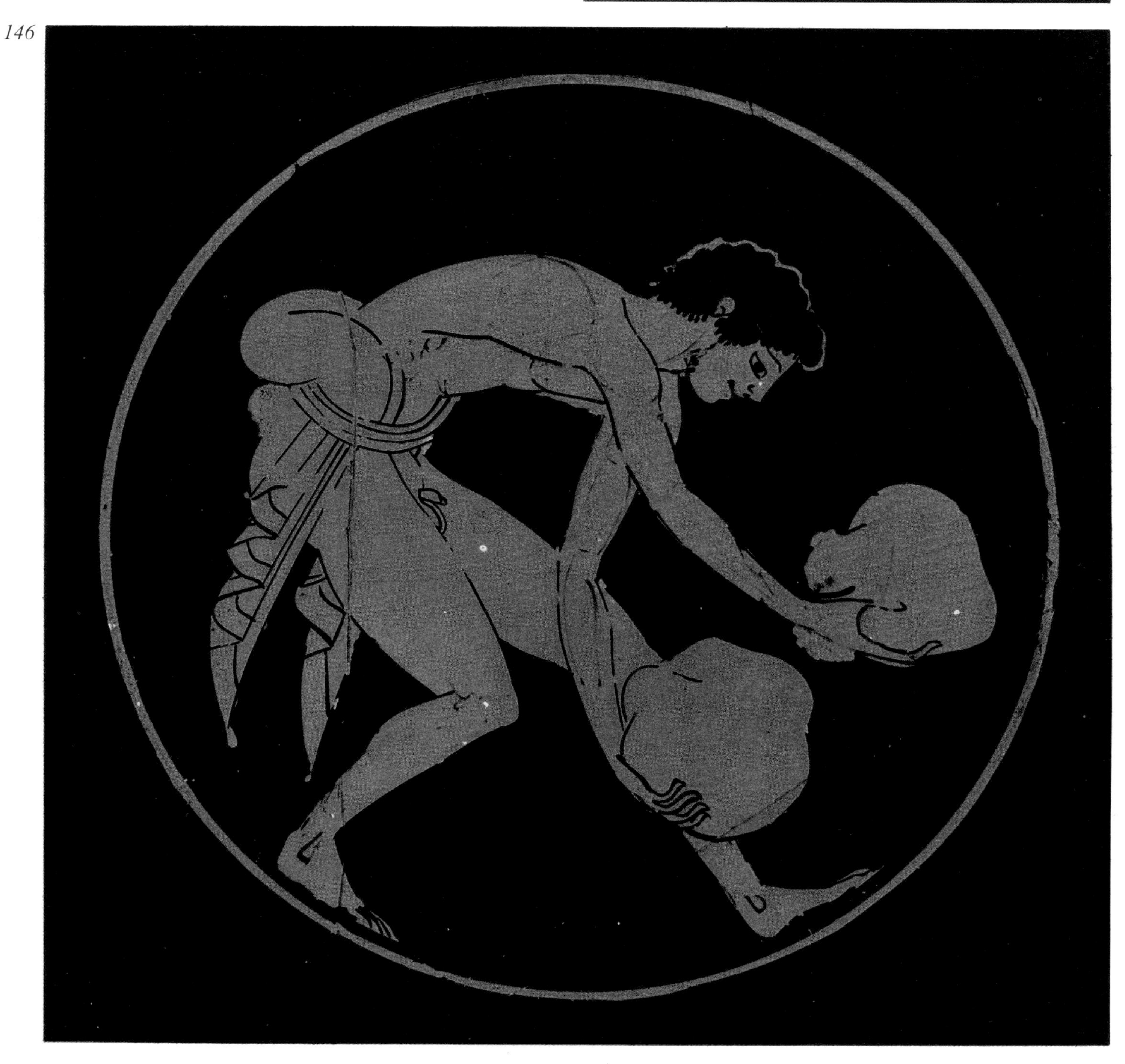

147. Ball games were particularly popular in the wrestling schools and the gymnasia. One of them, sphaira episkyros, *is depicted on a relief base discovered built into the Themistoklean wall. It is played by two teams, who try to throw the ball (here held by the first player on the left) over the heads of the players of the other team (Athens, National Archaeological Museum).*

148. Another ball game was keretizein, *a game similar to hockey. Two players hold sticks with hooked ends, and each tries to drag the ball, which is between them, towards himself (Athens, National Archaeol. Museum).*

147

148

superhuman achievements. Famous athletes had from an early date (7th and 6th centuries B.C.) cultivated their reputations in places where crowds gathered, mainly on the fringe of the great games at the Panhellenic sanctuaries, by displays of this kind, often challenging their rivals — if there were any — to an open contest. The famous Milon of Kroton, mentioned in another chapter, sent the crowds at Olympia wild with enthusiasm when he lifted a four-year-old heifer on his shoulders and carried it around inside the stadium. At an even earlier period (early 6th century), another athlete named Bybon had performed a similar feat of strength, also at Olympia: with one hand he lifted above his head, and threw, a massive cylindrical stone, which was discovered during the excavations and is now kept in the Museum at Olympia. It weighs 143.5 kilos, and has an inscription incised on it narrating the event. We can, of course, hardly conceive a feat like this to be humanly possible.

Jumping over obstacles was also one of the special exercises. One common form of this was the pole-vault (see "Jumping"), which could involve covering either distance or height. This exercise clearly had a practical application in the field of war, for crossing rivers, leaping over earthworks etc. The *epheboi* practised this either in the *gymnasia,* near the pit for the other jumps, or in the open, near natural obstacles. This exercise too, however, was one which never established itself as an event. In the pseudo-Panathenaic amphora of the "acrobat" from Rhodes, referred to in a previous chapter, the pole-vault is shown taking place at a public gathering and in an area that could be a stadium, along with other exercises of an acrobatic nature.

There were various kinds of games that made ex-

149. Relief scene of a youth demonstrating his skill with a ball (Athens, National Archaeological Museum).

149

150. In the ball game called ourania *the players threw the ball to each other without letting it fall to the ground. The loser became an "ass" and had to carry the winner, who was called "king," on his shoulders. A scene of "kings" and "asses": Three youths are sitting on the shoulders of three others, and stretching their hands excitedly towards the trainer, who is sitting opposite them (London, British Museum).*

150

cellent exercises, since they not only brought physical powers into play and developed qualities like courage, readiness, endurance, the desire to excel etc., but also provided amusement. They were therefore cultivated on a wide scale, particularly the ball-games *(sphairiseis),* and were played not only by boys and youths in the *gymnasia* and the wrestling-schools, but also by women in the *gynaikonites.*

The type of these games varied according to the age and sex of the players. A great number of names of ball-games is known from the literary sources, and there is an equally large number of representations of ball-players in works of art, mainly on vases; but there are very few of them that can be described with any accuracy, or whose rules are known at all. The ball itself was usually small, about the size of an apple, and made of material or leather, with a large number of "leaves" sewn together, and coloured or decorated with a variety of designs. It was stuffed with horse-hair, sheep's wool or down, and was firm and hard so that it would bounce, which was an essential, especially in the game called *aporrhaxis.* They threw the ball hard at the ground, caught it again when it bounced, and then threw it again, and so on. The bounces were counted and the winner was the player with the most. This game could also be played against a wall.

In the game called *ourania,* one of the players threw the ball as high as he could, and the others tried to catch it as it fell. This was the game played by the Phaiakians Laodamas and Halios in honour of Odysseus. Sometimes they threw the ball from one to the other without allowing it to fall to the ground. The one who lost became an "ass" and had to carry on his shoulders the winner, who was called "king."

A vivid scene with "kings" and "asses" is preserved on a black-figure *lekythos* from the end of the 6th century. It takes place in one of the courts of the *gymnasia* that were reserved for the purpose, and were called *sphairisteria,* or ball-games areas. Three lads are sitting horseback on the shoulders of three others and stretching out their hands eagerly to the *paidotribes* standing opposite them. With impatient cries of "give the order," they are urging him to throw the ball, which he is holding in his hand, to one of the three. Each in turn will try to catch it in the air and throw it back. If he drops it, the pair will change places and he will become the "ass" and the other "king." It is precisely the same game as one played by children in Greek villages a few years ago, which was called "ball on horseback."

The most commonly found team ball-game for youths was the *sphaira episkyros* (ball on the line), which was played by two teams having the same number of players. Using a stone *(skyros)* they scratched a line on the ground to separate the two opposing teams; the line was called *skyros* (after the stone), and they put the ball on it (hence the name of the game). A line was also drawn behind each team, thus limiting the playing area. The side who took the ball first, threw it above the players of the opposing team, who tried to catch it in the air and throw it back, and so on. Each team attempted to send the ball as far as possible, in order to compel the other side to retreat towards their boundary line. If the ball crossed the boundary line and went out, they lost.

This description derives from the 2nd century A.D. lexicographer Julius Pollux, and is supplemented by a relief representation of about 510 B.C. on the side of one of the three *kouros* bases found in 1922 built into the Themistoklean wall in the Kerameikos. The two opposing teams of three are facing each other. The first player on the left is getting ready to throw the ball hard in the direction of the opponents. The second player in his team is watching him attentively and, as he runs towards the centre, is urging him to throw it as far as possible. The third player is running towards the central dividing line where he will wait, as the first man in his team, in order to catch the ball when the opponents throw it back in their direction; he is also taking up a position opposite the corresponding player from the other side, who is the fourth figure from the left. This last is rushing towards the same spot from the opposite direction, and has even crossed the dividing line and is standing in the territory of the first team. There, however, he is being compelled by the third player, who is moving threateningly towards him, to stop and retreat to his proper position. The action of this player is, of course, illegal, but it is nonetheless deliberate, for the purpose of the game was to drive the opposition beyond their boundary line, and this was achieved most easily with a throw from a forward position, so that the nearer the player was to the central line the more dangerous were his throws to the opposition. The movement of the fifth man in clear: he is waiting to return the ball, while the sixth, the back member of his team, is quietly confident that the fifth man will in fact return it, because this time the ball will be coming from a great distance.

A more lively team ball-game was that known by the rather obscure name *phaininda* (or *pheninda*). This was played by two teams, and the team in possession of the ball threw it to each other, while their opponents tried to take it from them. To avoid this, they had to deceive the opposition, and the man who held the ball would pretend that he was going to send it to one player, but in the end throw it to another. If the ball fell to the ground, the player lost points. Everyone therefore had to be alert and ready to run in any direction to catch the ball, and also to make his opponent lose it by deceiving him.

The game *harpaston* (handball) was the same as *pheninda* according to some ancient authors, but others disagree. What is certain is that the aim of the player was to "snatch" (whence the name) the small ball in flight, amongst a crowd of opponents, by means of violent pushing, running and feinting. It was one of the violent, occasionally even dangerous, games recalling modern rugby which were known by the general name *sphairomachiai* (ball-fights).

The second of the three bases from the Themistoklean wall, referred to above, is decorated on the front side with a scene of the type of ball-game known by the ancient Greeks as *keretizein*. Here each of the ball-players has a short stick ending in a curved hook, that enables him to take possession of the small ball used in the game. The game was a form of hockey played in pairs. In the scene just mentioned the two players are depicted at the moment they are stooping, facing each other, and trying to drag the ball, which is on the ground between them, towards their own area, with the hooked end of the rod. The left hand is held parallel to the right, perhaps ready to help the movement. Their colleagues, who frame the two players, are watching with interest, making comments and encouraging them, as they wait their turn.

The Athenians were ardent admirers of ball-games, and distinguished men from time to time had their names connected with them. Sophokles was warmly applauded for his dexterity on an occasion when he himself was playing the part of Nausicaa in a tragedy, in the scene where she plays ball with her companions; and Isokrates was portrayed playing "hockey" in the bronze statue set up on the Acropolis, in the *sphairisterion* of the *Arrephoroi*, next to the Erechtheion. The Spartans too, however, who were the "inventors" of the ball-games according to one tradition, gave special attention to this type of exercise in their own particular form of physical education. The senior class of *epheboi* (19-20 years old) were called *sphaireis*, after these games, and it seems that the rules of their *sphairomachiai* were particularly severe.

Swimming and Rowing

Given the geographical position of Greece and the physical configuration of its terrain, it must be self-evident that swimming and rowing were basic features of daily life in ancient Greece.

The Greeks looked on swimming essentially as a physical activity with a practical use, both in times of peace and in war, and not only for the crews of trading or military vessels. It is known that fishing for oysters or sponges formed an important means of earning a living on many of the islands and coasts of the Aegean, and this led many of the inhabitants of these areas to become divers. It is also known that in a number of specific instances, naval hostilities demanded the use of under-water swimmers. The achievements of the under-water swimmers in the sieges of Sphakteria and Syracuse, during the Peloponnesian War, and the ventures against the Persian fleet on the eve of the battle of Artemision were in no way inferior to the activities of modern frog-men.

Most of the Greeks knew how to swim; this emerges from the comments of Herodotos on the small number of Greeks lost during the naval battle of Salamis, in comparison with the Persian losses. The Athenians, in particular, who were taught letters and swimming from an early age, considered a man who could do neither as uneducated. The need to learn and master swimming did not, of course, derive solely or primarily from its practical usefulness. The healthy feeling that goes along with this kind of physical exercise, and the range of beneficial effects it has on a man's constitution, were even more powerful reasons which made swimming part of the daily life of the Greeks. It was valued as a physical exercise and was adopted enthusiastically by both sexes as a recreational activity.

In Greece the most convenient place for swimming was, of course, the sea-shore. The rivers were not suitable for this purpose, generally speaking — though the Spartans are known to have swum in the Eurotas — and swimming-pools were not widely used; they were confined to the open pools used by the athletes in the wrestling-schools, and these were generally small and rather unsuitable for swimming. The pool, or bath, discovered in one part of the *palaistra* at Olympia measured 4.19 m. × 3.02 m., and was a mere 1.38 m. deep. One exception is the swimming-pool, also discovered at Olympia, west of the *palaistra,* near the banks of the river Kladeos. This was an open-air construction measuring 24 m. × 16 m. and 1.60 m. deep — the only genuine swimming-pool known in Classical Greece. Other kinds of constructions, such as artificial platforms for diving in places where the coast was not rocky enough for the purpose, were even rarer. The only example known is the artificial diving platform, over 2.60 m. high, with a projecting board, depicted in a wonderful fresco from a 5th century B.C. tomb at the Greek colony of Poseidōnia (Paestum) in Southern Italy. It was built of rows of cubical stones and the supports must have had the shape of a "T" or a cross. Amongst the features that produced this shape, there must have been means of climbing up it, possibly a vertical ladder to reach the fixed diving board, which was also made of stone.

The style of swimming and diving was free and natural, and swimming was generally what is called "freestyle" today. The arms moved alternately, describing the motion of oars (the common expressions in ancient Greek mean "to row the hands"); the body and head followed this movement, turning from side to side, and the feet trailed behind, striking the water with small movements or, in rare cases (like the swimmer on the François *krater),* kept together and motionless. The men and women swimmers depicted in ancient works of art usually hold their heads up out of the water, in a way that is unorthodox and against the modern rules for freestyle swimming.

There does not appear to have been a special technique for diving and swimming, nor any established rules or standards. These could only have developed as a result of a long period of systematic training for athletic competition; but neither swimming nor diving were ever practised as sports by the Greeks. According to modern athletic standards, the diver in the fresco of the tomb at Paestum should, at the point he is depicted, have his body in one straight line, from fingers to toes, and however impressive his dive may be, it cannot fail to appear amateurish.

The only role certainly played by swimming in the field of sport was as a training technique by which the athletes could keep in good physical condition; this was why there was a "swimming-pool" near the *palaistra* at Olympia, and this was why Tisandros, the famous boxer from Naxos in Sicily (6th century B.C.), used to swim around the headlands of the island. Even this was as free exercise rather than as part of a training programme.

The lack of interest displayed by the Greeks in swimming as a sport, which is perhaps somewhat surprising today, must be considered in conjunction with the fact that regular public swimming contests were never organised in the ancient Greek world.

By contrast, boat races existed in the Greek world long before the Roman period. Aetiological legends at a later date ascribed the origins of this event to the heroic age, and speak of a contest at the Isthmian games, won by the Argonauts in the Argo. The earliest certain testimony for them however, is from the 5th century B.C.

The texts refer to contests between ships or boats

151. Swimming was highly valued in ancient Greece as a physical exercise and as a means of recreation, in addition to its practical uses. The swimmer in the picture is moving her arms, and at the same time turning her head and body, while her feet make small rhythmic movements in the water (Paris, Louvre).

151

or triremes on the programme of regularly established games, such as the Panathenaia, the Diisoteria and the Mounichia in Piraeus, the Aianteia on Salamis, the Aktia at Nikopolis, etc.; and also on special occasions, like the funeral games held in 374 B.C. in honour of Euagoras of Salamis in Cyprus, or the various military naval exercises, which were held as competitions in order to keep up the interest of the crews. Contests like these were organised for the Athenian fleet by Iphikrates, during the course of his campaigns along the Peloponnesian coast in 372 B.C., and by Alexander the Great on a river near Babylon, shortly before his death.

The boats used for these occasions, until the beginning of the 1st century B.C., were the triremes used in war. From this period on, however, the contest began to develop in the direction of the modern boat race, and vessels built especially for the purpose made their appearance, with only one row of oarsmen, and also with a limited number of them, fluctuating between three and eight men.

The event was probably held in a manner similar to the exercises of Iphikrates, which are described by Xenophon. The ships put out to sea, drew up in a line with their prows facing the shore, and moved at full speed towards the land, which was the finishing point. This was the simple form of the competition. There was possibly another form, however, in which the course did not simply run in one direction but, in imitation of the chariot races, set off from the shore, had some landmark in the open sea, such as a small islet, as a turning point around which the boats had to row, and finished at the same point on the coast from which it had started. This is the type of race described by Virgil in the *Aeneid* and it certainly derives from Greek models. In other contests, speed could be combined with manoeuvrability, and the event took the form of a mock sea-battle. This must be what is meant by the "competitions for triremes" and the "contests between oarsmen and helmsmen" held by Alexander's fleet at Babylon, and the sea-battles at the Mounichia, and the Aktia in Roman times.

The competition was a team event, of course, in which muscular strength, co-ordination between the movements of the oarsmen, and the skill of the helmsman, all contributed towards the victory. In Athens, the contests were between the different tribes, and the victory and the prize went to the tribe that furnished the crew of the boat. The prizes, and the whole cost of getting a boat ready and training a crew, came from special contributions. A victory in the Sounion trireme race in the 5th century B.C. cost 15 minae, while the prize alone at the Panathenaia was worth 300 drachmai.

The competition was naturally enough held in high esteem in a city like Athens, which was a naval power. The Athenians included it in the Panathenaia, and in addition to the contests in Piraeus and Salamis already referred to, they also held a competition at Sounion. The crews on these occasions, oarsmen and helmsman alike, were *epheboi* from the competing tribes. At the Mounichia, where the contest was held in memory of the naval battle of Salamis, the *epheboi* were said to compete "in the sacred ships." If this is a reference to the famous sacred ships — the Paralos, the Salaminia, the Demetrias and the Antigonis — and if the city really entrusted these ships to its youth on these occasions, it is a measure of the importance of these displays in establishing the prestige of the Athenian state.

152. Diving, from the Poseidonia fresco. The "diver" plunges into the water from a high artificial platform (Paestum, Museo).

152

Famous Athletes in Ancient Greece

The Olympic Games endured for more than twelve centuries, and during these years, athletes of great quality appeared on the track and wrestling-pits of Olympia to astonish the crowds with their achievements. Mortal they may have been, but their Olympic victories won them immortality.

These illustrious athletes — the fleet *stadiodromoi, diaulodromoi* and *dolichodromoi,* the powerful wrestlers and boxers, the lithe *pentathletes,* and the indomitable *pankratiasts* — all left the mark of their passing indelibly on the sacred Greek valley of Olympia. There follows a selection of the most impressive figures of the ancient world, whose achievements made them legendary.

Theagenes of Thasos (pankratiast)

One of the most famous athletes in antiquity was Theagenes, son of Timosthenes, a priest in the temple of the god Herakles on Thasos. The Thasians believed that Theagenes was the son not of Timosthenes, but of the god, who assumed the form of Timosthenes and lay with his mother.

While Theagenes was still a boy of only nine years, he one day tore from its base the bronze statue of a god that stood in the square of Thasos, and carried it home on his shoulders, either because he liked the statue very much or because his young friends challenged him to do it. His fellow-citizens regarded his action as sacrilegious and wanted to put him to death for it. But the view which prevailed in the end was that of the more logical of them, who considered it a sufficient punishment to compel the boy to carry the statue back to its place. The young Theagenes did in fact take the statue back, and his compatriots were so astounded that the fame of his deed spread all over Greece.

Theagenes won his first victory in the boxing at the 75th Olympiad (480 B.C.), and in the *pankration* at the 76th (476 B.C.). He won three further victories in the Pythian games, nine in the Nemean and ten in the Isthmian, some of them in boxing and some in the *pankration.* He toured Greece in order to take part in the games held by various cities, and his many victories brought him great glory. Ancient sources record that the total number of crowns that he won in these games was as high as 1,400.

On one occasion, when he went for the games to Phthia, the home of fleet-footed Achilles, he did not compete in either the boxing or the *pankration,* since he knew that he was assured of victory in these events; instead he entered for the *dolichos,* which he won. He was motivated in this by a desire to gain a victory in a foot-race, in the homeland of Achilles, the swiftest of the heroes.

The Thasians were very proud of Theagenes, who had become a legendary figure and whose achievements passed from mouth to mouth throughout the whole of Greece.

The statue of Theagenes at Olympia was the work of the famous sculptor Glaukias of Aigina. Pausanias, who saw it, says that it stood in the Altis next to the statue of the kings Philip and Alexander, of Seleukos, Alexander's general and ruler of Syria, of Antigonos, also Alexander's general and father of Demetrios Poliorketes, and others.

The Thasians erected a large statue in their city after the death of Theagenes, who had brought so much fame to it by his many victories. Pausanias relates a very typical story connected with this statue; the incident occurred in Thasos. A man who had been an enemy of Theagenes during his lifetime, and who was himself an athlete, so they say, but one who could never win, since he had to face the invincible Theagenes, used to go every night and flog the statue, as though he were mercilessly beating the athlete himself. It appears that the statue came loose from its base and one night, while the madman was striking it, it fell on him and killed him, thus putting an end to his impious behaviour. The children of the dead man, however, had recourse to the law-court and brought a charge of murder against the statue, in accordance with the law passed by Drakon for the Athenians. The Thasians followed the law of Drakon, which prescribed exile for murder, even in the case of inanimate objects should they fall and kill a man, and took the statue and threw it into the sea. It then so happened that a great drought fell on the island of Thasos, as a result of which the crops did not grow, the fruit fell unripened from the trees, the earth grew no grass, the animals died and the people suffered great distress. Despairing of what to do, the rulers sent representatives bearing gifts to the oracle at Delphi. There, they prostrated themselves and sought advice: "What must we do to rid our country of the disastrous drought?" The oracle gave its response: "Bring back the exiles to their fatherland, to appease Demeter." The rulers then decided to send off ships to bring back all the exiles to Thasos. The drought and the famine continued, however, and the country suffered.

The Thasians, therefore, sent representatives again to the wise Pythia, and announced that they had done what they had been ordered, but the gods were still angry. The Pythia replied to them: "You have forgotten your great Theagenes, whom you threw in the sand, where now he lies, though before he won a thousand prizes." The authorities were greatly at a loss as to how they could find the statue of Theagenes in the sea, but some fishermen who had gone out fishing, caught it in their nets, hauled it in and carried it to the shore. The Thasians offered sacrifices in their joy and re-erected the statue in its former position, whereupon the drought ended. After this, the islanders sacrificed to Theagenes as a god of healing.

Leonidas of Rhodes (runner)

The achievements attributed to the athlete Leonidas of Rhodes are so great that they could be described as fantastic, when looked at from a modern viewpoint and in terms of man's capabilities today. However, the historical evidence for this runner with "the speed of a god" is firm and indisputable. Leonidas' achievement was so great that it was never equalled. In each of four successive Olympiads he won three victories in running events: the *stadion,* the *diaulos,* and the race in armour.

There were other famous athletes who won three victories, the first of them being Phanas of Pellene who won three crowns, in the *stadion,* the *diaulos* and the race in armour, during the 67th Olympiad (512 B.C.). A greater feat was that of Polites of Keramos who won three crowns at the 212th Olympiad (A.D. 69) in the running events of the *stadion,* the *diaulos* and the *dolichos,* all of them on the same day, and even the same morning, since these events were held one after the other. Other athletes won three victories not in the same Olympiad, but in one particular race at three successive Olympiads — athletes such as Astylos of Kroton, Krisson of Himera, Hermogenes of Xanthos, who won eight crowns in three Olympiads, and Chionis the Spartan, who won the *stadion* race at four successive Olympiads.

No one equalled the achievement of Leonidas, however. It is really difficult for a runner to retain his powers over a period of four successive Olympiads, whereas this is not difficult for an athlete competing in the heavy events, if nature has endowed him with a strong, muscular body. These events simply require good, intense training, and do not oblige the athlete to lead a careful life and observe a diet. The runner, however, is a slim athlete, and swiftness and endurance are both natural attributes that decline with the passage of time and with increasing age, since the joints and ligaments naturally lose their elasticity as the years go by. It is for these reasons that the feat of Leonidas of Rhodes remains unsurpassable.

Leonidas first won three crowns in the 154th Olympiad (164 B.C.) and was welcomed home with honour by the delighted Rhodians. Four years later, at the 155th Olympiad (160 B.C.), he won again three victories, and repeated his incomparable victory in the 156th Olympiad (156 B.C.). But when, at the age of 36 he won three events for the fourth time, thus having won twelve Olympic crowns for his city, his fellow-countrymen deified him, and Leonidas of Rhodes reached the height of good fortune.

Milon of Kroton (wrestler)

Milon, son of Diotimos, whose name was carved on the marbles of Olympia, was renowned amongst the renowned, the greatest of the athletes from Kroton, and is regarded by history as one of the most famous in the ancient world.

His glory was great. He first won at Olympia in the boys' wrestling, and was proclaimed victor a further five times in the men's wrestling. He made the rounds of the other games, winning seven times at the Pythian, nine at the Nemean, ten at the Isthmian, and gaining innumerable crowns during the course of his athletic career from the games at which he competed all over Greece.

The author Phylarchos illustrates the legendary strength of Milon by recounting an episode that took place at Olympia and to which a poet, Dorieus, devoted a poem. A translation is given here, since the incident is a typical one: *Such a man was Milon, when he raised from the ground the weight of a four-year-old heifer, at the festival of Zeus; and after he had lifted the enormous beast lightly onto his shoulders, like a small lamb, he carried it around, raising it in triumph, amongst the people celebrating; and all were amazed at this wonderful feat, as he carried the heifer and placed it at the feet of the priest of Pisa, who was performing the sacrifices. When he had carried this beast, which had no match, around the festival, he cut it into pieces, roasted it and ate it himself.*

The author Theodoros of Hierapolis also writes, in his book *About the Games,* that Milon used to eat twenty *minae* of meat, and as many loaves of bread. On one occasion at a festival on Aigina during the month of Anthesterion, when they were sampling the new wines, a large number of people were drinking together at a common table and made a bet as to who could drink the most wine "with a single movement." Milon succeeded in "downing in one" three *choai* (the equivalent of nine litres) and won the bet.

All the stories concerning Milon appear to be legendary. Once, the Sybarites, who always resented the prosperity of the neighbouring city of Kroton, declared war and arrived threatening to besiege and reduce the small town to submission. According to Theodoros, Milon came out into the square wearing a crown on his head and a lion-skin thrown over his shoulders. He brandished a club in his hands like a second Herakles and called on his fellow-countrymen to follow him. He himself went in front, and they all went out of the city together: their attack was so violent that the Sybarites took to their heels, leaving many dead behind them on the battlefield.

Milon of Kroton was a disciple of Pythagoras, and is said to have written a number of treatises. They say that once at a symposium of Pythagoreans the roof of the hall shook and would have crushed everybody, had not Milon succeeded in supporting the central pillar until his friends left the hall and were a good distance away. Milon, too, was able to dash out before the roof collapsed.

The stories preserved in the authors speak of Milon's superhuman strength, and surpass even the most fantastic legends. He used to hold a pomegranate in his clenched fist, and no one could open his fingers to take it away from him, nor could they make him crush the fruit by squeezing it. He would stand on an iron disc covered with oil, and no one had the strength to move him from it. He could tie a cord around his forehead, and then hold his breath so as to make the veins in the forehead stand out and break it. He used to hold his arm with the elbow locked into his side, and hold out his hand with the fingers spread and the thumb open, and no one could ever open his little finger.

Nonetheless, Milon was defeated by his fellow-countryman Timasitheos, when he appeared at Olympia to contest the victory for the seventh time, at the 67th Olympiad (512 B.C.), when it must be reckoned that he was at least 39-40 years old. His rival Timasitheos was a well-built and well-trained youth of 28. He beat Milon, the man of iron, not by strength but by guile, and tried to tame his intrepid opponent by wearing him out. The contest lasted for a long time, and Milon suffered and ultimately succumbed. Despite this, when the victory of the young Krotoniate was announced, the crowd rushed into the stadium, lifted Milon on their shoulders and carried him around in triumph, Timasitheos, the winner, being amongst those cheering.

The enormous statue of Milon that was set up in the Altis was carved by the sculptor Dameas. It is said that Milon himself lifted it and carried it to where it was erected. An epigram by Simonides was inscribed on the base: *This is the statue of Milon, best amongst the best, who conquered seven times at Olympia, without bending the knee.*

Fate willed, however, that the life of the most fortunate and glorious athlete should close with a tragic end. He went out once into the forest and saw there a newly cut tree-trunk into which wedges had been driven to open it. He decided to open the trunk with his strength: he put his hands into it and pulled them outwards, but the wedges flew out and the trunk closed up and trapped his hands. He was thus caught in a trap and had to stay in the wilderness, unable to free himself, and when night came, he was torn to pieces by the wild beasts.

Diagoras of Rhodes (boxer)

Diagoras, son of Damagetos, of Rhodes was a very famous boxer who won victories in all the great games — he was the most outstanding of all the ancient boxers, in the opinion of the historians of the period.

Pindar wrote for him one of the most splendid pieces of Greek lyric poetry. His Ode made such an impression that the Rhodians had it engraved in gold letters on the temple of Athena at Lindos. The great athlete's glorious career led his fellow-countrymen to trace his descent from the gods. His mother, they said, was in the countryside and was compelled to take refuge from the great heat in the sanctuary of Hermes, where the god found her asleep and lay with her. In fact, Diagoras came from a royal line, because his father was the grandson of Damagetos, king of Ialysos. Diagoras was an enormous man with a fine face, and his proud step and statuesque stance were much admired. Pindar calls him "immense" and the Scholiast on Pindar concludes that he must have been about 2.20 m. tall.

He won in the boxing at the 79th Olympiad (464 B.C.), twice at Nemea, four times at the Isthmus, several times in Rhodes and at many games held in Athens, Argos, Lykaion, Aigina, Pellene, Plataia, Thebes, Megara and elsewhere. He was called *euthymaches* (fair fighter), because when he was fighting he never stood side on, never stooped and never ducked away from an opponent. This direct style of fighting brought great pride to his many followers and admirers, and great pleasure and satisfaction to the spectators, who were capable of recognising and appreciating his directness and courage, his skill and the fair way in which he contested the crown, always observing the rules so as to put the victory beyond reproach.

Diagoras' character was full of majesty and nobility, modesty and dignity. For as long as he lived, he received great honours and achieved a glory which passed on to his descendants like a god-given heritage. The Altis itself hymned the good fortune of his line. The enormous statue of him stood there, with the statue of his eldest son Damagetos, an Olympic victor in the boxing, next to it. On the other side of it, was the statue of his second son, Akousilaos, an Olympic victor in the *pankration*. Further on, was the statue of his youngest and most notable son, Dorieus, who won three victories in the Olympic Games, eight in the Isthmian, seven in the Nemean, and one in the Pythian, all of them in the tough contest of the *pankration*. This was followed by the statues of his grandsons Eukles and Peisirodos.

The gods even granted this most fortunate man a sweet and honourable death. This was in 448 B.C., at the 83rd Olympiad. Diagoras, the proud father, was in the stadium watching his distinguished sons compete. The crowd surrounded him, embraced him and congratulated him, when his name echoed forth for the second time from the mouth of the herald, thanks to the victories of his sons. "Damagetos, son of Diagoras, of Rhodes, wins the boxing." "Akousilaos, son of Diagoras, of Rhodes, wins the *pankration*." The modest youths take their crowns, their manly faces alight with an uncontrollable joy. Forgetting the effort their eagerly sought victories have cost them, they run. There on the embankment, amongst the crowd, is their father Diagoras, the great Diagoras, the "fair fighter." With an impetuous gesture the sons place their victory crowns on their father's head. The crowd cheers: "Long live Diagoras." The youths, in their enthusiasm, lift him up onto their shoulders and go onto the track, wanting to show him off to the people, to show their pride and to take delight in his pride. The crowds cheer and shower them with flowers and laurel leaves. It is the triumph of Diagoras' life. Suddenly, from amongst the crowd, a Spartan's voice is heard: "Die now, Diagoras. There is nothing left for you but to ascend to Olympos."

The voice did not carry malice or envy, but was inspired by fear of the gods, lest this great joy should reach the point of impiety. And the voice was at once exhortation and advice. Enough Diagoras. After so much glory there is nothing left for you but to ascend to Olympos, to become a god.

The happy Diagoras heard the voice. And on the shoulders of his sons, in their embrace, and now thrice-happy, he bent his head, wearing the two crowns, and breathed his last. He did not ascend to Olympos, but he remained immortal.

Polydamas of Skotoussa (pankratiast)

Polydamas, or Poulydamas, came from the small city of Skotoussa in Thessaly.

Pausanias writes of his statue, which he saw in the Altis: *The figure on the high pedestal is by Lysippos; he was the biggest and the tallest of all human beings except for the heroes as they are called, and whatever race of mortals may have existed before the heroic age; of all the human beings of this age this man, Poulydamas, son of Nikias, was the biggest and the tallest.*

But Polydamas did not become well-known simply as a result of his Olympic victory in the *pankration*, at the 93rd Olympiad of 408 B.C. According to Pausanias' narrative, the great athlete's whole life was nothing but a continuous sequence of feats and exploits of all kinds that demonstrated his matchless strength and made him the equal of Herakles and the other legendary heroes. For all the deeds performed by Polydamas had never previously been achieved by a mortal.

The Thracian mountains up country from the river Nestos, says Pausanias, are stocked with wild beasts, including lions. These lions often range into the country round Olympos, and it was here that Polydamas, completely unarmed, killed a strong, wild lion of considerable size.

On another occasion he seized the biggest and most ferocious bull out of a herd of cattle by the hoof of one of its hind legs. The animal threshed and struggled in its attempt to get away and free its foot; it foamed at the mouth and bellowed in its despairing effort to escape, and in the end succeeded, but only by leaving its hoof in Polydamas' hands.

And Pausanias continues: Once a charioteer was driving his chariot at great speed. Polydamas got hold of the rear of the chariot with one hand and brought it to a complete stop.

Darius Ochus, the illegitimate son of Artaxerxes, who tricked the Persian people and seized power, hearing of the wondrous achievements of Polydamas, sent him rich gifts and invited him to his court to make his acquaintance. When the great athlete arrived, Darius Ochus proposed that he should fight with three picked Persians from his retinue, who were called the Immortals. Polydamas did not hesitate for a moment and fought the three of them in front of Darius. They appeared for the contest armed with the long Persian pikes and with swords, while Polydamas wielded only a club. He killed all three.

The invincible Polydamas came to a tragic end, however, destroyed by his own great strength. One summer he was relaxing with friends in the countryside, and they all took refuge in a cave to escape the unbearable heat. By ill chance, the roof of the cave began to break away and fall in large pieces, and it was clear that it would not last much longer. In the face of this deadly danger the others dashed outside and saved themselves, whereas Polydamas, trusting his own strength, stayed behind and raised his hands to the roof of the cave, confident that he could support it. But this proved fatal: the enormous rocks crushed him, and the famous Polydamas met with an inglorious death in the dark cave.

Melankomas the Karian (boxer)

Famous boxers competed at the Olympic, the Pythian, the Isthmian and the Nemean Games, men like the renowned Diagoras; the famous Glaukos, who was believed to be the son of the sea deity Glaukos of Anthedon; the youth Moschos from Kolophon in Asia Minor; Kleitomachos of Thebes; Kleoxenos, an Olympic victor who was never injured; Pythagoras of Samos who came to Olympia to compete in the boys' section, but was excluded and instead fought in the men's section and defeated them all; Hippomachos of Eleia, whom no opponent ever succeeded in getting close enough to hit; Tisandros of Naxos (Sicily), four times an Olympic winner; and many others.

The boxer that aroused the admiration of the ancient writers, however, was the amazing Melankomas from Karia in Asia Minor, who, as Dio Chrysostom relates, won many times without ever injuring his opponent and, of course, without being injured himself. It is, says the writer, a very strange thing for a boxer to be sound of limb and uninjured, for, as is well-known, boxers have broad noses, resulting from fractures of the bone in the nose, misshapen, flat ears, and faces full of marks left by old cuts, while Melankomas "is as healthy and unmarked as a runner." And Dio adds that he used to compel his opponents to give in and admit defeat, not only before he himself had received a blow, but even without striking them; for, he says, he believed that to strike someone, to injure or to be injured, did not constitute bravery.

Melankomas was unrivalled in the art of boxing, and his style of fighting was received enthusiastically by the spectators. His movements were light, free and simple. He used his hands only to defend himself against blows from his opponent, and continually changed position, avoiding the rough, violent and tough aspects of the sport. His whole comportment during the course of a contest had a particular grace and a severe harmony. One might claim that Melankomas had succeeded in changing the tough, hard sport of boxing into a genuinely noble contest. As a result of his tactic of not striking his opponent, the latter naturally grew angry after a short time, and lost his composure and control of his movements, so that he was repeatedly unsuccessful. In the end, despite his determination, the opponent would be drained and exhausted, and go off admitting defeat.

The same author writes that Melankomas could fight for two days with his arms held out before him, and nobody would see him change position.

Melankomas won his first Olympic victory in the

206th Olympiad (A.D. 45), and thereafter won many victories in most of the stadia of Greece.

Astylos of Kroton (stadiodromos)

Astylos of Kroton was an Olympic victor on many occasions, but it is not so much his many victories as his ill fate that has caused his name to survive in history. The goddess Tyche (Fortune) played a nasty game with him, for his city which had honoured and glorified him, denounced him and punished him harshly. He thus found himself without city and home, deserted by friends and relatives.

Pausanias writes: *Astylos of Kroton is by Pythagoras; he won the running race at Olympia three times in succession and scored victories in the diaulos race as well. Because in his two last victories he proclaimed himself as a Syracusan to please Hieron, son of Deinomenes, the people of Kroton decreed that his house be turned into a prison and they destroyed his portrait in the sanctuary of Lakinian Hera.*

The story of Astylos is typical. He was one of the most famous Olympic victors, with six crowns from three Olympiads (73rd in 488 B.C.; 74th in 484 B.C.; and 75th in 480 B.C.), and yet the gods reserved a humiliating end for him. Despite this, his name survived as one of the most famous track athletes, thanks to Simonides, who immortalised him with the following epigram:

Who of men today
has been adorned with so many petals and myrtles
and crowns of roses
thanks to his victories in the games?

Herodoros of Megara (trumpeter)

Apart from the athletes who distinguished themselves at Olympia, there were others that can also be regarded as competitors, for they, too, owed the privileged role they played in the ceremonial of the Games to competition.

Since there were many competent heralds and trumpeters who laid claim to the honour of announcing the events and the winners, or of blowing the trumpet in the hippodrome, competitions for these men, too, were established from the 96th Olympiad, and the victors won the prerogative of being the trumpeter or herald for the Olympiad (see "The First Day of the Games").

Herodoros of Megara is an example of a famous trumpeter. According to the Alexandrian writer Amarantos, quoted by Athenaeus, Herodoros was a man of enormous dimensions, excessively tall and with huge, powerful ribs. He used to sleep on a lion's skin which he spread on the ground, and he was a great eater and drinker. He would eat six *choinikes* of bread (about 7 kilos), twenty *litrai* of meat (about 7 kilos), and drink two *choai* of wine (6 litres). He won the competition for trumpeters at ten successive Olympiads, achieving his first success in the 113th Olympiad (328 B.C.), and the last at the 122nd (292 B.C.). A truly incredible achievement, for this huge man blew the trumpet at the Olympic Games for almost 40 years. During the second year of the 119th Olympiad, in 303 B.C., the gigantic trumpeter assisted the king Demetrios Poliorketes to capture Argos, by blowing so loud on two trumpets simultaneously that he inspired the soldiers to fight courageously.

Sport in the Hellenistic and Roman Periods

The Development of Sport in the Hellenistic and Roman Periods

The Development of Sport in the Hellenistic and Roman Periods

During the Hellenistic and Roman periods, athleticism followed the fortunes of Hellenism. The athletic ideal, that had its birth in the ancient city-states and reached its pinnacle during the period of the Persian wars, spread beyond the boundaries of the Greek world as a result of the conquests of Alexander the Great and the foundation of the Hellenistic kingdoms. Everywhere that Hellenism took root, the traditional buildings for training and exercise were erected, not only in the new great cities, but also in the smaller, more isolated settlements. At the same time, new festivals, modelled on the four Panhellenic festivals, were introduced in the new colonies in the East, along with smaller, local games. Both in Greece proper, and outside it, however, the new conditions had their effect on athletics and produced some significant changes, the seeds of which had made their appearance in scattered form as early as the 5th century B.C. The most important of these changes in the Hellenistic period was the rapid growth of professional athletics.

After the Roman conquest of Greece, the Roman attitude to sport, which differed from the Greek, and the economic decline in the Greek world, led to the decay of athletics. Despite this, the athletic ideal continued to be preserved in the gymnasia, the centres of Hellenism.

During the Imperial period, philhellene emperors attempted to give new life to the Panhellenic games and to sport generally, though in the sense they understood it. A certain revivification can, in fact, be observed, but it bore all the signs of the end. The Romans were in no position to breathe new life into the Greek athletic ideal, not only because the objective conditions had changed, but also because the Romans themselves had never essentially embraced this ideal.

Broadening out of Sport in the Hellenistic Period

One feature typical of the Hellenistic period is the great increase in the number of athletic buildings (gymnasia, wrestling-schools and stadia), and of athletic festivals, both in Greece proper, and in the states created by the successors of Alexander the

Great, and to some extent also in Magna Graecia. This increase was due to the spread of Hellenism, the new economic, political and social conditions, the brilliant reputation enjoyed by the Panhellenic festivals, and especially by the Olympic Games throughout the ancient world, and the ambition of the rulers of the Hellenistic states and other powerful figures to have their name connected with imposing deeds.

At the same time, the Greeks who had followed the spread of Hellenism and found themselves living amongst a wide range of nationalities, tried to cling to the main features of their culture, one of which was the athletic tradition, in close connection with religion and their heroic past. Once they had erected their holy buildings in their new homes in Asia, Syria and Egypt, therefore, their first thought was to build gymnasia, wrestling-schools and stadia, to organise games, and to send their best athletes to contest the victory in the Panhellenic games and bring honour to their new city. During this period, however, the athletic buildings were also multiplying in Greece proper, especially the gymnasia, for these were now centres of a more general training, open to a wider number of citizens (see "Athletics and Education").

This broadening out of sport was reinforced by the rulers of the Hellenistic states, who furnished vast sums of money for sporting installations and for the organisation of athletic festivals. Furthermore, they always kept their eyes turned to Greece proper, the cradle of their civilisation, and provided at their own expense for the improvement or adornment of existing sporting facilities there and for the erection of new ones.

The increase in the number of athletic festivals was of so great an order that, in addition to the four great Panhellenic games — the Olympic, Nemean, Pythian and Isthmian — a further 19 games that had virtually a Panhellenic character were held in the four years between two Olympiads. And this does not include the Ptolemaia at Alexandria, the Leukophrynia at Magnesia on the Maiandros, the Nikephoria at Pergamon, the Eumeneia at Sardis, the Asklepieia on Kos, the Erotideia at Thespiai, the Herakleia at Chalkis, the Eleusineia at Athens, and a host of smaller, local athletic festivals in cities great and small, that had roughly the same prestige. The Leukophrynia, in particular, which were organised on the model of the Pythian games and included gymnic, equestrian and musical competitions, achieved very great brilliance. They were even recognised as *isopythia* (i.e. equal to the Pythian games) and spectators travelled from all over the Hellenistic world to follow them.

The games of the Hellenistic period were characterised by their luxury, which contrasted with the austerity of the former times, and by the care taken to secure the greatest possible comfort for the spectators, during a period when the games increasingly lost their connection with religion and became purely a spectacle. The old and the new games included, basically, the events that had become established in the sporting tradition; but a number of events, such as the chariot races for foals, the youths' pentathlon, and the boys' pankration, came to be added to the programme, while the torch-races, that had been a local event at the Panathenaia,

153. Bronze statuette of a Roman pankratiast. At this period the athletes belonged to professional guilds which, unlike those of the Hellenistic period, had as their aim the advancement of their professional interests (Paris, Louvre).

16

gradually found their way into the new games. Many of the games, like the Attaleia, the Ptolemaia, and the Soteria at Megalopolis, served the ends of political expediency, but this in no way detracts from the importance of their contribution to the dissemination of athleticism and of Greek cultural values.

The Gymnasium

In the Hellenistic period too, gymnastics and training formed a fundamental element of education and, as in the Archaic and Classical periods, constituted one of the main features of the Greek way of life. The physical education of the young began at the age of about 8 years, though this varied from place to place and from period to period, and embraced both boys and girls. This education fundamentally followed the earlier patterns and took place in the traditional sporting areas, mainly the *palaistra* (Miletos, for example, had a "children's wrestling-school" at the beginning of the 2nd century B.C.). From a certain age, probably between about 14-18, many youths continued their physical education in the "gymnasium," the athletic, intellectual and political centre of the Hellenistic cities; this was under the general supervision of the *gymnasiarchos,* and was frequented by youths, grown men and even people of advanced age. The functions that in the past had been performed by a variety of athletic institutions (*gymnasion, palaistra* etc.) — that is, the physical education of the young, the training of athletes, mainly for the local games, and the cultivation of intellectual and moral values — were fulfilled in the Hellenistic period by the gymnasium. This was now a building complex, which embraced the athletic institutions named above, and whose size varied according to the city. The special position occupied by the gymnasium in the cities of the Hellenistic kingdoms is to be explained in terms of the socio-political role it played in the life of the Greeks: language, physical and intellectual education and culture, which were preserved and promoted within it, were the elements that allowed the Greeks to retain their identity as Greeks. At the same time, however, the gymnasium was a pole of attraction for the native inhabitants who aspired to become acquainted with and follow the Greek way of life.

The fact that during this period the gymnasium acquired an increasing number of areas for theoretical lessons (*exedra,* lecture-theatre, library) does not imply a neglect of physical education. Many scholars consider the extension of theoretical education in the gymnasia to be a sign of the decline of athletics. This was not the case however: as the vast numbers of surviving inscriptions connected with the games make clear, "the cultivation of the mind did not put an end to physical education," and the gymnasium at this period continued to be the nursery that produced young athletes both for the great Panhellenic games, and for the local athletics festivals.

Gymnastics was practised in the wrestling-school, which was normally private, as part of the general education of young children and consumed a large part of their daily activities. The time they devoted to it did not of course remain constant from period to period, but it appears that in Hellenistic times it had not decreased significantly. The person responsible for the physical education of the children was the *paidotribes.* These officials also existed in the public gymnasia, where they had assistants, such as the *hypopaidotribes,* the *sphairistes,* who taught a variety of exercises using the ball *(sphaira),* and the

154

154. Mosaic depicting women practising jumping, the discus and running which were part of the Olympic Pentathlon. Women's sport was quite widespread in the Roman period (Sicily, Piazza Armenina).

155

toxotes, akontistes and *hoplomachos,* who taught archery, the javelin and armed combat respectively. These officials are mainly known from the education of the Athenian *epheboi,* which was given systematic form as early as the 5th century B.C. The *paidotribes* and the trainers also prepared athletes who wanted to compete in the various games, and organised games for athletes of different ages.

A number of different athletic unions contributed to the promotion of sport. These usually consisted of the members of a gymnasium, and also of older men who had already left the gymnasium and embarked on a profession but who did not wish to lose contact with it completely. The unions had names such as "synod," "synod of the *xystos*," "the members of the gymnasium," and disposed of an administrative staff. It is certain, however, that they had broader cultural aims, in addition to sport.

Professionalism in Athletics

A distinction must be drawn at this point. When we speak of sport, we must separate the athletics of the gymnasium from professional sport, which dealt a fatal blow to the true spirit of competition that continued to be carefully and faithfully nurtured within the gymnasium as a national heritage.

From the 5th century B.C. onwards, despite the fact that the prize in the great Panhellenic games was simply a crown, a number of cities began to honour the victors by offering them goods or money, or exemptions that could be measured in terms of money (see "Honours Conferred on the Victors"). Cases are also known of athletes accepting money from an opponent in exchange for conceding the victory to him. Instances of this are even known from the Olympic Games, though heavy penalties were inflicted, since they represented deviations from the principles that had been laid down for the conduct of the Panhellenic games. It was during the Hellenistic period, however, that the phenomenon of athletes competing solely for money gradually took on serious dimensions — a development that it proved impossible to arrest. Professionalism in sport, however, was not an isolated phenomenon; it was a consequence of the political, economic and social life of the Greeks at that time, and was closely connected with the evolution of sport itself — that is with the improvement of training methods, the specialisation of athletes, and their great performances. An important role was also played in the development of professionalism by the fact that the financial rewards became greater and greater.

Improvement of Training Methods. Specialisation of Athletes. Great Performances

As we saw, methods of training and exercising for athletes had taken shape from the 5th century B.C., including a specific diet and basic rules of health, aimed at producing the best possible performance in the great Panhellenic games. This task was performed by the *paidotribai,* and later by the *gymnastai* (trainers), who were themselves usually veteran athletes and had an elementary knowledge of medicine. In the Hellenistic period, however, the athletes' training methods were determined by the state of knowledge — and mainly of medical science — of the age, and we have already referred to the "four-part cycle" or "system," which appears to have ultimately been the method most widely used (see "The Preparation of the Athletes"). Attention

155. Mosaic showing a statue of a boxer (Naples, Museo Archeologico Nazionale).

was also paid to the form and orientation of the competition areas, and to the type of exercise required for each event, so that the athletes would always be in form for competition. These improvements in the field of health and elsewhere were basically associated with the gymnasium. However, there also existed professional trainers, who promised young men endowed with natural gifts, or the parents of young children whose training they undertook, that if they followed the strict diet and tough training which they themselves prescribed, they would become unbeatable athletes.

The athletes who received this kind of training did in fact achieve very good performances. They usually preferred to specialise in one of the heavy events — wrestling, boxing or the pankration — and, treating sport as a profession, they travelled from contest to contest through the whole of the Hellenistic world, collecting crowns and financial rewards. The result of this was to discourage those who had neither the time nor the disposition to compete with them on what was now a professional level. The motives that encouraged young men to neglect their general education and turn to professional sport were the great financial rewards, and also the significant distinctions that made their position an exceptionally privileged one.

However difficult it may have been to compete with the professional athletes, there was no lack of non-professionals who made their way to the Panhellenic sanctuaries or to the local athletic festivals in order to compete with them solely for the crown of victory, and who, indeed, often succeeded in defeating them. It should also be observed that amongst the professional athletes, too, there were some who, though they practised sport as a profession, were still inspired by the true athletic ideal.

The Sporting Ideal and the Romans

The period following the subjection of Greece by the Romans in 146 B.C. was crucial for sport and the sporting ideal. To the ruins left by the continuous warfare between the Greeks, were added the fearful sackings and destructions of the Roman civil wars fought on Greek soil. During this period there was a general economic, moral and social collapse; most of the local games ceased to be held and the Panhellenic games fell into decay.

Two factors, however, made an important contribution to keeping alive the sporting ideal during this time of great difficulty for Hellenism. The first was the great prestige of the Panhellenic games. The Romans, despite their indifference to athletics and Greek athletic customs, did not suppress them, possibly for political reasons. The second was the preservation of the gymnasium as an institution. The important position occupied by the gymnasium in the life of the Hellenistic cities has already been indicated. After the Roman conquest, the enslaved Greeks used the small amount of autonomy left to them by the Romans to rally round the gymnasium, the centre of their national survival, and continued within it to engage in sporting, intellectual and social pursuits, in so far, of course, as the new conditions permitted; for although the Romans left the gymnasium as an institution untouched, they frequently intervened in its administrative organisation.

The authority of the games generally, and of Olympia in particular, was subjected to a severe test during this period by Sulla's plundering of Olympia during the Mithridatic wars, and by his transfer of

156. Fresco from Pompeii showing a Roman amphitheatre. In the Roman period athletic games gave way to savage and bloody spectacles (Naples, Museo Archeologico Nazionale).

156

the Olympic Games to Rome, where he made the athletes compete in order to add to the glory of his triumph. About a century later, the Olympic Games suffered a further testing from the high-handed, humiliating behaviour of Nero.

When conditions changed, from the Imperial period onwards, the two factors mentioned played a decisive role in the revival of sport by philhellene emperors like Hadrian and Antoninus. Local and other games were either held again, or new ones held for the first time, within the context of the gymnasium or with its help. These games were of enormous importance in preserving the true sporting ideal amidst the by now general climate of professionalism. As in the past, however, a number of those who eventually became professionals received their impetus to sport from the gymnasium.

Olympia rediscovered its old glory. The majestic temple of Zeus and other buildings were restored and the organisation of the Games was improved. Athletes came eagerly from all over the world and dedicated statues of themselves after their victories, while various powerful figures sent dedications and also set up statues of themselves. A similar situation prevailed at the other Panhellenic sanctuaries. Thanks to the liberality of Herodes Atticus, of Hadrian and of his successors, gymnasia and baths were built in Greece proper and elsewhere, derelict stadia were renovated, and a number of improvements were made, aimed at better residence and training facilities for the athletes.

At the same time new athletic festivals were instituted through the whole of the Roman Empire. Many of these were named after the Panhellenic games, though even at this period permission was sought from the sanctuaries after which the original games were named. Thus, there were Pythian games at Philippoupolis in Thrace and at Anazarbos in Kilikia, Nemean games at Anchialos in Thrace and Aitna in Sicily, Olympic games at Cyrene in North Africa and at Smyrna, and Isthmian games at Ankyra and Syracuse. The establishing of the Actia as a fifth Panhellenic athletic festival was a bad precedent. The subject cities began to flatter the Roman emperors by instituting athletic games in their names, like the Isolympia Augusteia at Naples, the Hadrianeia at Athens, and similar festivals at Pergamon, Halikarnassos, Sardis etc. These festivals, of course, did not have the splendour and prestige of the great Panhellenic games, and only existed for a short period — roughly speaking, as long as the lifetime of the emperor in whose honour they were established.

Despite this apparent flourishing of sport, the great Panhellenic games and the newly instituted ones that aspired to resemble them were (with the possible exception of the Olympic Games) very different from the ancient games, which had been closely connected with religion and the heroic past. They were simply imposing spectacles that the subjects of the vast Roman Empire came from east to west to see. In order to ensure the comfort of this great host, the stadia and other competition areas gradually took on enormous dimensions. The taste of this public was affected as time went on by the preferences of the Romans, who delighted not only in the heavy events (wrestling, boxing and pankration), to which the professionals had largely turned in the Hellenistic period, as we saw, but also in the more bloody contests between gladiators, or between men and wild beasts. Thus, at Antiocheia, at Corinth and elsewhere, armed combat came to be included in the programme of the games; but most distressing of all was the fact that these contests were also held in the theatre of Dionysos in Athens, where the works of the great tragedians had once been performed.

A great impulse was given towards professional

sport by the various professional athletic guilds, for which we have greater evidence from the Imperial period. These, however, differed from the earlier associations already referred to. The professional unions appeared to have cooperated with the actors troups, and to have received economic support from the emperors.

Herakles was usually regarded as the patron of these athletic unions, and their main centres were in the eastern provinces of the Roman Empire. Our most complete information, however, relates to one of these associations that was organised under Hadrian, with Rome as its headquarters, and survived until the dissolution of the Roman Empire.

As is clear from the designation "Itinerant synod of the *xystos*," which these unions usually adopted, their members travelled continuously from city to city to take part in the various games. There was great rivalry between them, and each athletic union was concerned to perfect its training methods so that its members were in form for competition.

These associations were instituted on the model of the other professional and religious guilds, and selected their officers from amongst retired athletes; their leader had a religious title ("high-priest of the whole *xystos*"), or was called *hieros* (sacred), a title that was frequently used in conjunction with the name of the union (e.g. "sacred synod of the *xystos*," "sacred synod of Herakles").

These professional associations undoubtedly did harm to sport. They bore no relation to the athletics of the gymnasium, nor to the local festivals, which preserved as far as possible the great athletic tradition of the Greeks.

The revivification of the Panhellenic games in the Imperial period began with Olympia and was to close at Olympia. Amongst the last lists of Olympic victors are to be found names from the most distant areas of the Empire, from Kappadokia, Assyria, Illyria etc., who show nothing of the modesty of the first Olympic victors, and adopt designations such as "first amongst men," "first and only," "unbeatable" etc. Moreover, Olympia, the sacred place had become a gathering ground for peoples and races who were bound together by nothing more than their love of the spectacle.

End of the Games (A.D. 393)

The lists of Olympic victors stop in A.D. 267. From this date until 361 there are no victors' lists, and we cannot be certain, therefore, that the Games were held. The preservation of the buildings, however, and the remodelling of the areas at this period, attested by archaeological evidence, suggests that the Games probably continued after a short interval. Scattered references relate that one Philoumenos of Philadelphia in Asia Minor won the wrestling in A.D. 369, and it is symptomatic that the last known Olympic victor was an Armenian prince, Barasdates or Artabasdos, who won the boxing in the 287th Olympiad (A.D. 369). The Olympic, like the other games, had already degenerated before they were officially abolished by the decree of the emperor Theodosius I, in A.D. 393.

Athletic games continued to be held in the Greek cities of the East, especially in Antiocheia, where Olympic Games were held until A.D. 510, when the emperor Justinian forbade them. These games were the last feeble presence on the field of sport. Lacking the support of ancient religion, removed from its mythical roots, and resting mainly in the hands of professionals, sport could not withstand the attack it received from the new religion, Christianity, which identified athletic games and festivals with the worship of the Olympian gods, against which it fought so passionately.

List of Ancient Olympic Victors

Bibliography
List of Illustrations
Index

List of Ancient Olympic Victors

The list of Olympic victors was compiled for the first time about 400 B.C. by the Elean sophist Hippias, who for the earlier Olympiads probably drew on the records at Olympia, oral traditions and the recollections of those still living. The Olympiad of 776 B.C., when the Elean Koroibos was victorious in the foot-race (the stadion*), is generally taken to be the beginning.*

Hippias' work was revised and continued in the 4th century B.C. by Aristotle and later by Eratosthenes, Phlegon of Tralles and others. It was transformed into a kind of Olympic chronicle and already in the 3rd century B.C. formed the basis of the ancient system of chronology. From among the later compilations the catalogue of victors in the stadion *race found in Julius Africanus (for Olympiads 1 to 249) is preserved complete in the* Chronicle *of Eusebios. The evidence for these lists comes from literary and historical sources, the relevant papyri from Oxyrrhynchos, the testimony of Pausanias, the catalogue of Julius Africanus, a number of coins and the inscriptions connected with the Games.*

The table below is based on Luigi Moretti, Olympionikai, I vincitori negli antichi Agoni Olimpici. *The first columns of figures give the successive numbers of the Olympiads together with their chronological equivalent. Then come the names of the victors, their cities, the contest in which they were victorious and (in brackets) the number of the victory, when the athlete won several times in the same sport. Olympic victories whose dating is not completely certain are marked with an asterisk.*

1	776	Koroibos of Elis: stadion
2	772	Antimachos of Dyspontion: stadion
3	768	Androklos of Messene: stadion
4	764	Polychares of Messene: stadion
5	760	Aischines of Elis: stadion
6	756	Oibotas of Dymai: stadion
7	752	Daikles of Messene: stadion
8	748	Antikles of Messene: stadion
9	744	Xenodokos (or Xenokles) of Messene: stadion
10	740	Dotades of Messene: stadion
11	736	Leochares of Messene: stadion
12	732	Oxythemis of Kleonai: stadion
13	728	Diokles of Corinth: stadion
14	724	Dasmon (or Desmon) of Corinth: stadion
		Hypenos of Pisa: diaulos
15	720	Orsippos of Megara: stadion
		Akanthos of Sparta: dolichos
16	716	Pythagoras of Sparta: stadion
17	712	Polos of Epidauros: stadion
18	708	Tellis of Sikyon: stadion
		Lampis of Sparta: pentathlon
		Eurybatos of Sparta: wrestling
19	704	Menos of Megara: stadion
20	700	Atheradas of Sparta: stadion
21	696	Pantakles of Athens: stadion (1)
22	692	Pantakles of Athens: stadion (2) and diaulos
23	688	Ikaros (or Ikarios) of Hyperesia: stadion
		Onomastos of Smyrna: boxing
24	684	Kleoptolemos of Sparta: stadion
		Phanas of Messene: dolichos
25	680	Thalpis of Sparta: stadion
		Pagondas (or Pagon) of Thebes: tethrippon
26	676	Kallisthenes of Sparta: stadion
		Philombrotos of Sparta: pentathlon (1)
27	672	Eurybates (or Eurybotos or Eurybos) of Athens: stadion
		Philombrotos of Sparta: pentathlon (2)
		Daïppos of Kroton: boxing
		State victory of the Eleans of Dyspontion in the tethrippon
28	668	Charmis of Sparta: stadion
		Philombrotos of Sparta: pentathlon (3)
29	664	Chionis of Sparta: stadion (1) and diaulos (1)
30	660	Chionis of Sparta: stadion (2) and diaulos (2)
31	656	Chionis of Sparta: stadion (3) and diaulos (3)
32	652	Kratinos of Megara: stadion
		Komaios of Megara: boxing
33	648	Gylis (or Gygis) of Sparta: stadion
		Lygdamis of Syracuse: pankration
		Myron of Syracuse: tethrippon
		Krauxidas (or Kraxilas) of Krannon: horse race
34	644	Stomas of Athens: stadion
35	640	Sphairos of Sparta: stadion
		Kylon of Athens: diaulos
36	636	Arytamas of Sparta: stadion
		Phrynon of Athens: pankration (?)
37	632	Eurykleidas of Sparta: stadion
		Polyneikes (or Polynikes) of Elis: boys' stadion
		Hipposthenes of Sparta: boys' wrestling
38	628	Olyntheus of Sparta: stadion (1)
		Eutelidas of Sparta: boys' pentathlon
39	624	Ripsolaos of Sparta: stadion
		Hipposthenes of Sparta: wrestling (1)
40	620	Olyntheus of Sparta: stadion (2)
		Hipposthenes of Sparta: wrestling (2)
41	616	Kleondas (or Kleonidas) of Thebes: stadion
		Hipposthenes of Sparta: wrestling (3)
		Philytas (or Philotas) of Sybaris: boys' wrestling
42	612	Lykotas of Sparta: stadion
		Hipposthenes of Sparta: wrestling (4)
43	608	Kleon of Epidauros: stadion
		Hipposthenes of Sparta: wrestling (5)
44	604	Gelon of Sparta: stadion
		Hetoimokles of Sparta: boys' wrestling
45	600	Antikrates of Epidauros: stadion
		Hetoimokles of Sparta: wrestling (1)
46	596	Chrysamaxos of Sparta: stadion
		Polymestor of Miletos: boys' stadion
		Hetoimokles of Sparta: wrestling (2)
47	592	Eurykles of Sparta: stadion
		Hetoimokles of Sparta: wrestling (3)
		Alkmaion of Athens: tethrippon
48	588	Glaukias (or Glykon) of Kroton: stadion
		Hetoimokles of Sparta: wrestling (4)
		Pythagoras of Samos: boxing
		...... Lenaios, in a special event
49	584	Lykinos of Kroton: stadion
50	580	Epitelidas of Sparta: stadion
51	576	Eratosthenes of Kroton: stadion
52	572	Agis of Elis: stadion
		*Tisandros of Sicilian Naxos: boxing (1)
		Arrichion of Phigaleia: pankration (1)
		Kleisthenes, tyrant of Sikyon: tethrippon

53 568 Hagnon of Peparethos: stadion
*Tisandros of Sicilian Naxos: boxing (2)
Arrichion of Phigaleia: pankration (2)

54 564 Hippostratos of Kroton: stadion (1)
*Tisandros of Sicilian Naxos: boxing (3)
Arrichion of Phigaleia: pankration (3)
Kallias, son of Phainippos, of Athens: tethrippon

55 560 Hippostratos of Kroton: stadion (2)
*Tisandros of Sicilian Naxos: boxing (4)
*Miltiades, son of Kypselos, of Athens: tethrippon

56 556 Phaidros of Pharsalos: stadion

57 552 Ladromos of Sparta: stadion

58 548 Diognetos of Kroton: stadion
*Euagoras of Sparta: tethrippon (1)

59 544 Archilochos of Korkyra: stadion
Praxidamas of Aigina: boxing
*Euagoras of Sparta: tethrippon (2)

60 540 Apellaios of Elis: stadion
Milon of Kroton: boys' wrestling
[Leo]kreon of Keos: boys' boxing
*Euagoras of Sparta: tethrippon (3)

61 536 Agatharchos of Korkyra: stadion
Rexibios of Opous: pankration
Kimon, son of Stesagoras, of Athens: tethrippon (1)

62 532 Eryxias (or Eryxidas) of Chalkis: stadion
Milon of Kroton: wrestling (1)
*Eurymenes of Samos, in a heavy event (boxing, wrestling or pankration)
Peisistratos, tyrant of Athens: tethrippon (2)

63 528 Parmenides of Kamarina: stadion
Milon of Kroton: wrestling (2)
Kimon, son of Stesagoras, of Athens: tethrippon (2)

64 524 Menandros of Thessaly: stadion
Milon of Kroton: wrestling (3)

65 520 Anochos (or Anochas) of Taras: stadion and diaulos
Damaretos (or Demaretos) of Heraia: race in armour (1)
Milon of Kroton: wrestling (4)
Glaukos of Karystos: boxing
*Philippos of Kroton: event unknown
*...... of Thebes: tethrippon

66 516 Ischyros of Himera: stadion
Damaretos of Heraia: race in armour (2)
Milon of Kroton: wrestling (5)
*Timasitheos of Delphi: pankration (1)
Kleosthenes of Epidamnos: tethrippon

67 512 Phanas of Pellene: stadion, diaulos and race in armour
Timasitheos of Kroton: wrestling
*Timasitheos of Delphi: pankration (2)
Pheidolas of Corinth: horse race

68 508 Ischomachos (or Isomachos) of Kroton: stadion (1)
*Kalliteles of Sparta: wrestling
Phrikias of Pelinna: race in armour (1)
*Pantaros of Gela: tethrippon
......, sons of Pheidolas of Corinth: horse race

69 504 Ischomachos of Kroton: stadion (2)
Thessalos of Corinth: diaulos (?)
*Philon of Korkyra: boys' stadion
Phrikias of Pelinna: race in armour (2)
*Damaratos, king of Sparta: tethrippon
*Titas: event unknown

70 500 Nikeas (or Nikasias) of Opous: stadion
Akmatidas of Sparta: pentathlon
Philon of Korkyra: boxing (1)
*Meneptolemos of Apollonia: boys' stadion
*Agametor of Mantineia: boys' boxing
*Kallias II of Athens: tethrippon (1)
Thersios of Thessaly: apene

71 496 Tisikrates of Kroton: stadion (1)
Exainetos of Akragas: wrestling
Philon of Korkyra: boxing (2)
Kallias II of Athens: tethrippon (2)
Empedokles of Akragas: horse race
Pataikos of Dymai: race for mares

72 492 Tisikrates of Kroton: stadion (2)
*Hieronymos of Andros: pentathlon
Kleomedes of Astypalaia: boxing
Hippokleas of Pelinna: a track event (1)
Kallias II of Athens: tethrippon (3)
*Krokon of Eretria: horse race

73 488 Astylos of Kroton: stadion (1) and diaulos (1)
*Euthykles of Lokroi: pentathlon
*Diognetos of Crete: boxing
*Asopichos of Orchomenos: boys' stadion
*Agiadas of Elis: boys' boxing
Hippokleas of Pelinna: a track event (2)
Gelon of Gela: tethrippon

74 484 Astylos of Kroton: stadion (2) and diaulos (2)
*Dromeus of Stymphalia: dolichos (1)
*Theopompos of Heraia: pentathlon (1)
*Telemachos of Pharsalos: wrestling
Euthymos of Lokroi: boxing (1)
*Agias of Pharsalos: pankration (1)
*Epikradios of Mantineia: boys' boxing
*Mnaseas of Cyrene: race in armour
*Polypeithes of Sparta: tethrippon

75 480 Astylos of Syracuse: stadion (3), diaulos (3) and race in armour
*Dromeus of Stymphalia: dolichos (2)
*Theopompos of Heraia: pentathlon (2)
Theagenes of Thasos: boxing
Dromeus of Mantineia: pankration
[Xe]nopithes of Keos: boys' stadion
[...]kon of Argos: boys' wrestling
[...]phanes of Heraia: boys' boxing
[Dai]tondas and Arsilochos of Thebes: tethrippon
State victory of Argos in the horse race
*Anaxilas of Region: apene

76 476 Skamandros (or Skamandrios) of Mytilene: stadion
Dandis of Argos: diaulos
[......] of Sparta: dolichos
[......] of Taras: pentathlon
[......] of Maroneia: wrestling
Euthymos of Lokroi: boxing (2)
Theagenes of Thasos: pankration (2)
[......] of Sparta: boys' stadion
Theognetos of Aigina: boys' wrestling
Agesidamos of Lokroi: boys' boxing
[Zop]yros of Syracuse: race in armour
Theron, tyrant of Akragas: tethrippon
Hieron, tyrant of Syracuse: horse race (1)

77 472 Dandis of Argos: stadion
[......]ges of Epidauros: diaulos
Ergoteles of Himera: dolichos (1)
[......]amos of Miletos: pentathlon
[......]menes of Samos: wrestling
Euthymos of Lokroi: boxing (3)
Kallias of Athens: pankration
[......]tandridas of Corinth: boys' stadion
[......]kratidas of Taras: boys' wrestling
Tellon of Orestheia: boys' boxing
[......]gias of Epidamnos: race in armour
State victory of Argos in the tethrippon
Hieron, tyrant of Syracuse: horse race (2)

78 468 Parmenides of Poseidonia: stadion and diaulos
[......]medes of Sparta: dolichos
[......]tion of Taras: pentathlon
Epharmostos (or Eparmostos) of Opous: wrestling
Menalkes of Opous: boxing
[E]pitimadas of Argos (?): pankration
[Lyk]ophron of Athens: boys' stadion
[......]emos of Parrhasia: boys' wrestling
[......]nes of Tiryns: boys' boxing
[......]los of Athens: race in armour

Hieron, tyrant of Syracuse: tethrippon
*Leophron: horse race (?)
*Agesias of Syracuse: apene

79 464 Xenophon of Corinth: stadion and pentathlon
Ergoteles of Himera: dolichos (2)
Diagoras of Rhodes: boxing
Ephotion (or Ephondion or Ephendion) of Mainalos: pankration
*Pythagoras of Mantineia: boys' stadion
Pherias of Aigina: boys' wrestling
*Protolaos of Mantineia: boys' boxing
*Kratisthenes of Cyrene: tethrippon
*Echekratidas of Thessaly: horse race

80 460 Torymbas (or Toryllas or Torymnas) of Thessaly: stadion
*Ladas of Argos (?): dolichos
Amesinas of Barke: wrestling
*Timodemos of Athens: pankration
Sostratos of Pellene: boys' stadion
Alkmedon of Aigina: boys' wrestling
*Kyniskos of Mantineia: boys' boxing
*[......]adas: event unknown
*Kordaphos of Lepreon: event unknown
Arkesilaos IV, king of Cyrene: tethrippon

81 456 Polymnastos of Cyrene: stadion
[......]nomos: pentathlon
Leontiskos of Sicilian Messene: wrestling (1)
Anthropos: boxing
Timanthes of Kleonai: pankration
*Ikadion of Crete (?): boys' stadion
Phrynich[os] of Athens: boys' wrestling
Alkainetos of Lepreon: boys' boxing
*Linas of L[......]: race in armour
Diaktorides: tethrippon
Aigias of Na[......]: horse race
Psaumios of Kamarina: apene

82 452 Lykos of Larisa: stadion
Euboulos: diaulos
Hippobo[los]: dolichos
Pythokles of Elis: pentathlon
Leontiskos of Sicilian Messene: wrestling (2)
Ariston: boxing
Damagetos of Rhodes: pankration (1)
Lachon of Keos: boys' stadion
Kleodoros: boys' wrestling
Apollodo[ros]: boys' boxing
Lykos of Thessaly: race in armour
Psaumios of Kamarina: tethrippon
Python of I[......]: horse race

83 448 Krison of Himera: stadion (1)
Eukleides: diaulos
Aigeidas of Crete: dolichos
Keton of Lokroi: pentathlon
Cheimon of Argos: wrestling
Akousilaos of Rhodes: boxing
Damagetos of Rhodes: pankration (2)
Lacharidas: boys' stadion
Polynikos of Thespiai: boys' wrestling
Ariston: boys' boxing
Lyk(e)inos: race in armour
*Arkesilaos of Sparta: tethrippon (1)

84 444 Krison of Himera: stadion (2)
Ikkos of Taras: pentathlon
Taurosthenes of Aigina: wrestling
Alkainetos of Lepreon: boxing (2)
*Charmides of Elis: boys' boxing
*Arkesilaos of Sparta: tethrippon (2)

85 440 Krison of Himera: stadion (3)
Theopompos II of Heraia: wrestling (1)
*Gnathon of Dipaia: boys' boxing
*Polykles of Sparta: tethrippon

86 436 Theopompos of Thessaly: stadion
*Theopompos II of Heraia: wrestling (2)
Pantarkes of Elis: boys' wrestling
Philippos of Arkadia: boys' boxing
Megakles of Athens: tethrippon

87 432 Sophron of Ambrakia: stadion
Dorieus of Rhodes: pankration (1)
*Lykinos of Elis: boys' wrestling
*Lykinos of Sparta: tethrippon

88 428 Symmachos of Sicilian Messene: stadion (1)
Dorieus of Rhodes: pankration (2)
*Alexandros of Sparta: tethrippon

89 424 Symmachos of Sicilian Messene: stadion (2)
*Kleomachos of Magnesia on the Maiandros: boxing
Dorieus of Rhodes: pankration (3)
Hellanikos of Lepreon: boys' boxing
*Leon of Sparta: tethrippon
*Da[masi?]ppos: event unknown

90 420 Hyperbios of Syracuse: stadion
*Aristeus of Argos: dolichos
Androsthenes of Mainalos: pankration (1)
*Amertas of Elis: boys' wrestling
Theantos of Lepreon: boys' boxing
Lichas of Sparta: tethrippon
Xenombrotos of Kos: horse race

91 416 Exainetos of Akragas: stadion (1)
*Lakrates of Sparta: event unknown
*Androsthenes of Mainalos: pankration (2)
*Nikostratos of Heraia: boys' wrestling
Alkibiades, son of Kleinias, of Athens: tethrippon

92 412 Exainetos of Akragas: stadion (2)

93 408 Eubatas (or Eubatos or Eubotas) of Cyrene: stadion
Poulydamas of Skotoussa: pankration
Archelaos, son of Perdikkas, king of Macedonia: tethrippon
Euagoras of Elis: synoris

94 404 Krokinas (or Kroukinas) of Larisa: stadion
Lasthenes of Thebes: dolichos (?)
*Symmachos of Elis: wrestling
*Eukles of Rhodes: boxing
Promachos of Pellene: pankration
*Peisir[rh]odos of Thourioi: boys' boxing

95 400 Minos of Athens: stadion
*Baukis of Troizen: wrestling
*Demarchos of Parrhasia: boxing
*Antiochos of Lepreon: pankration
*[...]krates: boys' stadion
*Euthymenes of Mainalos: boys' wrestling
*Xenodikos of Kos: boys' boxing
*Timon of Elis: tethrippon
*Aisepos (or Aisypos or Aisipos or Aigyptos): horse race
*[......] of Argos (?) or Tegea (?): event unkown

96 396 Eupolemos (or Eupolis) of Elis: stadion
Krokenas of Larisa: diaulos
[...]onios of Crete: dolichos
[...]os of Corinth: wrestling
[......] of [...]u[...]: boxing
[......] of [...]nan[......]: pankration (?)
*Epichares of Athens: boys' stadion
*Archedamos of Elis: boys' wrestling
*Bykelos of Sikyon: boys' boxing
*Lampyrion of A [......]
*[......]s of A[......]: event unknown
*Kyniska of Sparta: tethrippon (1)
Timaios of Elis: trumpeters' competition
Krates of Elis: heralds' competition

97 392 [......] of Terina (or Terinaios of Elis): stadion
*Euthymenes of Mainalos: wrestling
Phormion of Halikarnassos: boxing
*Dikon of Kaulonia: boys' stadion
Neolaïdas of Pheneon: boys' boxing
*Kyniska of Sparta: tethrippon (2)

98 388 Sosippos of Athens (or Delphi): stadion
Aristodemos of Elis: wrestling
Eupalos of Thessaly: boxing
Antipatros of Miletos: boys' boxing
*Xenarchos of Sparta: tethrippon
*Kleogenes of Elis: horse race

99 384 Dikon of Syracuse: stadion and diaulos or race in armour
Sotades of Crete: dolichos (1)
*Hysmon of Elis: pentathlon
*Narykidas of Phigaleia: wrestling
*Damoxenidas of Mainalos: boxing
Lykinos of Heraia: boys' stadion
Alketos of Kleitor: boys' boxing
Eurybiades (or Sybariades or Eurybates) or Sparta: tethrippon

100 380 Dionysodoros of Taras: stadion
Sotades of Ephesos: dolichos (2)
*...... of Samos: boxing
*Xenophon of Aigai: pankration
*Deinolochos of Elis: boys' stadion
*Hippos of Elis: boys' boxing

101 376 Damon of Thourioi: stadion (1)
*Stomios of Elis: pentathlon
*Labax of Lepreon: boxing
Kritodamos of Kleitor: boys' boxing

102 372 Damon of Thourioi: stadion (2)
Xenokles of Mainalos: boys' wrestling
*Thersilochos of Korkyra: boys' boxing
*...... Two men from Methydria: event unknown
Troïlos of Elis: synoris and foals' tethrippon

103 368 Pythostratos of Athens (or Ephesos): stadion
*Aristion of Epidauros: boxing
*......of Stratos: pankration
Damiskos of Messene: boys' stadion
Euryleonis of Sparta: synoris

104 364 Phokides of Athens: stadion
Sostratos of Sikyon: pankration (1)
Eubatas of Cyrene: tethrippon
*Archias of Sicilian Hyblaia: heralds' competition (1)

105 360 Poros of Cyrene: stadion (1)
Philammon of Athens: boxing
Sostratos of Sikyon: pankration (2)
*Xenon of Lepreon: boys' stadion
*Agenor of Thebes: boys' wrestling
Theochrestos I of Cyrene: tethrippon
Archias of Sicilian Hyblaia: heralds' competition (2)

106 356 Poros of Malia: stadion (2)
*Pyrilampes of Ephesos: dolichos
*Chairon of Pellene: wrestling (1)
Sostratos of Sikyon: pankration (3)
Philip II, king of Macedonia: horse race
*Archias of Sicilian Hyblaia: heralds' competition (3)

107 352 Smikrinas (or Mikrinas) of Taras: stadion
*Chairon of Pellene: wrestling (2)
*Athenaios of Ephesos: boys' boxing
*Philip II, king of Macedonia: tethrippon (?)
*Timokrates of Athens: synoris
*Dionysodoros of Thebes: event unknown

108 348 Polykles of Cyrene: stadion
*Chairon of Pellene: wrestling (3)
*Aischylos of Thespiai: boys' wrestling
*Philip II, king of Macedonia: synoris

109 344 Aristolochos of Athens: stadion
*Chairon of Pellene: wrestling (4)
*Damaretos of Messene: boys' boxing
*Kallikrates of Magnesia on the Maiandros: race in armour (1)
Arybbas of Epeiros: tethrippon

110 340 Antikles of Athens: stadion
*Asamon of Elis: boxing
*Telestas of Messene: boys' boxing
*Kallikrates of Magnesia of the Maiandros: race in armour (2)
*Kalliades: an equestrian event

111 336 Kleomantis of Kleitor: stadion
Mys of Taras: boxing
*Dioxippos of Athens: pankration

112 332 Grylos (or Eurylas) of Chalkis: stadion
Kallippos of Athens: pentathlon
*Cheilon of Patrai: wrestling (1)
*Satyros of Elis: boxing (1)

113 328 Kliton of Macedonia: stadion
Ageus of Argos: dolichos
*Cheilon of Patrai: wrestling (2)
*Satyros of Elis: boxing (2)
*Demades of Athens: an equestrian event
*Herodoros of Megara: trumpeters' competition (1)

114 324 Mikinas of Rhodes: stadion
Astyanax of Miletos: pankration (1)
Douris of Samos: boys' boxing
*Herodoros of Megara: trumpeters' competition (2)

115 320 Damasias of Amphipolis: stadion
Astyanax of Miletos: pankration (2)
*Hermesianax of Kolophon: boys' wrestling
*Pyttalos of Elis: boys' boxing
*Herodoros of Megara: trumpeters' competition (3)

116 316 Deinosthenes of Sparta: stadion
Astyanax of Miletos: pankration (3)
*Choirilos of Elis: boys' boxing
*Herodoros of Megara: trumpeters' competition (4)

117 312 Parmenion (or Parmenides) of Mytilene: stadion
*Alexibios of Heraia: pentathlon
*Aristophon of Athens: pankration
*Herodoros of Megara: trumpeters' competition (5)

118 308 Apollonides of Tegea: stadion
*Seleadas (or Seleidas) of Sparta: wrestling
Antenor of Miletos (or Athens): pankration
*Theotimos of Elis: boys' boxing
*Nikagoras of Lindos: synoris and horse race
*Herodoros of Megara: trumpeters' competition (6)

119 304 Andromenes of Corinth: stadion
*Nikandros of Elis: diaulos (1)
*Leontiskos: pankration
*Sophios of Messene: boys' stadion
*Kallon of Elis: boys' boxing
*Lampos of Philippoi: tethrippon
*Herodoros of Megara: trumpeters' competition (7)

120 300 Pythagoras of Magnesia on the Maiandros: stadion (1)
*Nikandros of Elis: diaulos (2)
Keras of Argos: wrestling
*Archippos of Mytilene: boxing
Nikon of Anthedon (Boiotia): pankration (1)
*Timosthenes of Elis: boys' stadion
*Hippomachos of Elis: boys' boxing
[...]s of Magnesia on the Maiandros: race in armour (1)
*Theochrestos II of Cyrene: tethrippon
*Herodoros of Megara: trumpeters' competition (8)
*Eubalkes of Sparta: event unknown

121 296 Pythagoras of Magnesia on the Maiandros: stadion (2)
Apollonios of Alexandria: diaulos
Pasichoros of Boiotia: dolichos
Timachos of Mantineia: pentathlon
Amphiares of Sparta: wrestling
Kallippos of Rhodes: boxing
Nikon of Anthedon (Boiotia): pankration (2)
Antipatros of Miletos: boys' stadion
[So]siades of Tralles: boys' wrestling
Myrkeus: boys' boxing
[...]s of Magnesia on the Maiandros: race in armour (2)
Archidamos of Elis: tethrippon
Pandion of Thessaly: horse race
Tlasimachos of Ambrakia: synoris and foals' tethrippon
*Herodoros of Megara: trumpeters' competition (9)

122 292 Antigonos of Macedonia: stadion (1)
*Herodotos of Klazomenai: boys' stadion
*Philippos of Arkadia: boys' boxing
*Eperastos of Elis: race in armour
Telemachos of Elis: tethrippon
*Herodoros of Megara: trumpeters' competition (10)

123 288 Antigonos of Macedonia: stadion (2)

124 284 Philomelos of Pharsalos: stadion

125 280 Ladas of Aigion (Achaia): stadion
Paraballon of Elis: diaulos

126 276 Idaios of Cyrene, also called Nikator: stadion
*Attalos of Pergamon: foals' tethrippon

127 272 Perigenes of Alexandria: stadion
*Nikarchos of Elis: wrestling
*Kratinos of Aigeira (Achaia): boys' wrestling
Glaukon of Athens: tethrippon

128 268 Seleukos of Macedonia: stadion
Alexinikos of Elis: boys' wrestling
......: race in armour
Karteros of Thessaly: tethrippon
M[......] of Krannon: horse race
...... of Thessaly: synoris
Belestiche of Macedonia: foals' tethrippon

129 264 Philinos of Kos: stadion (1) and diaulos (1)
Belestiche of Macedonia: foals' synoris

130 260 Philinos of Kos: stadion (2) and diaulos (2)

131 256 Ammonios of Alexandria: stadion
*Philinos of Kos: diaulos (?)
*Eikasios of Kolophon: boys' wrestling
Hippokrates of Thessaly: foals' race

132 252 Xenophanes of Amphissa: stadion
*...... of Elis: pentathlon

133 248 Simylos of Neapolis: stadion
*Lastratidas of Elis: boys' wrestling
*[...]s of Elis: event unknown
......, event unknown
Euryades of Elis: event unknown

134 244 Alkidas of Sparta: stadion
*......: wrestling

135 240 Eraton of Aitolia: stadion
Kleoxenos of Alexandria: boxing
*Euanoridas of Elis: boys' wrestling

136 236 Pythokles of Sikyon: stadion

137 232 Menestheus of Barke: stadion
*Gorgos of Messene: pentathlon
*Aratos of Sikyon: tethrippon

138 228 Demetrios of Alexandria: stadion
*Emaution of Thelphoussa (Arkadia): boys' stadion
*Pantarkes of Elis: horse race

139 224 Iolaïdas of Argos: stadion

140 220 Zopyros of Syracuse: stadion
Agesidamos of Messene: pankration
...... of Nibis (Egypt): event unknown

141 216 Dorotheos of Rhodes: stadion
Paianios of Elis: wrestling
Kleitomachos of Thebes: pankration
*Thrasonides of Elis: foals' race

142 212 Krates of Alexandria: stadion
Kapros of Elis: wrestling and pankration
Kleitomachos of Thebes: boxing
*Akestorides of Troy: synoris or tethrippon for foals

143 208 Herakleitos of Samos: stadion
*...... of Argos (?): diaulos (1)
*Damatrios of Tegea: boys' stadion

144 204 Herakleides of Salamis in Cyprus: stadion
*...... of Argos (?): diaulos (2)
*Damokrates of Tenedos: wrestling
*Sodamos of Assos: boys' stadion

145 200 Pyrrhias of Aitolia: stadion
*...... of Argos (?): diaulos (3)
*Damatrios of Tegea: dolichos
*Timon of Elis: pentathlon
Moschos of Kolophon: boys' boxing
Phaidimos of Alexandria in the Troad: boys' pankration

146 196 Mikion of Boiotia: stadion
*...... of Argos (?): diaulos (4)

147 192 Agemachos of Kyzikos: stadion
Kle[it]ostratos of Rhodes: wrestling

148 188 Arkesilaos of Megalopolis: stadion

149 184 Hippostratos of Seleukeia: stadion
* Epitherses of Erythrai: boxing (1)

150 180 Onesikritos of Salamis: stadion
* Epitherses of Erythrai: boxing (2)

151 176 Thymilos of Aspendos: stadion

152 172 Demokritos of Megara: stadion
* Agesistratos of Lindos: boys' wrestling
Diallos of Smyrna: boys' pankration

153 168 Aristandros of Antissa (Lesbos): stadion

154 164 Leonidas of Rhodes: stadion (1), diaulos (1) and race in armour (1)
* Lysippos of Elis: boys' wrestling

155 160 Leonidas of Rhodes: stadion (2), diaulos (2) and race in armour (2)
* D[...]gonos: boxing (1)

156 156 Leonidas of Rhodes: stadion (3), diaulos (3) and race in armour (3)
Aristomenes of Rhodes: wrestling and pankration
* D[...]gonos: boxing (2)
* Amyntas of Eresos (or Ephesos): boys' pankration

157 152 Leonidas of Rhodes: stadion (4), diaulos (4) and race in armour (4)
* Apollodoros of Samos: boys' stadion
* [......]s: a boys' event

158 148 Orthon of Syracuse: stadion
* [......]s of Elis: wrestling

159 144 Alkimos of Kyzikos: stadion
* Xenothemis of Miletos: boxing

160 140 Diodoros (or Anodokos or Anodoros) of Sikyon (or Kyzikos): stadion

161 136 Antipatros of Epeiros: stadion

162 132 Damon of Delphi: stadion
* Menodoros of Athens: wrestling

163 128 Timotheos of Tralles: stadion

164 124 Boiotos of Sikyon: stadion

165 120 Akousilaos of Cyrene: stadion
Agesarchos (or Haimostratos or Damostratos or Archestratos or Amestratos) of Tritia: boxing

166 116 Chrysogonos of Nikaia (Bithynia): stadion (1)

167 112 Chrysogonos of Nikaia (Bithynia): stadion (2)

168 108 Nikomachos of Philadelphia (Lydia): stadion

169 104 Nikodamos of Sparta: stadion

170 100 Simmias of Seleukeia on the Tigris: stadion
* Nikokles of Akrion (Lakonia): diaulos, dolichos and race in armour
* [......]s: foals' synoris

171 96 Parmeniskos of Korkyra: stadion (1)
* Nikokles of Akrion (Lakonia): stadion and/or diaulos or dolichos or race in armour
*......: boxing
* Antigenes of Elis (?): foals' synoris
* Aristodamos of Elis: event unknown

172 92 Eudamos of Kos: stadion
Protophanes of Magnesia on the Maiandros: wrestling and pankration

173 88 Parmeniskos of Korkyra: stadion (2)

174 84 Demostratos of Larisa: stadion
* Strogianos of Elis: horse race
* [T]elemachos of Elis: horse race
* [Prax]agoras of Elis: tethrippon
* Timareta of Elis: synoris
* Philistos of Elis: synoris
* Theodota of Elis: foals' tethrippon

175 80 Epainetos of Argos: boys' stadion

176 76 Dion of Kyparissia (Lakonia): stadion
* Philonikos of Elis: event unknown
* ...... of Elis: tethrippon
* Lasthenes of Elis: horse race

177 72 Hekatomnos (or Hekatomnas) of Miletos: stadion, diaulos and race in armour
Hypsikles of Sikyon and Gaius of Rome: dolichos
Aristonymidas of Kos: pentathlon
Isidoros of Alexandria: wrestling
Atyanas of Adramyttion: boxing
Sphodrias of Sikyon: pankration

Sosigenes of Asia: boys' stadion
Apollophanes of Kyparissia (Lakonia): boys' wrestling
Soterichos of Elis: boys' boxing
Kalas of Elis: boys' pankration
Aristolochos of Elis: tethrippon
Hegemon of Elis: horse race
Hellanikos of Elis: synoris and foals' tethrippon
Kletias of Elis: foals' synoris
Kallippos of Elis: foals' race

178 68 Diokles of Hypaipa: stadion
Straton (or Stratonikos) of Alexandria: wrestling and pankration

179 64 Andreas of Sparta: stadion
Straton of Alexandria: wrestling or pankration

180 60 Andromachos of Ambrakia: stadion
* Menedemos of Elis: synoris

181 56 Lamachos of Tauromenion: stadion
* Charopos of Elis: equestrian event for foals

182 52 Anthestion of Argos: stadion
Marion of Alexandria: wrestling and pankration
* Agelochos of Elis: equestrian event for foals
* [......]os: event unknown

183 48 Theodoros of Messene: stadion (1)
* [......]chos of Elis: tethrippon or synoris for foals
*...... of Elis: event unknown

184 44 Theodoros of Messene: stadion (2)

185 40 Ariston of Thourioi: stadion (1)
* Thaliarchos of Elis: boys' boxing

186 36 Skamandros of Alexandria: stadion
* Lykomedes of Elis: horse race

187 32 Ariston of Thourioi: stadion (2)
* Thaliarchos of Elis: boxing

188 28 Sopatros of Argos: stadion

189 24 Asklepiades of Sidon: stadion
* [Phili]ppos Glykon of Pergamon: pankration
* Demosthenes of Miletos: trumpeters' competition (1)

190 20 Auphidios of Patrai: stadion
...... of Miletos: diaulos
* Demosthenes of Miletos: trumpeters' competition (2)

191 16 Diodotos of Tyana: stadion
* Demosthenes of Miletos: trumpeters' competition (3)

192 12 Diophanes of Aiolia: stadion
Polyktor of Elis: boys' wrestling

193 8 Artemidoros of Thyateira: stadion
* Nikophon of Miletos: boxing

194 4 B.C. Demaratos of Ephesos: stadion (1)
* Polyxenos of Zakynthos: boys' wrestling
* Tiberius Claudius Nero of Rome: tethrippon

195 A.D. 1 Demaratos of Ephesos: stadion (2)
* Damaithidas of Elis: foals' synoris
* Archiadas of Elis: equestrian event for foals

196 5 Pammenes of Magnesia on the Maiandros: stadion
* Gnaeus Marcus... of Rome: event unknown (equestrian?) (1)

197 9 Asiatikos of Halikarnassos: stadion
* Gnaeus Marcus... of Rome: event unknown (equestrian?) (2)

198 13 Diophanes of Prousa (Bithynia): stadion
Aristeas of Stratonikeia (or Maiandria): wrestling and pankration

199 17 Aischines of Miletos, also called Glaukias: stadion
Tiberius Germanicus Caesar of Rome: tethrippon

200 21 Polemon of Petra: stadion

201 25 Damas (or Damasias) of Kydonia (Crete): stadion
* Demokrates of Magnesia on the Maiandros: boxing (1)
* Hermas of Antiocheia (Syria): pankration (1)

202 29 Hermogenes of Pergamon: stadion
* Demokrates of Magnesia on the Maiandros: boxing (2)
* Hermas of Antiocheia (Syria): pankration (2)

203 33 Apollonios of Epidauros: stadion
* Demokrates of Magnesia on the Maiandros: boxing (3)
* Heras of Laodikeia (Phrygia): pankration

204 37 Sarapion of Alexandria: stadion
Nikostratos of Aigai (Kilikia): wrestling and pankration
* Hermogenes of Philadelphia (Lydia): event unknown
* Apollonios: event unknown (1)

205 41 Euboulidas of Laodikeia: stadion
*......: diaulos and race in armour (1)
* Apollonios: event unknown (2)

206 45 Valerius of Mytilene: stadion
*......: race in armour (2)
* Apollonios: event unknown (3)

207 49 Athenodoros of Aigion (Achaia): stadion (1)
* Tiberius Claudius Patrobius of Antiocheia (Syria): wrestling (1)
Melankomas of Karia: boxing
*......: race in armour (3)
Publius Cornelius Ariston of Ephesos: boys' pankration

208 53 Athenodoros of Aigion (Archaia): stadion (2)
* Tiberius Claudius Patrobius of Antiocheia (Syria): wrestling (2)
* ...... of Stratonikeia (Karia?) pankration
Tiberius Claudius Aphrodisius of Elis: horse race
Kallippos Peisanos of Elis: equestrian event for foals

209 57 Kallikles of Sidon: stadion
* Tiberius Claudius Patrobius of Antiocheia (Syria): wrestling (3)
Publius Pompeius Eutyches of Philadelphia (Lydia): event unknown (1)

210 61 Athenodoros of Aigion (Achaia): stadion (3)
* Publius Pompeius Eutyches of Philadelphia (Lydia): event unknown (2)

211 65 Tryphon of Philadelphia (Lydia): stadion
Xenodamos of Antikyra: pankration
Nero, emperor of Rome: competitions for heralds, tragedy, lyre-playing; chariot race for foals; chariot race; race for ten - horse chariot.

212 69 Polites of Keramos: stadion, diaulos and dolichos
Tiberius Claudius Artemidorus of Tralles: pankration
* Diogenes of Ephesos: trumpeters' competition (1)

213 73 Rhodon of Kyme: stadion
* Diogenes of Ephesos: trumpeters' competition (2)

214 77 Straton of Alexandria: stadion
* Diogenes of Ephesos: trumpeters' competition (3)

215 81 Hermogenes of Xanthos: stadion and diaulos or race in armour (1)
* Tiberius Claudius Rufus of Smyrna: pankration
* [Prato]melidas of Sparta: event unknown
* Diogenes of Ephesos: trumpeters' competition (4)

216 85 Apollophanes of Tarsos, also called Papes: stadion
* Hermogenes of Xanthos: diaulos and race in armour (?)
* Titus Flavius Metrobius of Iasos: dolichos
* Titus Flavius Artemidoros of Adana: pankration (1)
* Diogenes of Ephesos: trumpeters' competition (5)

217 89 Hermogenes of Xanthos: stadion and diaulos or race in armour (2)
* Titus Flavius Artemidoros of Adana: pankration (2)
Sarapion of Alexandria: boys' boxing
Nikanor of Ephesos: boys' pankration
* Pankles of Tenos (?): event unknown

218 93 Apollonis (or Heliodoros) of Alexandria: stadion
Herakleides of Alexandria: boxing
* Athenaios of Athens: event unknown

219 97 Stephanos of Kappadokia: stadion
Marcus of Antiocheia (Syria): boys' wrestling

220 101 Achilles of Alexandria: stadion

Titus Flavius Archibios of Alexandria: pankration (1)

221 105 Theonas of Alexandria, also called Smaragdos: stadion
Titus Flavius Archibios of Alexandria: pankration (2)

222 109 Kallistos of Sidon: stadion

223 113 Eustolos of Sidon: stadion
*...... of Rhodes: dolichos (1)

224 117 Isarion of Alexandria: stadion
*...... of Rhodes: dolichos (2)
Publius Aelius Aristomachus of Magnesia on the Maiandros: boys' pankration

225 121 Aristeas of Miletos: stadion

226 125 Dionysios Sameumys of Alexandria: stadion (1)
D(e)idas: boxing
* Moschos of Pergamon: event unknown

227 129 Dionysios Sameumys of Alexandria: stadion (2)
* Marcus Ulpius Domesticus of Ephesos: pankration
* [Dei]philos of Aigai (Aiolid): event unknown
Lucius Minucius Natalis of Rome: tethrippon

228 133 Loukas of Alexandria: stadion
* Aelius Granianus of Sikyon: boys' stadion

229 137 Epidauros of Alexandria, also called Ammonios: stadion
* Aelius Granianus of Sikyon: diaulos, race in armour and pentathlon (1)
[Herma?]goras of Magnesia on the Maiandros: wrestling
Publius Aelius Artemas of Laodikeia: heralds' competition

230 141 Didymos Klideus of Alexandria: stadion
* Aelius Granianus of Sikyon: pentathlon (2)
* Marcus Tullius of Apameia (Bithynia): boxing (1)

231 145 Kranaos (or Granianos) of Sikyon: stadion
* Marcus Tullius of Apameia (Bithynia): boxing (2)

232 149 Attikos of Sardis: stadion
Dionysios of Seleukeia: wrestling
Sokrates: pankration

233 153 Demetrios of Chios: stadion and diaulos
* Marcus Aurelius Demetrios of Alexandria: pankration
* Kasia M[nasithea] of Elis: foals' tethrippon

234 157 Heras of Chios: stadion

235 161 Mnasiboulos of Elateia: stadion and race in armour

236 165 Aeithales of Alexandria: stadion
*......: diaulos (?)
* Marcus Aurelius Chrysippos of Smyrna: wrestling
* Titus Aelius Aurelius Apollonius of Tarsos: heralds' competition

237 169 Eudaimon of Alexandria: stadion
* [...] of Philadelphia: a foot-race

238 173 Agathopous of Aigina: stadion (1)
* Photion of Ephesos: boxing
* Marcus Aurelius Demostratos Damas of Sardis: pankration (1)

239 177 Agathopous of Aigina: stadion (2)
* Marcus Aurelius Hermagoras of Magnesia: wrestling
* Marcus Aurelius Demostratos Damas of Sardis: pankration (2)
* Gaius Julius Bassus of Miletos: heralds' competition

240 181 Anoubion of Alexandria, also called Pheidos: stadion
Marcus Aurelius Asklepiades of Alexandria: pankration
* K[..]ktabenos (?) of Ephesos: race in armour (?) (1)

241 185 Heron of Alexandria: stadion
* K[..]ktabenos (?) of Ephesos: race in armour (?) (2)
* Titus Aelius Aurelius Metrodorus of Philadelphia (Lydia): event unknown

242 189 Magnos of Cyrene: stadion
* Claudius Apollonius of Smyrna: event unknown (wrestling, boxing or pankration)
* Titus Julius Septimius Julianus of Smyrna: event unknown
* Marcus Aurelius Philosebastus of Ephesos: event unknown

243 193 Isidoros of Alexandria, also called Artemidoros: stadion (1)
* Marcus Aurelius Asklepiades of Alexandria: wrestling (1)
* Theopropos of Rhodes: horse race

244 197 Isidoros of Alexandria, also called Artemidoros: stadion (2)
Aurelius Metrodorus of Kyzikos: pentathlon
* Marcus Aurelius Asklepiades of Alexandria: wrestling (2)
*...... of Ephesos (?): boxing (?)

245 201 Alexandros of Alexandria: stadion
*...... of Ephesos (?): boxing (?)
* Marcus Aurelius Hierokles of Nysa: event unknown

246 205 Epinikos of Kyzikos, also called Kynas: stadion
* Ploutarchos: boxing
*......: boys' stadion

247 209 Satornilos of Gortys: stadion
* Gerenos of Naukratis: wrestling
* Gaius Perelius Aurelius Alexandrus of Thyateira (Lydia): pankration

248 213 Heliodoros of Alexandria, also called Trosidamas: stadion (1)
*...... of Bithynia, also called Graos: dolichos (1)
* Aurelius Aelix of Phoenicia: wrestling
* Lucius Silicius Firmus Mandrogenes of Magnesia on the Maiandros: pankration

249 217 Heliodoros of Alexandria, also called Trosidamas: stadion (2)
*...... of Bithynia, also called Graos: dolichos (2)
* Aurelius Aelix of Phoenicia: pankration
* Publius Aelius Aurelius Serapion of Ephesos: trumpeters' competition

250 221 * Publius Aelius Alkandridas of Sparta: stadion (1)
*...... of Bithynia, also called Graos: dolichos (3)
* Aurelius Phoibammon of Egypt: pankration

251 225 * Publius Aelius Alkandridas of Sparta: stadion (2)
Publius Aelius Granianus Fannius Artemidorus of Miletos: event unknown

252 229 * Demetrios of Salamis: stadion (1) and pentathlon (1)
* Claudius Rufus, also called Apollonius: event unknown (wrestling, boxing or pankration) (1)

253 233 * Demetrios of Salamis: stadion (2) and pentathlon (2)
* Claudius Rufus, also called Apollonius: event unknown (wrestling, boxing or pankration) (2)

254 237 * Demetrios of Salamis: stadion (3)
*......: wrestling or pankration

255 241 Publius Asklepiades of Corinth: pentathlon
* Aurelius Germanus of Antinoe (Egypt): event unknown
* Titus Domitius Prometheus of Athens: tethrippon

256 245 * Tiberius Claudius Diodorus of Hermopolis (?): event unknown
Valerius Eklektus of Sinope: heralds' competition (1)

257 249 * ...... of Athens: event unknown
* ......: event unknown
* Marcus Aurelius Pius of Daldis: event unknown

258 253 Valerius Eklektus of Sinope: heralds' competition (2)

259 257 Valerius Eklektus of Sinope: heralds' competition (3)

260 261 Valerius Eklektus of Sinope: heralds' competition (4)

261 265

262 269 Dionysios of Alexandria: stadion

263 273

264 277 * Aurelius Sarapammon of Oxyr-

		rhynchos, also called Didymos: event unknown
265	281	
266	285	
267	289	
268	293	
269	297	
270	301	
271	305	
272	309	
273	313	
274	317	
275	321	
276	325	
277	329	
278	333	
279	337	
280	341	
281	345	
282	349	
283	353	
284	357	
285	361	
286	365	
287	369	* Philoumenos of Philadelphia: event unknown (boxing, wrestling or pankration) * Barasdates of Armenia: boxing

OLYMPIC VICTORS OF UNCERTAIN DATE

Ainetos of Amyklai (Lakonia): pentathlon
Aischines of Elis: pentathlon (twice)
Anauchidas of Elis: boys' wrestling and wrestling
Ageles of Chios: boys' boxing
Aristeides of Elis: race in armour
Brimias of Elis: boxing
Boutas of Miletos: boys' boxing
Chaireas of Sikyon: boys' boxing
Charinos of Elis: diaulos and race in armour
Dionysid[oros] of Mylasa: boys' wrestling
Eualkidas of Elis: boys' boxing
Euanthes of Kyzikos: boxing
Eurydamas of Cyrene: boxing
Gorgos of Elis: diaulos, race in armour and pentathlon (4 times)
Klearchos of Elis: pentathlon
Kleinomachos of Elis: pentathlon
Kriannios of Elis: race in armour
Menalkes of Elis: pentathlon
Neolaïdas of Elis: boys' stadion and race in armour
Nikosylos of Rhodes: wrestling
Pherenikos of Elis: boys' wrestling
Philles of Elis: boys' wrestling
Prokles of Andros: boys' wrestling
Rufus: event unknown
Theodoros of Elis: pentathlon
[...]nos of Elis: event unknown
...... of Kroton: event unknown
...... of Rhodes: boys' wrestling
...... of Rhodes: dolichos
......: wrestling (twice)
......: diaulos (?) (4 times)
......: event unknown

OLYMPIC VICTORS OF UNCERTAIN AUTHENTICITY

* Amphilochos of Antiocheia: dolichos
* Annikeris of Cyrene: tethrippon
* Anoubion of Egypt: event unknown
* [A]ristarch[os]: event unknown
* Marcus Aurelius Abas of Adai: dolichos
* Marcus Aurelius Pappus of Myra: boxing
Marcus Aurelius Silvanus of Hermopolis: trumpeters' competition (ten times)
Aurelius Toalius of Oinoanda: pankration (twice)
* Epigonos of Tralles: event unknown (4 times)
* Eudaimon of Egypt: boxing
* Marcus Justius Marcianus Rufus of Sinope: boxing
* Leukaros of Akarnania: pankration
* Lykos of Messene: pentathlon
* Marcianus of Thyateira: event unknown
* Mnasiadas of Argos: unknown equestrian event
* Periandros of Corinth: tethrippon
* Phorystas of Tanagra: heralds' competition
Platon of Athens: wrestling
* Marcus Popillius Sotys of Perge: diaulos (?)
* Skopas of Krannon: tethrippon (?)
* Thrasym[...]: event unknown
* Timarrhas (?): event unknown
*...... of Sparta: boxing (?)
* ...... of Larisa: equestrian event
* ...... of Egypt: event unknown
*...... of Bithynia: event unknown
*...... of Miletos: wrestling
*......: event unknown

Bibliography

BENGTSON, N., *Die Olympischen Spiele in der Antike*. Zürich, 1971.

BERVE, H.- GRUBEN, G.- HIRMER, M., *Griechische Tempel und Heiligtümer*. München, 1961.

BILINSKI, B., *L'agonistica sportiva nella Grecia antica: aspetti sociali e ispirazioni letterarie*. Roma, 1960.

BLÜMEL, C., *Sport der Hellenen. Ausstellung griechischer Bildwerke*. Berlin, 1936.

BLÜMEL, C., *Sport und Spiel bei Griechen und Römern. Bildwerke aus den staatlichen Museen zu Berlin*. Berlin, 1934.

BRONEER, Oscar, *Isthmia, Topography and Architecture, Vol. II*. Princeton, 1973.

CONDORELLI, C., *Le antichi Olimpiadi e gli Olimpionici della Magna Grecia*. Catania, 1964.

DELORME, J., *Gymnasion; étude sur les monuments consacrés à l'éducation en Grèce*. Paris, 1960.

DEUBNER, L., *Attische Feste*. Hildesheim, 1966.

DIEM, G., *Olympiaden 776 v. Chr. bis 1964. Eine Geschichte des Sports*. Stuttgart, 1964.

DIEM, G., *Weltgeschichte des Sports. Band I. Von den Anfängen bis zur Französischen Revolution*. Stuttgart, 1971^{3}.

DIEM, G., *Alexander der Grosse als Sportsmann*. Frankfurt/Main, 1957.

DREES, L., *Der Ursprung der Olympischen Spiele*. Schorndorf bei Stuttgart, 1962.

DREES, L., *Olympia; Götter, Künstler und Athleten*. Stuttgart, 1967.

EBERT, J., Zum Pentathlon der Antike. *Abhandlungen der Sächsischen Akademie der Wissenschaften zu Leipzig*, 56 (1963), Heft I. Berlin, 1963.

FÖRSTER, H., Die Olympischen Sieger, I-II. *Gymnasium zu Zwickau Berichte* 1891 καὶ 1892.

GARDINER, E.N., *Athletics of the Ancient World*. Oxford, 1971^{5}.

GARDINER, E.N., *Greek Athletic sports and festivals*. London, 1910.

GRÜNDEL, *Die Darstellung des Laufens in der griechischen Kunst*. Würzburg, 1935.

HARRIS, H.A., *Greek Athletes and Athletics*. London, 1971.

HARRIS, H.A., *Sport in Greece and Rome*. London, 1972.

HARRIS H.A., An Olympic Epigram. *Greece and Rome*, VII (1960), p. 3-7.

HERMANN, H., *Olympia, Heiligtum und Wettkampfstätte*. München, 1972.

HÖNLE, Augusta, *Olympia in der Politik der griechischen Staatenwelt*. Tübingen, 1968.

HYDE, W.W., *Olympic Victor Monuments and Greek Athletic Art*. Washington, 1921.

JÜTHNER, J., *Philostratus über Gymnastik*. Leipzig/Berlin, 1909.

JÜTHNER, J., *Die athletischen Leibesübungen der Griechen (F. Brein)*, vol. I: 1965, vol. II: 1968, Wien.

JÜTHNER, J., *Antike Turngeräte*. Wien, 1896.

JÜTHNER, J., Kalokagathia, *Fetschrift Rzach, p. 99-119*. Reichenberg, 1930.

KARIOTAKI Z.N., *Ἱστορία τῶν βαρέων ἀγωνισμάτων καὶ τῆς ἀθλήσεως τῶν ἀρχαίων Ἑλλήνων*. Athens, 1975.

KITRINIARI K.S., *Φιλοστράτου Γυμναστικός*. Athens, 1961.

KUNZE, E., *100 Jahre Deutsche Ausgrabungen in Olympia*. München, 1972.

LEONARDOS, B., *Ὀλυμπία*. Athens, 1901.

MALLWITZ, A., *Olympia und seine Bauten*. München, 1972.

MARROU, H.I., *Histoire de l'Éducation dans l'antiquité*. Paris, 1965.

MEHL, E., *Antike Schwimmkunst*. München, 1927.

MEHL, E., *Weltgeschichte der Ballspiele*. Wien, 1956.

MEULI, K., Der Ursprung der Olympischen Spiele. *Die Antike*, 17 (1941), p. 189-208.

MEZÖ, F., *Geschichte der Olympischen Spiele*. München, 1930.

MORETTI, L., *Iscrizioni Agonistiche Greche*. Roma, 1953.

MORETTI, L., Olympionikai, i vincitori negli antichi agoni olimpici. *Atti della Accademia Nationale dei Lincei 1957*

NILSSON, M., *Griechische Feste*. Leipzig, 1906.

NILSSON, M., *Die hellenistische Schule*. München, 1955.

Olympia Berichte, vol. I-IX, Berlin, 1937-1967.

Olympische Forschungen, vol. I-VII, Berlin, 1944-1966.

PAPAHATZIS, N., *Παυσανίου Ἑλλάδος Περιήγησις: Μεσσηνιακὰ - Ἠλιακά*. Athens, 1965.

PATRUCCO, R., *Lo Sport nella Grecia antica*. Firenze, 1972.

POPPLOW, U., *Leibesübungen und Leibeserziehung in der griechischen Antike*. Schorndorf bei Stuttgart, 1960^{2}.

ROBERT, K., Die Ordnung der Olympischen Spiele und die Sieger der 75. bis 83. Olympiade. *Hermes*, 35 (1900), p. 141-1951.

RUDOLF, W., *Olympischer Kampfsport in der Antike: Faustkampf, Ringkampf und Pankration in den griechischen Nationalfestspielen*. Berlin, 1965.

SCHÖBEL, H., *Olympia und seine Spiele*. Leipzig, 1964.

SCHRÖDER, B., *Der Sport im Altertum*. Berlin, 1927.

WEIRICH, R., *Körper und Körpererziehung bei Platon*. München. 1932.

YALOURIS, N., *Olympia*. München, 1972.

YALOURIS, N., Athena als Herrin der Pferde. *Museum Helveticum*, 7 (1950), p. 27.

ZSCHIETZSCHMANN, W., *Wettkampf- und Ubungsstätten in Griechenland. I. Das Stadion. II. Palästra — Gymnasion*. Schorndorf bei Stuttgart, 1961.

List of Illustrations

B.C. London, British Museum. Phot. M. Holford.

90. Panathenaic amphora. Ca. 540 B.C. Paris, Bibliothèque Nationale.

91. Red-figure amphora. Early 5th century B.C. Munich, Antikensammlungen.

92. Bronze engraved discus. Early 5th century B.C. West Berlin, Staatliche Museen.

93. Bronze engraved discus. 3rd century A.D. Olympia, Archaeological Museum. Phot. Sp. Tsavdaroglou.

94. Bronze statuette. Early 5th century B.C. Bologna, Museo Civico. Phot. M. Pucciarelli.

95. Red-figure amphora. 490 B.C. Musei Vaticani. Phot. M. Pucciarelli.

96. Red-figure kylix. Ca. 460 B.C. Rome, Villa Giulia. Phot. M. Pucciarelli.

97. Fragment of a red-figure vase. Mid-5th century B.C. Würzburg, Martin von Wagner Museum.

98. Panathenaic amphora. 450 B.C. Naples, Museo Archeologico Nazionale. Phot. M. Pucciarelli.

99. Copy of the Diskobolos by Myron. Mid-5th century B.C. Rome, Museo Nazionale Romano. Phot. M. Pucciarelli.

100. Bronze engraved discus. Mid-5th century B.C. West Berlin, Staatliche Museen.

101. The attachment of the thong. Drawing K. Iliakis.

102. Red-figure amphora. Ca. 500 B.C. Munich, Antikensammlungen. Phot. C. Moessner.

103. Red-figure kylix. Ca. 420 B.C. East Berlin, Staatliche Museen.

104. Red-figure oinochoe. Mid-5th century B.C. Paris, Louvre. Phot. M. Chuzzeville.

105. Panathenaic amphora. Late 5th century B.C. London, British Museum. Phot. M. Chuzzeville.

106. Red-figure amphora. Mid-5th century B.C. Munich, Antikensammlungen. Phot. C. Moessner.

107. Red-figure pelike. Ca. 500 B.C. Leningrad, Hermitage Museum.

108. Red-figure kylix. 430 B.C. London, British Museum. Phot. M. Holford.

109. Red-figure amphora. Ca. 525 B.C. West Berlin, Staatliche Museen.

110. Red-figure psykter. Ca. 500 B.C. Turin, Museo di Antichità. Phot. Chomon-Perino.

111. Black-figure amphora. Late 6th century B.C. Musei Vaticani. Phot. M. Pucciarelli.

112. Red-figure amphora. Ca. 525 B.C. West Berlin, Staatliche Museen.

113. One side of the relief base of Poulopoulos. Ca. 500 B.C. Athens, National Archaeological Museum. Phot. Sp. Tsavdaroglou.

114. Bronze group of wrestlers. 16.5 cm. long. 2nd - 1st century B.C. Munich, Antikensammlungen. Phot. C. Moessner.

115. Red-figure psykter. Early 5th century B.C. Boston, Museum of Fine Arts, H.L. Pierce Fund.

116. Red-figure kylix. End of the 6th century B.C. London, British Museum. Phot. M. Holford.

117. Red-figure kylix. Ca. 430 B.C. London, British Museum. Phot. M. Holford.

118. Black-figure kylix. Mid-6th century B.C. Florence, Museo Archeologico. Photo Scala.

119. Panathenaic amphora. Late 6th century B.C. London, British Museum. Phot. M. Holford.

120. Bronze statue of a boxer by Apollonius. Late Hellenistic period. Rome, Museo Nazionale Romano. Phot. M. Pucciarelli.

121. Three kinds of thongs. Drawing K. Iliakis.

122. Red-figure amphora. Early 5th century B.C. Vienna, Kunsthistorisches Museum. Phot. E. Meyer.

123. Black-figure amphora. 530 B.C. London, British Museum. Phot. M. Holford.

124. Black-figure amphora. 525 B.C. Paris, Louvre. Phot. M. Chuzzeville.

125. Panathenaic amphora. 336/5 B.C. London, British Museum. Phot. M. Holford.

126. Red-figure kylix. Early 5th century B.C. London, British Museum. Phot. M. Holford.

127. Red-figure amphora. Early 5th century B.C. Athens, National Archaeological Museum. Phot. M. Skiadaresis.

128. Pankratiasts. 2nd century A.D. Florence, Galleria degli Uffizi. Photo Scala.

129. Panathenaic amphora. 332 B.C. London, British Museum. Phot. M. Holford.

130. Red-figure kylix. 490 B.C. London, British Museum. Phot. M. Holford.

131. Panathenaic amphora. Early 5th century B.C. New York, Metropolitan Museum of Art.

132. Panathenaic amphora. 520 B.C. Paris, Louvre. Phot. M. Chuzzeville.

133. Panathenaic amphora. 530 B.C. Boston, Museum of Fine Arts, H.L. Pierce Fund.

134. The Jockey of Artemision. About the middle of the 2nd century B.C. Athens, National Archaeological Museum. Phot. Sp. Tsavdaroglou.

135. Panathenaic amphora. End of the 5th century B.C. London, British Museum. Phot. M. Holford.

136. Black-figure amphora. Ca. 540 B.C. Munich, Antikensammlungen. Phot. C. Moessner.

137. Black-figure amphora. Late 6th century B.C. London, British Museum. Phot. M. Holford.

138. The hippodrome at Olympia. Reconstruction K. Iliakis.

139. Panathenaic amphora. Early 5th century B.C. London, British Museum. Phot. M. Holford.

140. Panathenaic amphora. 540 B.C. London, British Museum. Phot. M. Holford.

141. Coin of Thebes. London, British Museum. Phot. M. Holford.

142. Panathenaic amphora. 530 B.C. Madrid, Museo Arqueologico Nacional.

143. Red-figure choe. Late 5th century B.C. Paris, Louvre. Phot. M. Chuzzeville.

144. Red-figure krater. 410 B.C. London, British Museum. Phot. M. Holford.

145. The inscribed stone of Bybon. Late 7th century B.C. Olympia, Archaeological Museum. Phot. Sp. Tsavdaroglou.

146. Red-figure kylix. Ca. 500 B.C. Würzburg, Martin von Wagner Museum.

147. Relief from a statue base. Ca. 500 B.C. Athens, National Archaeological Museum. Phot. M. Skiadaresis.

148. Relief from a statue base. Ca. 490 B.C. Athens, National Archaeological Museum. Phot. M. Skiadaresis.

149. Marble lekythos with relief. Mid-4th century B.C. Athens, National Archaeological Museum. Phot. Sp. Tsavdaroglou.

150. Black-figure amphora. 525 B.C. London, British Museum. Phot. M. Holford.

151. Red-figure amphora. 510 B.C. Paris, Louvre. Phot. M. Chuzzeville.

152. Fresco from the tomb of the diver at Poseidonia. Ca. 480 B.C. Paestum Museum. Photo Scala.

153. Bronze statuette of the Roman period. Paris, Louvre. Phot. M. Chuzzeville.

154. Mosaic floor. A.D. 350-400. Piazza Armerina, Sicily.

155. Mosaic floor. Ca. 60 A.D. Naples, Museo Archeologico Nazionale. Photo Scala.

156. Fresco from Pompeii. Naples, Museo Archeologico Nazionale. Photo Scala.

Index